THE BRITISH MUSEUM

Maritime History
of Britain and Ireland

c.400–2001

THE BRITISH MUSEUM
Maritime History
of Britain and Ireland
c.400–2001

Ian Friel

THE BRITISH MUSEUM PRESS

To my mother, Lorna, and to
the memory of my grandparents,
Alice and Fred.

Published in 2003 by The British Museum Press
A division of The British Museum Company Ltd
46 Bloomsbury Street, London WC1B 3QQ

British Library Cataloguing in Publication Data
A catalogue record for this book is available
from the British Library

ISBN 0 7141 2718 3

Designed and typeset by James Shurmer

All maps and line drawings by Lynne Friel

Printed in Spain by Grafos S.A.

Contents

Acknowledgements

Anyone writing a survey such as this owes a great debt to a very large number of historians and writers, both past and present. I can only express my thanks to those whose work I have read and enjoyed in the course of researching this book; any errors are my own. At the very least, I hope that what I have written will encourage others to follow up particular subjects in greater detail through the works cited in the bibliography.

I wish to pay tribute to my editor at British Museum Press, Carolyn Jones. Carolyn has been a staunch supporter of the book since it was first mooted, and has seen me through the ups and downs of its writing. I could not have had a better editor. Thanks are also due to Carolyn's colleague, Martha Caute.

My wife, Lynne, has drawn the maps and illustrations in the book, for which I am profoundly grateful. Lynne and our children, Helen and David, have had to live with this book for far longer than was ever intended. Without their love, support and tolerance it would never have been finished.

Ian Friel

'The Merchants are a pack of sharpers, masters of ships arrant knaves, a vessel but a doubtful confidant, and the sea a mere lottery.'

Dispirited shipowner in the *London Spy*, 1698[1]

'In every mess I finds a friend
 In every port a wife.'

Charles Dibdin (1745–1814), *Jack in his Element*

'What a poor miserable trade a sailor's life is.... A farm labourer is far better off in every respect.'

Captain Robert Thomas, SS *Merioneth*, 1883[2]

'But the standing toast that pleased the most
 Was " The wind that blows, the ship that goes,
 And the lass that loves a sailor!"'

Charles Dibdin (1745–1814), *The Round Robin*

'Here he lies where he longed to be;
 Home is the sailor, home from the sea.'

Robert Louis Stevenson (1850–94), *Requiem*

'The death of Nelson was felt in England as something more than a public calamity; men started at the intelligence, and turned pale, as if they had heard of the loss of a dear friend.'

Robert Southey (1774–1843), *Life of Nelson*

'...*nothing* will ever compensate us for the men we have lost, not even the way so many of them died. They were ready to die because they wanted to save their children and their children's children from future wars.'

Lieutenant-Commander Peter Scott MBE, DSC & Bar, RNVR,
The Battle of the Narrow Seas, 1945[3]

Introduction

Nowadays most English-speakers are not English, or even 'British' by the current definition of that term. In fact, the total number of English-speakers outside the British Isles probably overtook the Anglophone population of these islands somewhere in the second half of the nineteenth century, largely due to the mushrooming population of the United States. The days of Britain as a great seapower have come and gone (so far as we know), but the maritime activities of the peoples of the British Isles have certainly left their mark upon the globe, for both good and bad. Perhaps one of the most remarkable of these effects is the spread of English.

English belongs to the western branch of the Germanic family of languages, and is closest in structure to Frisian, the language once spoken on what is now the northern coast of the Netherlands. It was slow to rise to prominence as a European language. As late as 1534 a multilingual dictionary published in the great port of Antwerp (in modern Belgium) did not include English.[1] From these small beginnings it has risen to being the second most-spoken language in the world, used by over 470 million people and the official or dominant language in over sixty countries. Much of the current pre-eminent position of English is due to political, economic and cultural clout of the United States of America, but the creation of an English-speaking America started as an English maritime enterprise.[2]

The subject of this book requires definition: the term 'maritime history' is not used here as a code for 'naval history', nor for a history of seafaring activity which avoids the naval side. 'Maritime history' in this book means 'the history of human activities relating to the sea and seafaring'. Major themes such as seafarers, warfare, sea trade, fishing and ship development will by turns occupy centre stage, although there has not been the space to give attention to certain areas, such as culture and the sea, smuggling, or yachting and other seaborne leisure pursuits. However, the work does try to give an idea of the great range of maritime activities in which the people of Britain and Ireland have taken part, and of the many ways in which what happened to the comparatively few at sea affected the lives of the many ashore. Whether or not it achieves this aim is for the reader to judge.

CHAPTER ONE

A boat to the island of ghosts, *c.*400–700

The sixth-century Byzantine historian Procopius was perhaps one of the best-informed people of his age, but even he knew only a handful of things about Britain. Some were just plain wrong, and at least one was unbelievable. Procopius was a court historian to the Emperor Justininian, who ruled the surviving eastern half of the Roman Empire from the great city of Constantinople (*Byzantium*: now Istanbul in Turkey). The western part of the empire had collapsed in the fifth century, wrecked by internal feuding and barbarian invasions. The province of Britain had been the first part to go, officially abandoned by Rome in 410, because it could no longer be defended.

The eastern empire was able to reconquer some of the lost western territories, but Britain remained outside its grasp. However, Byzantine merchant ships did reach there, and Procopius may have got his information about these remote islands from a sailor who had been on the long and dangerous run to north-western Europe. According to Procopius there were two islands, one called *Britannia* and the other *Brittia*. Whatever the historian meant by *Britannia*, it is clear that *Brittia* was Britain, for he described it as facing the mouth of the river Rhine and as the home of the *Angili*, the *Phrissones* and Britons. The first two were Germanic immigrants (Angles and Frisians) who began arriving in Britain in the fifth century; the Britons were the original Celtic inhabitants.

Procopius' Britain was a place for ghosts. According to him, the fishermen on the coasts facing the island had to go through a strange and frightening nightly ritual. A knocking at the door would rouse them, but no one would be there. However, the fishermen then had to go to down to the shore, where they would find strange boats waiting, that they had to row to Britain. The boats appeared to be low in the water, as if laden with invisible passengers, but the moment that they touched the opposite shore the craft would rise in the water, seemingly freed of their load. The passengers were the souls of the dead, and they had just been ferried to the next world.[1]

Ends and beginnings

Roman sea power and trade in north-western Europe had kept Britain linked to the imperial realms on the Continent. Both collapsed in the early fifth century, catastrophes that must have done as much – if not more – to cut Britain off from the failing empire as the official withdrawal of the Roman legions. These and other changes proved to be irrevocable, and that is why this book begins in about 400.

- ● Coastal fort
- ▢ Coastal signal station
- ■ Selected walled towns

1 Late Roman Britain (after Snyder 1998, pp 10–11).

Hadrian's Wall

● Ravenglass

? Caer Gybi

Brancaster

London

Saxon shore forts

Portchester

| 0 | | 100 | | 200 miles |
| 0 | 100 | | 200 km | |

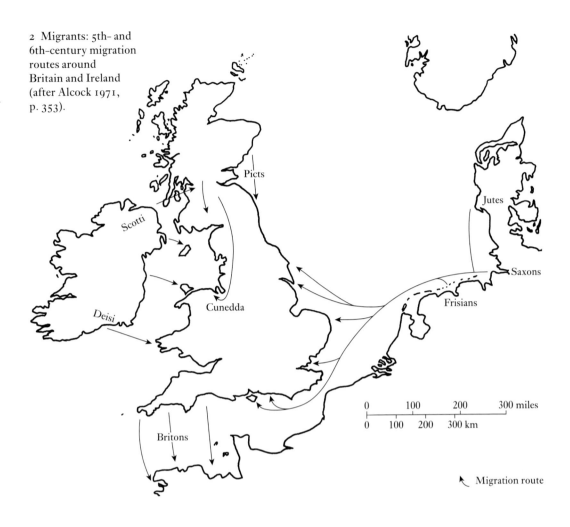

2 Migrants: 5th- and 6th-century migration routes around Britain and Ireland (after Alcock 1971, p. 353).

Picts

Jutes

Scotti

Saxons

Frisians

Deisi

Cunedda

Britons

| 0 | | 100 | | 200 | | 300 miles |
| 0 | 100 | | 200 | 300 km | | |

↖ Migration route

Although the sea was clearly very important to Roman Britain, the evidence for the maritime history of these islands in the late Roman period is rather thin. Sea trade of some sort existed, although the volume is unknown. In the fourth century the imperial government sent shiploads of grain and olive oil direct from North Africa to Britain to supply the troops, but these shipments had ceased by about 400. Most of the seaborne trade that existed in the early fifth century was probably restricted to cross-Channel routes, where piracy was a major problem. In the third and fourth centuries the Roman army had constructed ten large coastal forts, from Portchester in Hampshire to Brancaster in north Norfolk, as part of a defence scheme that also took in the Channel coast of Gaul (modern France). Known as the forts of the 'Saxon Shore', they appear to have been intended primarily as army and naval bases for defence against Saxon attackers, although pirates from Ireland and Scotland may also have been a problem.

The *Classis Britannica*, the fleet guarding Britain and the English Channel, survived into the fourth century, and there was enough shipping left in Roman

Britain in 407 to enable the usurping emperor Constantine III to lead an army from Britain to Gaul to attack Germanic invaders. However, it is unlikely that any organized fleet survived long into the fifth century, for the tax and supply systems that supported it probably ground to a halt soon after 410. The seaways around Britain were left open for others to use.[2]

In the year 448 or 449 three ships are said to have landed at Ebbsfleet in Kent, not far from the old Roman fort at Richborough. They carried two Germanic chieftains, Hengest and Horsa (meaning 'stallion' and 'horse'), and their followers, who had been summoned to fight as mercenaries by Vortigern, a ruler of the Britons in southern England, against the invading Picts from the north. The mercenaries soon proved to be a menace. Recognizing both the potential wealth of Britain and its military weakness, Hengest and Horsa sent for many more men from their homeland, the border-area between modern Denmark and Germany. They began a campaign that gradually subdued Kent and opened the way to massive immigration into Britain by Angles, Saxons and Jutes.

That, more or less, is the story told by the *Anglo-Saxon Chronicle*, the name given to a number of histories, probably first set down in the late ninth century.

3. View of part of the Saxon Shore fort at Portchester, Hampshire. Standing on Portsmouth Harbour, Portchester was the most westerly of the great 3rd/4th-century system of coastal forts built in Roman Britain.

The chronicle drew on a variety of written and oral sources, making it possible to piece together some aspects of the early centuries of English history.[3] It is impossible to be certain about the reliability of the details, but the sixth-century British monk Gildas also mentions the arrival of three 'keels' bearing treacherous mercenaries, so the dramatic arrival of the three ships at Ebbsfleet may have actually happened. If Vortigern did call in Germanic mercenaries, he was only following a long-established Roman practice. What is undeniable is that between the fifth and seventh centuries the Germanic tribes succeeded in overcoming many of the post-Roman British kingdoms. Starting from the east and south coasts, they had pushed into the areas of modern Yorkshire, the Midlands, Gloucestershire and Sussex by the end of the sixth century. They created a patchwork of tribal lands and small kingdoms that ultimately came together to form what we now call Anglo-Saxon England.

Anglo-Saxon society was dominated by a warrior élite, but historians and archaeologists vary as to whether Anglo-Saxon expansion was a matter of conquest, subjugation and extermination or a relatively peaceful process of assimilation. 'Ethnic cleansing' is certainly not a new phenomenon. However, as the scholar Christopher Snyder has recently remarked, contemporary writers and chroniclers all 'leave no doubt that fear and hatred dominated most relationships between Britons and *Saxones*'. The sea was a part of the life of the Anglo-Saxons, at least in the coastal regions, as the pagan Anglo-Saxon ship-burials at Sutton Hoo and Snape in East Anglia testify. For example, the great ship barrow or burial mound at Snape, possibly built about 550, was not just a grave marker. As W. Filmer-Sankey points out, the burial mound was visible from the nearby river Alde and from the North Sea. It may well have functioned in part as a sea-mark or navigation point for sailors, like the barrow of the eponymous hero Beowulf in the great Anglo-Saxon epic poem.[4]

England – 'the land of the Angles' – was not so-called until about the year 1000. However, four hundred years before this Aethelbert of Kent (*c*.560–616) was styling himself *rex Anglorum*, 'king of the Angles'. Some notion of a generalized English land or *Anglia* seems to have taken hold in the seventh century, although England as a political reality was still a long way off.[5]

The rise and fall of the British West

The Anglo-Saxon conquest was not a rapid one and it proceeded by fits and starts. The Britons survived for a long time in the Celtic west – in what later became Wales and Cornwall – and the north. They maintained some of the old Roman ways, although it is clear that their world was changing from the urbanized civil society of Roman times to one of tribes and kings. Large numbers of emigrants seem to have left Devon, Cornwall and Dorset in the late fifth and sixth centuries to settle in the former Roman province of Armorica, which became Brittany. It is believed by some scholars that the Breton language did not develop from the native Gaulish tongue but was actually taken to Brittany by these emigrants.[6]

Despite their seemingly isolated position, sea transport ensured that the Celtic

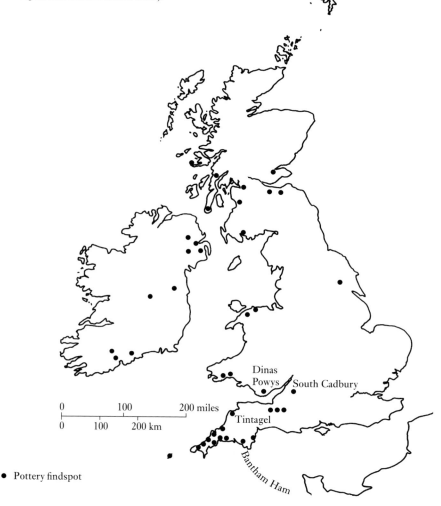

4 Findspots of imported 5th–7th-century Mediterranean pottery (after www.potsherd.uklinux.net/atlas).

Dinas
Powys South Cadbury

0   100   200 miles
0   100   200 km

Tintagel

Bantham Ham

● Pottery findspot

kingdoms of the west were not completely cut off from what was left of the old Roman world. Archaeological evidence has shown that fine pottery, including amphorae for wine or olive oil, tableware, and other goods were still reaching parts of Britain and Ireland between the fifth and seventh centuries from places as distant as Carthage, Alexandria and Palestine. Such fragments have been found in locations as far apart as the Scilly Isles and Strathclyde in Scotland. Although some odd potsherds have also turned up in London and St Albans, the bulk of them have been found in the west of Britain.

Most of the pottery found came from the north-east Mediterranean, the Byzantine heartland. The amphorae are difficult to date closely, but the tableware has been dated to about 475–550. Some pottery also came from North Africa and other places in the western Mediterranean, but it has been found in much smaller amounts than the eastern Mediterranean material. As M.G. Fulford has pointed out, this would have been consistent with eastern ships taking small additional cargoes on board at western Mediterranean ports as they voyaged to Britain. The voyages themselves were probably never very numerous, but the trade was consistent and seems to have lasted for about two centuries. It may have been at its height between about 475 and 550: a stone from Penmachno in Conwy (Wales) carries a Byzantine inscription dated to 540. Procopius' ghost story may well have come from a sailor who had been to Britain.

The main landfalls for the Mediterranean ships were in what is now western England and south Wales, with Tintagel in Cornwall as the main port of call,

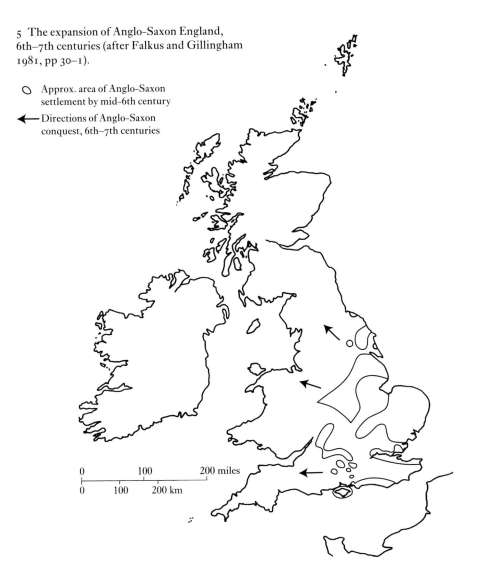

5 The expansion of Anglo-Saxon England,
6th–7th centuries (after Falkus and Gillingham
1981, pp 30–1).

O Approx. area of Anglo-Saxon
    settlement by mid-6th century

←—Directions of Anglo-Saxon
    conquest, 6th–7th centuries

0   100   200 miles

0   100   200 km

judging by the number of pottery fragments found there. Tintagel later played a major role in the Arthurian myth, but in reality it seems to have functioned as a trading post for the rulers of the Celtic kingdom of Dumnonia. The rocky cliffs and other physical features of the place would have made it unsuitable as a year-round port, so most of the trading must have taken place in the spring and summer. In any case storms would have made it very difficult for Mediterranean shipping to move north in autumn and winter. The risks of the long-distance trade from the Mediterranean were considerable; the round-trip must have taken months, with the danger of pirates added to that of storms.

Tintagel has yielded most Mediterranean pottery finds, followed by the major hillfort settlements at South Cadbury, Cadbury-Congresbury in Somerset and Dinas Powys in south Wales. Aside from Tintagel, it is difficult to identify many specific ports. One exception is the haven of Bantham Ham, at the mouth of the Avon in south Devon a few miles west of Salcombe. The Bantham site is on a promontory in a sheltered harbour and probably had little or nothing in the way of port facilities. Mediterranean and Gaulish pottery was found on the site decades ago, and more recent discoveries have indicated that feasts were held on the beach at Bantham while goods were exchanged. The image of boozy 'Dark Age' beach barbecues is difficult to resist, but sober reflection suggests that the exchange of goods may have been a much more formal matter than the 'party animal' detritus might suggest. The trade was a high-value business and anyone trading without a clear head was likely to be cheated.

The trade was centred on the exchange of luxury goods from the Mediterranean, such as wine, olive oil and fine pottery (and apparently sometimes also grain), for coins, treasure and Cornish tin. Tin, an ingredient in the manufacture of bronze, must have been the main reason for the trade, for Cornwall appears to have been the only source of tin in the Western world between the third and thirteenth centuries (see p. 63). Some Devon towns may also have owed their early development to the trade. A seventh-century saint's life has a reference to a ship carrying a cargo of corn from Alexandria that is blown off course and ends up in Britain (possibly at Exeter, but certainly at some port in Dumnonia), where the corn is traded for tin. The British end of the trade was probably controlled by the Celtic kings and aristocracy, who undoubtedly were the last consumers in Britain of the Roman 'good life'. Like the Italian galley trade of the thirteenth to sixteenth centuries (see Chapter 3), such voyages relied on the movement of low-volume, high-value goods.

There were shorter-range contacts between Britain, Ireland and Gaul between the fifth and eighth centuries, possibly centred on a trade in wine from the river Loire in what is now western France (British and Irish woollen cloth and leather may have gone the other way). Professor Thomas describes it as 'a jerkily continuous story of contact through three or four centuries'. Gaulish sailors were reaching as far afield as the west of Scotland coast by the second half of the sixth century, and in the Irish language the word *Gallus*, which at first meant 'a Gaul', later came to denote any foreigner. Small amounts of wheel-thrown Gaulish tableware have been found at many sites in western Britain and Ireland: such pottery was valuable in places where the old Roman pottery industries had long since collapsed or had never existed. The rise in Gaulish imports in Ireland and the west of Britain took place in the seventh and eighth centuries. Trade with the Mediterranean ceased in the seventh century, probably killed off by the rise of Islam, which conquered North Africa and the Middle East, and by the advance of the Anglo-Saxons in Britain. More than 600 years were to pass before regular direct trade started again between the British Isles and the Mediterranean.[7]

People on the move

The Anglo-Saxons who came to Britain in the fifth century did not give up sea-faring when they set about conquering and settling the land. Anglo-Saxon piracy remained a problem until the seventh century. Indeed, the historian John Haywood sees strong similarities between the activities of the Anglo-Saxons and those of the later Vikings. In the case of the former, the initial phase of seaborne raids (*c*.280–430) was followed by a stage in which raiding colonies were established on enemy territory (*c*.430–60). This was succeeded by a long period of settlement and consolidation (*c*.460–600), and an ultimate phase in the seventh century in which naval activity came under the control of kings and was used for wider political ends.[8]

One should not imagine that the coastal waters outside the practical reach of the Anglo-Saxons were peaceful. There is evidence of the refortification of prehistoric hillforts in locations close to the sea or a river, such as at Chun Castle and Castle Dore in Cornwall, and Dinas Powys in south Wales, indicating a waterborne threat. It has been suggested that a Roman-style fort built at Aberffraw on Anglesey was not Roman at all but was actually constructed by the kings of Dyfed in the fifth or sixth century as a defence against Irish pirates.[9]

The growing Germanic kingdoms pushed further west into areas controlled by Britons, and also clashed with one another. One of the largest of the kingdoms was Northumbria, which stretched from a line between the rivers Dee and Humber into what is now southern Scotland. Northumbria is the earliest-known Anglo-Saxon naval power, conquering the islands of Man and Anglesey in the reign of King Edwin (r. 616–32) and later, in 684, sending a naval expedition to Ireland. However, the richest and most successful of the Anglo-Saxon kingdoms of this era was Mercia. Between the early seventh and the late eighth century Mercia established hegemony over a swathe of land running from the Welsh border (the line of the famous Offa's Dyke) to the North Sea, as well as the kingdoms of Essex, Sussex, Kent and others. The power of Mercia was very probably enhanced by the flow of wealth from the trading ports of Kent and elsewhere. Mercian power was fractured by dynastic strife in the early ninth century and by the rise of Wessex; had it not been, the English resistance to the later Danish attacks might have been more effective.[10]

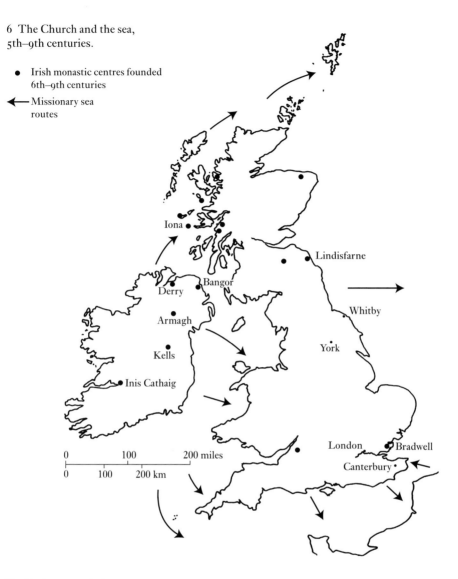

6 The Church and the sea,
5th–9th centuries.

- Irish monastic centres founded
  6th–9th centuries
- ← Missionary sea
  routes

Iona

Lindisfarne

Derry · Bangor

Armagh

Whitby

Kells

York

Inis Cathaig

0   100   200 miles
0   100   200 km

London · Bradwell

Canterbury ·

Religion and the sea

Besides invasions and raids, the best evidence for sea travel around the British Isles between the fifth and ninth centuries comes from the activities of saints, priests and penitents. Christian missions already existed in Ireland by the early fifth century, pointing to some peaceful sea contact with the late Roman Empire. People crossed the Irish Sea and perhaps also traded. Migration from Ireland in the Roman and early post-Roman periods brought Irish people and their language to western Wales, Scotland, Cornwall, Devon and to the Isle of Man, and stones inscribed with fifth- or sixth-century Irish ogham script have been found in Wales and Cornwall, some of them explicitly Christian in nature. One epoch-making link was inadvertently made by pirates. In the fifth century the future

St Patrick (*c*.389–*c*.461) was kidnapped as a boy by Irish raiders from his home in western Britain and taken to Ireland as a slave. He escaped after six years, but felt a powerful call to return and convert the pagan Irish to Christianity. By Patrick's own account, Ireland was then regarded as standing literally at the ends of the Earth, with nothing beyond but the sea into which the setting sun descended.[11]

The Celtic church in Ireland began 'exporting' religion to other parts of the British Isles and the Continent. St Columba (*Colum Cille*, *c*.521–97) was a son of an Irish royal house from what is now County Donegal. In 563 he took twelve adherents with him from Ireland to found a monastery on the island of Iona, near Mull in the west of Scotland, in the kingdom of Dalriada. Iona and its daughter churches played an important role in converting the Picts to Christianity, and established influence over the Anglian royal house of Northumbria in the seventh century. King Oswald of Northumbria (r. 634–42) was converted to Christianity at Iona while in exile in Scotland, and it was at his initiative that in 635 Aidan travelled from Iona to found a monastery at Lindisfarne, off the Northumbrian coast. Iona's influence in Northumbria did not decline until after 664, when the Synod of Whitby decided on the use of the Roman method of calculating the date of Easter rather than the Celtic one. Roman ideas about the issue eventually crossed the Irish Sea via Admonan, ninth abbot of Iona, who was converted to them during a visit to Northumbria in the 680s.

One of the most famous of the travelling Irish churchmen was St Brendan (*c*.486–*c*.575), who appears to have had links with Scotland, Wales and Brittany. The story of his *Navigation* into the Atlantic, with a small group of monks, in search of a blessed land seems to have been put together some five centuries or so after his time. Whether or not it represented a real voyage is difficult to say. The story was very popular in medieval times, and the legend of an Island of the Blessed in the western Atlantic undoubtedly provided some of the stimulus for the early exploratory voyages from Bristol in the late fifteenth century.[12]

Other Irish churchmen converted Mercia to Christianity in the seventh century, and worked to reconvert the kingdom of Essex, which had lapsed into paganism after the initial conversion by Augustine had failed to 'take'. St Columbanus (d. 615) took Irish missionary activity further afield, travelling to Gaul in about 590. He appears to have had a sophisticated notion of a Christian Europe with Rome as its centre, and he founded several monasteries there and in Italy, some of which in their turn sent missions to Britain.

The Irish Church played a crucial role in the conversion or reconversion of the pagan Anglo-Saxon lands to Christianity, a role that would have been impossible had sea travel around the British Isles not been a normal part of life in the sixth and seventh centuries, for all its apparent dangers.

However, it was the Roman Church, not that of Ireland, which came to control Christianity in England. In 597 Pope Gregory the Great sent the monk Augustine to convert the English. Augustine landed in Kent, a pagan Jutish kingdom that had dynastic and trade links with the Franks in Gaul. The Franks had also been Germanic invaders, but by this stage the Frankish kingdom was officially

Christian. King Aethelbert of Kent was married to a Frankish princess, which undoubtedly facilitated his conversion and that of his kingdom. Over the next two decades or so, the Archbishopric of Canterbury was established, along with bishops' sees at London, Rochester and York. Essex, East Anglia and Northumbria were also ostensibly converted, although the English kingdoms rapidly reverted to paganism. This, in turn, was soon reversed, largely through the efforts of Irish holy men rather than those from Rome. However, after the Synod of Whitby in 664, ecclesiastical power in England was based on Canterbury and through it on Rome.

The Christian Anglo-Saxon kingdoms began sending out their own missionaries and religious thinkers. Between the 670s and the 770s a number of major missionary enterprises left England for the Continent. In 678, for example, St Wilfrid left Northumbria to preach to the Frisians; in 716 Boniface crossed the Channel to begin his mission to the pagans in Germany; the theologian Alcuin of York, one of the greatest scholars of his day, was invited in 782 by the Emperor Charlemagne to oversee a Carolingian palace school.

It seems banal to point to connections of such cultural and religious significance as evidence of sea transport, particularly when they could all have been accomplished by the use of a handful of fishing boats. However, they do suggest that movement by sea between the British Isles and the Continent was at least possible at this period, despite pirates and raiders. Such contacts continued even during the era of the Viking raids and invasions, between the ninth and eleventh centuries, although the dangers of travel were probably much greater.

Early medieval Scotland, Ireland and Wales

The outlines of the future ethnic and political boundaries of the British Isles began to emerge in the centuries following the collapse of Roman rule. Ireland had never been conquered by the Romans, although it is apparent that it had sea contacts with Roman Britain and other parts of the empire. An Irish immigrant was living in the Roman town of Silchester (Berkshire) in the fourth or early fifth century, and by 432 there was at least one Christian community in Ireland that had links with Rome. Inscribed stones left by Irish settlers of the fifth century have been found in south-west Wales, and later cross-decorated stones probably of the seventh to ninth centuries found in Ireland, Man and Wales point to later Irish expansion across the Irish Sea. Some, if not all, of this expansion took the form of military conquest. The Gaelic peoples of Dalriada in Antrim, in the north of Ireland (known as the 'Scots'), invaded the west of Scotland and established three tribal groups in Argyll, Arran and Bute, driving the Picts out of these areas. The kingdom of Dalriada became a formidable regional naval power. Between the 560s and the 730s it sent out eight major seaborne expeditions, and a document of about 660 suggests that it could have, in theory, raised a fleet of 177 small warships (the law specified that every twenty households were to supply two warships with fourteen oarsmen each). Dalriada was not the only northern kingdom using naval force: in the seventh century the Picts were actively raiding the Western Isles. By

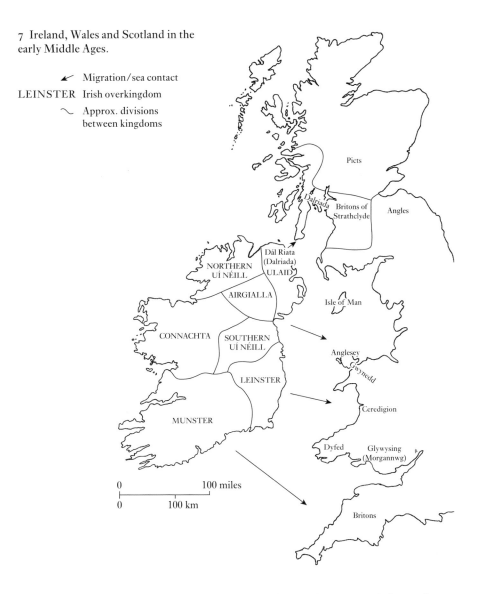

7 Ireland, Wales and Scotland in the early Middle Ages.

⟍ Migration/sea contact
LEINSTER   Irish overkingdom
⟍ Approx. divisions
     between kingdoms

Picts

Dalriada Britons of
          Strathclyde

Angles

Dál Riata
(Dalriada)
ULAID

NORTHERN
UÍ NÉILL

AIRGIALLA

Isle of Man

CONNACHTA   SOUTHERN
            UÍ NÉILL

Anglesey

Gwynedd

LEINSTER

Ceredigion

MUNSTER

Dyfed   Glywysing
        (Morgannwg)

0   100 miles

0   100 km

Britons

the eighth century Scotland was split between four main groups: Britons, Scots, Picts and English.[13]

Early medieval Ireland was no more united than any other part of the British Isles. Although some concept of a 'high king' of Ireland existed by the seventh century, it does not appear to have denoted the ruler of a centralized kingdom. The reality seems to have been much more complex, with a number of regional kingdoms ruling other, smaller kingdoms or tribes, their boundaries shifting with wars or changes in allegiance.

Early medieval Wales was likewise politically fractured. Apart from the south-eastern region, much of the Roman presence in Wales had been military in nature. The fifth and sixth centuries saw the appearance of a number of kingdoms, which

8. Porth Clais, Dyfed. Porth Clais was the medieval port of St David's, the centre of the Welsh Church. However, the narrow, rocky inlet at Porth Clais is a natural harbour and may well have been in use before the 11th century, one of many landing places around the coast of Britain and Ireland. Porth Clais was the reputed site of the baptism of St David, and features in the Welsh medieval epic, the *Mabinogion.*

by the eleventh century had become three major political units: Glywysing or Morgannwg in the south and south-east, Dyfed in the west and Gwynedd in the north-west. Anglo-Saxon military pressure in the form of raids and Offa's Dyke (built in the eighth century), as well as language and other cultural differences, helped to define the Welsh lands as separate from England, although the Welsh kingdoms also fought with each other and sometimes allied with the English. However, linguistic and cultural links overcame the political fragmentation of Wales and served to give both the Welsh and outsiders a sense of Wales as a country, if not a unified nation. The Britons of Wales and northern Britons were already describing themselves as *Cymry*, 'people of the same region', by the mid-seventh century and by the eleventh and twelfth centuries, notions of the rough geographical extent of Wales were fairly well established.[14]

Ships and shipbuilding

There is still a great deal that is not known about medieval boats and ships. Evidence for early medieval vessels in the British Isles is particularly sparse, but it is probable that log boats (canoes made from hollowed-out tree trunks) and skin boats were common, and were used as ferries, fishing boats, trading vessels and even for war. Skin boats, which survive today in the form of the paddled Welsh coracle or the rowed Irish curragh, can be very effective craft. Tim Severin's famous voyage of the 1970s, re-creating St Brendan's sixth-century voyage, showed that it was possible to sail across the North Atlantic in a skin boat. In 891 three 'Scots' (meaning Irish) were washed ashore on the Cornish coast in a boat made from two and a half skins. Trusting to the love of God to keep them safe, they had taken food for seven days, but had no means of propelling or steering the boat. They said that they had drifted for seven days before making land. This was regarded as such a miraculous feat that the three men were taken to meet King Alfred.[15]

Ships and boats made from wooden planks leave much more in the way of archaeological remains than skin boats, but few early medieval examples have been found in the British Isles. The most famous find is undoubtedly that of the Sutton Hoo ship, discovered in an Anglo–Saxon royal burial mound near Woodbridge in

9. The Sutton Hoo ship burial. Discovered in the 1930s, the 7th-century Sutton Hoo ship burial included a fabulous Anglo-Saxon treasure and the outlines of a large, double-ended ship which had been built clinker-fashion.

Suffolk. The ship was filled with magnificent treasures and was perhaps the last resting place of King Raedwald of East Anglia (d. *c*.625/6). The hull itself had rotted away, leaving only an impression in the soil and a large pattern of iron clench-nails. Careful recording and reinvestigation has shown that it was just over 27 metres in length, with a maximum beam of 4.5 metres and a depth amidships of 1.5 metres. The hull was clinker-built and double-ended, and was composed of nine runs of planking on each side. Clinker construction is a technique by which a hull is built up from a shell of overlapping planks, fastened at the edges by nails. The nails are driven in from outside, and are held in place by clenching their ends over metal washers called roves. Although the hull is stiffened by internal frames and beams, it is the shell of planks that is the main load-bearing element. Double-ended hulls, in which the stem and stern resembled each other, were commonplace until the later Middle Ages.[16]

It used to be thought that, due to lack of positive evidence of masts and rigging, the use of sail died out in northern Europe between the fifth and seventh centuries. This seems very unlikely. Sails were known in northern Europe before the Romans came and, as the historian John Haywood points out, it seems unlikely that the Saxons would have been much of a seaborne menace to the late Roman Empire if they had only possessed oar-driven boats. It is not known if the Sutton Hoo ship would normally have carried a mast and sail, but studies of the reconstructed hull have suggested that it could have performed well under sail. We do not know if the Sutton Hoo ship was built in England, but its general type – clinker-built and double-ended – seems to have been the predominant one in the waters of the British Isles until the thirteenth century, as it was in much of northern Europe. Old English, the term used for the language of the Anglo-Saxons, had over thirty words for different types (or usages) of ships or boats, plus nearly fifty more that may have been purely poetic in character. A prosaic trading ship might be called a *ceapscip*, for example, but a ship with a beaked prow (probably possessed by many vessels) could be the poet's *hornscip*.[17]

Almost nothing is known of the ships of the Dalriada or of the Picts, or of the other naval powers of the early medieval British Isles. It is quite possible that remains of some of these vessels survive somewhere on or off the coast; perhaps one day someone will even find the wreck of a sixth- or seventh-century Byzantine trading ship that never made it back to the Mediterranean.

Eighth-century Britain and Ireland were not peaceful places, as internal wars were common, but there were signs of growing stability. The Christian conversion, if only skin-deep in some places, was at least very widespread. International trade was developing and small towns were beginning to reappear. For such things to happen, the dangers of widespread piracy and sea war must have been receding. The ninth century was to show just what happened when they returned.

CHAPTER TWO

Wics, wars and 'heathen men',
*c.*700–1066

The first ports of Anglo-Saxon England

The clearest evidence for the international links of any early English kingdom comes from Kent. Kent was in contact with the Germanic kingdom of Frankia, which reached from modern Belgium to the south of France and from the Atlantic to western Germany. The Merovingian kingdom of Frankia even had pretensions to hegemony over the Angles, and in the late sixth century the pagan King Aethelbert of Kent married a Christian Frankish princess, who came along with her own bishop. Frankish-made items have been found in sixth- and seventh-century Kentish burials, but these could have got there by means of gift-exchange or raiding, rather than trade. Other Anglo-Saxon kingdoms, such as East Anglia, had links with Frankia and with places further afield, like Scandinavia. Trade, rather than aristocratic gift-giving, seems to have been getting under way in the seventh century. Amongst other things, Anglo-Saxon imitations of Frankish coins began to appear in the 630s, but English international commerce does not seem to have really flowered until the eighth century. By the late 700s commerce between England and Frankia was important enough for the two great rulers of the day, Offa of Mercia and Charlemagne, to have trade disputes (see p. 29).[1]

As settlement and centralized political control became more established in the seventh and eighth centuries, the first English towns began to appear, and a significant number of these were seaports. However, the growth of seaports was not an isolated phenomenon peculiar to England: ports, of course, had to trade with other ports in order to grow. The economic history of this period is marked by the development of settlements on both sides of the North Sea and English Channel with the Germanic word-element *wic*, meaning 'trading place', incorporated in their names. On the other side of the sea these included Schleswig (*Sliaswich*), now in Germany, Wijk-bii-Duurstede at the mouth of the Rhine (in Holland) and Quentovic, which stood near Boulogne. Their English counterparts included Fordwich and Sandwich in Kent, London (called *Lundenwic* in the 680s), Ipswich, Norwich and York (*Eorforwic*). All of these places were sited either on navigable rivers or in good coastal harbours. Wics were clearly among the most significant settlements where goods were exchanged, but not all port names, however, incorporated the *wic* element and coin finds scattered around the coast suggest that trading went on in all sorts of places. One such locality was the rural settlement of Sandtun, situated by a sea inlet near West Hythe in Kent. Sandtun was occupied between about 700 and *c.*850–75 and appears to have been on both coastal and international trade routes. Pottery found there came from Ipswich and

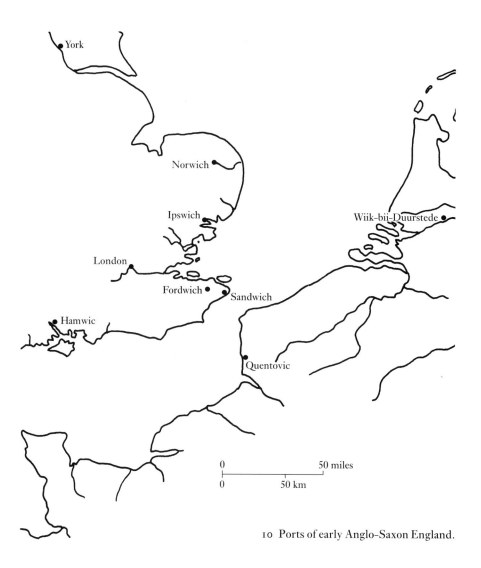

York

Norwich

Ipswich

London

Fordwich

Sandwich

Hamwic

Quentovic

Wiik-bii-Duurstede

| 0 | | 50 miles |
| 0 | 50 km | |

10 Ports of early Anglo-Saxon England.

the Thames Estuary, as well as from France and Flanders, and other activities carried on at this site included fishing, bone-working and salt-making.[2]

Sea trade, and the prosperity that went with it, operated as a major engine of economic growth in the eighth century. For instance, it is reckoned that of the ten places in late Anglo-Saxon Kent that could be regarded as towns, nine were ports. The one exception was Canterbury, which was of course a major religious centre and the capital of the old Kentish kingdom, but Canterbury had its own port at nearby Fordwich. Anglo-Saxon towns were tiny by modern standards, but in their day they seem to have been busy, cosmopolitan places with people coming from distant places to conduct their business. It is not always easy to see how some ports grew up, for nowadays they have little or no access to the sea, but early medieval coastlines were very different from those that we know today. Sandwich in Kent, for example, now has a rather restricted access to the sea, but it was once a great port. It was established on a sandbank on the edge of the wide Wantsum Channel, which once separated the Isle of Thanet from the mainland. Even if Sandwich had been sited at the end of a small creek, some of the small early medieval trading vessels could have reached the place. Most ships of the time could probably operate in very shallow waters, and as far as harbour installations went, needed little more than a convenient beaching point. As late as the eleventh century the limits of Sandwich harbour were defined rather alarmingly as the distance inland that an axe could be thrown from a boat drawn close inshore at high tide.[3]

The growth of ports was probably stimulated deliberately by local rulers. From the earliest times, it seems, government was involved in trade in some way. A king did not have to be a genius to make the connection between trade and wealth, and to see that some of this wealth could make its way to the royal coffers. The corollary was that trade had to be regulated and protected. In Kent King Hlothere (r. 673–85) appointed the earliest-known royal official, or reeve, to administer a wic settlement. It is likely that the reeve's duties included ensuring that a good proportion of the wealth flowing through the port ended up in the king's hands. By the 730s, if not earlier, the kingdom of Kent was levying tolls on ships using the port of London. In the 740s there is a clear reference to an official who collected these tolls, perhaps the first recorded customs officer in English history.[4]

At the beginning of the eighth century, four of the greatest Anglo-Saxon kingdoms had their wics. London, or Lundenwic, served Mercia; Ipswich catered for East Anglia; Hamwic for Wessex; and York (*Eoforwic*) for Northumbria. The short-lived Hampshire port of Hamwic, now covered by modern Southampton, may have owed its foundation in about 680–690 to the kingdom of Wessex, which had its capital at nearby Winchester. Archaeological evidence suggests that Hamwic, built on the eastern side of the peninsula between the rivers Itchen and Test, was a planned town with streets set in a north–south, east–west grid. It covered an area of about 45 hectares, and is estimated to have had a population of about 4,000–5,000 at its peak. Finds show that the port was home to many different craft-workers and had direct or indirect trading links with Frankia, Spain, Scandinavia and other places. It flourished for over 150 years, but declined at the time of the Viking attacks of the ninth century, like many other wics. The location was a good one for sea trade, and the town of Southampton later grew up on the western side of the peninsula.[5]

London was the largest of the English ports, a position of dominance it was to retain for most of the following 1,300 years. One of the clearest signs of early port growth comes from London. The city seems to have been more or less deserted between the mid-fifth century and 604, when King Aethelbert of Kent founded the first St Paul's Cathedral. However, a new settlement grew up to the west of the old Roman city, on a site now called the Aldwych (meaning 'old port' or 'trading settlement'). The first written evidence of the post-Roman port of London comes in 672–4, with a mention of 'the port of London, where ships tie up'. The historian Bede refers to a Frisian trader buying slaves at London in 679, and in the 680s the port was being called Lundenwic. Excavations have revealed a large eighth- to ninth-century settlement, between 55 and 60 hectares in extent, with a grid-pattern of streets. It is ironic that some of the earliest *English* towns (as opposed to redevelopments based on Roman foundations) seem to have resembled modern American cities in their layout rather than having the meandering street patterns that we regard as being 'typically' English. This London stood along the Strand (itself an Old English word meaning 'shoreline'), and may have housed as many as 5,000 people. It traded internationally as well as along the English coast (much of the pottery used in Lundenwic was made in Ipswich).

There is archaeological evidence of a decline in London's growth in the second half of the eighth century, but the reasons are not known. Trade fluctuations are the likeliest explanation at this date, but in the ninth century commerce was strangled by war. Viking activity from the 840s is liable to have made the Thames unsafe for regular trade, and between 871 and 886 London was occupied by the Danes. King Alfred refounded London in 886, but as a port within the old Roman walls, away from Lundenwic which declined and vanished. Alfred's initial idea may well have been to use London as another *burh* or fortress, but by the 890s there are clear signs that a trading harbour was being re-established, with new buildings, shipping tolls and the other features of a port. However, as Ian Walker points out, the Thames was probably not really secure from the Danes until 917. Thirty years or more may have passed from the time of the Viking occupation before London was really back in business.

Trading wharves were in use at London between the late 800s and 1000, with names such as Queenhithe and Billingsgate making their appearance, and excavations have shown that harbour works were built on the (modern) New Fresh Wharf site between the late ninth century and the mid-tenth century. Other archaeological discoveries point to rapid urban growth in London from the mid-tenth century. By about 1000 (or slightly later) the English government had developed a relatively complex list of harbour dues charged on merchandise reaching London. Different types and sizes of ships paid differential tolls, and the goods subject to local customs duties included planks, cloth, wool, 'blubber fish'(probably walrus or whale) and foodstuffs. Foreign merchants from France and elsewhere also paid dues according to where they came from. Late Saxon London was trading with the Low Countries, the Rhineland and northern France, and also received goods indirectly from the Byzantine Empire and even China. In the 730s Bede had written that London was 'a trading centre for many nations who visit it by land and sea', a description that would hold true until the invention of air travel. The city's future as the capital city of England, and later Britain, was intimately linked with its status as the greatest seaport in England.

Records of English trading voyages are almost non-existent before the thirteenth century, but archaeological finds and documentary evidence do make it possible to fill in some of the picture. English imports in the eighth and ninth centuries (and later) included wine and millstones from France and Germany, timber and foodstuffs. English exports over the same period are known to have included salt, cloth, hides and lead, as well as slaves. Pope Gregory the Great famously encountered Anglian slaves in Rome in the sixth century, and slavery was part and parcel of life in England and many other parts of Europe in the early medieval period. English and foreign merchants seem to have routinely traded in people, and this north European slave trade may have survived as late as the twelfth century. However, not all trade was so cruel. Ships carried scholars and books as well as goods and slaves, and sea trade enabled thinkers from England and other parts of the British Isles to play a part in the growing intellectual life of the Church in continental Europe.

Trade clearly had a major role in English international relations by the 790s, for by then it was important enough to be used as a political weapon. The Frankish Emperor Charlemagne banned all shipping movements and trade between England and Frankia after he discovered that the Mercian king Offa (r. 757–96) had been involved in an underhand scheme for a dynastic marriage between his son and Charlemagne's daughter. Relations were eventually patched up, but the two monarchs were in dispute again in 796, this time directly over trade. Offa complained about the size of millstones sent from Frankia, and Charlemagne made counterclaims that English export cloaks were shorter than they used to be. Charlemagne also claimed that some English merchants had been trying to pass themselves off as men of religion in order to avoid paying tolls. The dispute was settled amicably, with promises to protect each other's merchants. Minor though these episodes may seem, they underline just how important sea trade on both sides of the English Channel had become. It was about to be brutally disrupted.[6]

'Heathen men': the Viking wars[7]

The 'Viking Age' in Western Europe lasted from the late eighth century to the eleventh century. In the Norse language the word *víkingr* denoted a man who fought at sea, while *víking* could also mean sea warfare or raiding. Although Viking fleets often contained men from all of Scandinavia, in north-western Europe the Norwegians and Danes predominated, with the Swedes looking more to Russia and the east.

The Vikings were axe-wielding, bloodthirsty barbarians who slaughtered all in their path. They were also great seamen, shipbuilders and craftsmen, superb artists and builders, as well as being ordinary farmers and traders. There are elements of truth and caricature in both views; they represent both the older notion of the Vikings as mere pirates, and more recent ideas, derived in large part from archaeology, that see them more in the round. One thing at least we can be sure of: Vikings did not wear horned helmets as they charged into battle! This impractical headgear was invented by archaeologists and illustrators in the nineteenth century. The era was characterized by raiding, conquest and settlement that spread Scandinavian people and their culture from Russia to Ireland. Viking settlement changed the face of half of England and gave Ireland its first port towns. Viking society was dominated by aggressive and successful warriors who exploited their seaborne mobility to run rings round their enemies, to plunder and kill them, and to conquer their lands.

Various explanations have been put forward for the relatively sudden eruption

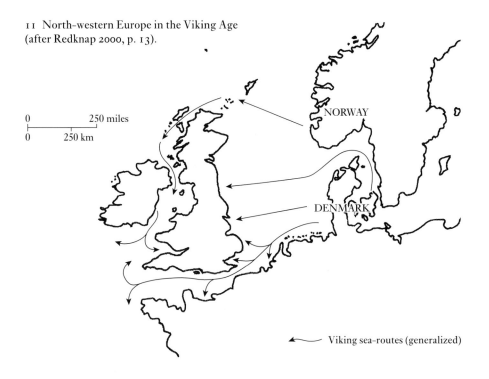

11 North-western Europe in the Viking Age
(after Redknap 2000, p. 13).

Viking sea-routes (generalized)

of Scandinavian sea-raiding in the late eighth century and for its recurrences over the next few hundred years. Over-population and political strife in Scandinavia are among the possibilities. It is also true that eighth-century Scandinavia was far poorer than contemporary western Europe and the lure of easy pickings drew many Vikings. Western Europe was totally unprepared to resist determined attack from the sea. The Vikings had several different types of ship, including the famous longships that spearheaded their attacks. However, they also possessed large cargo vessels that carried the settlers who moved in behind the armies. These ships and Viking seafaring skills were the keys to Viking expansion. Without them Scandinavia would have remained on the edge of the medieval world.[8]

The first recorded victim of the Scandinavian raiders in England was a reeve, Beaduheard, a servant of the king of Wessex, who arrogantly challenged some 'Northmen' or 'Danes' when they landed at Portland in Dorset in 789. Thinking they were ordinary merchants, he seems to have made the fatal mistake of asking three shiploads of Vikings if they had anything to declare.

The undefended religious houses of Europe presented the Vikings with lucrative targets. Like violent tourists they sacked Lindisfarne Abbey, off the north-east coast of England, in 793 and St Columba's Abbey on Iona, off western Scotland, in 795. The Vikings also made their presence felt on the coasts of Ireland and France in the 790s. The ease with which they were able to take wealthy churches and abbeys in exposed coastal positions strongly suggests that the seas around much of western Europe had been fairly peaceful in the eighth century. The great English scholar Alcuin wrote to Aethelred, king of Northumbria, after the

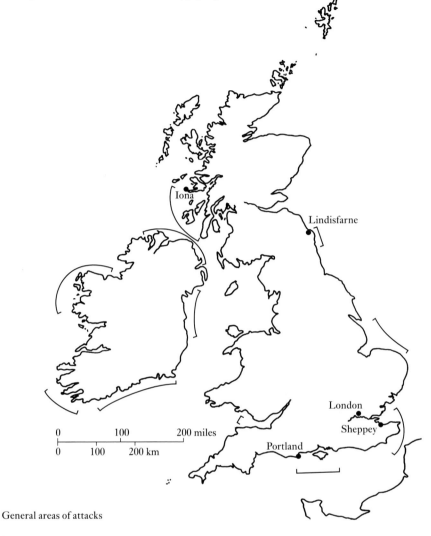

{ General areas of attacks

first attack. He lamented that the church of St Cuthbert at Lindisfarne had been 'spattered with the blood of the priests of God' and looted. 'Lo, it is nearly 350 years that we and our fathers have inhabited this lovely land, and never before has such a terror appeared in Britain as we have now suffered from a pagan race, nor was it thought that such an inroad from the sea could be made.'[9]

In the ninth century the Vikings involved themselves in the dynastic conflicts of Frankia, which was weakened by political crises, and raided widely in France, Frisia and Saxony. Dorestad, formerly a great Low Countries port, was raided heavily in the mid-830s (and on at least four other occasions in the next thirty years). Quentovic, the most significant Frankish port for English trade, was attacked in 842. In such conditions, normal sea trade must have declined sharply.

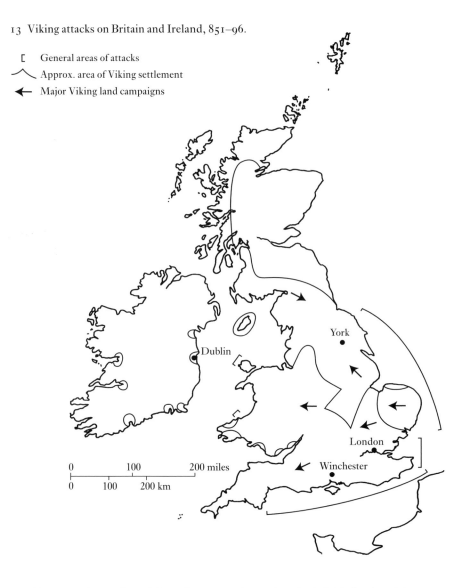

13 Viking attacks on Britain and Ireland, 851–96.

[General areas of attacks

∧ Approx. area of Viking settlement

← Major Viking land campaigns

York

Dublin

London

Winchester

0   100   200 miles

0   100   200 km

Viking attacks on the British Isles petered out after the initial shocks of the 790s. They returned with a vengeance in the 830s, probably at first as a by-product of Viking incursions into the Frankish Empire. In 835 'heathen men' raided the Isle of Sheppey in Kent. The following year King Egbert of Wessex fought and lost a battle against thirty-five shiploads of Danes at Carhampton in Somerset, an unlucky place that was to attract the attention of Danish raiders several times. Between 836 and 848 Danish seaborne 'raiding-armies' attacked the south and east coasts at various points, including Cornwall, Southampton, Portland, Romney Marsh, Lincolnshire, East Anglia, Kent, London and Somerset (twice more). English victories in battle, when they came, took place on land. There is little evidence before the time of King Alfred of any attempt at a coherent naval defence.

The nature of Danish activity in England began to change. The one saving grace of the early Danish attacks was that the raiders left England at the onset of the bad autumn and winter weather. In 851 their attacks moved beyond the stage of piracy when a Danish army stayed the winter in Kent, with either Thanet or Sheppey as their base. At about the same time, a huge fleet – said to comprise 350 ships – entered the Thames. Both London and Canterbury were attacked and the kings of Mercia and Wessex were beaten in battle. In 853 men from Kent and Surrey seem to have made some sort of seaborne attack on Thanet, inflicting defeat on the Danes in a pyrrhic victory that left many butchered or drowned on both sides.

In 865 a 'great raiding army' from Scandinavia landed in East Anglia. Over the next few years they conquered the kingdoms of Northumbria, East Anglia and Mercia, and between 876 and 880 began dividing up the conquered lands for settlement. The only surviving independent English kingdom was Wessex, ruled by King Alfred (r. 871–99). Alfred took a force to sea in 875 and fought seven Viking ships, capturing one and driving off the others, but this was an isolated early success. By 878 he was on the run in the Somerset marshes, and it was only his land victory at Edington in Wiltshire in that same year that turned the tables on the Danes and forced their leader Guthrum to make a temporary peace. Alfred made further attempts to fight the Danes at sea. He won a small but bloody battle over four Viking ships in 882, and in 884 his fleet wiped out sixteen shiploads of Danes at the mouth of the Stour in East Anglia. However, his victorious fleet battled with a large Viking force on the way home and lost.

In 886 Alfred reoccupied the city of London and concluded a treaty with Guthrum that recognized a huge swathe of eastern and northern England, later called the Danelaw, as Danish territory. Crucially, the treaty also brought the English lands outside Danish control under Alfred's rule. The Danish wars were far from over, however, and Alfred soon began constructing a series of *burhs* (fortified settlements) to defend his lands.

Although masters of the sea, by settling the land and accepting pitched battles the Danes became easier to defeat. Large-scale Viking raiding resumed in the 890s, and the south coast of Wessex was hit by sea-raids mounted from Northumbria and East Anglia, but they came up against strong and often successful English resistance. One effective English tactic was to separate the Danes from their ships, as this made them much more vulnerable. At Chichester in Sussex and Benfleet in Essex in 894, and near Hertford in 895, Viking forces were driven off, leaving their ships to be either captured or destroyed.

Alfred was set on fighting the Scandinavians by sea. He was given the overblown title of 'The Father of the Royal Navy' by later historians because of a famous passage in the *Anglo-Saxon Chronicle* relating to the year 896, in which the king is recorded as having large oared warships built (see pp 45–6). At least nine of his warships were ready to go to sea the same year, and they caught six Danish vessels in an estuary somewhere along the south coast. A fierce land and sea battle ensued, leaving 62 dead on the English side and 120 among the Danes. Only three damaged Danish ships, with badly-wounded crews, made it out of the estuary, and of those only one shipload got back alive to East Anglia. It was scarcely a Trafalgar, but may well have come as something of a shock to the Danes.

It is also possible that the Danes settled in Northumbria and East Anglia were starting to run low on ships. There are no overall figures for ship losses on either side, but the capture or destruction of Danish vessels at Chichester and elsewhere may have been making serious inroads into the Viking fleet. The *Anglo-Saxon Chronicle* states that the fleets that raided the south coast in 896 included significant numbers of warships that 'they had built many years before', which suggests that they were not building or acquiring many new vessels. English tactics were reducing the Vikings' manoeuvrability and throwing them on the defensive. The construction of forts, better military organization, and the targeting of beached ships meant that Wessex was becoming a much more dangerous opponent.

14 Map of the Viking wars, 975–1016

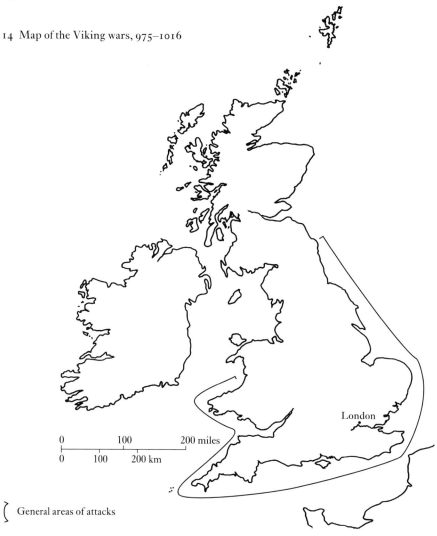

London

| 0 | 100 | 200 miles |
| 0 | 100 | 200 km |

(General areas of attacks

Alfred died in 899, but his successors carried on the fight. They extended the system of burhs, either taking over captured Danish fortifications or building new ones. When King Edward the Elder (r. 899–924) moved into the north-west, he built forts at Thelwall and Manchester (919), and at Rhuddlan in north Wales, to help protect the area against the attacks of Norse-Irish from Dublin. Inland forts on navigable rivers also had a role in maritime defence, given the ease with which the Vikings used rivers to move troops. By the 920s the forces of Wessex had pushed into the Midlands and the north-west.

The wars against the Danes turned Wessex into a naval power. We do not know the strength of Alfred's new fleet, but by 911 his son Edward was said to be able to raise a fleet of a hundred ships on the south coast. Chronicle figures for fleets are often questionable when they talk of 'a hundred' or 'hundreds', but in this case the fleet was big enough to fool a Danish land force invading Mercia into thinking that Edward had embarked most of his army and taken it to Kent. In fact, mobilizing the fleet was a strategic deception. Most of the English troops in Mercia and Wessex had stayed ashore and went on to kill many Danes.

Seaborne warfare became a familiar tool for the kings of Wessex. In 934 King Athelestan used a land force and a fleet to attack Scotland, a strategy that would be repeated by English kings later in the Middle Ages. In 945 King Edmund I raided Cumbria (which at this date included Strathclyde), then ceded it to King Malcolm of Scotland on condition that he would be his ally 'both on sea and land'. In 954 the Scandinavian kingdom of York fell with the death of its last ruler, Eric Bloodaxe. The kings of Wessex had effectively created the kingdom of England.

One of the great symbolic acts of early English history was carried out on water. Although *de facto* king of England from 959, King Edgar was not crowned until 973, when a ceremony was held at Bath. He then took his fleet to Chester, where he was met by six (or eight, the sources vary) under-kings from Cumbria, Scotland and Wales, who promised to be his allies on sea and land. In a brilliant act of political theatre the under-kings then rowed down the river Dee, in a boat steered by Edgar, to an abbey where prayers were said. The event had more show than substance, for within a few years the English kingdom was fighting for its life against the Scandinavians. However, a boat was a telling choice of symbol for the nation. No English ruler could afford to ignore the sea.

Edgar died in 975. He had two surviving sons by different wives. He was succeeded by his son Edward, but he was murdered in 979, allegedly at the instigation of Aelfrida, mother of his half-brother Aethelred. Aethelred II became king in what proved to be a terrible time for England, Wales and other parts of western Europe. There was a general renewal of Viking attacks. Norse-Irish from Dublin and the Isle of Man raided the Welsh coast between St David's and Anglesey between 978 and 999, but the heaviest and most frequent blows fell on the English West Country, the south coast and East Anglia. These were mounted by a combination of Norse-Irish, Norwegians and Danes.

The raids were disastrous. Between 980 and 982 attacks were made on places as far apart as Southampton, Thanet, Cheshire, Cornwall, Devon and Dorset, and in 982 London was burned. Preventing attacks of this nature was all but impossible in

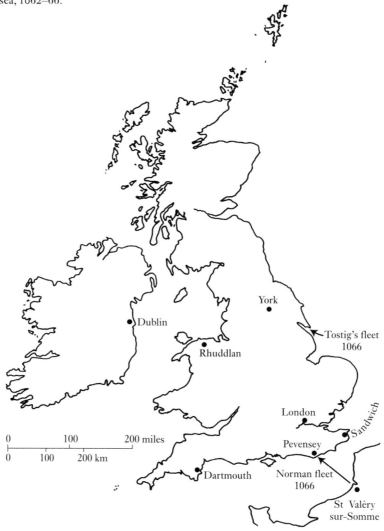

York

●Dublin

Tostig's fleet
1066

Rhuddlan

London

Sandwich

Pevensey

0   100   200 miles
0   100   200 km

Dartmouth   Norman fleet
1066

St Valéry
sur-Somme

a pre-industrial society. There was generally no warning until the Viking sails appeared over the horizon. Although some beacon systems did exist to alert those living inland (chains of fire-beacons set on hilltops within sight of each other), it was impossible to concentrate naval forces to intercept a fleet already in sight of the shore. However, destroying a fleet already known to be on its way was a possibility. In 992 Aethelred and his councillors decided to concentrate 'those ships that were worth anything' at London, with the aim of meeting and defeating at sea the fleet of the Norwegian Olaf Tryggvason (Olaf had arrived in 991 and defeated an English army at Maldon). But Aethelred's trap failed because a treacherous English commander warned Olaf, who was able to escape.[10]

The Scandinavians did not have it all their own way. Expecting easy pickings,

Olaf attacked London in 994 but was beaten off by fierce resistance from the Londoners. There was a strong opportunist element in Viking activity and Olaf's fleet moved off to attack the east and south coasts instead. Attempts were made to buy off the Vikings with *danegeld* (tribute payments) which provided short-term relief. Aethelred was not the first English king to try this, but paying 'protection money' was ultimately self-defeating. Like modern gangsters the Vikings only came back for more.

Aethelred and his councillors seem to have been well aware of the importance of naval forces in combating the Danes, but later attempts to muster naval forces against the Scandinavians also failed. In 999 Aethelred raised a fleet and an army to fight the Danes, but delays in preparation led to the force doing nothing, wasting time and money, leaving the soldiers and sailors demoralized. In 1008 the king ordered the construction of a national fleet. The fleet was stationed off Sandwich in 1009 but it was split when Wulfnoth, one of the English fleet commanders, was accused of treason. He broke away with twenty ships and went off to raid the south coast. A force of eighty vessels which pursued him was driven ashore by a storm: Wulfnoth then reappeared and burnt the ships. In the ensuing confusion Aethelred took the remainder of the fleet back to London, leaving nothing to oppose the Danes. The *Anglo-Saxon Chronicle* bitterly accuses him of wasting the nation's effort by lightly setting this deterrent aside.

In 1013 King Swein of Denmark invaded England. Although he encountered some resistance, much of the country rapidly accepted him as *de facto* king of England, underlining the depth of demoralization amongst the political class during Aethelred's reign. Aethelred fled to Normandy. Swein's death in 1014 allowed Aethelred to return, but he died in 1016 and Swein's son Cnut became king of England (known in legend as King Canute). England fell under Scandinavian rule from 1016 to 1042. However, the situation was markedly different to that in the ninth century. England was now ruled as one kingdom and the Scandinavian kings were Christians. It was not, as then, a pagan territory carved out of the remnants of the old Anglo-Saxon kingdoms.

Cnut's government was far more stable than Aethelred's had been. The king felt secure enough to lead four expeditions to Scandinavia between 1019 and 1028 in ventures to secure his interests there. Cnut was briefly ruler of Norway as well as of England and Denmark. England was a major power base for him, with greater reserves of manpower and wealth than his native Denmark. Among other things Cnut used the resources of the English kingdom to maintain a standing navy of sixteen ships. The fleet is estimated to have cost between £3,000 and £4,000 per year, and included the king's own 120-oar longship, as well as smaller vessels. Creating a standing fleet gave the king's seamen some political clout, for when Cnut died in 1035, 'the men of the fleet in London' sided with those in the royal council who successfully proposed a regency as the solution to a succession dispute.[11]

Cnut's sons ruled successively until 1042, when Edward, later called 'the Confessor', became king. Ships and fleets continued to play a significant role in Edward's time. Naval forces were mustered in 1045, 1046 and 1047 to meet threatened Norwegian invasions that did not materialize. In 1049, at the request of the Holy Roman Emperor, a fleet was stationed at Sandwich to prevent the Count of Flanders from escaping in that direction during a war with the Emperor. Sandwich was a key strategic port in the eleventh century, giving any fleet using it a sheltered anchorage and easy access to the English Channel, the Thames Estuary or the North Sea.

Edward paid off the fourteen ships of his navy in 1050 and 1051 when the threat of invasion from Norway seemed over. The land taxation required to support the field army and ships had proved to be a severe burden on the country and in 1051 he abolished the *heregeld* tax (which maintained military forces), first levied by Aethelred in 1012. These changes did not lead to peace. Eleventh-century Europe was a place where private warfare was common and disputes between a king and his nobles could rapidly lead to bloodshed.

In 1051 the powerful Earl Godwine and his sons were forced to leave the country for Ireland and Flanders after clashing with Edward. They used ships and soldiers to force their way back, bringing death and destruction to parts of Somerset and the south coast as they gathered supplies. Godwine raised men, ships and further supplies from his lands in Wessex. Accompanied by his son Harold (later Harold II of England) and ships from Romney, Hythe, Folkestone, Dover and Sandwich, he sailed to London to confront King Edward. Godwine arrived at Southwark where he waited for high tide. The Southwark people held the southern end of London Bridge and Godwine bargained with them to secure safe passage for his ships through the bridge. His ships were on the south side of the river, and then moved as if to encircle the king's ships on the north bank. A tense showdown ensued, but there was no battle. According to the *Anglo-Saxon Chronicle*, the sailors and soldiers on both sides did not want to fight fellow Englishmen as this would weaken the country and lay it open to foreign attack. This scene becomes less heart-warming when one remembers the murder and looting that Godwine's family had inflicted on fellow Englishmen, but the sentiments of the fleet and army on this occasion do seem to have averted a major bloodbath. Negotiations followed, Edward capitulated, and Godwine got his lands and rights back.

The latter years of Anglo-Saxon England were marked by further seaborne conflict. In 1054 Earl Siward of Northumbria invaded Scotland and defeated the Scottish king Macbeth. The basic English strategy, as in later centuries, was to use both a land army and a naval force in the invasion. In 1055 and 1058 a rebel English nobleman called Aelfgar allied himself with the Norse-Irish of Dublin and Gruffydd ap Llewelyn, king of Gwynedd and Powys in Wales, and made shipborne attacks on western England. The second attack also involved a fleet led by Magnus, son of Harold Hardrada, king of Norway.

Gruffydd ap Llewelyn was the most powerful ruler in Wales, having eliminated the last of the south Welsh princes who opposed him in 1055. He possessed a naval force of some sort and was clearly a serious threat to England. In 1062 Earl Harold marched overland from Gloucester and destroyed Gruffydd's main base at Rhuddlan, burning his ships and their gear, and leaving Gruffydd on the run.

In May 1063 Harold sent a fleet from Bristol round the Welsh coast, stopping at various points and taking hostages. A land invasion of north Wales followed, led by Harold's brother Tostig. In August of that year Gruffydd was killed by his own men, and both his head and the figurehead of his ship were presented to King Edward by Harold. Gwynedd and Powys were given to two Welsh princes by Edward in return for pledges to serve him by land and sea.

Despite these victories, the English kingdom was in extreme danger. There was a continuing threat of invasion from Norway and a growing likelihood of attack from Normandy. Some years before the Norman invasion of 1066, Duke William of Normandy seems to have manoeuvred Earl Harold into taking an oath that he would support William's claim to the English throne in succession to Edward. This, at least, is what Norman sources claimed. True or not, it helped to supply a pretext for William's invasion, for when Edward died in January 1066 it was Harold who became king of England.

Large-scale invasions had been defeated before, and if William had been beaten at Hastings the course of English history could have been very different. However, in the spring of 1066 Harold's brother Tostig, who had been exiled in 1065, had appeared off the south coast with a naval force, making raids and extorting supplies. He gathered further ships at Sandwich and sailed north. He attempted to land on the east coast, but was driven off and retreated to Scotland. He later joined up with King Harold of Norway, who crossed the North Sea with a force said to number between 300 and 500 ships. Harold raised an army to guard the south coast and positioned his fleet at the Isle of Wight for the same purpose. Subsequently he had to race north to face Harold Hardrada and Tostig, who had sailed up the river Ouse and landed near York. He defeated and killed them in battle, but then received news that Duke William of Normandy had landed at Pevensey in Sussex on 28 September with a large army.

William's plan to invade England and seize what he claimed as his crown is said to have been met with dismay by his vassals, the Norman aristocracy. They feared Harold as a wealthy and powerful king with 'a numberless fleet with expert crews long experienced in maritime dangers and battles'. They were also concerned that Normandy did not have sufficient ships or sailors for an invasion fleet, and that the cost of building such a fleet would be crippling. Whether this was just a story designed to increase the magnitude of William's victory or not, the reference suggests that the Anglo-Saxon navy enjoyed a formidable reputation.[12]

William went ahead with his plans. A fleet was built on the river Dives in Normandy and then moved north to St Valéry at the mouth of the river Somme. The wind may have forced the fleet to go in this direction, but it also put it much closer to the English coast. Chronicle sources suggest that William's invasion was delayed by contrary winds, which is entirely credible. However, as the historian N.J. Higham points out, it is also very possible that William simply waited until he was certain that the English army and fleet in the south had been disbanded. This happened in early September when their supplies ran out. The fleet was sent back to London, but many ships were apparently lost *en route*. There was nothing to stop William crossing the Channel. Harold moved south with remarkable speed, but met William in battle by a 'grey apple tree' near Hastings. Harold was killed and the English army collapsed. William marched on London where, on Christmas Day 1066, he was crowned king of England.

The Norman Conquest succeeded mainly because it was a large-scale land-grabbing exercise. The Anglo-Saxon nobility, gentry and clergy were ousted and their lands and rights given to the Norman magnates and others who had taken part in the Conquest. England was decisively pulled out of the Scandinavian orbit and became part of a cross-Channel kingdom.

Viking-age Scotland[13]

The pattern of Viking activity in Scotland was similar to that in England and Ireland: initial scattered raids followed by settlement. The first raids in Scotland came in the 790s, with attacks on Orkney in 794 and Iona and Skye in 795. There were further raids on Iona in 802 and 806. By about the mid-ninth century Norse settlements were established in Orkney, Shetland and the Hebrides, and by the tenth century the Norse had footholds on the northern and western Scottish main-land, although settlement may have been more intensive on the islands than on the mainland. The Norse place names on the mainland tend to be more topographical in character, suggesting that they were used to denote waymarkers for ships, rather than settlements. On the islands, however, settlement names are common. Norse settlement in Scotland was entirely rural in character, although some places, such as the religious centre at Whithorn in south-west Scotland, may have functioned as Norse trading-stations in the eleventh and twelfth centuries.

Viking attacks between the ninth and eleventh centuries weakened the Picts, Britons and English in Scotland, to the long-term benefit of the Scots. From the 840s the Scots, under Kenneth Mac Alpine and his successors, pushed back their enemies, creating a strong Scottish kingdom that covered the area of the southern part of modern Scotland. By 1018 the southern Scottish border had assumed something like its modern form.

Norse sea trade around Scotland was probably fairly limited. It seems to have included slaves, soapstone (from Shetland, a carving stone prized by the Vikings), and perhaps also timber and iron for building ships and boats on the rather barren Scottish islands. Farming was undoubtedly important, and there are signs by the eleventh and twelfth centuries of large-scale deep-sea fishing.

Viking Ireland, the Irish Sea and Wales

The first Viking raid fell on Ireland in the mid-790s. As in other parts of Europe, the earliest targets were typically religious houses, where concentrations of wealth could be found without any military defences. Ireland did not begin to suffer large-scale incursions until the 830s, when sizeable fleets started to range far inland along rivers such as the Liffey, Boyne and Shannon. In 841 two Viking bases were established on the east coast of Ireland, at Dublin and at Annagassan, some way to the north. Called *longphorts*, these were sheltered and defended ports for ships and

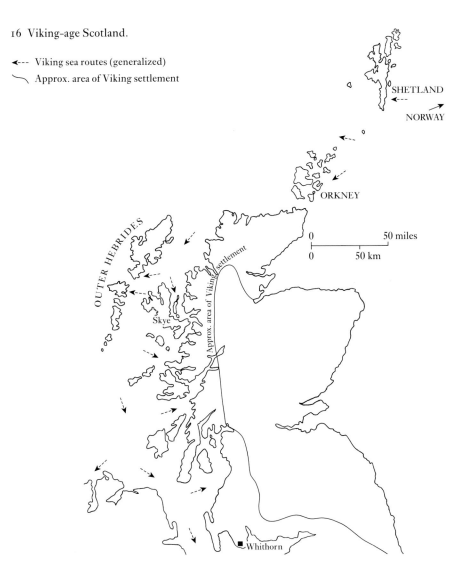

16 Viking-age Scotland.

◄--- Viking sea routes (generalized)

⌐ Approx. area of Viking settlement

SHETLAND

NORWAY

ORKNEY

OUTER HEBRIDES

Skye

Approx. area of Viking settlement

0   50 miles
0   50 km

Whithorn

became permanent versions of the winter camps that the Vikings established in England. Other longphorts were established at Cork (ninth century), Waterford (early tenth century), as well as at Wexford, Limerick, Arklow and Wicklow.

Ireland suffered many Viking attacks, but Viking settlement never extended much beyond the immediate area of the longphorts. In the course of time the longphorts developed as trading centres, and Dublin in particular thrived as a slave-trading port for slaves captured in the Viking wars. This trade lasted into the eleventh century and is known to have involved other ports of the Irish Sea zone such as Bristol. Dublin also developed strong links with the Scandinavian kingdom of York, which was established in 867 and remained mostly in Viking hands until it finally fell to the English in 954. These links were maintained through traffic across the sea to Cumbria and north-west England, as well as via a partially-overland route through Scotland. The Isle of Man was certainly settled by the Vikings by the late ninth century, possibly earlier, and was well connected with Dublin and other parts of the Scandinavian world. Norse settlers began colonizing Galloway, Cumbria and north-east England in the early tenth century, so that from coast-to-coast the north of England was under Scandinavian control.

As in the rest of contemporary Europe, warfare was rife in Ireland between individual kingdoms, but the Irish rulers did make alliances from time to time against the Vikings. In 902 the *Ostmen* (as the Vikings came to be called) were driven out of Dublin by an Irish assault. The Vikings returned in force with a fleet in 914 and the Dublin base was re-established in 917. New raids followed, and Dublin grew in wealth and importance, but Olaf Sigtryggsson, the last independent ruler of Dublin, was defeated at the battle of Tara in 980 by Mael Sechnaill II, king of Meath. It was this battle, and not the more famous battle of Clontarf in 1014, which brought the Ostmen under Irish rule. However, the

17 Viking-age Ireland and Wales.

Ostmen remained a distinctive and influential group for some time, playing a part in English and Welsh conflicts in the eleventh century, and trading with Normandy in the twelfth century.

Viking assaults on Wales began in about 852. They were destructive but sporadic, and no major long-term conquests were made. The hills, mountains and deep valleys of the Welsh landscape favoured defenders. Also the resources in terms of food and loot may well not have been as great as in England or Ireland, giving less incentive for campaigns.

Viking settlement in Wales was very thinly spread. Whilst it has so far yielded little in the way of archaeological evidence, there are just over fifty English place names in Wales that are of Scandinavian origin. Twenty-one of these are settlement names (such as Angle in Milford Haven), most close to the coast, but thirty-five are the names of islands or other coastal features, including Anglesey, Fishguard, Stack Rocks, Swansea, Tusker Rocks, Flat Holm and Steep Holm. As in north-west Scotland, Scandinavian names for coastal features unerringly mark out the Viking coastal sea-routes.

Scandinavian settlement in Ireland, the Isle of Man, Cumbria and Scotland effectively turned the Irish Sea into a Viking lake. As the archaeologist Mark Redknap suggests, the low-lying and fertile island of Anglesey was in a prime strategic position for Viking seafarers. It was within a half-day or day's sail from Man, Dublin or Chester, and offered a sheltered landfall on the direct route between these last two places. It was an important centre for the kings of Gwynedd, and its fertility led to its Welsh description as *Môn mam Cymru* (Mona, mother of Wales). Anglesey suffered many raids, and in 987 a successful attack from the Isle of Man led to the enslavement of (according to the chronicle sources) two thousand people. No Viking port towns have so far been discovered in Wales, but the site of a possible trading station has been discovered on Anglesey at Llanbedrgoch, about one kilometre inland from the good natural harbour of Red Wharf Bay. The site may have been briefly occupied by the Vikings, and has chillingly yielded the hastily buried remains of five people who may have died by violence in the ninth or tenth century.

From about 904 to about 950 most of Wales was brought under a single rule by Hywel Dda ('the Good'). He acknowledged the overlordship of the English kings Edward the Elder in 918 and Athelstan in 927 because of the Viking threat, but the greater part of his reign coincided with a decline in Viking activity. Hywel's rule flourished in these conditions of comparative security. He may have codified some of the Welsh laws, and in 928 matters were peaceful enough to allow him to make a pilgrimage to Rome. His death in about 950 was followed a few years later by the renewal of Viking attacks on the British Isles. His kingdom disintegrated. As before the coastal areas suffered worst from Viking attacks, with monasteries and churches being raided. St David's Cathedral, the mother-church of Wales, was attacked on eleven occasions between 967 and 1091, and in 998 the bishop of St David's was killed.[14]

Trade, merchant shipping and fishing during the Viking era

The Viking attacks undoubtedly caused serious damage to the seaborne trading networks that existed in northern Europe in the eighth and ninth centuries, along with many of the ports that served them. However, there are signs that trade revived during periods when the Viking threat declined. Archaeological evidence suggests that England's existing trade routes still mostly functioned in the ninth century, but that a lower volume of trade passed along them. The Vikings themselves operated as traders, although the extent to which they engaged in trade has been questioned. For example, the Viking settlement of Jorvik, capital of the Scandinavian kingdom of York, has yielded finds that point to links with Byzantium and the Middle East, but the actual volume of surviving imported goods is very low. No Scandinavian pottery emerged from the famous Coppergate site at York, and out of 15,000 other artefacts found, just over 3 per cent came from abroad. Jorvik and other Scandinavian settlements clearly kept in contact with other parts of the Viking world, such as Dublin, Scotland and Scandinavia, but the role of the Viking as merchant may be somewhat questionable.

It is possible that the fall of the Scandinavian kingdom of York in the 950s may not have been an entirely bad thing for the Vikings in Ireland. Dublin seems to have enjoyed an economic upsurge in the late tenth century, and the collapse of the link with Jorvik may have enabled Dublin merchants to develop new trades, to places such as Bristol and even France.

London was gradually re-established as a port, and by the early 1000s tolls were being levied on shipping (see p. 47). The existence of large English war fleets in the tenth and eleventh centuries suggests that there was probably a fairly large trading fleet too. By the time of the Domesday Book survey in 1086 there was enough trade to make it worthwhile for even a small port like Arundel in Sussex to be levying tolls on shipping.

Much of the archaeological evidence for fishing in Viking-era England – beyond finds of fish-bones themselves – relates to fish-weirs placed in rivers to trap fish. However, fish-bone evidence from London, Nottingham, Lincoln and York does indicate that the consumption of riverine species declined in the early eleventh century (possibly due to increasing river pollution around urban sites) in favour of a move towards eating more marine species of fish such as cod, herring and mackerel. This, in turn, implies an increase in sea fishing activity. Whale bones are sometimes also found on Anglo-Saxon sites, but these seem to have come from animals that were accidentally stranded, and claimed as a rare treat by the king or nobility. There is no real evidence of deliberate whaling activity in England until after the Middle Ages.[15]

Sea travel of other kinds also survived during the Viking era. The kingdom of Wessex maintained sea contact with the papacy in Rome even at some of the most difficult times. For example, in 853 the young Alfred went to Rome and in 890 the Abbot of St Augustine's in Canterbury took offerings from Alfred and Wessex to Rome. Alfred himself was keen to hear travellers' tales, and is known to have received a number of exotic voyagers, including Irish mystics and the Scandinavian visitor Ohthere, who brought back stories of voyaging to the Arctic Circle and other places.[16]

Ships and shipbuilding

There is very little evidence for specific types of ships used in England, Scotland, Wales and Ireland during the Viking era. In some areas, such as the Danelaw and Ireland, local wooden shipbuilding traditions may have been completely overlaid by Scandinavian ones. Certainly, as late as the 1290s the technical terminology used by shipwrights in Newcastle and York (both deep in the former Danelaw) had a distinctly Scandinavian flavour when compared with that used in East Anglia or further south.[17]

The basic type of Viking ship had a clinker-built, double-ended hull with a deep keel. It was steered by a side-rudder and carried a single square sail. The best Viking ships combined technology and art in ways seldom equalled in the history of shipbuilding. The oared longship (or 'snake' or 'dragon', to give it some of its contemporary names) was the most famous Viking craft, but the Scandinavians constructed many other types, including cargo vessels.

The English and other indigenous inhabitants of north-western Europe between the eighth and eleventh centuries had their own types of vessels. They appear to have had general similarities with Viking craft – they were clinker-built, double-ended, had one mast and a side-rudder – so it is probably true to say that they all belonged to the same broad technological 'family'. Nevertheless, beyond these resemblances there may well have been significant differences of design and technical capability. In describing the new warships that King Alfred of Wessex had built in 896, the *Anglo-Saxon Chronicle* said that they were different from

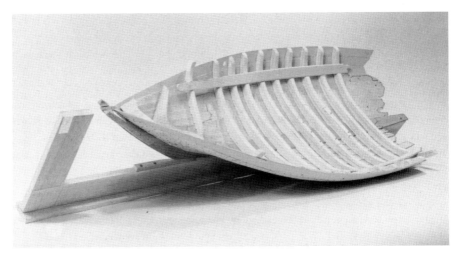

18 Model reconstruction of part of the late 9th/early 10th-century Graveney boat. Found in Graveney Marsh (Kent), this clinker-built craft was a trading vessel.

those of the Danish and the Frisians (the English used some Frisian mercenaries) and were made 'as it seemed to himself [i.e. Alfred] that they might be most useful'. The brief details of these ships given in the chronicle have given rise to considerable debate. Some of the ships had sixty oars or more, and they were nearly twice as long as other types, as well as being faster and steadier. They may also have been 'higher' or 'more responsive', but the description is debatable. For all the passage's problems, it does identify a specifically English type of warship that was, apparently, designed by Alfred himself.

At least nine of these ships were ready to take part in a battle against the Danes later that year. The most interesting thing that emerges from this passage is less the nature of the ships themselves than the clear implication that late ninth-century Wessex had sufficient expertise, shipwrights and shipbuilding materials to

19 Partial incised image of a ship found at Christchurch Place, Dublin, 11th century. The image shows a one-masted ship, perhaps double-ended (the stern is missing), with a sailor sitting on the yard.

produce sizeable warships in a fairly short space of time. Building a war fleet has never been a cheap or easy thing to do. Four hundred years later, in the mid-1290s, it took seven major English ports (one of them London) to produce eight large galleys for Edward I.[18] The English undoubtedly also used captured Danish ships, and perhaps adopted some of their designs. In 895, for example, London men seized a significant number of Danish warships abandoned in the river Lea and took them back to London.

The large numbers of ships that the English could field in the eleventh century indicate that the country had a viable shipbuilding industry, which must have built for both war and trade. Chronicle references to ships are generally concerned with warships, but none has yet been found by archaeologists. The one late Anglo-Saxon wreck so far known was a merchant vessel, found at Graveney in the north Kent marshes (see fig. 18). This late ninth- or early tenth-century clinker-built ship is estimated to have been about 14 metres in length, and roughly 3.9 metres in the beam. The vessel appears to have been very stable, and calculations have suggested that it could have achieved 3.5 knots under oars (with six oarsmen) and about 7 knots under sail. The floor-timbers in the bottom of the hull were heavy and close-set, and it is possible that the 'Graveney boat' was a bulk-carrier, intended for weighty cargoes such as stone or salt. Finds in the hull show that it was also used to transport hops for brewing, and it may well have traded across the North Sea.

Despite the wide vocabulary of Old English ship-type names (see p. 24), distinguishing between different kinds of Anglo-Saxon or foreign ships can be problematical, beyond the well-known examples. For example, the early eleventh-century harbour dues at London listed four types of vessel: the small ship, paying one halfpenny as toll, the larger ship 'with sail(s)', rated at one penny, and the keel and the hulk, each paying fourpence. The different rates cannot necessarily be taken as indicators of relative size except in the vaguest way, for the keel and the hulk might have been identified more with foreigners, and hence subject to higher duties.

Very little can be said about shipbuilding in other parts of the British Isles at this period, although it is clear that the Vikings built ships or boats in the areas where they settled, including Ireland. In 1962 five eleventh-century Viking ships were excavated in Roskilde fjord in Denmark. Wreck 2 was a vessel of about 30 metres in length, constructed of eastern Irish oak in about 1060, perhaps at Dublin. It was a warship, a *draka* ('dragon') or *esneca* ('snake' or 'serpent') rowed by about thirty pairs of oarsmen. A longship of the type that descended on so many north-west European coasts, it is comparable in size to some of the warships for which the English were taxed so heavily in the first half of the eleventh century. Repairs with Danish oak suggest that the vessel spent a good deal of time in Scandinavia before it was sunk as a block-ship.[19]

The Anglo-Saxon navy

Alfred the Great's fleet was the starting-point for a state navy, although he was far from the first Anglo-Saxon king to use naval forces. The fleet evolved into an equivalent of the fyrd (the national army raised by a 'call-up' of freemen) that provided armies for the king, based on specific territories. The contribution of inland areas to the ship fyrd was probably restricted to money to build and maintain warships (through a tax called ship-scot) and the men to man them. Some ports also owed ship-service to the Crown for specified periods of time each year, such as Maldon in Essex and the original Cinque Ports ('five ports': Hastings, New Romney, Hythe, Dover and Sandwich) of Kent and Sussex. These were granted in return for privileges.

In 1008 King Aethelred ordered that each land unit of 310 hides (a unit of assessment equal in many places to 120 acres/48.6 hectares) should produce sufficient resources to support one warship, with each 10 hides producing a small craft and 8 hides funding a helmet and armour for the crew members. Five hides were to produce one sailor. On this basis Wessex alone would have been able to field about ninety ships and nearly 5,400 fighting sailors, nearly two-thirds of them equipped with helmets and armour. It is evident that a system of this kind existed earlier than 1008. St Paul's Cathedral in London in the mid- to late 990s raised a crew of forty-six by taking individuals or small numbers of men from twenty-seven of its estates in coastal and inland locations in Middlesex, Hertfordshire, Essex, Surrey and Kent. Such a 'folk-navy' system was far from unprecedented in northern Europe (see p. 20).[20]

By the mid-eleventh century Anglo-Saxon England had a substantial naval force. It could be drawn from the ships and men of the king and his earls, from the ship-sokes (a unit of three administrative districts or 'hundreds', providing a warship and crew) and ship fyrd, from particular seaports, from mercenaries and by the impressment of merchant vessels. In theory at least, the ship fyrd was summoned for a part of each year, and in the time of King Edgar (r. 959–75) there are said to have been annual manoeuvres. The summoning of the ship fyrd may have declined in the eleventh century, but naval forces – whether they belonged to the king or to leading nobles like Earl Godwine – played an important role in pre-Conquest English politics. Like the army in some twentieth-century Third-World nations, the fleet was a political as well as a military weapon, and the opinions of ordinary sailors mattered to those in power in a way that they would not do again for many centuries. After the Conquest William I summoned the ship fyrd on a number of occasions, including his assault on Scotland in 1072. The system gradually died out and by the early twelfth century the navy had all but disappeared.[21]

CHAPTER THREE

War and trade, 1066–c. 1500

Politics, war and fleets

The Norman Conquest of 1066 reorientated England towards continental Western Europe and away from the Scandinavian world. The Anglo-Norman empire, consisting essentially of the Duchy of Normandy and England, existed until 1154 when the accession of Henry II (r. 1154–89) led to a vast increase in its size. Henry Plantagenet (the family name) was duke of Normandy, count of Anjou and duke of Aquitaine (Gascony) before he became king. With the addition of these new territories, the empire (now called the Angevin Empire, after Anjou) stretched from the Scottish border to the Pyrenees. The Angevin Empire opened up new trading areas for England, including the important wine-growing region of Gascony.

The cross-Channel kingdom faced little in the way of external naval threats. The English Channel became a highway for the Norman and Angevin kings, with Southampton or Portsmouth in England and Barfleur and Dieppe in Normandy favoured transit ports. The crossings seem to have been unremarkable, apart from the famous wreck of the *White Ship* in 1120, when the sons of Henry I were drowned near Barfleur, along with many others from the royal court (one chronicler later claimed that the crew and passengers were drunk before the ship set sail).[1]

The year 1066 saw the beginning of a new phase of war and conquest in the British Isles. The Normans pushed into parts of Wales, and by the mid-twelfth century, held much of the south coast, including Gwent, Glamorgan, the Gower peninsula and Pembroke, as well as some other smaller areas. Henry II considered conquering Ireland in 1155 and even obtained papal authority to do so; he finally invaded in 1171 to bring some Anglo-Norman adventurers under control. However, he was also acknowledged as lord by a number of Irish kings, which gave substance to his claim of authority over Ireland and created a formal link that was to have a profound effect on the subsequent histories of Ireland and England. Although the Anglo-Norman 'conquest' of Ireland was never as complete as the Norman conquest of England, and vast swathes of Irish territory were to remain outside the control of English kings, the nature of Irish society was changed fundamentally. The Anglo-Normans and their successors introduced manorial institutions, stimulated the growth of towns and brought in English and Welsh settlers. They were also responsible for introducing the English language to Ireland.

Naval expeditions mounted from England were rare in the twelfth century. The largest one known was a force of 167 ships from England, Normandy and other parts of northern Europe that sailed from Dartmouth in 1147 on crusade against

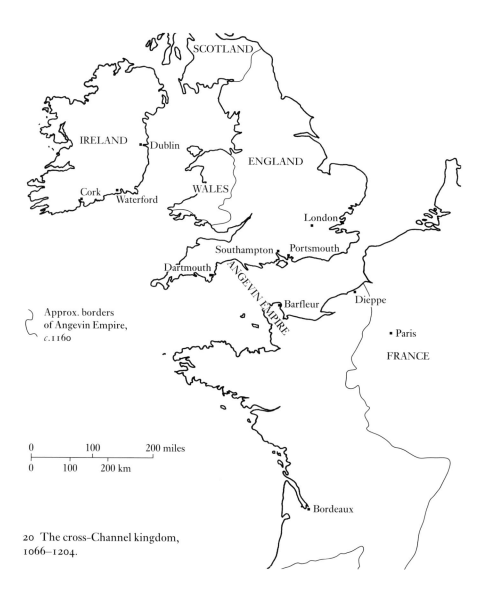

20 The cross-Channel kingdom,
1066–1204.

Islam. Much of the Iberian peninsula was still under Moorish control, and the
crusade fleet from Dartmouth helped the king of Portugal to capture Lisbon.
Another large English crusade fleet left Dartmouth in 1190 to take part in the
Third Crusade, which was led by the Angevin king Richard I.[2]

Richard I (r.1189–99) maintained the Angevin Empire through his enormous
energy, together with superior military and diplomatic skills. When he returned to
northern Europe from crusade, he built a fleet that was used successfully to help
resist French encroachments into Normandy. This fleet probably formed the basis
of the impressive naval force that his brother John (r.1199–1216) was to wield. The
English fleet of the late 1100s and early 1200s was the first substantial national navy
since the extinction of the Anglo-Saxon fleet following the Norman Conquest. The

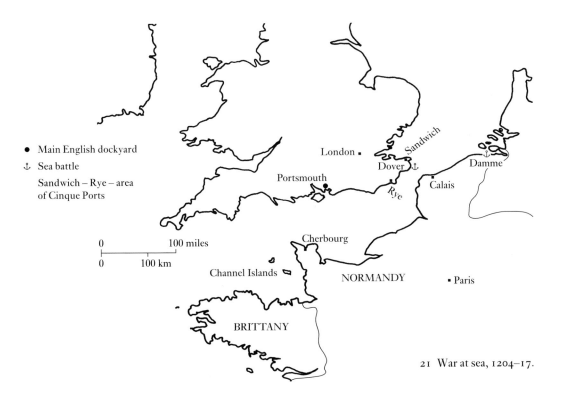

London

Sandwich

Dover

Damme

Portsmouth

Calais

Rye

0   100 miles

0   100 km

Channel Islands

Cherbourg

NORMANDY

Paris

BRITTANY

21 War at sea, 1204–17.

Cinque Ports (the original five were later joined by Rye and Winchelsea, along with other, smaller places) of Kent and Sussex, despite a commitment originating in Anglo-Saxon times to provide ships and men for royal service, were only of intermittent importance in royal naval activity in the Middle Ages (see p. 52).

The kingdom of France and the Angevins were regularly at odds, and by the early thirteenth century the French were winning. A combination of French military pressure and John's political ineptitude meant that, by the end of 1204, Normandy and most of the central Angevin territories had been lost, including Anjou itself. Because of the French threat and King John's desire to reconquer his lost lands, England saw its largest naval build-up since the eleventh century during his reign. By 1206 there were 50 royal galleys, based in different ports in England and Ireland. A large stone-walled galley base was constructed at Portsmouth, with what may have been a dock with a constant water level allowing vessels to stay afloat whatever the state of the tide. Other facilities for warships were built at Southampton, Rye and Winchelsea. It is known that between 1209 and 1211 over £5,000 was spent on the royal fleet (a massive sum for the period), with building and repair activity concentrated on the coasts of Hampshire and Sussex. From 1209 to 1212 54 vessels were built for the king, including 20 galleys. The galleys sometimes had 50 or 60 oars or more, and seem to have been the main combat vessels. Large numbers of sailing ships were also constructed, probably to act as troop and supply transports. The war fleets of the period could be quite large: one force, for example, had 1,291 sailors who manned 20 galleys and 40 sailing ships.[3]

In 1213 Philip II of France invaded Flanders, supported by a large fleet. Flanders had long been recognized as a good location from which to invade England and, according to one thirteenth-century chronicler, John determined to destroy Philip's armada before it could reach England. Whether by accident or design, the English fleet (probably composed of both royal and merchant ships) caught the French ships at anchor in the Flemish harbour of Damme. Large numbers of French ships were looted and burned, and the French destroyed the rest to prevent their capture. The returning English fleet was laden with loot; one chronicler later boasted that 'never had so much treasure come into England since the days of King Arthur'.[4] However, the following year John sailed to La Rochelle and campaigned in western France, but was forced to retreat. At the same time his allies in Flanders were defeated at the battle of Bouvines. Any hopes that John had nurtured about recovering his lost lands on the Continent were now gone.

The baronial rebellion of 1215 that led to the signing of Magna Carta was aided by French support, as well as by the defection of the Cinque Ports to the rebels. In May 1216 the French Dauphin Louis was able to land an army in Kent in a bid to assert his claim to the English throne. Louis' task was made easier because the English royal fleet had been damaged in a storm and the Cinque Ports had effectively left the door open to the French. John died in 1216 and was succeeded by his young son Henry III (r.1216–72). With England ruled by a regent and the French advancing into England, things looked bleak for the Angevin monarchy, but naval power turned the tide. In the spring and summer of 1217 a French army was besieging Dover Castle. A French resupply fleet was driven off in May, and a second French fleet sent in August was defeated and mostly captured. The French force was led by a renegade priest-turned-pirate known as Eustace the Monk, who had operated in the Channel for over a decade. Hubert de Burgh brilliantly commanded the English squadron opposing Eustace, allowing the French to pass his force at Sandwich, then sailing out behind them so that he was able to get to windward and choose the place and time of his attack. Rightly described by Nicholas Rodger as 'one of the most decisive medieval naval battles in northern waters', the battle forced the French army to withdraw from England, preventing a French conquest.[5]

The navy of John's time largely ceased to exist after his death for lack of money. Poitou finally fell to the French in 1224, leaving Gascony as the sole English possession in France. These losses left southern England facing a potentially hostile French coastline, and helped to set an important part of England's strategic agenda for centuries ahead. Probably relying mostly on merchant shipping, John's son Henry III staged a number of naval expeditions to south-western France between 1225 and 1254, aiming either to retake Poitou or defeat French incursions into Gascony. Henry's forays enjoyed mixed results.

Plantagenet imperialism in the British Isles revived in the 1270s with Edward I (r.1272–1307). Anglo-Norman expansion into Wales had, by the thirteenth century, reduced the surviving independent Welsh princedoms to shrinking zones in the west and north. Llewelyn ap Gruffudd of Gwynedd (d.1282), the most important Welsh leader of the period, united the native Welsh in ways that threatened Plantagenet interests. Llewelyn had been recognized by Henry III as 'Prince of Wales' in 1267 in a vain attempt to turn him into a docile feudal subject of the English Crown. Edward I fought two wars with Llewelyn in 1277 and 1282. Llewelyn was killed in the second war and, although Wales was far from finally pacified, its independence was ended.

Edward I's Welsh wars involved land invasions of north Wales, supported by ships. The ships carried supplies for the army but were also used to occupy the fertile island of Anglesey. The island's harvests were seized to deny them to Edward's Welsh enemies. The Welsh rulers had some ships, but they were neither numerous nor strong enough to successfully oppose Edward at sea. English sea power played an important role in Edward's victory, and some years later it had to be deployed again to rescue Edward's vaunted Welsh castles during a rising in 1294.[6]

Dynastic ambition lay at the root of many medieval wars. 'Claims to the throne' of this or that place might have a quaintly Ruritanian air to a modern reader, but in the Middle Ages they shaped politics, moved armies and fleets, and often ended in large-scale slaughter. In 1286 Alexander III of Scotland died in a fall from his horse. His heir, the infant Margaret of Norway, died in 1290, which left the way open for Edward I to pursue his claims to control of Scotland as its feudal overlord. These claims took material form in March 1296 when Edward invaded Scotland and captured the port and town of Berwick. This began the long and bloody Scottish wars of independence, a conflict that poisoned Anglo-Scottish relations for centuries. The war saw rapid changes of fortune. A rising of 1297 led by William Wallace severely damaged the English forces and their Scots supporters, and was followed by an invasion of northern England. The Scottish kingdom was temporarily revived, at least in name.

Edward's Scottish campaigns between 1297 and 1304 highlighted once again the critical importance of seapower. Scotland had ships and traded internationally, but it lacked any sort of state navy and its merchant fleet was small. England's shipping industry was far larger and merchant ships were crucial for the resupply of English land forces operating in Scotland, as they had been for those in Wales. English ships operated on both the east and west coasts (the west coast campaigning also involved the use of Irish troops and ships). Edward's invasions of 1301 and more particularly of 1303–4 overcame the Scots, but the English hold on Scotland was a temporary one. Robert Bruce was crowned king of Scotland in 1306 and rose against Edward. Bruce survived the initial stages of his campaign in part because of naval support from the Flemish in the North Sea and from the Lord of the Isles on the west coast (see p. 60), who commanded a large number of 'Viking-style' galleys that made the Isles into a formidable regional naval power.

Edward I died in 1307, and the disastrous political and military leadership of his son Edward II (r.1307–27) enabled Bruce to win back more and more of Scotland. The resounding Scottish victory at the battle of Bannockburn in 1314 was the most visible sign of English failure, but with the assistance of the Flemish and the Lord

1 Invasions of Anglesey, 1277, 1282 & 1295

2 Seaborne re-supply of English castles 1294

3 Irish ships supply English campaigns on
west coast of Scotland 1300 & 1301

4 English fleet support for east coast
invasions

5 Isle of Man captured &
recaptured 1313–33

6 Scots invasions 1315 & 1318

7 Scottish naval blockade 1318

8 Scottish ships attack east coast
of England 1310s–30s

Berwick

Anglo-Scottish border

Anglesey

22 Sea power and the English
wars against Wales and Scotland,
13th–14th centuries.

of the Isles, Scotland was able to use sea power to project its forces in a way that was seldom seen at any other time in its history. In 1313 a Scots force retook the Isle of Man from the English, losing it soon after but recapturing it again in 1317 (it was finally lost to the English in 1333). In 1315 and 1318 the Scots were able to invade Ireland, and in 1318 a Scottish sea blockade of Berwick led to its fall. Scots and Flemish ships attacked the east coast of England. Scottish military success on land continued into the 1320s, and in 1328 Edward III (r.1327–77) was forced to recognize Robert I as king of Scotland. Scottish ships were active against English shipping and coastal settlements in the 1330s. The ultimate defeat of England in the medieval wars against Scotland can be explained in part by the failure of English kings and commanders to secure their seaborne supply-lines.[7]

23 'King, ship and sword, and power of the sea': gold noble of Edward III, struck 1351. The image of an armed king in a ship is said to have commemorated the English naval victory at Sluys in 1340; it was certainly a symbol of naval power. The theme was repeated from time to time on English coins until the 16th century.

France became more of a naval threat to England in the thirteenth century. War broke out again in 1293, in the same year that a large dockyard for oared galleys and barges, the Clos des Galées, was completed at Rouen, and in 1295 and 1297 there were fears of a French invasion. The danger of galley attacks by the French and their allies in the mid-1290s prompted Edward I to order a national galley-building campaign of his own, which seems to have produced only eight vessels. Anglo-French conflict dominated the maritime affairs of England from the thirteenth to the fifteenth centuries, the worst period of warfare being the so-called Hundred Years War. This broke out in 1337 when Edward III claimed the French throne, a claim that he later abandoned. The war was in fact a series of conflicts, not always fought for the same reasons, which lasted until 1453 when the French finally conquered Bordeaux, leaving England with the port of Calais as its sole continental possession.

The Hundred Years War was won and lost on land, but its maritime aspect was of critical importance to England, although English seapower was not always up to the job it was called upon to do. English royal fleets, called 'the king's ships', were generally small in size and, apart from King John's short-lived Portsmouth base, there was never a medieval English equivalent of the Clos des Galées. The Crown had to rely on its subjects to provide warships and transports for any great expedition.

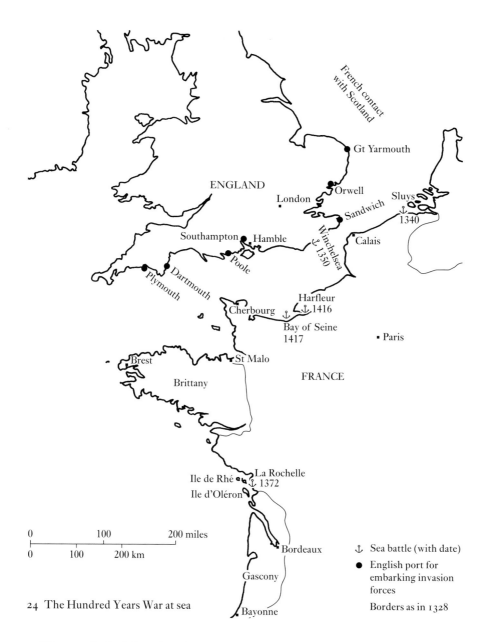

French contact with Scotland

Gt Yarmouth

ENGLAND

London   Orwell
Sandwich   Sluys
1340

Southampton   Hamble
Winchelsea 1350
Calais
Poole
Plymouth   Dartmouth
Harfleur 1416
Cherbourg
Bay of Seine 1417
Paris

Brest   St Malo
FRANCE
Brittany

Ile de Rhé   La Rochelle 1372
Ile d'Oléron

0   100   200 miles
0   100   200 km

Bordeaux

⚓ Sea battle (with date)
● English port for embarking invasion forces
Borders as in 1328

Gascony

24 The Hundred Years War at sea

Bayonne

The naval administration that supported the English royal fleets in the four-teenth and fifteenth centuries was very limited in size and scope. Although John had a 'Keeper of the King's Ports and Galleys', the office soon lapsed. A 'Clerk of the King's Ships' was appointed in 1336, but the post was principally concerned with administering the upkeep of the fleet. In times when the royal fleet was expanding (for instance, during the reign of Henry V), additional officials were appointed to carry the administrative burden, but the clerks were never people of major importance.

In the late thirteenth century the naval defence of England was divided into the Northern and Western Fleets, the Northern normally covering the coast from the Thames to Scotland and the Western covering the seaboard from the Thames to Bristol. In 1300 the gentry assigned to command these fleets were called 'admirals' for the first time, a word of Arabic derivation that was already used in the Mediterranean. The posts were more administrative than military in nature, for the admirals were chiefly concerned with raising and controlling fleets of merchantmen. War fleets were invariably commanded by aristocrats (or the king, if he was present), as was the case in land campaigns. The permanent post of Lord Admiral of England was created in 1408, but English lord admirals did not really become significant as operational commanders until the sixteenth century.[8]

The naval expedition, the sea patrol and the coastal raid were the commonest types of naval operations that English ships undertook in the Middle Ages. Naval expeditions generally required the movement of large numbers of troops, horses and supplies, and considerable numbers of private ships had to be seized by the Crown for such enterprises since the king's ships were never numerous enough for big campaigns. The impressment of merchant shipping must have been a considerable hindrance to trade. For example, major fleet musters for expeditions took place in England on at least twenty-one occasions between 1338 and 1360.[9] Although some shipowners and masters attempted to avoid royal service, by and large medieval English kings were able to get hold of enough ships to move their armies when they needed to (see Table 1).

Sea patrols were used for reconnaissance, for attacks on enemy merchant shipping and for small-scale actions against enemy warships. They were also sometimes used for the suppression of piracy, although with limited success as the most successful English pirates were often exactly the same people who provided the Crown with ships and men for naval activity. Seamen had a major share in any ships and cargoes that were taken as prizes, and one wonders if medieval sea patrols were sometimes not more akin to shopping expeditions than war voyages.

Coastal raiding was the most brutal manifestation of sea warfare, for the targets were often civilians. The English, French and their allies all committed terrible

Table 1 Numbers of ships impressed for medieval English war fleets[10]

Date	Destination	Ships
1230	Brittany	288
1297	Flanders	305
1342	Brittany	440+
1345	Gascony	152
1346	Normandy	750+
1347	Calais	738

acts of this kind during the Hundred Years War. The war opened with extensive French raiding. Portsmouth was burnt in March 1338, and one Sunday morning in October of that year some fifty French and Genoese galleys sailed into Southampton Water. They took the port by surprise, while the townspeople were at Mass, and are said to have killed many and raped considerable numbers of girls and women. Before departing for Dieppe with large amounts of loot, the raiders set fire to the town, razing much of its southern part. Areas of Southampton destroyed in the raid are said to have been still in ruins nearly seventy years later.[11]

Raids on Harwich, Hastings, Plymouth and other places followed in 1339, and in 1340 the English visited destruction on Boulogne, Dieppe and Tréport. Coastal raids became a familiar part of the wars between England and France from the 1330s to the 1450s, and the fear they engendered must have been considerable. During the Peasants' Revolt of 1381 the Kentish rebels decided that some of their number should stay behind rather than marching on London, to 'keep the sea-coasts free from enemies'.[12]

Large-scale naval battles were very uncommon during the Middle Ages and all of those in the Hundred Years War took place near the coast. Attacking a fleet in an anchorage or a restricted waterway, or intercepting a fleet passing close to the coast, was possible. If the attacker's luck held, an anchored fleet would stay put long enough for the attacking fleet to arrive; and a force sailing close inshore would at least give some time for the alarm to be raised and an intercepting squadron to weigh anchor. The English victories at Damme (1213), Sluys (1340) and Harfleur (1416) are examples of the former type of battle, while the battles of Dover (1217), Winchelsea (1350) and Calais (1458) were of the latter kind. Sluys was famous because the English fleet, led by Edward III, annihilated a French invasion force, destroying about 190 of the 250 vessels that Philip VI had mustered there and killing more than 16,000 men. A grim joke evidently circulated round the English fleet after the battle to the effect that if God had allowed the fish of Sluys to speak, they would have spoken perfect French as the result of eating so many French bodies.[13]

Sea battles themselves were fairly rudimentary affairs, fought as boarding actions with bows, arrows and other hand weapons. Sailors knew that getting to windward of an opponent enabled one to choose the best time and position to board (see p. 52), but otherwise tactics were very basic and sometimes involved deliberate ramming. Shipboard guns were used in small numbers by the English and others from the 1330s, but they were essentially small anti-personnel weapons. Even Henry V's biggest gun-armed ship only had seven cannon. The numbers of guns on ships increased markedly in the second half of the fifteenth century, but these were still fairly small-calibre weapons. Most warships could not carry big guns until the sixteenth century (see p. 118).[14]

Despite English victories such as Sluys, the French and their Iberian and Mediterranean allies had effective professional naval forces based on oared galleys and barges, while the English in the main did not. One of the few exceptions was the navy put together by Henry V (r. 1413–22) for his war with France. Henry clearly knew that if he was going to be able to conquer France, he would have to destroy the naval power of the French and their Genoese allies in the English Channel (the Genoese had huge sailing ships called carracks). By means of construction, purchase and capture, Henry increased the size of the royal fleet from six ships in 1413 to thirty-nine in 1417/18 (more than one-third captured from enemies). This included three 'great ships' (English carracks) in the 500–1,000 ton range (joined in 1420 by the 1,400-ton *Grace Dieu*, the biggest ship built in England before the sixteenth century), and a number of captured Genoese carracks. Henry also had some twenty-eight shipmasters, who served on a salaried basis, the closest approach so far in England to a naval officers' corps. This group included men like Ralph Huskard, master of the royal balinger *Anne* (a balinger was a fast fighting ship with oars and sails) in 1416, who was still in royal service in 1431, or William Payn, who captained one of the great Genoese carracks captured by the English, and in 1418 became the master of the *Grace Dieu*.[15]

The king's ships, normally based on the Thames near the Tower of London, were mostly shifted to Southampton in Henry's time to be closer to France. Stores were constructed at Southampton, and the nearby river Hamble became a major anchorage for the fleet, defended by a wooden tower called the 'Bulwark' and with a windlass-mounted iron chain across the river mouth to prevent the entry of enemy ships. Henry used royal and merchant ships to mount a small-scale invasion of Normandy in 1415, which led to the battle of Agincourt and the capture of the port of Harfleur. A Franco-Genoese fleet attempting to recapture Harfleur in 1416 was beaten by an English fleet led by the Duke of Bedford, and in 1417 the Earl of Huntingdon destroyed the remainder of French sea power in a battle off the Chef de Caux in the bay of the Seine. With the way clear, Henry sailed to Normandy with his main invasion force. Within three years the French king had capitulated and Henry was recognized by treaty as the heir to the French throne. His young son Henry VI was later crowned king of a dual Anglo-French monarchy. The destruction of the Clos de Galées in 1418 and the capture of Normandy wiped out French sea power in northern Europe for more than a generation.

Henry died in 1422, and, with the sea war at an end, most of his fleet was rapidly sold off. Even in victory the government could not afford to maintain a large standing naval force. By the mid-1430s the royal fleet consisted of one small balinger and the rotting hulks of the great ships. The fleet declined to almost nothing in the mid-fifteenth century, and although it was revived somewhat in the time of Edward IV (r. 1461–83), England did not again have a sizeable royal navy until the sixteenth century. Attempts to reinforce English possessions in Normandy and Gascony came too little and too late, and by the end of 1453, the port of Calais was all that remained of England's continental possessions. England's final defeat in France in 1453 was the result of political ineptitude, military reverses on land and the revival of the French monarchy. The English merchant fleet, deprived of the Bordeaux wine trade which had created a demand for large, defensible ships, declined in size and importance.

The increasing instability of Henry VI (r. 1422–61, 1470–1) and his government led to civil war, the 'Wars of the Roses', which took place in three major phases, 1455–64, 1469–71 and 1483–87. The English political class was largely tied up in internal plots and mayhem. The wars were essentially land conflicts, although a string of both successful and doomed usurpers used the sea to stage landings in different parts of the British Isles over these years. The one major foreign expedition of this period came in 1475, when Edward IV invaded France as a means of uniting the kingdom, but found that his Breton and Burgundian allies had deserted him. The French king Louis XI effectively bought him off and Edward returned home without, so to speak, a shot being fired, but a good deal richer.

Medieval Scotland

Although Scotland suffered badly from English invasions in the thirteenth and fourteenth centuries, the period between the eleventh and fifteenth centuries saw the Scottish kingdom gradually develop from an entity confined to the south and east, with very limited control over the Highlands, to a country that had more or less the same borders as the modern state. The Western Isles, along with Orkney and Shetland, belonged to Norway, a relic of earlier Norse settlement (the Western Isles had been formally ceded to Norway by Scotland in 1098), and in the thirteenth century the Norwegian kings were still powerful enough to make their presence felt.

The Western Isles themselves (along with the Isle of Man) were under the more immediate rule of the Lords of the Isles, men who commanded significant galley fleets. In 1263 King Haakon IV took a large fleet to the west of Scotland with the aim of raising revenue, looting and asserting his power there. Reinforced by ships from the Isles and from Man, Haakon attacked Scottish possessions in the west of Scotland. A small battle ensued at Largs on the coast some thirty miles south-west of modern Glasgow, after some Norwegian ships ran aground. The Norwegians burnt their ships and retreated, and the Scots accounted it a victory. Haakon died in Orkney on the return journey, having failed to assert Norwegian control. Negotiations began, and in 1266 the Western Isles and Man were ceded to Scotland, although the Scottish Crown did not secure final control of the Western Isles until the late fifteenth century. Orkney and Shetland became part of Scotland in 1469, as part of a royal marriage settlement.

From the late thirteenth century to the 1500s Scotland's most important and consistent ally was France. The 'Auld Alliance' was first concluded in 1295, and was renewed on nine occasions between then and 1548 (Scotland finally abandoned it in 1560). It lasted so long because England was often a common enemy of both countries over this period, and it was of strategic benefit to both partners. It gave the Scots some military and naval assistance against England and, by forcing the English to secure their northern border before launching major attacks on France, hampered English military ambitions against France. It held considerable potential danger for England. In 1383, for example, the Admiral of France, Jean de Vienne, took an army to Scotland as part of a plan for a co-ordinated Franco-Scottish assault in the north and the landing of a major invasion force in Kent. The plan miscarried because the French fleet was diverted by a rising in Flanders, and Vienne's raid only amounted to a limited cross-border incursion.[16]

Masters and mariners

Most of what we know about the day-to-day business of seafaring in the medieval British Isles comes from English records, which survive in greater numbers than those for other parts of these islands. Even this picture is far from complete, but it does give some idea of the nature of life at sea in English ships in the Middle Ages.

As in later centuries a ship was always commanded by a master, a man who in many cases was the owner or part-owner of the ship in which he sailed. Few other shipboard officers are known before the sixteenth century, apart from constables who seem to have functioned mainly as leaders of troops shipped aboard for war service, and were commonly found in war fleets. By the early fifteenth century constables served on most ships engaged in royal service, whether in war or trade. Aside from a few specialists such as clerks, carpenters or gunners (the latter not recorded before the late fifteenth century), this is as much as is known of the command structure of medieval English ships. Medieval shipmasters are mostly shadowy figures at best, and almost nothing is known of the ordinary seamen of the period. No doubt experienced mariners were valued for their skills, but the only sign of any 'career structure' was that ships often carried complements of boys in their crews, some presumably serving as apprentices of some sort. On most voyages only one or two boys were present. Thus, when the 104-ton *Griffyn* of Cardiff took part in a (non-military) royal voyage to Brittany in 1402, the crew consisted of one master, one constable, twenty-six mariners and two boys.[17]

The basic pay-rate for sailors in royal service was established in the early 1200s, as follows:

Table 2 Basic pay rates in the early 1200s

Rank	Daily pay
Master	6d
Constable	6d*
Mariner	3d
Boy	1½d

* (Paid at the same rate, although the master was evidently recognized as the ship's commander.)

Pay levels did fluctuate, particularly in the wake of the Black Death of 1348–50 when labour was much scarcer (and hence able to hold out for higher wages), but the seamen of Henry V's day were back at the pay rates of their predecessors of two hundred years before, albeit with some additional weekly pay as a 'reward' or bonus. At the very least, the pay rates must have made sailors even keener on looting any ships they captured.[18]

Seafaring was a lowly occupation in the Middle Ages, and in England it did not have the strong organization of other crafts. For example, only six shipmen's guilds (seamen's guilds) are known to have existed (at Bristol, King's Lynn, Grimsby, Hull, York and Newcastle) in the fourteenth and fifteenth centuries. They were maintained by contributions from their members, but there is little evidence that they enforced training or professional standards to any great degree.[19]

Shipboard discipline was based, at least in theory, on the Laws of Oléron. This was a law code apparently first set down in the thirteenth century and seems to have originated from laws which regulated the Gascon wine trade (the Ile d'Oléron lay on the route). The Laws gave protection to the mariner from unjust and arbitrary punishment by the master. For example, a mariner was only obliged to take one blow from the master, although if he hit back he was to be fined £5 and lose the hand that struck the blow. Mariners were also allowed to seek sanctuary at the ship's shrine, which was usually set up near the mainmast. On a less violent level, sailors were allowed to load their own small cargoes into the hold on trading voyages. They had to be consulted by the master as to the best day to set sail (in case of stormy weather) and in the settlement of shipboard disputes, although the master could ignore their decisions. Sick mariners were to be set ashore and a woman paid to nurse them. This seems a long way from the image of a tyrannical 'master under God' of later centuries, but it is impossible to say how widely the laws were honoured. The most that can be said is that they were widely known, but since many working relationships in medieval society were governed by force and fear, life at sea may have been no exception.

The 'Shipman' who features as one of the Canterbury pilgrims in Geoffrey Chaucer's late fourteenth-century *Canterbury Tales* is often taken as a sort of archetype of the medieval English mariner, partly because sailors feature so seldom as significant characters in surviving medieval literature. Chaucer's Shipman came from Dartmouth, a sunburnt 'good fellow' (the term could mean 'rogue') wearing a knee-length garment of coarse woollen cloth and armed with a dagger hung on a strap under his arm. He was credited with intimate knowledge of tides, coasts and dangers from the Baltic to the Mediterranean, but he was also dishonest and utterly ruthless, drowning anyone he defeated in combat. He sailed in a barge called the *Maudelayne*. Various attempts have been made to identify him with a specific person. If he was based on a real mariner, it was probably the elder John Hawley of Dartmouth, a notorious pirate (see p. 83).[20]

English sea trade

England was the wealthiest and most populous country in the medieval British Isles, but compared with the sophisticated, urbanized economies of the contemporary Mediterranean, it was 'out in the sticks'. The English export market was mainly characterized from the twelfth to the fifteenth centuries by the export of raw materials in trades mostly controlled by foreigners – a symptom of classic economic 'underdevelopment' in more recent times. However, a minority in England grew rich on the profits of trade, including the Crown. In the thirteenth century English kings clearly became aware of the possibilities of taxing trade as

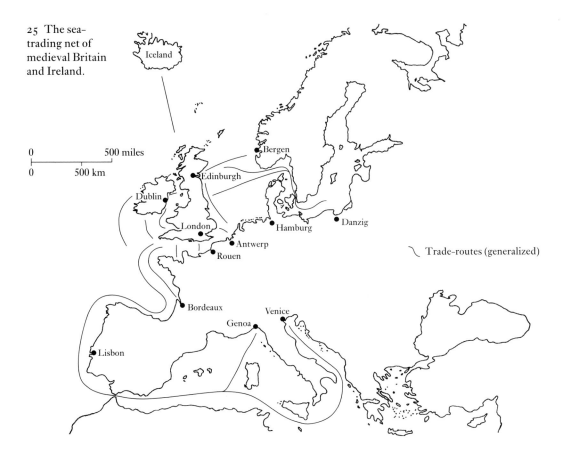

25 The sea-trading net of medieval Britain and Ireland.

Iceland

Bergen

Edinburgh

Dublin

London

Hamburg

Danzig

Antwerp

Rouen

⟍ Trade-routes (generalized)

Bordeaux

Venice

Genoa

Lisbon

0 ___ 500 miles
0 ___ 500 km

a source of profit, and in 1275 Edward I imposed the first successful national customs system.

England's main raw material exports were wool, followed by tin, lead and coal. Cloth was the only really significant manufactured export, taking over from wool as England's leading export between the 1420s and 1440s. None of these were high-volume exports needing many ships to move them, and much of the trade in raw materials was in the hands of foreign merchants who may not have favoured using English vessels. Nevertheless, the wool and cloth trades made certain places rich: in 1334, six of the ten wealthiest towns or cities in England, including London, were east coast ports engaged in the wool trade.

In some areas English merchants fought foreign competition. Much of the cloth trade was eventually captured by the economic power of the London merchants. By the mid-1400s, about 60 per cent of all English export trade was passing through the capital. The cloth trade settled down into a relatively cosy pattern, run by the so-called Merchant Adventurers, that saw most cloth exports channelled into the short sea route from London to Antwerp, the great continental cloth market. This ultimately damaged the trade of other English ports. The situation was ended by the collapse of the Antwerp market in the mid-sixteenth century.

26 The Wool House, Southampton. Built *c*.1406, this great warehouse testifies to the profits that arose from the wool and cloth trades.

The most significant trade for the English shipping industry was undoubtedly the import of wine from Gascony. The wine trade needed a good proportion of large vessels capable of carrying bulk wine cargoes. Such vessels could also be converted into effective warships, and in this way the trade added to the country's potential stock of naval shipping. In addition, Gascony contributed large amounts of money through customs and other duties to the Crown, and Gascon ships (particularly those of Bayonne) made an important contribution to English war fleets. Although wine was imported from other places, Gascony was England's main supplier. Wine was a luxury product, consumed mainly by the gentry and aristocracy, but the wine-drinking habit was very widespread across the country. Even very small towns are known to have had wine-sellers.[21]

The largest container for transporting wine was a barrel called the tun, which contained 252 gallons of wine (roughly the equivalent of 1,500 modern 75 cl bottles). In the thirteenth century, if not earlier, the tun became the standard measure for the carrying capacity of English ships; this is why a ship today is still measured in terms of its 'tonnage', even though the modern units are very different. Tonnage was being used as a measure of a ship's military potential by the thirteenth century. An order of 1214, for example, called for all ships of Bristol and other counties, capable of carrying 80 tuns of wine or more, to be notified to the Crown.[22] This underlines the importance of the wine trade for English shipping; no-one ever seems to have thought of rating a ship on the basis of how many wool-sacks or broadcloths it could carry.

The medieval wine trade was at its height in the early fourteenth century. In the year from September 1304, shipping arrivals (of all nationalities) at Bordeaux peaked at 1,020, with over 86,000 tuns exported. Many of these were ships making more than one voyage, but this still meant that Bordeaux was a very busy port. In the early 1300s, about one-fifth of Gascon wine exports (around 20,000 tuns annually) went to England. The main wine trading ports were Bristol, Southampton, London and Hull, but unlike the wool trade much of the wine coming to England seems to have come in English-owned ships used by English merchants. War, plague and piracy hit the Gascon wine trade badly in the fourteenth century. There were fewer producers, fewer consumers and transport became riskier and more expensive. English imports of wine in the fifteenth century never reached more than half the levels of the early 1300s. As the historian Christopher Dyer points out, it is probable that the decline in wine imports into England during the Hundred Years War was not only due to war directly affecting supplies. Transport costs also soared, more than doubling the price of wine per gallon, and this could deter even aristocratic consumers from buying as much as they once did.[23]

In the fourteenth century sailing times were rather haphazard, at least in peacetime, with English ships putting in at Bordeaux between August and the following April, and sailing even in the stormy winter months. Wartime sailings were more organized in order to provide mutual protection, and convoys were first used during an Anglo-French conflict in 1324. Undoubtedly the convoy system, necessary as it was, played a major role in pushing up costs. By the mid-fifteenth century there were normally two sailings to Bordeaux each year, in early November and March, to coincide with the two wine seasons.

As the trade declined so did the numbers of ships needed to move the wine. Total annual shipping arrivals at Bordeaux between the 1350s and 1440s seldom rose above 250, and on at least one occasion fell below 100. However, one sideeffect of the Hundred Years War was that most foreign shippers withdrew from the Gascon wine trade, leaving the field open for English merchants and vessels. Ships from Devon became particularly important in the trade, carrying between about one-sixth and just over one-quarter of the wine exported from Bordeaux between the 1350s and the 1440s. Dartmouth was generally the leading Devon port, followed by Plymouth, but most of the wine went to ports outside the West Country which itself was too poor to be a major market for the product.

The English wine trade from Gascony was almost killed off when the region fell to the French in 1453. It did not resume on a normal basis until after England and France had concluded a durable peace in 1475. However, it was not until the late 1490s that English wine imports from Gascony again reached 10,000 tuns per year.[24]

Salt, canvas and iron were other significant imports. The salt came from Bourgneuf Bay in the west of France, and was of major importance in England and elsewhere because salting was one of the few effective ways of preserving meat and fish. 'Bay salt' was not of very good quality, but was cheap and plentiful. The Dutch dominated the English salt trade until the late fifteenth century and probably not too much of it travelled in English ships.[25]

The sail canvas used by the English generally came from the Baltic, Brittany or south-western France, because canvas manufacture was not established in England until the sixteenth century. A native woollen cloth called 'bever' was sometimes used for sails until the late fourteenth or early fifteenth century, but it is clear that canvas was preferred, probably because it was stronger and more durable. The English also had a preference for Spanish iron from the Basque region of northern Spain. English iron was rather brittle, and the Basque variety was both better and cheaper. Iron imports are estimated to have reached an average of 3,500 tons per year by the 1490s. Besides these major products, medieval England also imported 'naval stores' (pitch, tar and timber) from the Baltic; although the level of the medieval trade is unclear, it was a major feature of Anglo-Baltic trade until the nineteenth century.[26]

The direct sea link between Britain and the Mediterranean, severed in the seventh century, was re-opened by the Venetians and Genoese in the late thirteenth century. They used oared galleys to move high-value, low-volume cargoes such as spices. After 1340 the Genoese used large sailing carracks with bulk cargoes such as alum, used for fixing cloth dyes. Southampton, Sandwich and London gradually became regular ports of call. Regular Italian sea trade continued into the sixteenth century, but finally died off in the 1530s. The English made occasional attempts to trade directly with the Mediterranean, but had little success until the second half of the sixteenth century.[27]

Most of the routes followed by English mariners in the Middle Ages involved either a comparatively short journey across the open sea or coastal sailing. The only one that required long-distance oceanic navigation using a magnetic compass was the Iceland trade. The voyages were undertaken in order to exploit the rich Icelandic fishing grounds and to purchase stockfish. Stockfish was cod or other fish that was preserved by being gutted, beaten with clubs and then dried in the cold northern air, without the use of salt. With so many meatless days decreed in the medieval religious calendar, fish was a vital source of protein, and the Iceland trade had the potential to make some men rich. It may have started in the fourteenth century, but there is no clear evidence of English ships off Iceland until 1408/9. The trade was first developed by east coast ports, but later ships from the West Country, Wales and Ireland took part. However, the trade, which may have been at its height between about 1430 and 1460, was dominated by Hull and Bristol, ports able to furnish the largish ships (of more than 100-tons burden or capacity) that seem to have been common in the Iceland trade. The trade was carried on in the face of official opposition from Denmark, which ruled Iceland. The English seamen had a bad reputation for kidnapping Icelandic boys and rustling cattle, and some of them went so far as to murder the Icelandic governor in 1467. This was one of the causes of the 1468–74 sea war between England, Denmark and the Hanse (see below), which the English lost and which led to a decline of the Iceland trade. Icelandic waters were reopened to the English by an Anglo-Danish treaty in 1490, and ships began sailing there in increasing numbers to fish for cod (using lines). In 1528, 149 English ships sailed for Iceland, but the fishery again began to decline in the 1530s because of increasing Danish port dues and restrictions on fish sales in England.[28]

27 Hanse Steelyard, King's Lynn (on the right). Built *c.*1474 to replace an earlier building (perhaps on the same site), the Hanse Steelyard in King's Lynn served as one of several warehouses and trading bases for the Hanse in England.

The impact of sea trade was felt mainly in the cities and towns of medieval England. River and road distribution, with the horse-drawn wagon as the heavy goods vehicle of the time, ensured that the valuables carried by ships reached those who could afford to pay for them. It is known, for example, that wine imported at Southampton in about 1440 went as far inland as Oxford, and that Mediterranean alum reached the cloth dyers of Leicester, over 120 miles to the north. However, the towns housed a minority of the population and the rural majority probably lived their lives as if the sea did not exist.[29]

England and the Hanse

The German Hanse or Hanseatic League was a massive trading union of towns in the Baltic, Germany, Scandinavia and Russia. Established in the thirteenth century, it was the economic superpower of northern Europe and achieved massive penetration of English trade. As early as 1157 German merchants operating in London were given protection by Henry II, a sign of their importance to the government. The later Hanse developed a system of trading stations or *kontore* in different towns, which the English came to call 'Steelyards' (after the original German hall in London). Hanseatic merchants enjoyed long-term royal protection in England and favourable customs exemptions because the trade that they brought meant extra income for the government. As a result the greatest concentration of *kontore* were in England: there were eight in English ports, at London, Ipswich, Great Yarmouth, King's Lynn, Boston, Hull, York and Newcastle, whereas in Scotland there was only one, at Edinburgh.

English relations with the Hanse were quite good in the 1430s, but these deteriorated because of indiscriminate attacks by English pirates. The most spectacular was Robert Wennington's capture of a convoy of a hundred ships belonging to the Hanseatic League as they returned from Bourgneuf Bay laden with salt in 1449. In 1458 the Earl of Warwick, then Captain of Calais, captured part of another Hanse Bay fleet. Attempts by English ships and traders to break into the Baltic trade were often resisted by members of the Hanse. Eventually relations broke down completely in 1468 when ships from Danzig (modern Gdansk) and Denmark seized English ships bound for Poland. The English closed the London Steelyard and war broke out between the English and the Hanse, with fighting between ships from the two sides. The Treaty of Utrecht, which ended the war in 1474, gave the Hanse back all their old privileges in England and more, but led to the virtual exclusion of English ships from the Baltic until the second half of the sixteenth century. The Hanse did not lose their privileges in England until 1598.[30]

English coastal trade

No national customs were payable on the medieval coasting trade, which makes it very difficult to find out much about its nature or volume. Coastal shipping did have to pay local port dues, but few records of these survive. Those that do suggest that, at least for some of the time, coastal trade flourished. For example, coastal shipping made up three-quarters of all shipping movements in the port of Exeter between 1383 and 1411. All sorts of goods seem to have been moved around the coast, from small household articles to complete ships' masts. Southampton, for example, imported tin and slate from the West Country by sea, wheat from Sussex and fish from the West Country and East Anglia. Piracy and war had adverse effects on coastal sea trade, particularly through the Straits of Dover. Ports such as Southampton and Sandwich prospered in part because shippers found it safer to unload goods bound for London at these places rather than make the potentially dangerous journey round the North Foreland of Kent and into the southern North Sea.[31]

The Newcastle coal trade is known to have been a big employer of coastal shipping in the eighteenth and nineteenth centuries, and it may also have been one in the Middle Ages. Coal was being shipped from Newcastle by at least the early 1290s, and probably much earlier. Some of this went to Scotland, Holland, Zeeland, Flanders and France, although Newcastle coal was unloaded in both the east and south coast ports of England, including London, which was probably the biggest domestic market for the coal. A 'sea-coal lane' existed in the capital in the 1220s and there are signs of coal imports in the 1250s. Some Newcastle customs accounts of the period 1377–91 suggest that much of the export trade at this time

28 English chart of Dover, *c.*1530. This was not a navigational chart, but gives an early image of one of England's chief Channel ports, as important in the cross-Channel passenger trade in the Middle Ages as now. The small ships in the foreground are somewhat distorted, but include perhaps the earliest illustrations of gunports.

went in ships from Holland, Zealand, Flanders and the Baltic, with little participation from Newcastle ships. It is possible that the local vessels were engaged mainly in the coastal trade. The loading of coal at Newcastle was generally carried out using river craft of about 21 tons called 'keels', which took coal from the quayside to ships anchored in the Tyne.[32]

Medieval English ports

London was far and away the largest port and the biggest city in the medieval British Isles. By the late thirteenth century its population may have numbered 80,000, at a time when a place with 2,000 people would have been regarded as a big town. The waterfront of the old Roman city of London lay roughly along the line of modern Thames Street, but excavation has shown that between the twelfth and fifteenth centuries it crept southwards, in places by over 100 metres. Such developments seem to have been the work of individual wharf-owners. Aside from a desire to create more building space, the process may have been driven by the periodic silting up of quaysides. As silt and rubbish built up against the waterfront, it became difficult for larger vessels to tie up, so a new quay had to be built further

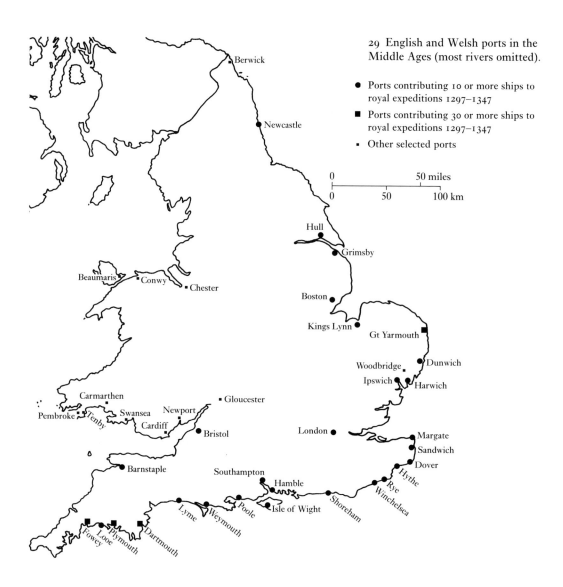

29 English and Welsh ports in the Middle Ages (most rivers omitted).

● Ports contributing 10 or more ships to royal expeditions 1297–1347

■ Ports contributing 30 or more ships to royal expeditions 1297–1347

▪ Other selected ports

| 0 | | | 50 miles |
| 0 | 50 | | 100 km |

Berwick

Newcastle

Hull

Grimsby

Beaumaris Conwy Chester

Boston

Kings Lynn Gt Yarmouth

Woodbridge Dunwich
Ipswich Harwich

Carmarthen Gloucester

Pembroke Tenby Swansea Newport
Cardiff Bristol London Margate
Sandwich
Dover
Barnstaple Southampton Hythe
Hamble Rye
Winchelsea
Lyme Weymouth Poole Isle of Wight Shoreham
Fowey Looe Plymouth Dartmouth

out into the river in order to provide sufficient depth of water. Evidence of a similar type of medieval 'creeping waterfront' has been found at Newcastle-upon-Tyne, amongst other places.

Larger ships were confined to the east of London Bridge because the bridge arches were too low to permit sizeable vessels to pass. The area in which they moored or anchored east of the bridge was known as 'the Pool' by as early as 1000. All of the wharves along the river were served by small craft, some called 'shouts', which plied the river in great numbers and were small enough to get through the bridge arches carrying coastal shipments or cargoes off-loaded from bigger ships. The names of some of the quays, such as Fishwharf, Timberhithe, Saltwharf, Oystergate and Woolwharf, advertised some of the commodities that passed through them. The economic boundaries of the port of London were already spreading beyond the limits of the City by the late Middle Ages. By the fourteenth and fifteenth centuries the north bank parishes of Wapping, Shadwell, Ratcliffe, Limehouse, Poplar and Blackwall, all to the east of the Tower of London, were providing building, repair and other services for the shipping using the port.

Cargo-handling in most ports was rudimentary. Some cranes did exist at places like Southampton and London, but much unloading was probably handled using blocks and tackles attached to a ship's yardarm, or by porters (the ancestors of dockers) tramping up and down gangways. At Southampton licensed porters were already in existence by the late thirteenth century, with set scales of charges for handling different cargoes such as wine, wool, salt, cheese and even millstones.[41]

The accounting entities of medieval English customs ports were based around a major 'head port' and its 'creeks' or lesser ports where trade revenue was collected. The customs port of Newcastle stretched as far south as Whitby, for example. It is apparent that most medieval ports were little more than 'creeks', too small and too poor to be able to afford or need harbour facilities. One hundred and fifty-five places in England contributed ships to English royal expeditions between 1297 and 1372, but the vast majority of these were tiny, two-thirds contributing less than five ships apiece (103 places) and only thirty able to contribute more than ten ships each. These were not absolute measures of numbers of ships in each port, but they probably give a pretty good indication of the general situation.[42]

For a town that had a significant inland trade and good communications, sea trade could be a key to wealth and major development. The 1334 lay subsidy (tax) returns show that of the fifty wealthiest regional towns and cities in England, sixteen were ports, with Bristol, York, Newcastle, Boston, Great Yarmouth, King's Lynn and Southampton among the top ten (the top eleven in reality, as Newcastle and York were 'level pegging' in terms of assessed wealth). However, wealth and shipping strength were not necessarily the same thing, for the comparatively poor West Country ports of Dartmouth, Plymouth and Fowey frequently fielded large numbers of ships (see Fig. 29). This may have been because of the poverty of the region, shipping being the only investment liable to yield significant returns.

If ports could grow, they could also die. Sometimes physical factors were the cause. A few examples will suffice: the Kentish port of Old Romney was killed off by silting even before the Norman Conquest; the silting of the Dee Estuary in the fourteenth century left Chester effectively stranded; after years of battering by storms, Old Winchelsea in Sussex finally disappeared in a terrible storm of 1287; floods and storms destroyed Edward I's new victualling bases on the Cumberland coast at Wavermouth (1301) and Skinburgh (1305).

Some ports were killed by the actions of men. Most places raided during the Hundred Years War recovered, but not all. New Winchelsea, founded in 1288, failed to develop as hoped because of devastating French raids between 1337 and 1380, although silting also played a part. The tiny port of Gosford, on the River Deben in Suffolk, seems to have lost all or most of its ships to attacks by the French and Flemish in 1403, and it disappears from the records as a trading place.[43]

Welsh sea trade

The development of towns came slowly to medieval Wales, but it was spurred on by Anglo-Norman settlement in the twelfth and thirteenth centuries. By 1300 there were about eighty towns in the country, some of which, such as Cardiff, Carmarthen and Tenby on the south coast, were ports. Further north, the main crossing-point from Anglesey to the mainland was the port of Llan-faes, a trading harbour said to be receiving an average of thirty ships per year in the thirteenth century. Welsh ports traded with Ireland, England and Brittany, taking wool and leather to England and hides to Brittany. Welsh ships were also to be found in the Gascon wine trade and the Bay salt trade, although their numbers were probably fairly small.

Archaeological finds can help to broaden the picture of the medieval coasting trade. In 1995 the wreck of a thirteenth-century clinker-built ship was discovered on the south-east coast of Wales at Magor Pill, just across the Severn from Bristol. The ship was probably a coastal trader and was carrying iron ore that seems to have been mined in Glamorgan. Land-based excavations have found thirteenth-century pottery from the west of England at Welsh coastal sites, complementing

30 Fishermen: *c.*1120 carving on a column capital from Lewes Priory, Sussex. Fishermen net fish from a double-ended wooden boat. Other images from the capital recall Jesus calling Peter and Andrew from their nets to be 'fishers of men'.

documentary evidence of cross-Severn contacts at this period and suggesting that there was active trading between the Welsh and English sides of the Severn Estuary.[33]

Coastal fishing

Very little is known about fishing in the British Isles before the later Middle Ages, although local inshore fishing has been practised around the coasts of Britain and Ireland since prehistoric times. From the Middle Ages onwards, and perhaps before, particular types of small craft were developed to cope with local conditions and different sorts of catches. Excavations have suggested that herring and cod were significant parts of the diet in some parts of England, but it is possible that sea fishing before 1200, although widespread, was on a fairly small scale. There were two main English fisheries, the larger one on the east coast with herring as the main catch. The smaller fishery was in the south-west, but caught a wider range of species. The east coast fishery, which had Great Yarmouth and Scarborough as it main centres, began to decline in the fourteenth century, due to war, population decline and foreign competition (particularly from the Dutch). The south-western fishery rose in importance in the fifteenth century, but did not make up the short-fall in the lost yields on the east coast.

The medieval English fishing industry apparently could not provide England with all of its fish supply. It is certain that commercial fishing was developing in England from the thirteenth century, and for this fishermen were going further and further out to sea, in the fifteenth century to Icelandic waters (see p. 66).[34]

Medieval Ireland and the Irish Sea: trade and ports

Ireland became part of the Angevin Empire in the 1170s, although firm political control of the country eluded English rulers for centuries. The Irish ports of the south-east were key factors in the conquest and settlement. They became 'beach-heads' for the Anglo-Normans and other immigrants. Ports such as Dublin, which had been created by the Scandinavians and run for centuries by their 'Ostmen' descendants, were further developed by the Anglo-Norman incomers and their English successors. The greatest concentrations of towns or boroughs lay in the areas that saw the most intensive Anglo-Norman settlement and about half of the 163 boroughs lay on the coast or on a navigable river. As in other places, the availability of water transport was a key factor in urban development. The south-eastern port of New Ross, for example, was sited where the rivers Nore and Barrow met, and both rivers stretched far inland into the area settled by the Anglo-Normans. Data for medieval Irish trade is rather thin, but cumulative customs receipts for Ireland between 1276 and 1333 suggest that New Ross, Waterford and Cork were the leading ports, followed by Dublin and Drogheda (see Fig. 31).

Although Dublin had a poor harbour and many goods had to be off-loaded some way from the port and transhipped in boats, it was the key Anglo-Norman town in Ireland and as a consequence received a greater level of trade than would have been

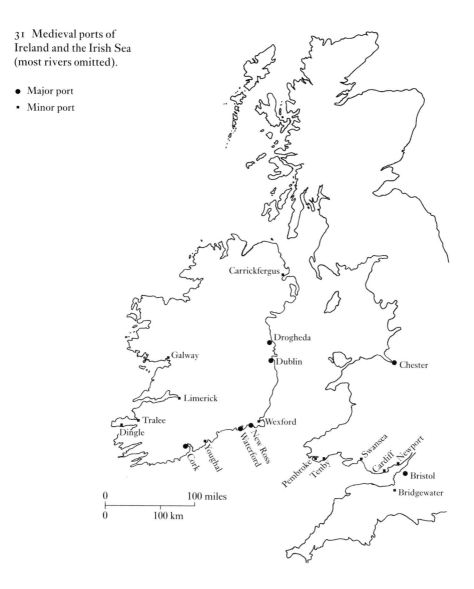

31 Medieval ports of
Ireland and the Irish Sea
(most rivers omitted).

● Major port
▪ Minor port

Carrickfergus

Drogheda

Galway

Dublin

Chester

Limerick

Tralee

Wexford

Dingle

New Ross

Waterford

Youghal

Cork

Pembroke

Tenby

Swansea

Cardiff

Newport

Bristol

Bridgewater

0   100 miles
0   100 km

the case had it been just another port. Access to the hinterland was one factor in the success of the south-western ports, but they were also closer to Bristol and France than Dublin or Drogheda. It is known that medieval Ireland had trading links with Portugal, Spain, Gascony, France and Flanders, but there is little doubt that the most important trade-link for Ireland lay across the Irish Sea.

Wool, woolfells and hides seem to have been the main exports from Ireland in the thirteenth century. These appear to have declined in the fourteenth century, to be replaced by the export of fish, some cloth and other items. The majority of the cargoes on the Ireland–Bristol route were moved by English ships, for the Irish merchant fleet was very small in the Middle Ages, both in terms of numbers and sizes of ships. Irish ships did take part in the Bordeaux wine trade but, as with

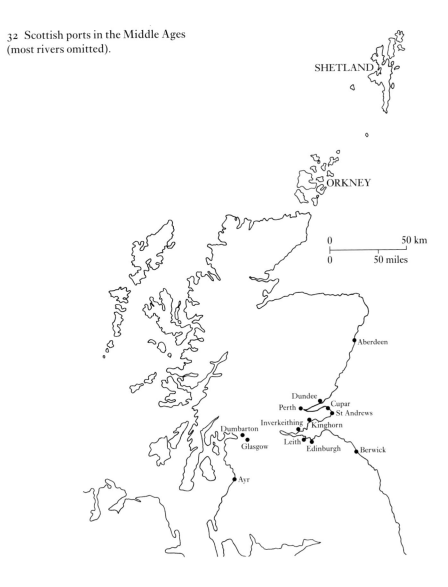

32 Scottish ports in the Middle Ages
(most rivers omitted).

SHETLAND

ORKNEY

0   50 km

0   50 miles

Aberdeen

Dundee
Perth   Cupar
St Andrews
Inverkeithing   Kinghorn
Dumbarton
Leith
Glasgow   Edinburgh   Berwick

Ayr

English shipping, the high point was probably reached in the early 1300s, when Irish cargo sizes averaged 90 tuns. Cargoes on other Irish routes were generally small, in the order of 20–30 tons or less. Customs records of the 1480s suggest that probably no more than about 130 Irish vessels were operating in the Irish Sea, although lack of Irish ships did not always mean a lack of Irish traders. After Bordeaux fell to the French in 1453, Breton shipping filled the vacuum left by the departure of the English, but Irish wine merchants often sailed in ships owned by Bretons and others. In the late fifteenth and early sixteenth centuries something like 150 Irish traders were operating in this trade.

    Bristol and Chester were the main English ports for Irish trade. Bristol had been mixed up in slave trading with Ireland in the early eleventh century, and the

Anglo-Norman conquest gave Bristolians a firm base in Dublin. In about 1171/2 Henry II actually granted Dublin to the men of Bristol, possibly in return for help given in his crossing to Ireland. Irish trade went to other Bristol Channel ports such as Bridgwater in Somerset and to Tenby in Wales, but the second English port for Irish trade was Chester, which was also the greatest port in the north-west of England in the Middle Ages and was said to have been trading with Dublin in the early twelfth century. During the thirteenth-century English campaigns in Wales, Chester functioned as a supply base for the armies and castles in north Wales, often acting as an entrepôt for grain, fish and other supplies sent from Ireland. Chester, like Bristol, also served from time to time as an embarkation port for troops being sent across the Irish Sea. They were also the two main points of departure for civilian travellers to Ireland, though crossing the Irish Sea was not always an easy or safe proposition. In the early 1320s the Earl of Pembroke petitioned Edward II for a particular royal order to be taken to Ireland. In view of the dangers of crossing the Irish Sea, he asked that duplicate copies should be made, one copy to be taken by a lawyer sailing from Pembroke and the other carried by a lawyer from Chester![35]

Scottish ports and sea trade

The east coast ports of Scotland were far more important than those on the west coast in the Middle Ages. The former were closer to the Continent and much more accessible to the shipping of nations that were either allies of the Scots or at least neutral in the Anglo-Scottish conflict. The closest overseas trading destination

33 A reconstruction of part of the 13th-century Magor Pill Boat, found on the Welsh side of the Severn Estuary.

from the west coast was Ireland, which was poor and subject to fluctuating levels of English control.

However, many of the east coast ports also stood directly on one of the English invasion routes. Berwick was the leading Scottish port until 1296 when it was taken by Edward I. A century later, Edinburgh (through its outport Leith) had the greatest trade of any Scottish seaport, followed by Dundee, Perth, Cupar, Inverkeithling, Kinghorn and St Andrews. Overseas trade was controlled by the Convention of Royal Burghs, and a Scottish Staple was established at Bruges in 1407.[36]

The shipbuilding industry

Although shipbuilding undoubtedly went on in medieval Scotland, Wales and Ireland, most of the surviving evidence relates to England. However, wooden ship-building was probably very similar in nature in all these countries. Shipwrightry was not a high-status trade in medieval England and it appears to have been a rather small industry. In the 1350s officials had to be sent to East Anglia to conscript ship-wrights for a royal shipbuilding project on the Thames, a few miles from London, the country's biggest port. When the Henry V's great ship *Grace Dieu* was built at Southampton in 1416, additional shipbuilders had to be fetched from the West Country to assist; even a major seaport like Southampton seems to have not had enough shipwrights.

Financial accounts between the late thirteenth and early fifteenth centuries make it clear that shipbuilding craft structure was based on the technology of clinker construction:

Table 3 The organization of English shipwrightry

Worker	Probable function	Daily pay-rate, early 15th century
Master shipwright	designer and site manager	8d
Boarder	shaping and fitting timbers; overseers	6d
Clenchers	used hammers to clench over the nail-heads inside the hull	5d
Holder	worked outside the hull, holding in the nails that were being clenched	4d
Boy/servant	general assistants	3d

The work of clenchers and holders in particular must have been dull and repet-itive in the extreme. This trade structure is found fully formed in the 1290s in places as far apart as Lyme in Dorset and Newcastle-upon-Tyne; given its close relationship to clinker technology, it may have been in existence in the days of the Sutton Hoo ship.

A number of other kinds of worker were also involved in shipbuilding. Smiths were always needed to make nails and other ironwork for vessels, and from the 1340s, if not earlier, there was a new craftsman, the caulker. Caulkers were people who filled the gaps between planks with waterproofing materials; in earlier periods this job seems to have been done by shipwrights and it is not clear why a separate trade should have emerged. However, it was to remain a part of the shipbuilding trade for as long as wooden seagoing vessels were built.

It is difficult to find evidence of established shipyards in medieval England, although Smallhythe in Kent functioned as a rural shipbuilding centre between the early fifteenth and mid-sixteenth centuries. The location of shipbuilding sites seems to have been rather haphazard and the sites themselves were rudimentary, although it is known that ships were being built in simple docks by at least the 1330s. These were holes dug in the ground by a waterway, with the water kept out by an earthen dam. The ship was built inside. When completed, the dam was broken down and the ship was floated out at high tide. The process was taken a step further in 1495 with the construction at Portsmouth of the world's earliest-known dry dock. This great structure, built for repairing Henry VII's warships, had a large dam like a tidal dock, but also had a pump to empty out water. This made its reuse much easier and would have dealt with any leaks in the dam (see p. 97).[37]

The development of ships

Seagoing ships of any size in Britain and Ireland (and the rest of northern Europe) were built clinker-fashion until the late fifteenth or early sixteenth century. Shapes no doubt varied enormously, but the ancient 'double-ended' hull form was widespread until the fourteenth century, when vessels that were asymmetrical, with stems and sterns of different shape,

34 Cast of the town seal of Dunwich, Suffolk, late 12th century. A double-ended ship fitted for war with fore- and aftercastles, and a topcastle at the head of the single mast. Vessels of this hull-form were found right across northern Europe in the 12th and 13th centuries. The fish swimming in the sea give a clue to one of the sources of Dunwich's prosperity. Many medieval port towns carried ships or other maritime images as symbols of the source of their economic wealth.

gradually supplanted it. To put it crudely (and somewhat inaccurately) they had a 'sharp end' and a 'blunt end'. This change in form appears to have been related to the introduction of the stern rudder, which first appeared in the twelfth century and eventually supplanted the side or quarter rudder. It was less vulnerable to storm or battle damage than the side rudder and, more importantly, was probably better suited to deep-hulled merchant ships. The stern rudder may have first appeared on types with straight sternposts, although by the thirteenth century it was being adapted for use on the curved sterns of ships with the double-ended hull form.

Like hull construction, sailing-ship rig in northern Europe followed the same general pattern until the fifteenth century. The one-masted rig with a single square sail was ubiquitous in the north. The square sail worked well with the wind from behind or from the beam, but its windward sailing capabilities were somewhat limited. Sailing to windward was helped by a tacking-boom or '*lof*', which pushed out the windward edge of the sail to stop it collapsing. In the thirteenth and four-teenth centuries the lof (probably a Viking invention) was gradually replaced by bowlines, movable ropes running from both vertical edges of the sail to the bowsprit, a spar projecting out over the bow. Other sail- and yard-control ropes were being developed in the thirteenth and fourteenth centuries, to the extent that

35 Outline drawings of medieval ship-types: keel, cog, hulk and carrack (based on medieval images: approximate relative sizes, but not to scale).

a sailor in, say, 1800 would have had little difficulty in understanding how to control a sail of 1400. Many of the names given to this gear, such as tack, sheet and brace, originated in the Middle Ages and are still used to describe the gear of modern square-riggers.

The general lines of development of medieval ships are clear, but it is much harder to be specific about ship and boat types. By the fifteenth and early sixteenth centuries, English waters were being used by at least sixty different types of craft, or at least craft of sixty different *type*-names. With most of these vessels it is possible to distinguish whether they were small boats, sea-going merchantmen or warships, but beyond that it is difficult to be certain about what they looked like. Added to this is the problem that the meanings of type-names changed over time or varied from region to region. For example, the word 'barge' nowadays can denote a canal boat or a Thames sailing barge; in late medieval England the name was applied to an oared warship. That said, we can pin names to certain types of merchant vessel, such as the cog and hulk (see Fig. 35).

Although it appears that most late medieval hulls were asymmetrical, one of the last hold-outs of the ancient double-ended hull form was in the Western Isles of Scotland. Here elegant Highland galleys and birlinns (a smaller version of the galley) were still in regular use in the early seventeenth century, and the MacLeods of Dunvegan Castle on Skye built their last birlinn as late as 1706. Suspiciously 'Viking-looking' stems can still be seen on modern Scottish cobles (a type of small fishing vessel).[38]

Elsewhere the decline of the double-ended ship may have been hastened by military considerations. Defensive castles were appearing on ships by the late twelfth century. These were at first rather makeshift-looking structures, not unlike the watchtowers of twentieth-century wartime prison camps. The forecastle was positioned at the bow (the origin of the term 'foc's'le') and the aftercastle at the stern. Many ships also had topcastles positioned on the mast, just above the yard, and reached by climbing the standing rigging that supported the mast on either side. The castles, typically shown in medieval illustrations with crenellations, were used for combat. Medieval sea battles were normally resolved by boarding actions and, in such a situation, being higher than your opponents conferred a distinct advantage. It has been suggested that castles may have first appeared on the comparatively low-built, double-ended vessels in an attempt to nullify the height advantage of deep-hulled ships like the cog. It was an 'arms race' that the lower ships could never win, for castles were fixed to the higher-sided ships, thus compounding their advantage. Over the course of time castles became a normal part of the structure of some vessels, particularly warships, although many medieval merchantmen may have sailed without them. By the late fifteenth century large warships had multi-stage castles (with two or three decks, or perhaps more) as a matter of course, a change perhaps largely dictated by the massive increase in the number of guns carried by big combatants.

The rise in gun power was not the only major change in European shipping in the fifteenth century. From the 1430s small skeleton-built Portuguese caravels began to appear in north European waters. Northerners called these ships 'carvels', a term that rapidly became synonymous with skeleton construction. Skeleton construction involved nailing the hull planks to a pre-erected skeleton of strong frames; the planks did not overlap, but were laid against each other, giving the hull a smooth exterior. Clinker construction has its own good qualities, but it may have been more expensive than skeleton construction; in addition, skeleton-built hulls appear to have been tougher, more durable and easier to repair. The skeleton construction 'revolution' may have taken as much as seventy or eighty years to spread across all of northern Europe, but by the early to mid-sixteenth century it had mostly supplanted clinker construction as means of building sea-going vessels of any size. Carvels are first noted in English waters in 1448, in Ireland in 1449, and by 1450 both a Portsmouth pirate called Clais Stephen and the king of Scotland owned carvels. Whether through imitation of captured ships or through the teaching of itinerant shipwrights, the technique of skeleton construction spread fast. The earliest-known English-built carvel, Sir John Howard's *Edward*, took to the water at Dunwich in Suffolk in 1466.

Given its close relationship to the clinker-building process, the shipbuilding trade in England and other parts of northern Europe is liable to have been badly disrupted by the introduction of Mediterranean skeleton construction in the mid-fifteenth century. As one might expect, the old names such as 'clencher' and 'holder' begin to disappear from the sources by the early sixteenth century. Pay rates suggest that the sixteenth-century trade structure was much more fragmented, but whether the change was a crisis or an 'opportunity' for shipwrights is difficult to say.

The *Edward* was also a three-masted ship, a result of the other fifteenth-century shipping revolution. Until the early fifteenth century English ships (and probably most ships in the northern Europe) appear to have had only one mast. The northern square sail and the hull form of the cog had spread to the Mediterranean in the late thirteenth or early fourteenth century. The resulting square-rigged *cocha* (later called a 'carrack' in the north) was generally a large vessel. In the mid-fourteenth century a second, smaller mast was added to the type. Set behind the mainmast, this mizzenmast carried a small triangular lateen sail to assist with manoeuvring. The lateen, like the modern yacht sail, is a fore-and-aft rigged sail with much better windward performance than the square sail, but is less well adapted to sail with the wind from behind. Combining the two increased the manoeuvrability of the cocha or carrack.

This two-masted rig spread to northern Europe, certainly by the decade 1410–20. The first-recorded English-built two-master was Henry V's balinger *Anne*, launched at Southampton in 1416, and the English Crown acquired other two-masters about this time. A third mast and sail, the foremast and square foresail, had been developed by the 1430s, and this may even have been an English invention. The foresail, sited just behind the bow, was probably in origin just a manoeuvring sail, but over the next three or four decades it grew in size, eventually becoming one of the main propulsive sails of the ship, second only to the mainsail. A square-rigged topmast was added on top of the mainmast by the 1460s to give more propelling power, and a square spritsail was also rigged on a yard under the bowsprit (the main topsail may originally have been intended to counter the tendency of the spritsail to bury the ship's bows in the sea). A topmast and sail soon appeared on the foremast and even the mizzenmast (the latter usually carrying a lateen topsail), and by the 1480s some larger vessels even had a fourth lower mast, the bonaventure, carrying a lateen perched on top of the stern. By about 1510 a large warship could carry up to a dozen sails, including 'topgallants' set on masts fixed to the heads of the topmasts. The whole arrangement was supported and worked by a forest of standing and running rigging. (Standing rigging supports the mast; running rigging uses pulleys and other gear to move the yards and sails).

That said, by 1500 the commonest type of sea-going rig was more modest: square-rigged fore and mainmasts (with topmasts), and a lateen-rigged mizzen. This type of rig made a ship of that time much more manoeuvrable than its one-masted predecessor of 1400, and it also made the vessel somewhat safer to operate. In a one-masted ship, if the mainmast or mainsail went, the ship was utterly at the mercy of the elements; if a three-master lost a mast or a sail it was in trouble, but the two additional masts meant that all was not necessarily lost. The three-masted rig gave sailors more options, increased their chances of survival, and thus added to the chances of safe return in trading and other voyages. The three-masted rig was united with the skeleton-built hull in the fifteenth century, and the type became the mainstay of the European transoceanic voyages of the fifteenth and sixteenth centuries. Despite major changes in hull form, size and rig configuration, it remained the basic type of European sea-going vessel until the nineteenth century.

One other major phenomenon of European shipping in the second half of the fifteenth century was a sharp decline in the numbers of large ships. The numbers of such vessels seem to have increased in England in the first half of the fifteenth century, and by about 1450 there was a significant number of English merchantmen in the 300–400-ton range. The decline of the large ship was doubtless due to many factors, one of which (in northern Europe, at least) may have been the introduction of skeleton construction: carvels were generally of less than 100 tons. In the case of English ships, the cessation of the Gascon wine trade deprived many of the larger ships of their *raison d'être*. The export of cloth, England's other main sea trade, only required small vessels. Large ships carried on in the Iceland trade for some decades, but even they fell out of use by the 1490s. Merchant ships of more than 100 tons burden were not common again in England until the late sixteenth century, when they were again constructed for long-distance bulk trade and for war.[39]

Trade, shipping and law

English merchants in the fourteenth and fifteenth centuries were keenly aware that they would derive much more benefit if English sea trade was carried mainly in English ships, and if the trade was under their control rather than that of foreigners.

The first attempts at navigation laws in England date back to the reign of Richard II in the late fourteenth century. Laws were passed in 1382, 1383 and

1391, aimed at making English merchants freight their cargoes in English ships if any were available at reasonable rates (or, in the wine trade, to use English or Gascon ships). It is very doubtful if these laws had much effect. The fact that English merchants did make inroads into the foreign domination of English sea trade in the fourteenth and fifteenth centuries may indicate that the English merchant marine was growing, but if so, it seems to have been at a slow rate. Laws of similar intent were passed in 1485 and 1489 with respect to trade with south-west France, and they were reiterated in the sixteenth century. Finally, in 1563 the coasting trade was closed to foreign ships. The legislation of Richard II's time was still said to be in force in the seventeenth century, but it took the very different conditions of that time to make a navigation law effective (see pp 154–9).

Marine insurance developed in the medieval Mediterranean, but was little known in fifteenth-century northern Europe. Generally, however, medieval shippers used other methods to reduce risk: practical measures such as travelling in convoy; legal measures such as safe-conducts and licences; financial measures such as avaries, or general averages, which meant collective contributions to dividing cargoes between several ships.[40]

Pirates and piracy

Piracy was endemic in medieval Europe. In some ways it is more accurately seen as the blackest form of a 'black economy' than as just crime. The dividing line between pirate and sea trader or even pirate and honoured citizen was sometimes blurred or non-existent. The truth was that the people who committed piracy were often also traders in their own right and exactly the same people that medieval governments relied on when waging a naval war.

The Hawley family of Dartmouth in Devon are a case in point. From at least the 1370s to 1436 the Hawleys were active pirates and privateers. John Hawley senior was a wealthy and respected Dartmouth seafarer, shipowner and merchant who undertook privateering voyages against foreign enemies for Richard II and Henry IV. He was also a well-known pirate, but never suffered any serious penalty for his activities. John Hawley's son, also called John, carried on the 'family business' until his death in 1436. This John endured a brief spell in jail in 1406, but seems to have experienced little further interruption to his career. Balingers, fast fighting ships equipped with both sail and oars, were favoured by medieval pirates, and in 1416 Hawley gave his 56-ton balinger *Craccher* ('Spitter') to Henry V, to serve in the king's fleet. One of Hawley's former shipmasters (and a former master of the *Craccher*), John William, rose to be master of the second largest of Henry V's 'great ships', the *Jesus,* despite committing at least one act of piracy when working for Hawley. He went on to become a respected member of the merchant community in Southampton, perhaps rising to be mayor and an MP.

Part of the problem lay in the thin line between piracy and privateering (privateers, loosely speaking, were individuals licensed by a government to attack the ships of state enemies). Piracy was a civil, not a criminal, offence in England until the sixteenth century, despite the fact that piracy was essentially theft, often accompanied by threats and violence or sometimes murder. The Admiralty Court had jurisdiction over piracy, but someone arrested for piracy could only be convicted if they confessed or if there was a firsthand witness against them. This made getting a conviction very difficult. If the pirate was foreign, a merchant might be able to acquire a letter of reprisal (or marque) that authorized the seizure of goods from the pirate's countrymen to the value of the pirated items (the late seventeenth-/early eighteenth-century letter of marque was rather different, an official licence to attack enemy shipping during wartime).

Much medieval piracy was probably small scale, at the level of stealing goods from anchored ships, a sort of 'nautical mugging', but some attacks were spectacular. In 1340, for example, a large Italian ship was intercepted and pillaged while *en route* to Flanders by sixty-two ships from Great and Little Yarmouth in Norfolk and Dunwich and Bawdsey in Suffolk. It was said that goods worth £20,000 were stolen, and the Crown had to pay £16,000 in compensation to the owners. Attempts were made to limit the activities of pirates, both home-grown and foreign. In 1442 and 1454 'sea-keeping' patrols were organized but, like an earlier scheme of 1406, these came to nothing. Acts of piracy could in effect become overt acts of war as when the pirates attacked ships belonging to the Hanse in the mid-fifteenth century (see p. 68).[44]

Pirates, of course, did not only operate on the sea. One tactic was to kidnap people on land and then ransom them. In March 1450 Margaret Paston wrote from Norwich to her husband John recounting attacks by foreign pirates (probably Flemings) on the Norfolk coast: 'There [have] been many enemies against Yarmouth and Cromer, and have done much harm, and taken many Englishmen, and put them in great distress, and greatly ransomed them; and the said enemies [have] been that they come up to the land, and play on Caister Sands.'[45]

The efforts of most medieval English governments to halt piracy lacked conviction: they often needed the pirates too much for naval service. Henry IV (r. 1399–1413), for example, appears to have used English piracy as a sort of diplomatic weapon, applying pressure on enemies that was just short of open war. Also, people like the Hawleys were important men in their localities and relatively far from the centre of power: no local jury would ever convict them. There is evidence that, with the French wars finally over and improvements in trade conditions in the second half of the fifteenth century, men were drawn back to more lawful ways of making money. Stable royal governments keen to assert their authority could also have an effect on helping to deter piracy, but it was not a problem that would be solved in British waters until the seventeenth century.[46]

Merchants and shipowners, thirteenth–fifteenth centuries

The word 'shipowner' is not found in English sources until 1540, but the concept itself is ancient, although very little is known about shipowners before the thirteenth century. In the Middle Ages the 'king's ships' were not a state navy as such, they were quite literally the possessions of the king. As such, they saw service as trading vessels or VIP transports, as well as warships. Aristocrats and members of the gentry also owned ships, as did some religious houses such as Beaulieu Abbey in Hampshire. However, the commonest ship-owning groups were probably merchants and shipmasters, operating on a small scale. No shipping companies existed in the modern sense, although there was at least one medieval shipping magnate, William Canynges of Bristol, who owned ten ships and ran his own dockyard in the 1460s.[47]

Most mercantile shipowners operated on a much humbler scale, but in relation to the general run of society they tended to be relatively wealthy people, usually concentrated in the places with the best trade. For example, of 233 Devon shipowners active between 1340 and 1408, two-thirds lived in Dartmouth and the Dart estuary or Plymouth. These were also the places where the majority of the men who owned more than one ship were to be found. Shipowning also went along with political power and, in the case of local magnates like the Hawleys of Dartmouth, shipowning and trading could also go along with piracy. For poorer people, shipowning partnerships were possible, with sometimes two or three individuals (including women) sharing the costs of running a vessel. Occasionally as many as nine people might have shares in a ship.[48]

Navigation up to 1600

Medieval navigation techniques were rudimentary. It is likely that much navigational lore was learned by heart and by experience, and was seldom put into writing because few medieval mariners could read. Sailing directions, which told the mariner what tides would run at such-and-such point or which headland followed which, probably developed as oral mnemonics which the sailor committed to memory, in much the same way that a modern London cab driver does the 'knowledge', memorizing the capital's street layout. The earliest written sailing directions in English date from the fifteenth century. Called a 'rutter' (after the French *routier*), such documents appeared in printed form in the sixteenth century (in France in 1520 and England in 1528), often with small maps or pictures of stretches of coastline.

Medieval navigational equipment was very basic. The magnetic compass was known from the twelfth century, if not earlier, but an equally if not more important device was the sounding lead, a solid lump of lead attached to a marked line that made it possible to measure the depth of water under a ship. Later leads had a small hole in the bottom that could be filled with tallow, to which seabed samples would adhere. Experienced navigators would be able to estimate their position from the nature of the sample, and it is quite possible that this practice was known in the Middle Ages. The other common medieval instrument was the sandglass or 'running glass', first developed in the Mediterranean in the thirteenth century and used to time a ship's run on a certain point of sailing or to time watches. All of these instruments were in use on English ships by the fourteenth century, although one cannot be certain how widely they were used. For example, the accounting records of 61 English royal ships in service between 1399 and 1422 show that while 49 (80 per cent) had sounding lines or leads and 29 had sandglasses (48 per cent),

36 Frontispiece by Theodor de Bry for *The Mariners Mirrour*, by Lucas Jansz Waghenaer (English translation London 1588). This is one of the first great chart atlases. The frontispiece illustrates, amongst other things, the sounding lead and line, the astrolabe, the crosstaff, the compass rose, the sandglass and the dividers used on charts.

only 16 had compasses (26 per cent). However, it is possible that compasses and other navigational gear were brought aboard as the personal property of the officers.[49]

Navigational instruments improved in the fifteenth century with the development in southern Europe of astrolabes, quadrants and cross-staffs, which were all devices used to measure the altitude (angle in the sky) of heavenly bodies, such as the sun, above the horizon. This made it possible to calculate latitude, a crucial step for transoceanic navigation. Despite many attempts, however, the determination of longitude had to wait until the development of accurate and stable shipboard timepieces in the eighteenth century (see p. 178).

Sea-charts were first developed in thirteenth-century Italy, but were probably not used in northern Europe until the sixteenth century (the earliest-known English sea-chart dates from the 1530s). It is very difficult to judge the extent of their use on English ships. John Aborough, the master of the *Michael* of Barnstaple in Devon in 1533, owned two charts, one of them for the Levant (eastern Mediterranean), along with four compasses, an English rutter ('which I John Aborough was a year and a half making of it'), a Spanish rutter, a Portuguese 'reportory' (probably an almanac), a lodestone (for magnetizing a compass needle), a 'running glass', as well as a quadrant and crosstaff. Aborough was equipped with most of the wherewithal for oceanic navigation, so it is clear that such techniques were known in England by the 1530s; however, decades were to pass before they were put to much use.[50]

Sailing directions relied in part on the recognition of coastal features, such as headland shapes, church spires and so on. At night, of course, such features disappeared, so in some places rudimentary lighthouses were erected, usually maintained by religious houses. The one at Hook in County Wexford is said to date from the fifth century, although certain evidence of lighthouses in the British Isles dates only from the twelfth century. At least thirteen lighthouses existed in medieval England, one in Wales, one in Scotland and two in Ireland, and there are indications of some thirteen more in these islands. The Hook light, like some if not all other medieval lights, was funded by local shipping tolls; in the fifteenth century, for example, Hull was granted a royal charter that allowed the port to collect shipping dues to build and maintain a lighthouse on Spurn Point. The marking of sea channels with buoys and poles, so that mariners could avoid shallow water, was practised in medieval England, but very little is known about it.[51]

The evidence for seamarks becomes much clearer in the sixteenth century, with the appearance of buoyed channels laid and maintained by organizations such as the Trinity House of Deptford. Founded in 1514, Trinity House survives today as the body responsible for lighthouses and other navigational features in England and Wales. Trinity House was awarded a charter by Henry VIII after a group of masters and mariners had petitioned the king that improvements had to be made to the quality of pilotage in the Thames. Pilotage, the guiding of ships into harbour by a local experienced pilot, remains a vital function. The Thames Estuary, with its shifting sands and winding river, was an especially difficult proposition for shipmasters and Trinity House took responsibility for pilotage in the Thames. Two seamen's guilds were later incorporated as Trinity Houses, on the model of the London Trinity House, at Newcastle (1536) and Hull (1541). In 1566 the Trinity House of Deptford was made responsible for seamarks and the licensing of watermen on the Thames. Trinity House was an influential organization, composed of shipmasters and owners, but despite its royal charters the Crown seldom consulted it on naval or shipbuilding matters until the time of Charles I (r. 1625–49).[52]

CHAPTER FOUR

Into the Ocean, *c.*1500–*c.*1600

The English navy: politics, war and privateering

The modern Royal Navy can trace its origins to the Tudor period (1485–1603) as the naval administration established in that period formed the basis for later developments. It is no accident that, in the late 1990s, three major fleet units, the submarines *Vanguard* and *Triumph* and the aircraft carrier *Ark Royal*, all bore names that had first been used in the sixteenth century.

As ever, the growth of the royal fleet was conditioned by political and military factors. Henry VII (r.1485–1509) undertook few foreign campaigns and so needed only a handful of royal ships. The single most important naval development of his reign was the construction of Portsmouth dockyard in 1495, with the world's first dry dock. Matters changed rapidly under his son Henry VIII (r.1509–47). He revived the English claim to the French throne, but his first two wars with the French, in 1512–14 and 1522–5, achieved little. Henry recognized that he needed a navy to fight his wars, and built his fleet up from a mere five ships in 1509 to thirty by 1514, including the huge carrack *Henri Grâce à Dieu* (1,500 tons) and the *Mary Rose* (600 tons).

The pattern of naval operations in Henry's first two wars with France was similar to that of the Hundred Years War. The English fleet was used to attack and capture enemy merchant shipping, raid the French coast and support land invasions. A new factor in naval warfare, which had not been present during the Hundred Years War, was the oared galley, equipped with one or two heavy guns placed in its bow. The low-built galleys could out-manoeuvre sailing ships and were ideally placed to blow holes in them at waterline level. The French had a strong force of galleys which, although not always well led, terrorized the English fleet and forced it to retreat from St Malo to Plymouth in 1513 after Sir Edward Howard, the new English Lord High Admiral, had died in a futile boarding action.[1]

Most of the royal fleet was laid up after 1525, with skeleton crews of shipkeepers aboard. A few ships stayed in commission, but there was little naval activity. Henry's break with the Roman Catholic Church in the 1530s had enormous implications for the redevelopment of the navy. Firstly, as a nation led by a heretic (the Pope excommunicated Henry in 1538), England was potentially at the mercy of the two great Catholic powers, France and the Holy Roman Empire, and had considerable need of a navy for defence. The continuance of foreign threats for much of the sixteenth century played an important role in the continuance of the navy. Secondly, the Dissolution of the Monasteries and the consequent sale of monastic

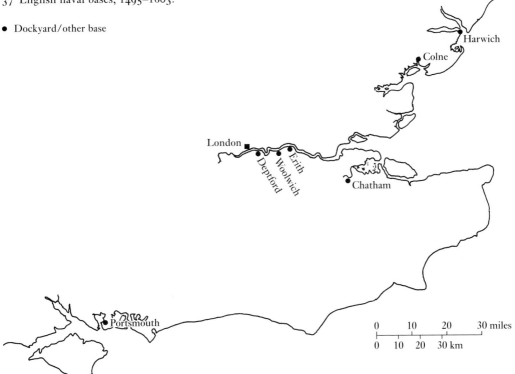

37 English naval bases, 1495–1603.

● Dockyard/other base

Harwich

Colne

London

Deptford
Woolwich
Erith

Chatham

Portsmouth

| 0 | 10 | 20 | 30 miles |
| 0 | 10 | 20 | 30 km |

land put a lot of money into the royal treasury to pay for men, ships and new coastal fortifications. Between 1536 and 1547 twenty-seven ships were built, rebuilt or bought for the navy, and eighteen new gun-armed forts and blockhouses were built on the coast of England and Wales. Although a few places, such as Dartmouth, had acquired purpose-built artillery forts in the fifteenth century, Henry's defence scheme was the first state programme of this kind.[2]

However, *realpolitik* outweighed religious dogma, and in 1543 England became an ally of Charles V, the Holy Roman Emperor, in a war against France. Henry invaded France in 1544 and captured Boulogne. Disastrously for England, Charles made a separate peace with France, leaving the English to face the French alone. Francis I of France brought together a huge fleet (comprising perhaps 200 to 300 ships, including many sailing warships and 25 deadly galleys) in the ports of Normandy in the spring of 1545 for an attack on England. The danger was acute. An English fleet of about 160 royal and private ships was assembled at Portsmouth, under the command of Lord Lisle, the Lord High Admiral. Despite these huge concentrations of forces, there was no climactic, Trafalgar-style battle in the Channel. As it was, the campaign consisted of skirmishes, small, vicious coastal raids and a few major disasters. The French anchored in the Solent in July and raided the Isle of Wight, but soon withdrew because of disease and dwindling supplies. The confrontation in the Solent was marked by a single catastrophe, the

38 Dartmouth Castle, built between 1481 and 1495. The great harbour at Dartmouth was one of the most significant havens in the medieval south-west. The coastal artillery fort was a local venture, built to control the narrow entrance to the harbour with heavy guns and a chain defence. The first great age of state-sponsored coastal fortification came later, in the 1530s and 1540s.

accidental loss of the *Mary Rose* and perhaps as many as seven hundred men, when the ship capsized as it was bombarding the French.

As in the Middle Ages, Scotland remained a potential source of danger to England, although less for its navy than its 'Auld Alliance' with France, which meant that England was faced with dangerous two-front wars during Henry's time. James IV of Scotland (r.1488–1513) created a small fleet in the early sixteenth century, with the help of French money, shipwrights and even timber. The fleet included the 1,000-ton carrack *Michael* (completed 1512), which for a brief period may have been the largest ship in Europe. A new royal dockyard, the 'New Haven of Leith' (Newhaven), was ready by about 1507. However, Leith was vulnerable to attack, as the sixteenth century was to show. A second dockyard was constructed over twenty miles up the Forth at the Pool of Airth, protected by a fortification at the Queensferry Narrows. Newhaven remained the building yard, but the Pool of Airth became a base for maintenance, repair and fitting-out. However, Scotland could not hope to match the financial or naval resources of England, and by the time James was killed at the battle of Flodden in 1513, the navy was eating up about one-fifth of his government's annual expenditure. Ironically, the most telling blows against English shipping were by Scots privateers, not the navy, which was never very much of a threat to England.

However, the military and political alliance between Scotland and France was a major worry for the English government. It was impossible for the English navy to stop or even seriously impede sea communication between Scotland and France. Spotting a ship at sea relied on eyesight alone, and, given the limitations imposed

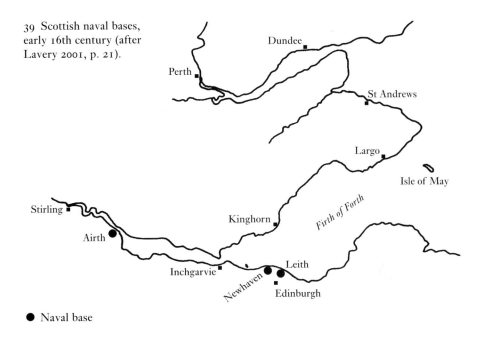

39 Scottish naval bases, early 16th century (after Lavery 2001, p. 21).

Dundee

Perth

St Andrews

Largo

Isle of May

Stirling

Firth of Forth

Kinghorn

Airth

Leith

Inchgarvie

Newhaven

Edinburgh

● Naval base

by weather and primitive maritime technology, obtaining 'command of the sea' was fairly short-lived unless one side could annihilate the other side's fleet in harbour. Blockades were likewise short-lived affairs, ended by lack of supplies or bad weather. Scottish fleets were able to reach France safely in 1513 and 1523, and shiploads of French supplies or troops were able to reach Scotland in 1543, 1545 and at other times.

The English were still able to mount devastating attacks on Scotland, however. In an attempt to drive the Scots out of his third French war, Henry assembled a massive raiding force of more than two hundred royal and merchant ships at Newcastle in April 1544. The fleet landed an army that defeated a Scots force and burnt both Edinburgh and its port of Leith. It was a savage action, but failed to force the Scots into making peace. The French war ended in 1546, but the conflict with Scotland continued. The English defeated a Scots army at Pinkie Cleugh in 1547, and went on to establish garrisons in Edinburgh and other locations. However, as before, English seapower could not sever the link with France, and the pro-French party in Scotland was able to secure the betrothal of the infant Mary, Queen of Scots, to the French Dauphin. In 1548 she sailed safely to France. Anglo-French war broke out again in 1549, with sea fighting off the Channel Islands (including a galley attack beaten off by English warships), but the war ended in 1550. The French bought Boulogne back and the Scottish war petered out.

The wars of the 1540s may have seen some military and naval victories for the English, but they also led to great loss of life and prohibitive expenditure. The French and Scottish wars between 1543 and 1547 alone are reckoned to have cost about £2 million, of which just under £300,000 was spent on the navy. By 1550 England was an exhausted country, plagued by unrest and political instability.

Despite this, the navy was not badly maintained during the reigns of Edward VI (r.1547–53), Mary I (r.1553–8) and the early years of Elizabeth I (r.1558–1603). It is somewhat ironic that Philip of Spain, who married the Catholic Mary I in 1554, regarded the English navy as one of his assets. In 1557 England was drawn into a Spanish war with France, but the navy achieved very little and England lost its one continental foothold, Calais, in 1558. The one truly unusual event of the naval war came in July 1558, when gunnery support from a small English squadron enabled a Spanish army to win a land battle with the French on the beach at Gravelines.

In 1558 the Protestant Elizabeth Tudor became queen of England. The early decades of Elizabeth's reign saw profound shifts in the international situation, which finally broke the old medieval patterns. The Franco-Scottish 'Auld Alliance' was shattered in 1560 when English military and naval support helped the Scottish Lords of the Congregation to stage a successful Protestant rising against the party of Mary, Queen of Scots, and the French troops that sustained them. France ceased to be much of threat as it sank into religious civil war, and England entered into alliance with the French Protestants, the Huguenots, who were a seapower in their own right.

From England's point of view, the biggest change on the international scene was the deterioration of its relations with Spain, which in 1585 led to a nineteen-year war. England was never at any time in the sixteenth century a serious threat to Spain. England was a country of just over 4 million people by 1600; the Spanish population alone at this time was double that and Spain was also the centre of a great and wealthy empire that stretched from the Mediterranean to the Americas. However, England was an aggressively Protestant nation – at least in its external relations – and it presented a potential challenge to Spain as the leading Catholic power. In the 1560s and 1570s English seamen attempted to break into the lucrative Spanish trade from the Americas, both as merchants and pirates, acts that were considered both illegal and highly provocative by the Spanish.

This period saw the rise of Francis Drake (c.1542–96). Drake was a man of very lowly origins, the son of a man who had worked as a preacher in the navy and had evidently imbued his son with a fierce belief in the rightness of Protestantism. Drake went to sea, and took part in his cousin John Hawkins' three slave-trading voyages from Africa to the Americas. The Spanish attack on Hawkins' ships at San Juan de Ulua in Mexico (1568) left Drake, Hawkins and others with a conviction that the Spanish were treacherous, deadly enemies of England.[3]

Drake raided Mexico and Panama in the 1570s, as well as Spanish shipping, and netted a fortune in bullion. His circumnavigation of the globe (1577–80), which the Queen privately supported, was not only a triumph of navigation, for Drake returned with something in the order of £150,000 in treasure. Not unreasonably, the Spanish began to see every English maritime venture as a form of covert state warfare, and the slide towards war began. Elizabeth gave support to the revolt of Dutch Protestants against Spanish rule in the Netherlands. Although there was good deal of sympathy for the Dutch in England, it was also in England's strategic interest to reduce Spain's hold on the Low Countries. Elizabeth did not seek war with Spain, but she came to be perceived by Philip II as a dangerous heretic. In the meantime, Philip became even more powerful, conquering Portugal in 1580. This gave Spain another colonial empire, a new fleet and important harbours on the Atlantic seaboard of Iberia. That same year, Spanish and Portuguese troops were sent to Ireland to support a rising against the English, which was suppressed by English land forces and a naval expedition.

Renewed English support for the Dutch rebels finally led to war with Spain in 1585. The first English action of the war was also the first English transoceanic campaign. Led by Drake, a fleet of twenty-two ships and 2,300 men raided Spanish settlements in the Cape Verde Islands (off Africa), the Caribbean and Florida. Despite extensive looting, the expedition failed to cover its costs, and two-thirds of its men were left unfit for duty by disease.

In April 1586 Philip II decided to send an *Armada* (fleet) to invade England and topple Elizabeth. The preparations took two years to complete, delayed in part by Drake's pre-emptive strike on the port of Cadiz in April 1587. The Spanish strategy was simple, but probably doomed from the start. The Armada would sail up the English Channel, avoiding battle with the English fleet, to link up with the Duke of Parma's army in Flanders in the Low Countries. The fleet would then convoy Parma's troops safely across the sea, to land somewhere in the vicinity of Margate, where the march on London would begin. The Armada that finally sailed from Lisbon on 18 May 1588 consisted of 141 ships from places as far apart as Dubrovnik in Croatia and the Baltic. Just over 20,000 soldiers were embarked, along with a huge range of supplies that included great siege guns.

Even four centuries on, the Armada story is surrounded by potent nationalist

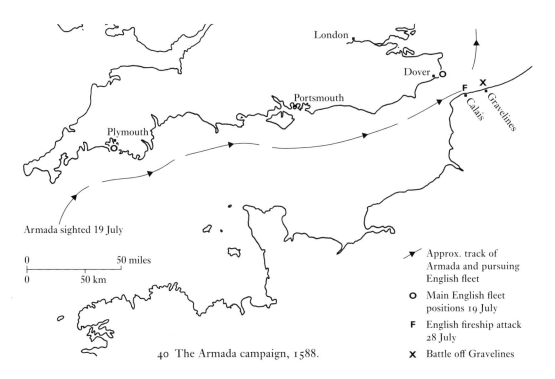

40 The Armada campaign, 1588.

Armada sighted 19 July

0 ____ 50 miles
0 ____ 50 km

⟋ Approx. track of Armada and pursuing English fleet

O Main English fleet positions 19 July

F English fireship attack 28 July

X Battle off Gravelines

myths, at least on the English side. When in 1987 the National Maritime Museum at Greenwich announced that its major 1988 commemoration of the campaign would take a scholarly and even-handed approach, bellicose elements of the right-wing press were incensed. A *Times* leader admonished the exhibition organizers for putting 'accurate, scientific history' before the perceived national myth, commenting that 'national anniversary festivities should properly be concerned with projecting myths not recording facts'.[4] One myth is that the Spanish were cowardly and disorganized: in fact, the reverse was true. Another myth is that Drake led the English fleet: in actuality, he was a vice-admiral under the command of the Lord High Admiral, Charles, Lord Howard of Effingham, and Drake's conduct (disobeying orders and leaving his station to capture a Spanish prize) was less than creditable. What is true is that the English fleet played a major part in the Armada's defeat.

The English mobilized 34 royal ships and 192 private ships against the Armada in the spring and summer of 1588, from the Queen's massive new galleon *Ark Royal* (540 tons burden) to the 25-ton *Gift* of Topsham and even smaller ships. The English fleet was not a bad match for the Armada, and included some large, modern fighting ships. The campaign was mainly fought by sailing ships: only four Spanish oared vessels reached the Channel and the English did not use any oar-driven ships in combat. The English fleet was split into two main sections, with 105 vessels under Howard at Plymouth, and a smaller force under Lord Henry Seymour, covering the Kent coast. On 19 July an English scout ship sighted the Armada off the Lizard and reported back to Plymouth. The English harried the Armada as it sailed up the Channel, but failed to break its formation. The Spanish fleet anchored off Calais, with the intention of linking-up with Parma (whose preparations were running late, a fatal flaw in the whole plan), but it was dispersed by an English fireship attack on the night of 28 July. The attack was the single most decisive action of the campaign, for it not only temporarily broke the Armada's formation, it pushed it into the southern North Sea, where the prevailing winds made it all but impossible to turn back towards the Channel and Parma. The battle off Gravelines on 29 July was a confused, bloody combat conducted at close range, that left the English almost out of ammunition. The Armada re-formed, but with the English fleet behind and in pursuit (the Spanish did not know that the English had used most of their shot), had little option but to sail north, with the aim of rounding Scotland and Ireland on the journey home. Twenty-nine of the weakened and battered ships of the Armada were to be sunk by the bad weather of that stormy summer.

The English lost few men in battle, but thousands died of disease shortly after the campaign, and the Spanish may have suffered 11,000 dead. A naval campaign on this scale was unprecedented, at least in northern Europe, and many years were to pass before the English had to fight battles against such a powerful enemy over such a wide area, with vast ammunition expenditure.[5]

The defeat of the Spanish invasion attempt in 1588 was the one major strategic victory for the English during the war. Spain remained a great power throughout. In 1596 and 1597 two more invasion Armadas were despatched, but both were sunk

41 *The English and Spanish Fleets Engaged*, English School, late 16th century.
A propagandist English portrayal of the defeat of the Armada, probably intended as a
representation of the battle off Gravelines. A Spanish galleass flying the papal banner
and bearing monks and jester, amongst others, is attacked at stem and stern by
broadside-firing English warships. In the background, English galleons fire on Spanish
warships. It is unlikely that the battle of Gravelines ever looked like this, but the
essential message was true: the English fleet defeated the Armada.

or dispersed by storms *en route*. English strategy involved preventing invasion and
raiding the Spanish Empire both in Iberia and overseas. The defence of England
was a considerable success: English ships raided Spanish towns and other settlements many times, but the Spanish only managed to make one successful attack on
England, when, in July 1595, four Spanish galleys operating from a base in Brittany
attacked and burned Mousehole, Newlyn and Penzance in Cornwall.

Direct invasion-prevention efforts had mixed success. An expedition led by
Drake and Sir John Norris to destroy surviving Armada ships in northern Spain in
1589 met with very little success because the commanders diverted the campaign
to their own ends. The problem was that in all campaigns there was a chance of
loot, and most of the English naval commanders were aggressive entrepreneurs
who saw no contradiction in mixing their religious, patriotic and military aims with
personal business. In 1596 a joint Anglo-Dutch raid on Cadiz, under the firm

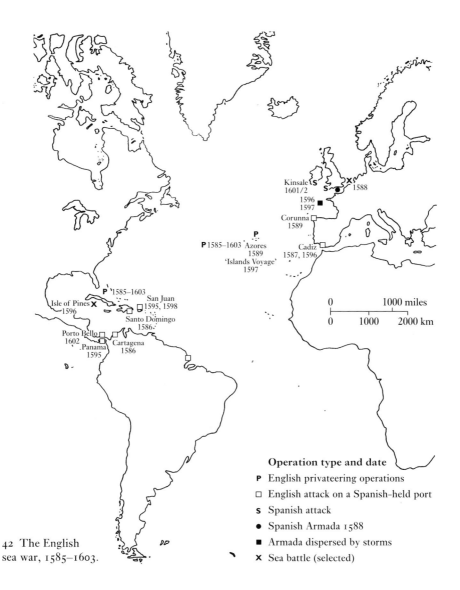

Kinsale **S** **X** 1588
1601/2 **S**
1596
1597 ■
Corunna □
1589

P
P 1585–1603 Azores
1589
'Islands Voyage'
1597

Cadiz □
1587, 1596

0   1000 miles
├────────┤
0   1000   2000 km

P 1585–1603
Isle of Pines **X**   San Juan
1596   □ 1595, 1598
Santo Domingo
1586
Porto Bello □   □
1602   □
Panama   Cartagena
1595   1586

Operation type and date

P English privateering operations
□ English attack on a Spanish-held port
s Spanish attack
● Spanish Armada 1588
■ Armada dispersed by storms
x Sea battle (selected)

42 The English
sea war, 1585–1603.

control of Lord Howard, had much greater success in forestalling Spanish invasion plans and hindering attempts to support Catholic rebels in Ireland. The attackers captured the port and town, and inflicted over £7 million pounds' worth of damage on the Spanish war effort. More than twenty-five Spanish ships were taken or destroyed, including eleven great Indiamen (ships engaged in trade to the Americas), and 1,200 cannon were captured. In many ways it was, after the Armada campaign itself, the single most effective naval English expedition of the war.

However, in the 1590s most English naval and privateering activity was directed against Spanish shipping routes. In 1590 an English force led by Hawkins and Frobisher staged a fairly effective blockade of the Spanish coast, disrupting sea trade for months. The English ships were kept supplied at sea, a tactic that anticipated the eighteenth century, but blockade offered little profit if it kept enemy ships penned in harbour. A privateering war on the high seas was much more suited to the buccaneering mind-set of most English sea captains. It is known that, between 1591 and 1598, more English ships were engaged in privateering than had been raised for the Armada campaign. The privateering voyages ranged in scale from single-ship cruises to major forays, like the Earl of Essex's 'Islands Voyage' to the Azores in 1597, in which about thirty ships sailed on an expedition (which failed) to seize an island as a privateering base. The larger fleets were joint ventures, and sometimes involved royal ships and royal investment. For example, Elizabeth invested about one-third of the £90,000 raised to sponsor a raiding voyage to the Americas commanded by Drake and Hawkins in 1595. The Spanish knew the expedition was coming, and it failed, with both commanders dying at sea. The last English actions of the war were privateering attacks, which had mixed success, although in 1602 Sir Richard Leveson and William Monson succeeded in taking a Portuguese Indiaman with a cargo worth £44,000.

The Anglo-Spanish war petered out. Philip II died in 1598 and Elizabeth in 1603. Neither side had anything to gain from prolonging the conflict, and a peace treaty was signed in 1604. The war showed the effectiveness of the Tudor navy and the administration that supported it, and saw the navy's transformation into a force able to mount operations across the Atlantic Ocean. The lure of loot also led to the development of an even larger privateering industry, with the construction of many large private warships that harried Spanish trade in northern Europe, and into the Caribbean and Mediterranean (see pp 92–3 and 109). It has been estimated that about half of the war effort against Spain between 1585 and 1604 was contributed by the privateers. Even if England still had nothing like the territories or wealth of the Spanish Empire, the last two decades of the sixteenth century saw England begin to emerge as a transoceanic power.

The administration of the English fleet underwent major changes in the sixteenth century. The expansion of the royal fleet under Henry VIII greatly increased the amount of financial and administrative business required to run the fleet, and necessitated the development of new shore facilities at Deptford, Woolwich and Erith on the Thames. The yards were probably sited there because of their proximity to the capital and because they were regarded as easier to defend than the existing yard at Portsmouth. As Brian Dietz has suggested, placing the main royal dockyards on the Thames probably played a very important role in the development of the London shipbuilding industry in the sixteenth century.[6]

Naval administration was at first run on a rather limited and *ad hoc* basis, with a small number of officials, until the mushrooming level of naval activity in the 1540s seems to have forced the government to create a larger and better-planned organization. This was described in a document of March 1545 as 'the King's Majesty's Council of the Marine', and was soon also being called 'the Admiralty'. The council included seven major posts (some of them new), including the Treasurer, Surveyor and Rigger and the Master of Naval Ordnance (an officer to oversee victualling was appointed in 1550). The changes were truly epoch-making. People with professional knowledge of the sea, logistics and organization had been involved in naval administration before, but these changes led to the appointment of professionals with discrete areas of reponsibility. The new council was the origin of what in the seventeenth century came to be called the Navy Board, which administered the navy until 1832. By any modern standard, the new administration was doubtless inefficient, corrupt and riddled with nepotism, but it was a significant improvement on what had gone before. The capacity to be able to plan and to budget, and the experience of the men who served in the naval administration, helped to keep the fleet in being after Henry VIII's death and played a central role in furnishing England with an effective navy.

The sixteenth century saw the English royal navy change from being an occasional wartime phenomenon to something permanent. By the second half of the sixteenth century, if not before, those in power had accepted the need for a standing naval force that did not simply disappear once the latest crisis was over.

Tudor seafarers: social and economic conditions

Despite the fame of great captains like Drake and Hawkins, the common sailor was at the bottom of the Tudor social heap. Commonly regarded by their social superiors with a mixture of fear and contempt, seamen were often said to be violent and difficult to control. Certainly the seafaring workforce was more mobile than most, and must have included a fair number of rootless drifters with no allegiance to any place. For example, in 1550 the Scottish merchantman *James* of Leith had a crew that included Scots, Englishmen from more than ten counties, as well as some Welshmen.

The pay of ordinary sailors reflected their low status. A seaman of 1537 earned 6 shillings per month, whilst a farmworker earned 8 shillings. Their counterparts some eighty years later earned 17–18 shillings and 24 shillings respectively. As Geoffrey Scammell remarked, the labourer only worked a six-day week; the sailor got his victuals for free, but he had to work every day of the week and his work involved a much greater risk to life and limb. Evidence from later periods suggests that most men went to sea because they had to, in search of a wage and their daily bread. There is little reason to believe that medieval or Tudor mariners were any different. Some individuals undoubtedly did go to sea out of ambition or a sense of adventure, but it is likely that they were in the minority.

The records of the High Court of Admiralty, which contain many depositions by ordinary masters and mariners, give some evidence about the ages of seafarers (samples of eighty-three men and thirty-six masters). Although the samples are rather small, they do suggest that the majority of ordinary sailors were in their twenties, and that men did not generally become masters until they reached their thirties. A rather similar sort of age-structure existed in the first half of the eighteenth century (see p. 190).[7]

Literacy levels may have been higher among sailors than in the general population. Cargo documentation and the growing prevalence of sea-charts made it a real advantage for a sailor to be able to read. Of eighty shipmasters and forty-six mariners who took part in appraising ships for the High Court of Admiralty

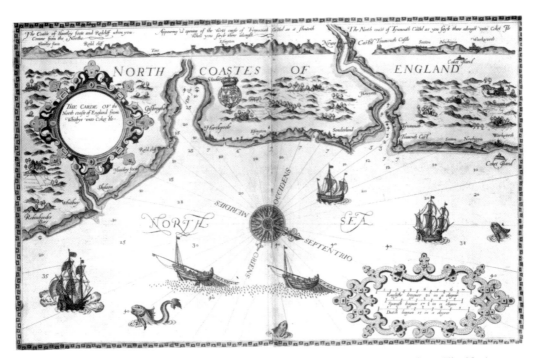

43 The north-east coast of England, from Whitby to Warkworth, from *The Mariners
Mirrour*, 1588. The chart gives a good idea of the sort of printed chart information
available to seafarers from the 16th to the 18th centuries. The herring busses (fishing
boats) in the foreground may well have been Dutch.

between 1579 and 1590, just over half of each group were capable of signing their
names.[8]

In the sixteenth century the range of office-holders on board ship seems to
increase markedly, although whether this was because of genuine new developments, or the lack of information for earlier periods, is difficult to say. As ever, the
master was in overall command, and on merchant ships often acted as an agent for
the merchants whose cargo he transported. The mate was the assistant ship's
commander; below him was the boatswain (pronounced 'bosun'), who had charge
of discipline, ship's gear and other matters, such as stowage. The ship's carpenter
was another important figure, who carried out running repairs and helped to maintain the vessel. Lesser officers called quartermasters are often encountered, who
worked for the boatswain or other officers, and who seem to have had particular
responsibility for different quarters of the ship. Armed ships generally had a
master gunner and his assistants, to maintain and operate the weapons, and ships
on long-distance voyages often had pilots (navigators) to help navigate the ship.
The purser was another office-holder, charged with looking after the ship's pay and
other expenditure; he also sometimes acted as a merchant's representative on
trading voyages. Barber-surgeons began to appear on larger warships from the
mid-1540s, and on merchant ships on long-distance voyages, but they were often

of doubtful quality. The leading English surgeon of the time, William Clowes (1544–1604), published the first English textbook on sea-surgery in 1588, *A prooved practise for all young Chirurgians*, but he seems to have had little influence on what he described as the many 'sorry surgeons' serving in the ships of his day, to the detriment of their unfortunate patients.[9]

Tudor England seems to have had enough seamen for its merchant shipping and for a moderately-sized navy undertaking smaller-scale operations. However, at times of crisis, such as the campaigns of 1545 and 1588, there are signs that resources were stretched to the limit. Men appear to have begun avoiding naval service in larger and larger numbers. One reason was that naval pay lagged far behind inflation for most of the sixteenth century. Another reason may have been the danger of disease. A large sailing warship carried hundreds of men, equivalent to the population of a small town, but in a far more confined space. Small wonder that disease was common and spread so quickly in these cramped, unhygienic conditions. Warships may have been two or three times as crowded as merchant vessels. This would not have encouraged merchant seamen to enter royal service and privateering offered better prospects for self-enrichment than the navy, as prize money was shared out more equally than in the navy. By the 1590s the popularity of privateering was being blamed as the reason for the great difficulties then being encountered in recruiting men for the fleet.

No doubt sailors were generally rough and tough people: the sea was a dangerous place, with danger from weather, accident, piracy and war, and the working day was long and hard. In theory, seamen were kept in line by a range of harsh and sometimes brutal punishments. However, if they were the bunch of thugs, incompetents and anarchists that they are sometimes portrayed as, one is left wondering how any merchant ships ever left port, let alone how fleets were raised and operated in wartime. Although merchant ship casualty figures are unknown in the sixteenth century, it is surely a telling point that out of the 115 or so warships owned by the English Crown between 1509 and 1603, only 11 are definitely known to have been lost, whether the cause was wreck, harbour accident, capture or destruction in combat. The dramatic and terrible ends of the *Regent* (1512), the *Mary Rose* (1545) and the *Revenge* (1591) became so famous partly because they were so rare. Similar evidence emerges from some of the trans-oceanic voyages. Out of twenty-two ships used on the voyages to Sir Walter Raleigh's failed Roanoke colony in what is now North Carolina between 1584 and 1590, only one ship was lost *en route*. Likewise, Martin Frobisher's three voyages, with a total of fifteen ships into the perilous Canadian Arctic between 1576 and 1579, saw the loss of only one ship.

Naval pay was not only increased in 1582 – probably to help attract more men – it was also given a much more detailed structure. Twenty-nine pay grades were created (three more were added in 1588), from master to seaman, and there were, for example, now four different ranks of gunner recognized for pay purposes. Also, very importantly, the pay structure divided the fleet into six 'rates' based on tonnage (not to be confused with seventeenth-century system of ship rates), with the largest ships in the first rate. While the pay of an ordinary seaman was the same whether he served in a first-rate ship or a sixth-rate one, the pay of the master of a first-rate vessel was 50 per cent higher than that of his sixth-rate counterpart.

Although some men volunteered for the navy, the majority seem to have been recruited by means of some form of compulsion. Sometimes this was done by commissioners sent out into the shires to raise enough men, and sometimes local authorities were called upon to fill quotas for sailors. Men pressed into service were given 'conduct money' to cover travelling expenses and told to turn up at a particular port by a given date. The impressment system does not seem to have been as harsh or as resented as the later press-gang. In 1544 it was thought sufficient to use the 'Common Cryer' of London 'to make proclamation that all mariners pressed should haste them on shipboard'.[10]

The danger of sickness was ever-present when a fleet went to sea. The triumph of the English fleet against the Armada in 1588 was marred by a devastating outbreak of sickness that hit parts of the fleet, and which would have gravely impaired England's ability to fight back if the Spanish had returned. Whatever the disease was, it was deadly. Howard, the Lord Admiral, commented that 'they sicken the one day and die the next. It is a thing that ever followeth such great services.' Out of five hundred men aboard the great ship *Elizabeth Jonas*, over two hundred had died. Howard recognized that if the men were not paid properly and the sick properly cared for, 'we should very hardly get men to serve'. However, he was also moved by the plight of his sick and destitute sailors from the campaign, for 'It were too pitiful to have men starve after such a service.'[11]

The tragic fate of so many English seamen in the anti-Armada fleet led to the establishment in 1590 of a scheme to provide for the support of injured seamen and the widows of men killed on active service. The scheme was based on seamen contributing 6d per month from their wages, the money being kept in the large, iron-bound 'Chatham Chest'. The Chatham Chest funds were eventually amalgamated with those of Greenwich Royal Hospital in 1814. 'Seamen's sixpences' later went to support Greenwich Royal Hospital, opened in 1705 as a home for elderly or disabled seamen who had served in the navy, a naval counterpart of the army's Chelsea Hospital. In the nineteenth century hospital residences declined as out-pensions became more common, and the institution closed in 1869 (the buildings were used, from 1873, for the Royal Naval College). Payments of sixpences by merchant seamen continued into the nineteenth century, although this caused great resentment, as it was only ever men who had served in the Royal Navy that benefited from the funds raised.

Organizations such as Trinity House also had a charitable aspect, giving help to aged or disabled sailors, sailors' widows and orphans. In 1618, for example, Trinity House is known to have been paying pensions to 160 people living on the Thames or Medway. Some men were granted rowing licences on the Thames by Trinity House, which gave them a living as watermen (riverborne taximen).[12]

The salty diet: sailors' food and drink

Standard shipboard rations did not change very much between the Middle Ages and the nineteenth century. Stories of bad or inadequate food and drink at sea are common enough, but had victuals had been as uniformly poor as the horror stories sometimes suggest, few ships would have ever left harbour. A recent study by the Canadian scholars Conrad and Nancy Heidenreich of the victualling of Frobisher's second expedition to the Canadian Arctic in 1577 indicates that it was possible in the sixteenth century for shipboard rations to be more than adequate, even on transoceanic voyages. The ration allowances worked out for this voyage were not dissimilar to those for contemporary naval operations. The Frobisher expedition was estimated to last for 168 days. The probable weekly 'menu' for each is reckoned to have been as follows:

Table 4 Weekly rations, 1577

Every day	Four meat days**	Three fast days*** (i.e. meatless)
1 lb (0.45 kg) biscuit*	1 lb (0.45 kg) beef	About 4 oz (115 g) fish
1 gallon (4.5 l) beer	8.9 oz (252 g) peas	4 oz (115 g) butter
(0.875 imperial gallons)	*or*	*or*
	1 lb (0.45 kg) pork	8 oz (226 g) cheese
	8.9 oz (252 g) peas	1.3 oz. (37 g) oatmeal
		2.6 oz. (74 g) rice

* Alternatively, there was an allowance of 1 lb (0.45 kg) of flour that could be made into biscuit. Biscuit, later aptly known as 'hard tack', was made from a slow-baked mixture that was one-part flour and two-parts water. It was tough and unpalatable, but for sea voyages had the advantage of lasting a long time if kept dry, although it was also famously a good environment for weevils.

** There was enough beef for only one out of every six meat days, but enough pork for the remaining five.

*** There was enough of these foodstuffs to ensure that there were equal numbers of 'fish' and 'cheese' days.

These four basic daily menus would each give between 4,000 and 5,000 kcal. The Heidenreichs have calculated that the average daily amount of energy expended by a seaman on these Arctic voyages would have been about 4,500 kcal, so the foodstuffs provided would have met these requirements and also provided most nutrients. The meat and fish was salted for preservation and had to be soaked before cooking to remove the salt. However, it is unlikely that even long-term soaking could remove all the salt, and the shipboard diet must have had a high salt content. The most serious nutrient deficiencies were in foods containing Vitamin

A and Vitamin C. Vitamin A deficiency can lead to a number of ailments, including night blindness, but Vitamin C deficiency ultimately results in scurvy.

Scurvy is a terrible disease that causes lethargy and leads to teeth falling out, the enlargement of the spleen, and subcutaneous bleeding. Left untreated, it will kill. Evidence from eighteen English and other Arctic and Greenland voyages between 1576 and 1632 indicates that men began to die from scurvy about eight to ten months after leaving port. Sixteenth-century sailors clearly had a practical knowledge that certain plants (rich in Vitamin C), sometimes called 'scurvy grass', could be used to treat or prevent the onset of scurvy, long before the medical profession recognized the cure in the eighteenth century. The problem for long-distance sailors was that this practical knowledge did not translate into an understanding of the vital importance of the regular feeding of the crew with fruit or other anti-scorbutants. Dr James Lind (1716–94), a naval surgeon, discovered that the juice of citrus fruits was a very effective anti-scorbutant, and published his findings in 1753. However, the Royal Navy did not make it mandatory for ships to carry lemon juice until 1795. This was later replaced by lime juice, the origin of the American term for a British person, 'limey'.

The official ration lists do not take account of private stocks of food carried on board, particularly by officers, and ships leaving port might often have fresh provisions available for some days. It is known that even in the sixteenth century ships might carry small amounts of spices, mustard, honey and wine, but it is probable that these were consumed more often by the officers than the men. However, it is clear that if ration allowances were kept to and the food was as good as it could be, the average seaman could at least be sure of being adequately fed, something that was far from certain ashore. Analysis of the skeletal remains of crew from the *Mary Rose* (sunk 1545) suggests that, although some had suffered from malnutrition in childhood, the men were strong individuals who were 'probably well fed' while in royal service. One of the principal attractions of going to sea for many men between the Middle Ages and the nineteenth century may have been that, despite all the risks of shipboard life, it offered the chance of a full belly.[13]

English sea trade and ports, *c.1550–c.1600*

The collapse of the Antwerp cloth market in the mid-sixteenth century was initially a shock for English merchants, particularly those in London, but in the longer term it proved beneficial. English traders were forced to start looking for new markets, a motive that underpinned many English long-distance voyages, from Willoughby and Chancellor's search for the north-east passage to Asia in 1553 onwards. English trade began to develop in other, less spectacular directions as well. In 1558, to reduce smuggling and regularize a chaotic situation as regards customs revenue, the English government produced a list of ports where goods could be loaded or unloaded, which would be subject to proper customs regulation ('Legal Quays').

English merchants returned to the Baltic in the 1570s and gradually succeeded in setting up bases there. The Hanse Steelyard in London was finally closed in

1598, and by the early 1600s the Hanse had given way to English pressure and allowed merchants from England to operate in the main Hanse ports. The trade in timber, 'naval stores' and other bulk goods from the Baltic became particularly important for the English ports closest to that region, east coast ports such as Newcastle, King's Lynn and Great Yarmouth.

English ships began to reappear in the Mediterranean in the second half of the sixteenth century, and the port of Leghorn in north-western Italy became a base for English merchants and pirates in 1573 (the Grand Dukes of Tuscany opened the port to both Protestant and Jewish merchants, in order to increase its trade). Ottoman Turkey welcomed English diplomatic and mercantile overtures as a way of countering their common enemy, Spain, and the Levant Company was established in London in 1581 to develop trade with Turkey. The Mediterranean as a whole proved to be a good market for English cloth, tin, lead and fish, and the wines, cotton, dried fruit and other luxury goods of the south found a ready sale in England. The Mediterranean trade was more valuable than that from the Baltic, and was very much centred on London, although it did involve some other English ports. Overall, the changes in the pattern of Tudor England's sea trade were slow – in 1606, for example, over 90 per cent of London's export trade was still with France and other parts of north-western Europe. London, with its growing population, its great mercantile wealth and the royal court, dominated both inter-

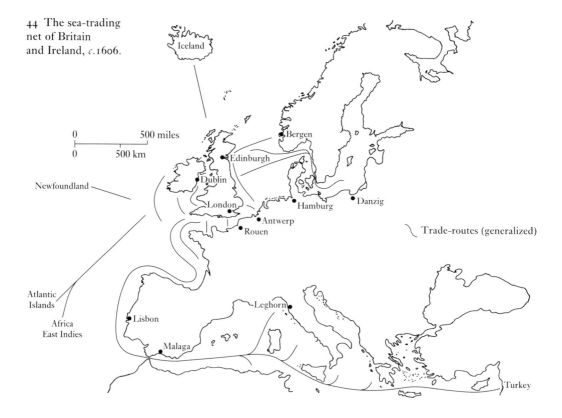

44 The sea-trading net of Britain and Ireland, c.1606.

national trade and coasting traffic, sucking in food and other goods from English ports and abroad. The total tonnage of shipping entering the port of London rose by 50 per cent between the late 1560s and 1600, from 34,600 tons to 52,300 tons.[14]

Irish and Scottish trade, 1500–1600

Irish trade in the sixteenth century was anything but parochial in nature, although on a much smaller scale than that of England. The nature of its trade was in some ways similar to that of England in the Middle Ages: raw materials, cloth and fish were exported, with wine, salt, iron and luxury goods coming the other way.

Dublin and Wexford traded principally with England (especially Bristol), but Waterford, Galway and the other ports of the south and west had extensive contacts with Spain, Gascony and Flanders. Galway was the principal Irish wine port until the late sixteenth century, when it had to start paying customs dues to the Crown. All Irish ports were adversely affected by the Anglo-Irish wars of the late Elizabethan period.[15]

Scotland's overseas trade was much smaller than that of England, but it ran along well-established routes to France, the Low Countries, Baltic and Scandinavia from the east coast ports, and to Ireland and France from the west coast. Scottish exports included fish, hides, wool and cloth, and Scottish vessels were regular visitors to the Baltic.[16]

Piracy and privateering

Until 1536 someone arrested for piracy could only be convicted if they confessed or if there was a firsthand witness against them. This made getting a conviction very difficult. In 1536 piracy became a common law offence, to be tried by the Lord High Admiral and common law judges at London. Piracy became somewhat riskier for pirates, but they had to be caught first, and some pirates had strong supporters in the form of wealthy and powerful individuals. It was not unusual, for example, for members of the aristocracy and the gentry to indulge in piracy, either directly or as sponsors. Getting stolen goods back through the courts could be a long and fruitless business, and foreign merchants sometimes resorted to getting letters of reprisal from their home government, which allowed them to seize goods to the value of those stolen from the countrymen of their assailants.[17]

Granting letters of marque against a wartime enemy's shipping could be a very effective way of harassing an opponent. It was a form of 'privatized' warfare that had no direct financial cost for the government issuing the letters. However, it could have serious political consequences in that it soured relationships with other countries. Seamen provided with letters of marque were often less than scrupulous about whom they attacked, be it enemy, neutral or even friend. English privateers were very active in the 1543–6 war with France, and, as well as going for French shipping, they also attacked that of Flanders (a Spanish possession) and Spain. Spain was at first an ally in the war, and later a neutral. The problem became so bad that in January 1545 the Holy Roman Emperor seized English vessels and embargoed trade with England. A few months later a Southampton merchant and pirate named Robert Reneger captured a Spanish treasure ship, the *San Salvador*, returning from the Americas, and took a cargo of gold worth about £4,300 – a huge sum. His spurious legalistic excuses for the crime were accepted by the king, who also got a share of the proceeds.

Piracy against foreign shipping was sometimes tolerated for political reasons. In 1548 Lord Seymour, the Lord High Admiral, during a time of nominal peace with France, encouraged English seamen to attack French merchantmen and fishing vessels, probably as a means of impeding French support for Scotland.

In the mid-1550s a number of English gentlemen, who had rebelled against the marriage of Philip and Mary, took refuge in France, and for a couple of years were active as pirates, with tacit support from the French government, which also opposed the marriage. The problem was greatly reduced, if not eliminated, when ships of the royal fleet captured six of the pirate vessels in a battle off Plymouth in July 1556.[18]

English piracy was widespread between the 1560s and 1580s. It is said that, over this period, English seamen took over £20,000 worth of goods from the Scots, although the Scots in their turn took over £9,000 worth from the English. The Scottish effort, if not commendable, suggests at the least that Scots pirates, with their much smaller numbers, were very effective. Piracy of English ships against other English ships was still a problem, as it had been in the Middle Ages.

The second half of the sixteenth century saw English piracy and privateering spread beyond the waters of north-western Europe. In the Caribbean and the Americas it often took the form of quasi-warfare against Spain, until the outbreak of open war in 1585 turned it into respectable privateering, one of the English growth industries of the 1590s (see p. 107). North European seamen were also increasingly active in the Mediterranean. Between about 1580 and the early 1600s the activities of Dutch, and particularly English, traders and pirates in the Mediterranean caused irreparable damage to the maritime trade of the great port of Venice.[19]

English oceanic voyaging and exploration, *c.*1480–1606

English overseas exploration and colonization had very little impact on the rest of the world until the seventeenth century, despite the fame of explorers such as John Cabot, Francis Drake and Martin Frobisher

Bristol ships started voyaging out into the Atlantic in 1480 and 1481, and it is possible that English ships were fishing off the Grand Banks of Newfoundland in the 1480s. John Cabot's famous 1497 voyage from Bristol, which probably made landfall in Newfoundland, was actually aimed at reaching China. Cabot returned a hero, and made a second voyage in 1498, but disappeared along with four of his five ships. Other English voyages were made to Newfoundland in the early 1500s, but English participation in the Newfoundland fishery, which came mostly from the south-western ports, did not really start to grow until the 1570s. Devon took the lead, with Dartmouth as the main port, and Fowey was the principal port in

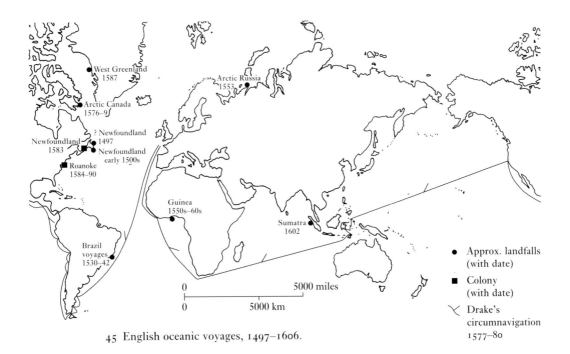

45 English oceanic voyages, 1497–1606.

Cornwall. The Basques and the French dominated fishing off the Grand Banks, although by 1620 some 300 English vessels (carrying about 6,000 fishermen) were operating in the area. An additional English fishery developed off New England in the early seventeenth century, but it was taken over by American fishermen from the 1660s.[20]

The problem for England and most European nations was that Spain and Portugal, under the Treaty of Tordesillas in 1494, carved up ownership of the New World between themselves, along with its vast wealth of gold, silver and slaves. These two imperial powers could not always enforce their rule over such vast territories, but the treaty made the presence of foreign ships in these regions at best illegal and at worst an act of war.

English transoceanic ventures were intermittent until the 1550s, and their chief value probably lay in the acquisition of navigational and geographical knowledge. As Professor Andrews pointed out, the oceanic voyages before the 1550s achieved very little, probably because they attracted little support from the nation's wealthiest traders, the London merchants. The London merchants were comfortably settled in the Antwerp cloth trade, which had few risks and offered good returns. This all changed in the mid-century when the Antwerp market collapsed.

Sebastian Cabot, the son of John Cabot, had returned to England in 1548 after decades in the service of Charles V in Spain, including a period as the Emperor's chief navigator (*Pilot Major*). Cabot may have helped to promote the idea of exploration as a way of finding new markets; certainly in 1553 he became governor of a company set up to promote an expedition to find a north-*east* passage to the Orient. It was a good time to do so and courtiers and London merchants subscribed £6,000 to the venture. Sir Hugh Willoughby and Richard Chancellor left London in 1553 with three ships. Separated *en route* by a storm, Chancellor failed to find any passage, but reached the White Sea and made his way overland to Moscow, where he met Ivan IV ('the Terrible'). Willoughby and the crews of the two other ships took shelter in a remote Lapland inlet, where they all froze to death. However, Chancellor returned safely, and in 1555 the Muscovy Company was founded and given a monopoly of trade with Russia. The Muscovy Company was, in effect, the first long-distance, joint-stock (shareholding) trading company in English history, the precursor of other transoceanic trading companies and, later, shipping lines. Its example came to be imitated, and its influence, in spreading geographical and economic knowledge, was enormous.

Spain and Portugal were the world leaders in transoceanic navigation in the mid-sixteenth century, and it was from them that the English began to learn up-to-date techniques. The English navigator Stephen Borough was allowed to study at the Casa de Contratación at Seville, the base for Spanish work in navigation. One of the fruits of his time there was an English translation of Martin Cortes' *Breve Compendio de la Sphera y de la Arte de Navegar* (1551), which had become the standard Spanish textbook for celestial navigation and was published in England in 1561 as the *Arte of Navigation*. It was an important work for English navigators and appeared in ten editions between 1561 and 1630.[21]

The period from the 1550s saw the real beginnings of English oceanic enterprise. A curiosity to understand more about the world, and in some cases a wish to spread Christianity, helped to motivate these enterprises, but there can be little doubt that the overwhelming inspirations were greed and the desire to compete with the great empires of Spain and Portugal and win fame and glory. As the Elizabethan poet, Thomas Churchyard, wrote in a eulogy of the seaman, Sir Humphrey Gilbert, departing on an abortive journey to the Americas:

> Then weighed I how immortal fame
> was more than worldly care
> And where great mind remains
> the body's rest is small
> For country's wealth, for private gain
> or glory seek we all.[22]

Transoceanic trade appeared to offer fabulous riches, in the form of precious metals and exotic materials and spices; the slave trade from Africa was developed to supply cheap labour to exploit the riches of the New World. The European impact on the wider world began in the fifteenth and sixteenth centuries with aggression and exploitation on a grand scale, creating a legacy that has played its part in making the inequalities of the modern world.

Not all of the long-distance voyages were ventures into the unknown. The Elizabethan government saw the Ottoman (Turkish) Empire, the Moslem enemy of Catholic Europe, as both a trading partner and a potential counterweight to Spain. Trade negotiations opened with the Turks in 1579, and in 1581 the Levant Company was established in London and given a monopoly in trade with Turkey (and, from 1592, with Venice). The Turkish trade was very valuable to England, offering goods such as cotton, carpets, silks, oils, wine and currants. 'Turkey merchants' became very rich, and although the opening-up of the East Indies trade in the early 1600s provided competition in the supply of exotic goods, the Levant Company survived until 1825.

English attempts to break into the lucrative Portuguese-controlled Guinea trade in West Africa from the 1550s had little success in the face of growing Portuguese opposition and the incredible health risks involved in going there (an English expedition to Guinea in 1553 lost nearly two-thirds of its men). John Hawkins' three slaving voyages from Africa to the Americas in the 1560s represented an early and abortive English attempt to break into the Spanish and Portuguese slave trade. Spanish resistance put an end to this, and nearly a century was to pass before English merchants again became slavers.

Seamen from the West Country – such as Francis Drake, John Hawkins, Humphrey Gilbert and John Davis, all Devonians – played a disproportionately large role in English overseas enterprise in the Elizabethan era. Devon and Cornwall had been important maritime counties in the Middle Ages, their experienced maritime populations perhaps having been driven to the sea by the relative poverty of the region. The widening horizons and fabulous opportunities for loot helped to make these men national and international figures, and to give them a lasting fame denied to their medieval forebears, who may have been terrors of the seas, but seldom operated very far from land.

From about 1570 much of the energies of Drake and other English maritime leaders was put into attacking and plundering the Spanish Empire. Hitherto the English had generally avoided direct assaults on the Caribbean, 'the Spanish Main' of later romantic fiction. Between 1570 and 1577 there were at least thirteen English expeditions to the Caribbean, raiding by sea and on land, all illegal even under English law since England and Spain were at peace. This was piracy and Drake was in it up to his neck. However, it is too easy to think of Drake as a simple pirate. He was a man of great intelligence and ambition. One of his ambitions was to take a ship into the Pacific to seek for riches there. This was the origin of what became his 1577–1580 circumnavigation, only the second in history. The expedition aimed to gather information as well as loot, although it also did the latter very efficiently: the £150,000-worth of Spanish silver that Drake brought back with him would have been enough to fund about two-thirds of the English naval effort against the Spanish Armada in 1588.[23] Drake had set out with five ships, but returned with just one, the 150-ton *Golden Hind*. Elizabeth knighted him aboard the ship at Deptford in 1581, where the vessel was dry-docked, perhaps the first ship in history to be used as an historic monument (although it was eventually left to rot away).

The search for the north-west passage was revived in the 1570s by the merchant Michael Lok, London agent of the Muscovy Company, and the seaman Martin Frobisher. Frobisher led a small expedition to Arctic Canada, where no passage was found, but Frobisher returned with an ore sample that he claimed was gold, a claim that was backed by an assay report (metallurgical analysis). Royal backing was secured and a larger expedition (including the royal warship *Aid*) returned in 1577, followed in 1578 by a full-scale mining fleet with fifteen ships. However, the ore proved to be worthless and Lok was ruined. The voyages did bring about the first, largely unhappy, encounters between Englishmen and the Inuit people, a story that was found to be still alive in Inuit tradition three hundred years later.[24]

The 1580s saw the first two English colonies in North America. Both were failures. Sir Humphrey Gilbert established a very short-lived colony at St John's in Newfoundland in 1583, but it quickly collapsed because of illness and desertion, and Gilbert drowned on the voyage home. Gilbert's half-brother, Walter Raleigh (*c*.1554–1618), tried to establish his own colony in the Americas, on Roanoke Island, off the coast of what is now North Carolina. The colony was set up in 1585, with 114 men, women and children. In August 1587 the birth took place of Virginia Dare, the first English child known to have been born in America. However, the Spanish war prevented the sailing of supply ships in 1588 and 1589; a return voyage in 1590 found the colony deserted, perhaps due to a food shortage. The colonists had probably sought shelter with local Indians, but they were not found.[25]

English enterprise in the Far East enjoyed rather more success. The English East India Company (EIC) was established in September 1599, with the aim of trading with the Far East. It began with a massive capital sum of just over £30,000, promised by 101 London merchants. A few English expeditions had gone to the Pacific in the 1580s and 1590s, but, as England and Spain were at war, their aim was generally plunder rather than trade. The Portuguese had led the way in establishing a network of trading posts and fortifications in the Far East, followed by the Spanish and later the Dutch, but no European nation had a monopoly on trade with the region. The Dutch made a number of profitable voyages to Bantam in Java between 1595 and 1599. Dutch success in the spice trade created considerable interest among the London merchants, which helped to lead to the formation of the EIC. The Dutch government, the States General, went on to form the United East India Company (VOC) in 1602 to regularize and control their own valuable trade.

The EIC's first royal charter gave it a monopoly of English trade beyond the Cape of Good Hope and Magellan's Strait (in regions not already controlled by a Christian ruler), for fifteen years. The company was also given the right to export £30,000 of silver every year, a major concession and a sign of the return in profits expected from the venture (the export of large amounts of 'treasure' abroad was traditionally regarded by governments and embryo economists alike with horror). The first voyage did not sail until February 1601, after a delay caused by abortive peace negotiations with Spain. The first fleet comprised five ships, led by the 600-ton *Red Dragon*, a total of 1,520 tons of shipping in all. There were about five hundred crew in total and the ships were well armed, although the voyage was explicitly undertaken for reasons of trade rather than privateering.

The EIC was not able to sort out the long-term joint-stock financing of its voyages until the early 1620s, which hampered some of its early ventures. English cloth was initially exported rather than silver, but the cloth did not sell well in the hot climates of the Far East. The first fleet traded to Sumatra, in the Indonesian archipelago, again following the Dutch example, and returned in September 1603 with cargoes largely consisting of pepper. A 'factory' (trading post) was established at Bantam, the first English foothold in the Far East. The voyage was not a financial success, and the English market was flooded with pepper, but the EIC persevered. The second voyage was not a great success either, although the aim this time was to try to balance pepper in the cargo with nutmegs, cloves and other spices, and it was marked by friction with the Dutch.

The Dutch eventually succeeded in driving the English out of the valuable spice trade in the Spice Islands in the Indonesian archipelago. After a local Anglo–Dutch war from 1618 to 1620, and the massacre by the Dutch of English merchants on the island of Amboyna in the Moluccas in 1623, the English withdrew. The conflict left a legacy of bitterness that was to resurface in the 1650s.[26]

Curiosities

Greed, a desire for conquest and jealousy of rival nations were the most powerful motives behind transoceanic voyaging, but they were not the only ones. Some harboured sincere notions of converting 'the heathen' to Christianity, although Christian charity was singularly absent from most of the early transoceanic encounters. Curiosity and a passion for the exotic also helped to send ships out on the oceans. Even in the early 1500s Bristol ships brought people and artefacts back from the other side of the Atlantic. Artists like John White and pioneer scientists such as the polymath, Thomas Hariot (1560–1621), sailed on some of the Elizabethan voyages, making maps and bringing back images of distant cultures and specimens of plants. In the seventeenth century the famous father-and-son gardeners, the John Tradescants, amassed a collection of exotic objects, plants and seeds that later went on to be the foundation collection of England's first public museum, the Ashmolean in Oxford.

Contrary to popular myth, Sir Walter Raleigh did not introduce tobacco into England, for it was already known to English seafarers. Hariot went to Roanoke (which Raleigh did not) and wrote the first English description of a herb called *Uppowoc* that the local Algonquian Indians smoked in pipes and was known to the Spanish as 'tobacco'. Indian pipes and tobacco were brought back to England and popularized at court by Raleigh. Hariot became an habitual smoker and died of cancer.

Raleigh was also later said to have introduced the potato into the British Isles; in fact, it was the Spanish who first brought the vegetable back to Europe – from Peru. Although it is known that some potatoes were being grown in London by 1596, it was in seventeenth-century Ireland that it became a widespread crop. Those other future staples of British and Irish consumption, coffee and tea, did not arrive in the British Isles until the 1650s, coffee probably coming from the Turkish Empire and tea from China via Holland.[27]

The shipping industry: ships and men

The Elizabethan government made the first really concerted attempt to collect data about the numbers of sailors and ships in England so that it would have a fairly good idea of what sort of force the merchant fleet could field in a military crisis. These maritime censuses did not always cover the whole country, but to judge from the fact that close on two hundred private vessels were raised for the campaign against the Armada in 1588, they were part of a system that worked fairly well.

The censuses are historically important because they give us the first fairly clear idea of just how many seamen (defined as sailors, fishermen and Thames watermen) and ships there were. The 1582 survey is the most comprehensive one from the Elizabethan period; when compared with a manpower survey from 1628, it illuminates a number of trends in the English shipping industry in the late sixteenth and early seventeenth centuries.

The 1582 survey lists 1,518 ships from 10 tons burden upwards, totalling 67,604 tons. The merchant fleet was still quite weak: 78 per cent of the ships were of less than 100 tons burden. London, Essex, Suffolk and Norfolk emerge from the survey as the most important seafaring region, with about half of the total tonnage and nearly two-thirds of the 178 'defensible' ships in the realm (i.e., ships of more than 100 tons burden, these being thought big enough to be militarily useful). The continued importance of this region is underlined by shipbuilding figures from the 1595–1618 period (see p. 115), and by the 1582 and 1628 manpower figures.[28]

As far as the human resources of the shipping industry went, the 1582 survey listed 16,283 seafarers, including fishermen and Thames watermen, of whom about 46 per cent lived in the London/Kent/Sussex/Essex/East Anglia region. However, about one-quarter of all English seafarers were listed in Devon and Cornwall – 4,083 men – helping to indicate why West Countrymen were so prominent in Elizabethan maritime enterprise. The 1628 manpower survey is far from perfect, for it leaves out certain counties like Sussex, and the unpopularity of naval service by this time may have led to people avoiding the count. However, certain trends stand out, the chief of which is that the London-Essex-East Anglia arc, which had had 36 per cent of the nation's seamen in 1582, possessed 56 per cent by 1628. Given that the total – 15,898 men – was slightly lower than in 1582, the growth of the London region may well have been at the expense of other places. Only Dorset, Hampshire and Bristol showed any absolute growth in figures, and all others were in decline. Devon and Cornwall's manpower was just under half what it had been in 1582, and was about 12 per cent of the total. London had been the greatest English port in the 1580s; by the 1620s it was even more significant.

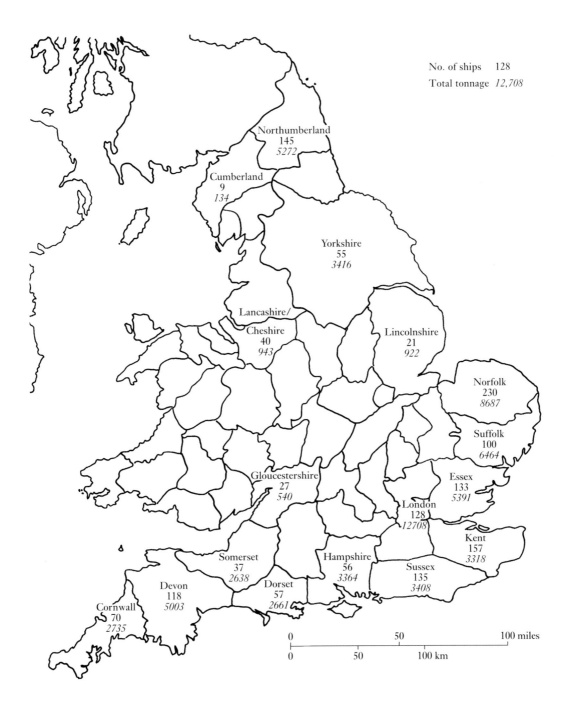

No. of ships   128
Total tonnage   *12,708*

Northumberland
145
5272

Cumberland
9
134

Yorkshire
55
3416

Lancashire/
Cheshire
40
943

Lincolnshire
21
922

Norfolk
230
8687

Suffolk
100
6464

Gloucestershire
27
540

Essex
133
5391

London
128
12708

Kent
157
3318

Somerset
37
2638

Hampshire
56
3364

Sussex
135
3408

Dorset
57
2661

Devon
118
5003

Cornwall
70
2735

0   50   100 miles
0   50   100 km

46 The distribution of the English merchant fleet, 1582.

851 No. of seafarers 1582

293 No. of seafarers 1628

Blank indicates not
counted in survey

Northumberland
851
293

Cumberland
212

Yorkshire
878

Lancashire/
Cheshire
324

Lincolnshire
449
192

Norfolk
1670
1036

Suffolk
1282
1130

South Wales
753

Gloucestershire
220
823

Essex
693
666

London
2286
6150

Kent
1195
412

Somerset
512

Hampshire
470
530

Sussex
513

Cinque Ports
892

Devon
2165
539

Dorset
645
1044

Cornwall
1918
1366

0   50   100 miles

0   50   100 km

47 Seafaring manpower of England and Wales, 1582 and 1628.

The shipbuilding industry, c.1500–c.1618

The medieval English shipbuilding industry presented a rather diffuse picture, with few obvious major centres of ship construction and relatively few shipwrights. When Henry VIII wanted to build his 1,500-ton *Henri Grâce à Dieu* at Woolwich in 1512, he had to conscript 252 shipwrights, caulkers and other workers from as far away as Cornwall and Yorkshire, this despite the fact that the site was just a few miles downstream from the largest port in the country.

The sixteenth century saw the Thames and its region grow to become the unchallenged shipbuilding capital of the country. This apparent change is not just the result of better documentation being available for the sixteenth century than earlier periods. The creation of royal dockyards on the Thames and later the Medway in the 1500s seems to have been a key factor in this development, for the yards created concentrations of knowledge and skilled workers who were also often available to the merchant shipbuilding industry. In early 1559, for example, 520 shipwrights were employed in royal yards on the Thames and at Portsmouth; given the rise and fall of the demand for royal ships, many of these men must have also worked in merchant shipbuilding.

The increased demand for the construction and repair of royal warships not only seems to have created more job opportunities, it helped to raise the status of the industry. Since the fifteenth century, English governments had intermittently paid a bounty of 3 shillings per ton for the construction of ships of 100 tons burden or more. The aim was to build up a stock of large, defensible merchantmen that could be used in war, rather than to encourage trade. The figures for the last twenty or so years of the bounty are thought to offer the clearest picture of this kind of shipbuilding in England. The period saw an explosion of ship construction that had started because of the Anglo-Spanish war of 1585–1603. Yards worked to satisfy a demand for large, well-armed vessels that could be used for privateering and long-distance trade. Between 1595 and 1610 the London shipyards alone built 174 vessels of 100 tons burden or more, totalling 40,978 tons, or roughly four times the total tonnage built or rebuilt for Elizabeth's navy during the Spanish war. To put this figure in context, between 1510 and 1603 about 90 vessels (totalling approximately 35,000 tons) were built or rebuilt for the English royal fleet. London's output in fifteen years exceeded nearly a century's worth of building for the royal navy.

London was the centre of a major shipbuilding region that stretched from the capital, along the Thames and up the east coast as far as Aldeburgh in Suffolk. Between 1595 and 1618, 508 ships of more than 100 tons burden each, totalling more than 102,000 tons burden, were built in England. Just over 55 per cent of this tonnage (256 ships) was built at London and other nearby ports on the Thames. Suffolk was the leading shipbuilding county, producing 22.5 per cent, with Ipswich as the most significant provincial construction centre. The next shipbuilding county was Essex, with a little over 8 per cent of the total. The rest of England outside of the London–Suffolk arc contributed the remaining 13 per cent or so. Devon, for all its Elizabethan fame as the home of Drake and Hawkins, constructed a mere 15 ships in the 100-ton-plus range, an average of less than one per year over this period.[29]

The sixteenth century also saw the beginnings of an English sailcloth industry. In 1547 some Breton canvas-makers were brought to England to teach others how to make their cloth, but it was not until 1558 that the first English sailcloth-makers are recorded, two Ipswich brothers called John and Richard Collins. The Ipswich industry really seems to have taken off in the 1580s. In 1590, probably because of the stress of the Spanish war, the English navy switched to drawing almost 90 per cent of its sailcloth from English, rather than foreign, sources (70 per cent of naval canvas was still coming from England in 1635). However, the quality of the Ipswich product seems to have declined: it was being called 'trash' in 1620 and the local industry sank to a low ebb.

The status of English shipwrights began to grow in the sixteenth century. This was perhaps partly a reflection of the growing demand for ships in the second half of the century, but it almost certainly also derived in part from the creation of royal master shipwrights. Medieval shipwrights, like John Hoggekyn, builder of Henry V's *Grace Dieu*, had occasionally received payments that recognized their status or efforts in royal service, but the Tudor master shipwrights attained an altogether different level of importance. The first to be appointed on a salary (4d per day) was James Baker (1538). His son, Matthew (c.1530–1613) also became a royal master shipwright (1572). He rose to be one of the leading figures in the shipbuilding trade, designing and building many important royal warships at a time when shipwrightry was starting to turn from a trade into a profession. Matthew Baker became the first Master of the Shipwrights' Company, incorporated in 1605.

There is little doubt that until the nineteenth century (and later in some places) the construction of most smaller wooden vessels did not involve the use of paper plans. Shipwrights relied on traditional knowledge and methods, gained in a long apprenticeship, and much work was probably carried out 'by eye', rather than by measurements. The few surviving English shipbuilding contracts from the sixteenth century contain dimensional figures, such as keel length or hull breadth, but often omit key facts that were clearly left up to the shipwright's skill, discretion and knowledge. Contracts for three large royal galleons drawn up in 1589, for example, fail to mention how many masts the ships should have. Matthew Baker is the first English shipwright known to have written a theoretical treatise on ship-building, which goes under the title given it by its later owner, Samuel Pepys, as *Fragments of Ancient English Shipwrightry*. The treatise consists of a number of disjointed pieces of text, together with luminously beautiful drawings of ships, and Baker probably had some idea of publishing his thoughts. The earliest-known technical treatises on shipbuilding come from fifteenth-century Italy, and it is apparent that Baker got at least some of his ideas from the Mediterranean, which he had visited. Baker's aim was to popularize the use of arithmetic and geometry in shipbuilding, although his designs may have represented the mathematization of ideas derived from practical experience rather than theoretical concepts. He railed against the ignorance of many of his contemporaries, but did have a major influence on some others, including Phineas Pett (1570–1657), the son of his contemporary and fellow royal master shipwright, Peter Pett (d. 1589). Phineas Pett later went on to design and build the *Sovereign of the Seas* (1637), the greatest ship of its age.

The English shipbuilding industry in 1600 was very much larger than it had been in 1500. By the early 1600s England may not have been as great a naval power as Spain, but it had a strong shipbuilding industry, capable of producing many large, defensible ships. However, as the seventeenth century was to show, this particular product – heavily manned and expensive to construct – was in the end not necessarily the best thing for the English shipping industry.[30]

Ships and guns, *c.*1500–*c.*1600

The three-masted ship may have been technologically superior to earlier types, but like them, it was still subject to winds, tide and currents. Even nowadays extreme bad weather can prevent merchant vessels from sailing; in the sixteenth century and, indeed, whenever sailing vessels were used, the weather had a profound effect on what could be accomplished at sea. The ships of this period could sail to wind-ward to some extent, but sailed much better with the wind behind or from the side. If the wind was in the wrong direction, it could make it difficult, if not impossible, for ships to get out of harbour. Even if ships managed to get to sea, the wind could make the going very difficult and frustrating. The start of Willoughby and Chancellor's tragic attempt to find a north-eastern passage to China in 1553 is a case in point. Their small fleet of three ships departed from Ratcliffe on the Thames on 10 May. Contrary winds meant that they were not able to leave the English coast for nearly six weeks. [31]

Shipping in England during the sixteenth century undoubtedly conformed to northern European norms. Clinker construction was still being used for building large ships in the late fifteenth and early sixteenth centuries. It seems to have fallen out of use as a technique for building the larger seagoing ships in the early decades of the sixteenth century, although clinker construction carried on being used for small craft up until modern times.

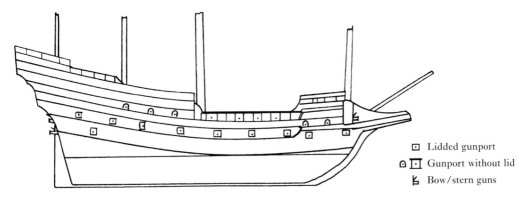

☐ Lidded gunport
◖ ⊡ Gunport without lid
↳ Bow/stern guns

48 Line drawing of an English galleon, late 16th century,
after a design by Matthew Baker (after Baynes and Pugh 1981, p. 76).

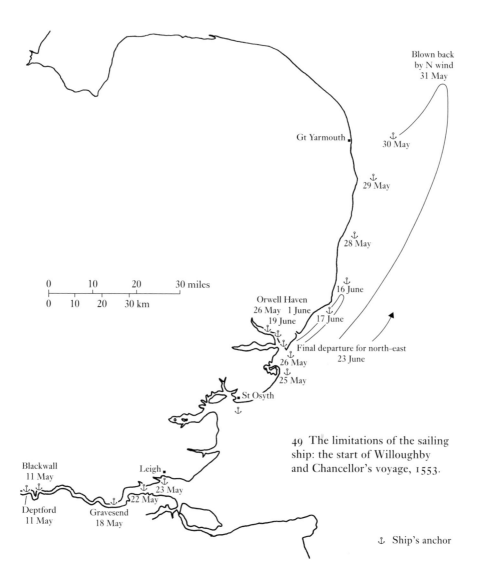

Blown back
by N wind
31 May

Gt Yarmouth

⚓ 30 May

⚓ 29 May

⚓ 28 May

⚓ 16 June

Orwell Haven
26 May 1 June
19 June   ⚓ 17 June

⚓ Final departure for north-east
26 May   23 June
⚓ 25 May

⚓ St Osyth
⚓

0   10   20   30 miles
0   10   20   30 km

49 The limitations of the sailing
ship: the start of Willoughby
and Chancellor's voyage, 1553.

Blackwall   Leigh
11 May   ⚓ 23 May
⚓⚓   ⚓ 22 May
Deptford   Gravesend
11 May   18 May

⚓ Ship's anchor

The most important change in naval gunnery in the first half of the sixteenth century was the development of the lidded gunport. Skeleton construction made it possible to cut rows of openings for guns in the sides of a ship without weakening the hull, something that was impossible in a clinker-built vessel (although clinker-built ships did occasionally have loading ports in their sides). The provision of a lid for the gunport made it possible to seal the port against the sea; this, in turn, made it possible to cut gunports much closer to the waterline, below the weather deck. Warships could now carry heavier armament than hitherto because larger guns could be shipped without the danger of upsetting the ship's centre of gravity, as would have happened if they had been placed on the weather deck or in the castles.

The chronology of this development is still poorly understood. The invention has been attributed to a French shipwright named Descharges in 1501, but lidded gunports may not have been common until the 1530s or 1540s. The change greatly increased the firepower of warships, and in theory made it easier for them to sink enemy vessels. By the mid-sixteenth century larger warships commonly had rows of gunports on both sides of the hull, giving them a slightly superficial resemblance to ships of the line of the seventeenth and eighteenth centuries. However, there the resemblance ends. Although the idea of firing guns from a distance to sink other vessels was known in the early sixteenth century, it was not commonly practised. In the 1540s, for example, English naval tactics were directed at boarding the enemy with hand weapons, which were always carried in large numbers by warships during the age of sail. Guns were an adjunct to boarding tactics, not the main weapon.

50 Reconstruction of the Pilgrim Fathers' ship, the *Mayflower*. No pictures and few details survive of the *Mayflower*, which carried the Pilgrim Fathers to New England in 1620. This reconstruction, built in the 1950s, is more a generalized re-creation of a small merchantman of the late 16th or early 17th century.

By the time of the Spanish Armada in 1588, the English had developed techniques for stand-off gunnery, probably to avoid being boarded by the heavily-manned Spanish vessels. The English rate of fire was much higher than that of the Spanish and they expended huge amounts of ammunition, but they failed to sink a single enemy ship by direct gunfire. Recent work by Nicholas Rodger has emphasized the importance of bow and stern guns in English ships (developed originally as a means of combatting oared galleys), as opposed to the gun batteries in the sides of the vessels (broadsides). It was only in the seventeenth century that naval gunnery techniques developed to the point where one sailing warship had a good chance of sinking another by gunfire.[32]

The established nature of the royal fleet in the second half of the sixteenth century undoubtedly made other new developments possible, allowing long-term practical experience to influence new designs and technology. The English galleon of the latter part of the sixteenth century is a case in point. The classic galleon was a ship with a low bow, a projecting beakhead like a galley, a hull designed for speed, three or four well-rigged masts and a large number of heavy guns. Once credited to John Hawkins, the galleon design in fact developed over decades from some of the oared galleasses (vessels equipped with oars and a full square rig) created in the 1540s to fight that perennial English fear, the galley. By the 1530s and the 1540s, as the wreck of the *Mary Rose* has shown, the lumbering carrack with huge superstructures was being superseded – in English service, at least – by a vessel with lower superstructures. Reduced superstructure height meant less wind resistance and improved manoeuvrability. The galleon was built for speed and manoeuvrability, but it was not well suited to oceanic voyaging, for the heavy guns and the fine lines meant a corresponding lack of storage space. The galleon could not go very far before it had to be revictualled.[33]

Like other European fleets in the first half of the sixteenth century, the English navy had made considerable use of oared warships (galleys, rowbarges and so-on), but the Elizabethan navy was essentially a sailing-ship force. A feared war machine in the early 1500s (see p. 88), by the late sixteenth century the galley was easy prey for well-handled sailing warships carrying heavy guns. In northern waters, aside from a few small areas, the day of the oared fighting ship was over by 1600.

CHAPTER FIVE

Fall and rise, *c*.1600–1815

Peace, war and navies, 1603–52

The reigns of James I (r.1603–25) and Charles I (r.1625–49) were marked by a decline in the effectiveness of the royal fleet. The seeds of this decline were probably already present in Elizabeth's time, with the queen's reluctance to spend money on the navy and the fatal blurring of private and public interests common in most bureaucracies of the period. Under James the problems got worse. Naval finances were in the hands of the devious and corrupt Sir Robert Mansell, a royal crony (Treasurer of the Navy, 1604–18), and the Lord Admiral, Charles, Earl of Nottingham, was a lax supervisor who stayed in office far too long (he retired in 1618, aged eighty-two, after thirty-three years in post). Two commissions of enquiry into abuses in the navy were held in 1608 and 1618. Nottingham departed after the second and the administration of the navy was put in the hands of the commissioners, with a five-year brief to reduce costs and increase the numbers of ships. They succeeded to some extent and Charles extended their brief indefinitely in 1625, but the navy still had enormous problems that became all too apparent in the 1620s.

Attempts to use the navy as an instrument of military and diplomatic power ended in failure. In 1620–1 Mansell staged a half-hearted and rather futile expedition to north Africa, directed against Barbary pirates who were preying on English ships. England joined the Netherlands in a war against Spain in 1624, but an expedition to Cadiz in 1625 failed due to inadequate command and poor supplies. For the same reasons, Buckingham's expedition to the Ile de Rhé in 1627, which attempted to relieve the besieged Huguenot port of La Rochelle, also failed. Thousands of English sailors and soldiers died from sickness. Buckingham, blamed by many as the principal cause of the nation's ills, was assassinated at Portsmouth in 1628 by a disgruntled army officer as preparations were underway for another La Rochelle expedition.

It was apparent that the English mercantile community, who had been enthusiastic investors in the privateering business in Elizabeth's reign, were now much more reluctant to support royal expeditions, and this contributed to the failures of the 1620s. Twenty years of peace had seen them use their well-armed merchantmen to develop new long-distance trades. As was the case with the East India Company, they were not averse to fighting bloody wars in distant places where there was hope of profit, but they saw little return in supporting the naval and military adventures of the Stuart monarchy. It was a part of the growing discontent with the Crown among the political class. Although the opinions of ordinary seafarers are far less easy to discern, it does seem that they too were somewhat disaffected. The débâcles of the 1620s must have convinced many men that serving the king meant poverty, starvation and death; certainly preparations for an expedition in 1626 were hampered by widespread fleet mutinies.

The navy that existed in the 1620s was not well equipped for the tasks it had to perform. Although the navy grew in size over the decade, many of the new ships were large, lumbering, prestige pieces, fit for a set-piece battle but not really suited for patrolling the seas. Piracy from Dunkirk-based raiders and Barbary pirates from north Africa was a real problem, and a group of ten small (120–140-ton) war-ships, the *Lion's Whelps*, were built in 1628 to help combat this problem. Named *First Whelp*, *Second Whelp* and so on, these vessels were perhaps the first approach to a real 'class' of warships in England. They were never as fast or effective as they were intended to be, but they saw a great deal of service and two of them survived to serve Parliament in the 1640s.

As the traditional merchant community could no longer be relied upon in the way that it had been in the sixteenth century, Charles decided to concentrate on building up the royal fleet. The result was the tax known as 'Ship Money', levied first on London and the port towns in October 1634, but extended to the inland counties in August 1635. It was a property tax, intended to fund the navy. Although presented as a policy that would enable the Crown to build a fleet that would offer better protection to merchant shipping, it proved very unpopular. This was all in the context of Charles' extra-parliamentary rule: he had dissolved Parliament in 1629 because it would not vote him the funding that he wanted. Ship Money helped to turn even some respectable country gentlemen against the royal government. The Kentish landowner Sir Roger Twysden wrote that 'truly the common people had been so bitten with Ship Money they were very averse from a courtier'. Ship Money by itself did not cause the Civil Wars, but it was a major example of Charles' attempts to gain greater political and financial control.

Despite rising opposition that eventually killed the tax, Ship Money did raise a great deal of money for the navy. Eight ships were built or rebuilt for the navy between 1635 and 1641, including the massive 100-gun *Sovereign of the Seas* of 1637, the largest English ship since the *Henri Grâce à Dieu* of 1514 and the first real three-gundeck warship. Naval patrols were sent out in the years from 1635 to 1641, but the navy proved to be a limited deterrent to foreign powers. In 1639 a Dutch fleet led by the Admiral Maarten Tromp sank most of a Spanish fleet in the Downs (the sea area between the Goodwin Sands and the Kent coast), ignoring a nearby English naval force. The battle of the Downs was a disaster for the Spanish and a humiliation for the English. The Dutch had behaved as if they owned the English coastal waters. English defences were not even strong enough to prevent emaciated Spanish survivors from landing, although some of the local Kentish people contrived to rob and beat them up.

Charles' policies eventually brought him into collision with Parliament. The Civil Wars started in 1642 with the Parliamentary side seeking to bring the king under control. By the time the wars ended in 1651, Charles had been beheaded and England had become a republic. The wars that were fought in England, Scotland

and Ireland in this period are conservatively calculated to have killed about 192,000 people through battle, disease or starvation, and more than two-thirds of the victims were Irish. In proportionate terms it was the bloodiest conflict ever waged in the British Isles, even taking Second World War bombing into account.

All the major battles of the Civil Wars took place on land, but there was also a continuous struggle around the coasts and out at sea that helped to decide the final outcome. Most of the navy sided with Parliament, a sign of the depth of its disaffection from the monarchy. Its loss was a great blow for Charles. As various historians have remarked, if the king had controlled the fleet, London would have been quickly blockaded and the trade and customs revenue that fuelled Parliament's war effort would have soon dried up.

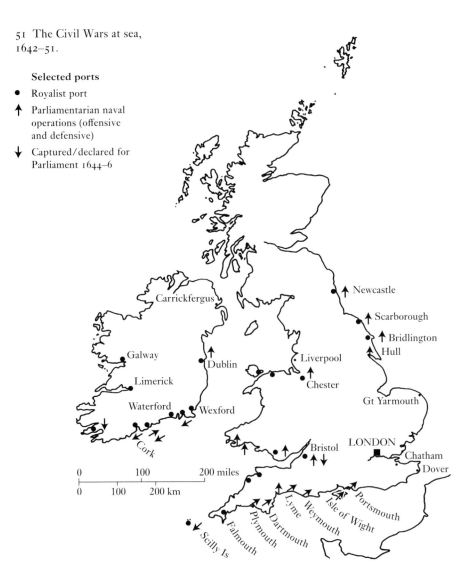

51 The Civil Wars at sea, 1642–51.

Selected ports
- ● Royalist port
- ↑ Parliamentarian naval operations (offensive and defensive)
- ↓ Captured/declared for Parliament 1644–6

Parliament rapidly took control of the fleet, replacing the principal administrative officers with a navy commission of twelve officials, which remained the navy's governing body until 1660. Parliament used the navy in a variety of ways: to help capture port towns (or resupply besieged ones) and to patrol the seas, trying to stop foreign supplies from reaching Charles. Also, most importantly, given that London merchants and their like were at the heart of the Parliamentary cause, the navy was used to protect trade and merchant shipping. The very existence of the navy may also have helped to dissuade foreign powers from meddling in English politics, although much of Europe at the time was consumed with its own agonies in the closing years of the Thirty Years' War.

The loss of the navy meant that the Royalists largely had to depend on privateers to wage war at sea, preying on the sea trade of the Parliamentarians. By 1643 over 150 English and foreign privateers were operating in Charles' name, from Dunkirk (until the port was taken by the French in 1646), Normandy, Brittany, the Channel Islands, the west of England (a major Royalist enclave until almost the end of the war) and Ireland. Charles did establish a small Royalist fleet at Bristol in 1643, but it never had the resources to take on the ships of the Parliamentary commander, the Earl of Warwick, head-to-head.

The 1640s also saw great upheaval in Ireland. Following a major rising in 1641, the Catholic forces joined together as the Confederated Catholics of Ireland with an assembly and administrative centre at Kilkenny. The Confederation levied taxes, organized military forces and even issued letters of marque against Parliamentary shipping. At one stage some 40 to 50 privateers were operating in the name of the Confederation, and it has been estimated that between 1642 and 1650 Irish-based privateers took at least 250 ships, nearly one-third of them English. The Confederation was at peace with the king from 1643 to 1646 – its official aim was Irish liberty under the Crown – but gradually fell apart due to internal disunity and, from 1647, military defeat.

Both sides in the Civil Wars relied on sea trade, or rather the revenue from it, to supply most of their finances. Parliament started off with the massive advantage of holding London and the huge government revenues levied on its trade. The king had Newcastle, with its coal trade, and the Cornish tin trade. After a ceasefire with the Confederated Catholics in 1643, Charles was able to get reinforcements from Ireland, and Irish ports were opened up as bases for Royalist privateers.

Sea ports were also vital for the supply of arms from abroad, particularly for the Crown which had lost control of the major gun-founding industry in the Weald. Despite the risks of gun-running into war zones, some foreign shippers and arms manufacturers grew rich on the English wars. Amsterdam alone exported over 125,000 hand weapons to England between 1642 and 1646, along with more than 12,000 suits of armour. For much of the First Civil War (1642–6), the main Royalist supply ports in England were Bristol, Newcastle, Falmouth, Dartmouth, Exeter and Weymouth. Parliament's main port was of course London, but in East Anglia the Parliamentary Eastern Association used King's Lynn as its main supply base, and both sides used rivers to move large quantities of materiel from the coast to armies operating inland.

There were no set-piece sea battles during the Civil Wars – the Royalist side seldom had enough big ships to make such encounters feasible – but Parliament's fleet saw hard and continuous service. Commanded by Robert Rich, Earl of Warwick, the fleet was organized into Summer and Winter Guards. Between 1642 and 1648 most Summer Guards had more than fifty state warships and merchant-men on hand. As well as patrolling against Royalist privateers and protecting merchant shipping, the Parliamentary fleet played a vital role in sustaining its coastal garrisons under siege, and helped to bring about the fall of Royalist enclaves. In 1642 and 1643, for example, seapower made it possible for Parliament to keep its besieged garrison at Hull supplied with men and reinforcements and so prevent its capture by the Royalists. If Hull had fallen at the start of the war, it would have given Charles one of the greatest arsenals in the country and a major supply route from the Continent. In such circumstances, Parliament would have probably lost the north of England entirely.

The Parliamentary fleet had little hold on the Irish Sea in 1642 and 1643, lacking much in the way of bases between Portsmouth and Liverpool. The situation began to change in 1644, when men and ships commanded by Captain Richard Swanley took several Royalist forts in west Wales, and so gained control of Pembrokeshire and Milford Haven, threatening communications between the Royalist port of Bristol and Charles I's supporters in Ireland, and eventually stemming the flow of men through patrols and blockades.

The fortunes of both sides fluctuated markedly during the First Civil War, but Parliamentary victories at Marston Moor (1644) and Naseby (1645) led to Charles' defeat. The Scots, allied with Parliament, took Newcastle in 1644 and in 1645 and 1646 other Royalist bases fell to Parliament, including Bristol. The Royalist priva-teering effort briefly revived in the West Country in 1645, but declined as Royalist ports were captured. Wexford and other Irish ports began to grow in importance as privateers shifted from England and Dunkirk (which surrendered to the French in 1646), and naval power alone was not sufficient to destroy them. It took the Cromwellian conquest of 1649–52 to secure control of the Irish ports.

Charles surrendered to the Scots in 1646 and was handed over to Parliament. However, he conspired with the Scots to invade England and restore him to the throne, and their invasion in 1648 caused the Second Civil War (1648–51). Revolts in Kent and other areas in 1648 were broken by the New Model Army, which went on to defeat the Scots. The Scottish conspiracy helped to seal Charles' fate. Important factions on Parliament's side had wanted to see him re-established as a constitutional monarch, but religious and political radicals such as Cromwell wanted to establish a republic. Charles was beheaded in January 1649, and little more than six weeks later the monarchy was abolished. The Commonwealth (1649–53), the short-lived English republic, had arrived.

However, the Republicans were in a minority and had aggravated many who wanted Parliament to negotiate with the king. In 1647 the radical religious Independents in the army had seized power, and they set about trying to purge the navy of officers with sympathies for Presbyterianism, a less radical form of Protestantism. The result was that in 1648 part of the fleet in the Downs mutinied. A dozen ships even blockaded the Thames for some days, and then sailed off to Holland to join the Royalist side. The revived Royalist fleet, although small, became a problem for Parliament. Under the command of Prince Rupert, it moved from Holland to Kinsale in Ireland in 1649. Rupert's force was later blockaded by one of the new republic's three generals-at-sea, Robert Blake, and then pursued by him first to Portugal and then to southern Spain. Most of the Royalist fleet was driven ashore by Blake and destroyed off Cartagena in 1651.

Parliament invaded Ireland in 1649 and Scotland in 1650. Both campaigns were heavily supported by resupply from the sea. The Scots invaded again in 1651 in support of Charles II, but their defeat at Worcester finally ended the English Civil Wars. Cromwell's England emerged from the Civil Wars with a strong, aggressive and experienced navy, led by a government determined to see England grow as a commercial, diplomatic and military power.

The military reduction of Ireland took until 1652. Initially led by Cromwell, the English invasions involved killing, destruction and dispossession on a vast scale, and Cromwell became one of the great 'hate figures' of Irish history as a result.[1]

The Dutch Wars and the 'Glorious Revolution', 1652–88

The seventeenth-century Netherlands was a powerful seafaring nation and a dangerous commercial rival for England, not least in the Far East where competition over the spice trade led to open war and bloody massacres in the late 1610s and early 1620s (see pp 110–11).

The Netherlands was at war with Spain from 1596 to 1609 and again from 1621 to 1648, which hampered the development of its trade. When peace with Spain came in 1648, the Dutch were soon were back in business with a vengeance. Dutch fishing vessels were to be seen operating off the English east coast in large numbers, fishing in waters that the English considered to belong to them. English participation in the Baltic trade dropped by half; Dutch ships were trading with the English colonies in America and appearing in the Mediterranean in ever-growing numbers.

In 1651 the English Parliament enacted the Commonwealth Navigation Ordnance, which became famous (or infamous) as the Navigation Act. The Act provided that all cargoes to England from outside Europe had to be carried in English ships, and that goods brought from their country of production had to be carried directly to England from that country (or from where they were normally first shipped) either in English vessels, in ships of the country of production or in ships from the country of first shipment. In practical terms it cut Dutch shipping out of much of its trade with England. It led to war.

The three Dutch Wars (in 1652–4, 1665–7 and 1672–4), saw naval combat of a new kind. The new tactics involved opposing fleets formed into lines, firing broadsides at each other, with fleet commanders exerting much greater control over individual vessels, and proportionately less initiative allowed to individual captains. The day of the seaman-adventurer in government service was not yet over, but fleet actions began to call for levels of discipline and professionalism that had real implications for the development of the profession of naval officer.

52 Battles of the Dutch Wars, 1652–74 (the battle of Bergen, Norway, 1665, is out of the map area).

0   50 miles

0   50 km

●   Battles of the First Dutch War 1652–4
■   Battles of the Second Dutch War 1665–7
▼   Battles of the Third Dutch War 1672–4
M   Dutch raid in the Medway 1667
H   'Holmes Bonfire' 1666

The battles involved much greater concentrations of firepower than were seen in the sixteenth century, with many large ships mounting heavier guns. Standards of gunnery also began to improve. The growing gap between the warship and the armed merchantman was not quite complete, but the latter was not suited to the line of battle and the sea battles were mostly fought by the state fleets of the Dutch provinces and the English navy. Although the boarding and capture of enemy ships were to remain significant in sea warfare until 1815, the Dutch Wars were marked by the destruction of growing numbers of ships. At the battle of the Gabbard Sands (or North Foreland) in June 1653, for example, the Dutch lost about twenty ships, of which eleven were captured, but six were sunk and three destroyed in explosions. After some 150 years of development, the broadside-firing warship was becoming a very powerful engine of destruction.

Powerful state navies could not exist without strong centralized states to create and maintain them. The end of the English Civil Wars saw Parliament in

53 *The Battle of the Gabbard Sands 1653*, by Heerman Witmont. This battle off the Suffolk coast was an early victory for the English.

possession of a navy of seventy-two ships, more than a quarter of which carried 32 guns or more, and of these, three had 70 or more cannon. Forty new ships were added to the fleet between 1650 and 1654 in what was, to date, the largest warship-building programme in English history. Officered by experienced seamen closer in origin and outlook to the merchants in Parliament, and supported by a high level of finance, the navy proved to be a powerful instrument of war and diplomacy for the Commonwealth (1649–53) and the Protectorate (1653–9) that followed it. It also ensured that when Charles II (r. 1660–85) was restored to the throne he had a fleet capable of carrying the sort of strategic and diplomatic weight that his father had wanted but failed to create.

After the first actions in the spring of 1652, the encounters of the summer and autumn of 1652 were convoy battles. In February 1653 Blake effectively closed the Channel to Dutch shipping after a three-day running battle. The following June the victory at Gabbard Sands off Orfordness in Suffolk forced the Dutch back into their home ports, where they had to endure a blockade. In late July Dutch attempts to break the blockade in fierce battles off the coast, near Katwijk and Scheveningen, ended in failure and the death of Admiral Tromp, who was killed by a musket shot. The English, who were employing some form of line-of-battle tactic in the war, lost two ships, while the Dutch lost at least fourteen, and possibly twice that number. The Dutch fleet was temporarily broken, and the war ended in 1654 with the Dutch acceding to the Navigation Act. Dutch losses amounted to more than 80 warships and 1,200 or so merchant vessels. The merchant vessels were snapped up by English owners, transforming the English merchant fleet and eventually leading to a major crisis in the shipbuilding industry (see p. 169).

English warships were soon in action again. In April 1655 Blake routed the Barbary pirates of Algiers, and in that same year the Protectorate government started a campaign against the Spanish in the Caribbean, the 'Western Design', which led to the capture of Jamaica in May and a five-year war with Spain. The English fleet operated much more successfully in this transoceanic war against Spain than it had in Elizabeth's time, but English losses of merchant ships to Spanish privateers exceeded the number of Dutch merchantmen captured by the English in the Dutch Wars. As Richard Harding has pointed out, it was privateering that tended to swing the balance in a naval war, chipping away at the shipping resources, sea trade and wealth of a nation, rather than the noisier and more spectacular actions of the big fleets. Certainly, the efforts of the English navy in the Dutch Wars were greatly aided by privateers.

The naval battles of 1652 and 1653 showed that, on the whole, the English fleet was more effective than that of the Dutch. The Dutch quickly learned the lessons of the first war with England. They began building heavier ships, armed with more big guns, and organized their fleets under much more centralized control. By the mid-1650s the Dutch navy was almost equal in numbers to the English fleet, although overall they still lacked the firepower of the English vessels.

The Second Dutch War (1665–7) was started by a powerful faction in England, which included James, Duke of York (later James II), Lord High Admiral of England, along with courtiers and London merchants. They feared Dutch ambitions and looked covetously on Dutch trade. Preliminary skirmishes in 1664 included the English capture of the Dutch settlement of New Amsterdam, which was renamed New York in honour of James. War was not actually declared until 1665. The first major sea battle came when two forces of around one hundred ships clashed off Lowestoft in Suffolk on 3 June 1665. The English, led by the Duke of York, had a major victory, sinking eighteen Dutch ships and taking another fourteen, for the loss of one English ship. English casualties amounted to about 800, whereas the Dutch lost more than six times this number. It was the worst Dutch defeat in all of the three wars, but the English allowed their enemies to escape and begin rebuilding their forces.

In 1666 the French and the Danish sided with the Dutch and declared war on England. The English fleet had problems with its victual supply and, in the wake of the Great Plague of 1665, both sides lacked manpower. The year 1666 also saw the first major English defeat of the Dutch Wars, in the Four Days' Battle (1–4 June) off the North Foreland of Kent. The battle was a prolonged, bloody and exhausting affair, in which the English under the Duke of Albemarle lost over 5,000 men and about twenty-two ships – three times as many ships as the Dutch. Despite this disaster the English were able to inflict a crushing defeat on the great Dutch Admiral de Ruyter (the victor of the Four Days' Battle) off Orfordness in July, driving the Dutch fleet home and gaining temporary command of Dutch waters. The resourceful English commander, Sir Richard Holmes, took this opportunity to destroy 150 Dutch merchant ships anchored inshore of the Frisian Islands in what came to be called the 'Holmes Bonfire'.

Faced with shortages of money and stores after the exhausting battles of 1666, and with a negotiated peace in the offing, the English did not fit out the main fleet in 1667. The Dutch took the opportunity to mount their own version of the 'Holmes Bonfire'. In June 1667 Admiral De Witt entered the Thames and the Medway and landed troops without meeting serious opposition. In the course of a few days they destroyed nineteen ships, including three big warships, and made off with two more, one of which was the 86-gun *Royal Charles*. It was one of the most humiliating episodes in English naval history. The war ended in 1667 with the Treaty of Breda, as neither side had much to gain from its continuation. One of the few material benefits derived from the conflict was that the treaty allowed both sides to retain any colonial possessions they had conquered. For the English, this meant increasing their foothold in North America by keeping New York and other former Dutch territories there.

However, the Anglo-Dutch conflict was not yet over. In 1670 Charles II made a secret treaty with Louis XIV of France for war against the United Provinces of the Netherlands. The French invaded the Netherlands by land in 1672 and the English declared war that same year. The war brought them few returns – and included a major English defeat in Solebay in Suffolk in 1672 – and Charles made peace in 1674. The Anglo-Dutch Wars were of little lasting benefit to either side and cost thousands of lives. They did, however, demonstrate that any nation wishing to be a big player on the international stage in Europe and beyond had to invest in a costly line-of-battle fleet and the infrastructure to support it.

In the latter part of the seventeenth century, English warships active in the Mediterranean fought often and successfully against the Barbary pirates from the north African states. This helped to make sailing conditions for English merchantmen safer, which encouraged more trade and raised English diplomatic status in the region.

The year 1688 is one of the more famous in English history, the time of the 'Glorious Revolution' that saw the Dutch William III of Orange drive his Catholic father-in-law James II from the throne in a bloodless coup. In the context of the Anglo-Dutch Wars this may seem a very peculiar turn of events, but the Catholic James (the former Duke of York), who succeeded his brother Charles II in 1685, had done much to alienate the political community of largely Protestant England – an effect intensified by the rampant religious bigotry of the period. The English navy did nothing effective to oppose the large Dutch invasion fleet that put William and his army ashore at Brixham. Its operations were perhaps compromised by officers wishing to wait and see who would win on land.[2]

'The second Hundred Years War': the Royal Navy and the wars of 1689–1815

The year following the Glorious Revolution saw England join the Grand Alliance with other European powers against Louis XIV's France, and this was soon followed by a French declaration of war. This was the beginning of a series of seven major Anglo-French conflicts, culminating in the Napoleonic War of 1803–15, which some historians have called 'the second Hundred Years War'. It was also the period that saw Great Britain (so-called from the time of the Anglo-Scottish Union in 1707) rise to be a global power.

France had developed a strong navy in the second half of the seventeenth century, due in large part to the drive of the French minister Colbert. However, France was first and foremost a land power, and in the late 1690s the French abandoned the strategy of building up a force of large warships in favour of the creation of expeditionary forces, cruising squadrons and privateering ships. This left the way open for the development of Britain as the greatest naval power in the world. By 1715 the British Royal Navy had 182 ships on its books that exceeded 300 tons, more than the fleets of France and Holland put together, and it had almost twice as many line-of-battle ships as France.[3]

Despite seemingly carrying all before him in 1688, William III was not secure as king. James II was still at large and bent on retaking the throne. In March 1689 the French navy landed James in Ireland. The subsequent Jacobite rising and its suppression by William's forces left many dead and a created a powerful Protestant mythology that still lives today. The early part of the war (1689–97) was marked by English naval failure. A near-disastrous attempt to attack French resupply ships at Bantry Bay in Ireland in 1689 was followed in 1690 by the defeat of an out-numbered Anglo-Dutch fleet off Beachy Head. Fortunately for the allies, lack of supplies and disease meant that the French could not exploit their victory and had to head for home. On the way they burned Teignmouth in Devon, the last time until 1914 that an enemy was able to inflict serious harm on an English coastal town.

The temporary French naval superiority in the Channel was ended in 1692, as was James II's attempt to reoccupy the English throne. The English sank most of his invasion force and fifteen French ships of the line in the battles on the Normandy coast, at Baie de Cherbourg and Baie de La Hogue. The invasion attempt was over. Even this great defeat did not break the French navy, but financial problems – France was also in the middle of a great land war – kept it in check. The French reorganized their strategy from one of *Guerre d'Escadre* (war against enemy fleets) to one of *Guerre de Course* (war against trade). French war-ships and privateers mounted a concerted and very damaging campaign against allied merchant ships, but by the time the war ended it was the English and Dutch who had command of the seas.

The War of the Spanish Succession (1702–13) against Spain and France was again fought by the English in alliance with the Dutch. The English (British from 1707) fleet grew in size during the conflict and much of the French effort at sea was in the form of commerce-raiding. The war had a number of important conse-quences for future British naval strategy and trade. Gibraltar was captured in 1704 and the island of Minorca in 1708; both became British naval bases and both were retained by Britain under the Treaty of Utrecht in 1713. Newfoundland and Nova Scotia were also acquired, and the Spanish Empire was opened up as a market for British slavers. Another outcome was that the war ended with the French battle-fleet in serious decline. A failure to defeat a French force off the coast of Colombia in 1702 was followed by a series of victories, which included the sinking of Spanish

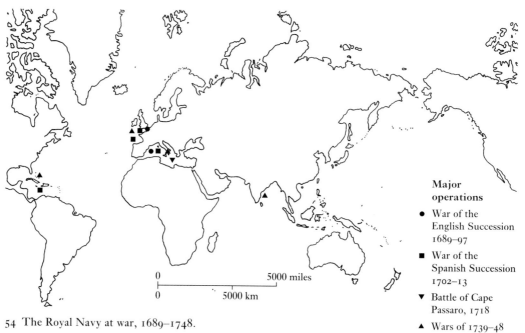

Major operations

- War of the English Succession 1689–97
- War of the Spanish Succession 1702–13
- ▼ Battle of Cape Passaro, 1718
- ▲ Wars of 1739–48

54 The Royal Navy at war, 1689–1748.

treasure fleets in 1704 and 1708 (Vigo Bay, Spain, and Cartagena, Colombia), and the defeat of enemy seaborne attempts to retake Gibraltar in 1704 and 1705. By 1713 Britain was the greatest seapower in the world.[4]

The period from 1713 to 1739 saw no major naval wars for Britain. Both France (in 1715–16) and Spain (in 1719) gave naval and other support to Jacobite risings in Scotland, but these were quickly crushed by land forces. The navy was used as a diplomatic 'sledgehammer' ('lever' is too inadequate a term) against Spain on a number of occasions. These included helping to end the Spanish occupation of Sicily in 1718 by defeating a Spanish fleet there, and in 1727 interrupting the flow of silver from Panama by a blockade of Panama, which forced the Spanish to end a siege of Gibraltar. The British fleet was also used against the Russians and the Swedish in the Baltic from 1715 to 1727 to protect the vital trade in naval stores.

The coronation of the Elector of Hanover as George I of Great Britain in 1714 presented Britain with an unwanted commitment to defend a continental territory. Hanover was a strategic liability, impossible to defend without strong European allies, and French attempts to acquire the province helped to lead to the Seven Years War (see p. 135). The troublesome link with Hanover was not broken until 1837, when Victoria became Queen of Britain (Salic Law did not allow a woman to inherit the Electorate).

The 1720s and 1730s saw a revival of the navies of Spain and France. Anglo-Spanish disputes over the slave trade in the Americas and other issues boiled over into war with Spain in 1739, which in 1740 became part of a general European conflict over the succession to the throne of the Austrian Empire (1740–8). Spain

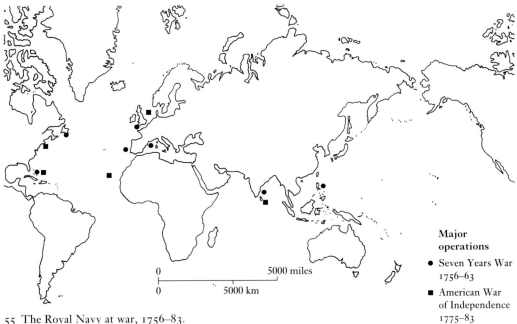

Major operations

● Seven Years War 1756–63

■ American War of Independence 1775–83

55 The Royal Navy at war, 1756–83.

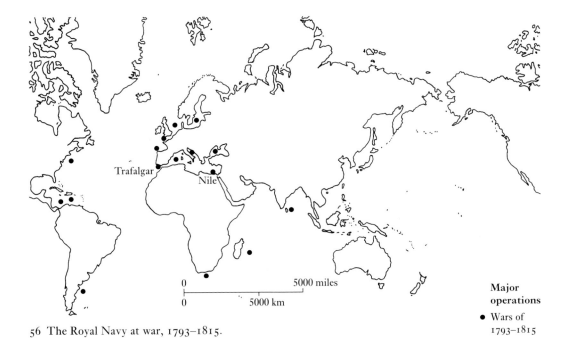

Trafalgar

Nile

Major operations

● Wars of 1793–1815

56 The Royal Navy at war, 1793–1815.

was an ally of France (which did not declare open war on Britain until 1744), and the presence of the French fleet restricted the Royal Navy's freedom of action. The early years of the naval war were mostly marked by failed operations on the British side. A French invasion fleet actually sailed for England in February 1744 (before the declaration of war), but was dispersed by a storm off Dungeness before the Royal Navy could attack it. As in 1596 and 1597 English Channel weather had proved to be more decisive than seapower.

The land war went badly for Britain and its allies, and the French made brilliant strategic use of Charles Edward Stuart, 'the Young Pretender' to the throne of Britain. Bonnie Prince Charlie landed in Scotland in July 1745, sparking a major Jacobite rebellion that saw the invasion of England, a triumphant advance as far south as Derby, and the recall of seasoned British troops fighting the French on the Continent. The presence of the Royal Navy probably dissuaded the French from making an invasion attempt, and British seapower certainly helped in the Jacobite defeat by convoying troops and stores to Scotland. The navy triumphed in two battles against the French off Finisterre in May and October 1747, taking a total of twenty-five vessels (including eight ships of the line) for the loss of no British ships. However, in both cases the French were escorting transatlantic convoys, the bulk of which escaped as the warships joined battle (the entire convoy escaped during the second battle). The British Admiral George Anson and Rear-Admiral Sir Edward Hawke gained great prestige from their victories, but not every British naval officer was so successful. In 1748 Rear-Admiral Charles Knowles on the Jamaica station was able to bring about the destruction of two large Spanish ships of the line off Havana, but was later court-martialled for the desultory manner in which he had brought his force into action.

The War of the Austrian Succession ended in 1748 in stalemate, with French military power undefeated in Europe. France, in fact, emerged from the conflict as a wealthier nation. The Royal Navy had done some damage to French trade, but its record was scarcely one of unalloyed success. Inevitably there was also a transoceanic dimension to the war, which saw British soldiers fighting in the Americas and India.

One of the key figures in the mid-eighteenth-century Royal Navy was George, Lord Anson (1697–1762). He first came to prominence as the commander of a small squadron of six ships sent to the Pacific in 1740 to raid Spanish settlements and trade. This terrible epic voyage saw many more men die from scurvy than from battle, and only one ship, Anson's *Centurion*, completed what became a voyage of circumnavigation. However, Anson returned in 1744 with over half a million pounds of Spanish treasure taken from a treasure ship off the Philippines, which made him a rich man and a national hero. Anson was promoted to admiral in 1745 and ennobled after his victory off Finisterre in 1747. With John Montagu, Earl of Sandwich (1718–92; First Lord of the Admiralty, 1748–51, 1763, 1771–82), Anson played a major role in the Admiralty Commissioners asserting their control over the Navy Board, a process that began in the mid-1740s and came to a successful conclusion some ten years later. The introduction of standard officers' uniform in 1748 was an outward sign of a growing professionalism. Although the navy, like other aspects of Georgian society, was prey to corruption and undue influence, it was, broadly speaking, left in the hands of experienced officers who knew what they were doing. Certainly, the Royal Navy that went to war against France in 1756 was a tighter and more formidable instrument of war than the navy of the 1740s.

The Seven Years War (1756–63) was fought in Europe's far-flung colonies as well as in Europe itself. Despite the changes in the navy, the war opened with a major humiliation for Britain. The British base at Port Mahon on Minorca surrendered in 1757, losing the navy one of its two Mediterranean stations. The government, trying to save itself, made a scapegoat out of the commander of the British relief force sent to Minorca, Vice-Admiral John Byng. Byng was court-martialled and shot. The government still fell, and William Pitt the Elder, a bellicose proponent of a maritime strategy against France, came to power.

One of the most effective strategies used by the British proved to be blockade, reducing France's ability to support its colonies and restricting the operational capabilities of its navy. French overseas possessions were lost to the British: Louisbourg in Canada, Fort Duquesne (renamed Pittsburgh) and the island of Guadeloupe in 1758, Quebec in 1759 and Montreal in 1760. Robert Clive's military victories in India against the French and their Indian allies consolidated the position of the English East India Company there.

The French government decided to try to finish the war by invading Britain, but in November 1759 the invasion force was defeated in appalling weather at Quiberon Bay in Brittany by a British squadron commanded by Admiral Sir Edward Hawke. The French navy, beset by a crippling lack of supplies and cash, was unable to take the offensive again. The war finally ended in 1763 with Britain in possession of Canada and Nova Scotia, as well as St Vincent, Grenada, Tobago and Dominica in the West Indies, and Senegal in Africa (a vital area for the slave trade). Minorca was also regained. Spain had entered the war against England in 1762, and both Havana in Cuba and Manila in the Philippines fell to British amphibious operations. Both were soon given back, but Havana was returned in exchange for Florida. In terms of territorial acquisitions, the Seven Years War was the most successful conflict ever fought up to that time by Britain.

However, the Royal Navy was not invincible, as the American War of Independence (1775–83) showed. When the American colonists rose in revolt they had no real navy with which to take on the British, but they soon acquired allies who did. France declared war against Britain in 1778, and by 1780 the country was also fighting Spain and Holland. The British army in America depended on supplies from Britain. The Royal Navy was enormously overstretched, protecting Britain from invasion at the same time that it was trying to defend the vital sugar trade from the West Indies and to support the army in America. In 1778 the American privateer John Paul Jones was even able to raid Cumberland and Northern Ireland. A threatened French and Spanish invasion of Britain in 1779 was only prevented by disease and a lack of supplies among the invasion forces.

Gibraltar was soon under siege, but was effectively saved in 1780 when Admiral Rodney defeated Spanish squadrons in two battles off Cape St Vincent (the second battle, known as the 'Moonlight Battle', was conducted at night, a rare event in the age of sail). Rodney was also victorious in the West Indies in 1782, where the French had gained maritime superiority. He defeated a Franco-Spanish force sailing to invade Jamaica. The battle took place off Les Saintes islands, and Rodney took advantage of a change in the wind to break the French line in two places, throwing them into confusion. This was a novel tactic, later used by Nelson, and although only five ships were captured, one of them was the French flagship, the *Ville de Paris*. The invasion fleet was forced to retreat.

The American colonies were lost because of the failings of the army and the ultimate impossibility of holding down a people prepared to fight to the death for their independence. However, if the navy had been able to do more to support the army and interdict American privateers and merchantmen, the war might not have ended in the humiliating débâcle for Britain that it did. As it was, in 1783 Britain had to recognize the thirteen American colonies as the United States of America (there was an additional loss, on a much smaller scale: Minorca was returned to the Spanish). Despite this, the Royal Navy did not end the American war in bad condition. By the close of the war the navy had defeated its enemies at sea, and the period from the early 1770s to the early 1780s, when the Earl of Sandwich was First Lord of the Admiralty, was one of reform, growth and innovation.[5]

The French Revolution of 1789 and the vast political changes in France that followed eventually led to another major European war. Although the 1793–1802 and the 1803–15 conflicts are, respectively, styled the 'French Revolutionary War' and the 'Napoleonic War', they were, in truth, one war with a brief period of peace in the middle that allowed the warring parties to re-arm. The war became a conflict to prevent France from dominating most of Europe and was conducted on a scale not hitherto seen.

The Royal Navy started the war with a frontline strength of 425 ships, and, apart from the major crisis of the Nore and Spithead mutinies, its conduct in the war was generally marked by professionalism and discipline. The French navy – particularly the officer corps – had been damaged by the Revolution, but it was not a negligible force and grew stronger over time. The Royal Navy could not prevent French military victories on the mainland of Europe, but it could, and did, ensure that Britain stayed in the war and could carry the offensive to the French coastline and French overseas territories. All of the major fleet actions of the war were British victories.

The first major battle of the war, later known to the British as 'The Glorious First of June', took place in 1794 on the eponymous date. This was, in effect, a 'convoy battle', as the French fleet had sailed out of Brest to protect a huge convoy of grain that had sailed from America for famine relief in France. The battle was fought about 400 miles off the coast of Brittany. The French lost seven ships in the battle and had to retreat, but still successfully defended the convoy, which arrived unscathed.

As in the American war, Britain's enemies began to multiply. Holland, transformed into the Batavian Republic by a French invasion, declared war in 1795, and Spain followed in 1796, both bringing their navies in on the French side. In February 1797 Admiral Jervis' Mediterranean fleet captured four Spanish ships of the line in a major action off Cape St Vincent against a fleet twice the size of his own. The battle brought Horatio Nelson to public attention, his wildly heroic actions playing a significant part in the British victory.

The Dutch fleet received a major blow in October of that same year. The British Admiral Duncan had blockaded the Dutch fleet in the Texel, despite major mutinies in the British fleet. However, bad weather forced Duncan's ships back to England, and the Dutch took the opportunity to sail out. Duncan was soon alerted to this and returned with sixteen ships of the line, the same number as in the Dutch fleet. In a battle off the Dutch port of Camperdown, Duncan divided his ships into two columns and used them to break the Dutch line. No British ships were lost, but nine Dutch ships were captured, including the flagship.

British naval history from 1797 to 1805 is dominated by the figure of Horatio Nelson (1758–1805). The son of a Norfolk rector, Nelson went to sea at the age of twelve and rose rapidly, becoming a post-captain (able to command a rated ship) at twenty. Nelson served in the Mediterranean in the early years of the 1793–1802 war, playing a notable part (publicized by his own efforts) in the Battle of Cape St Vincent. These years saw him lose his right arm and the sight of his right eye in combat, although he never wore the eye-patch of later caricature.

In 1798 Nelson was given a squadron to hunt for a large French force that had sailed from the south of France. The fleet carried Napoleon Bonaparte and an army destined for Egypt. Nelson correctly deduced the destination, but took some months to find the French ships. He finally located them anchored in Aboukir Bay, at the mouth of the Nile, and attacked on the evening of 1 August. Manoeuvring between the shallow water around Aboukir Island and the French fleet, some of the British ships sailed around the western end of the French line, pinning the stationary French vessels between fire from both sides. The battle went on through the night, and by dawn the French fleet in Egypt had virtually ceased to exist. Nine ships of the line were captured and two frigates and two battleships were sunk, including the 120-gun flagship L'Orient, which exploded with a flash visible for miles around. Once again, no British ships were lost. Cut off from resupply, Bonaparte was forced to leave Egypt a year later.

The Battle of the Nile made Nelson into more than just a famous commander: he became, in effect, a 'superstar', fêted for his brilliance as an admiral but also lampooned for his very public relationship with Emma Hamilton. No British seaman, before or since, has matched his fame and reputation. Nelson was undoubtedly vain and assiduously promoted his own myth, but as a fighting commander he had few equals and none with such a consistent record of success. However, Nelson's glory was bought at the price of many men's lives. Two hundred and forty-eight British sailors perished at the Battle of the Nile, but something in the order of 1,600 Frenchmen died, many of their burned and blasted bodies left floating in Aboukir Bay.

In 1800 Russia, Sweden, Denmark and Prussia made a pact to resist British claims to the right of searching neutral shipping in the hunt for French goods. In March 1801 the Danes closed their own ports and those in the Elbe to British shipping. British reaction was swift. Nelson was second-in-command to Admiral

Sir Hyde Parker in a British fleet sent to break the embargo. On 2 April the fleet attacked Danish ships and forts at Copenhagen, and so battered the Danish defences that the Danes were forced to conclude an armistice, negotiated by Nelson. At a critical point in the battle Nelson affected not to see a signal from Parker to withdraw (figuratively turning his blind eye), and so won through. Nelson's action led to the recall of Parker and his own promotion to fleet commander and a viscountcy. In 1803 Nelson was given command of the Mediterranean fleet, with HMS *Victory* as his flagship.

French invasion of Britain had first become a serious possibility in 1797, but the threat receded somewhat when Napoleon went to Egypt. However, Napoleon revived his invasion schemes in the early 1800s, and by 1805 a force of more than 160,000 men was ranged in six divisions along the Channel coast from Etaples to Calais. Just under 2,300 vessels had been gathered to transport the force. In England large volunteer forces were raised to garrison the coast and new fortifications were constructed, including many Martello towers. The Royal Navy had many smaller vessels in the English Channel – frigates, brigs, coastal gunboats and others – some of which patrolled the Channel, while others were kept in reserve. Some were manned by 'Sea Fencibles', a sort of seagoing Home Guard composed of fishermen and other seamen.

There were fears that a large French fleet at Toulon, commanded by Admiral Villeneuve, might escape and link up with other vessels in French or Spanish ports. Napoleon planned to use his main fleet to take command of the Channel, at least for long enough to cover the sailing of his invasion fleet. In 1805 Napoleon ordered Villeneuve to sail to the West Indies, where the various elements of the French and Spanish fleets were supposed to concentrate. The plan was for them to sail back to Europe and drive the Royal Navy from the Channel. Villeneuve was able to escape from Toulon in March 1805 and he headed for the West Indies. Pursued by Nelson, Villeneuve returned before the other ships could join his fleet. He fought a brief action off Cape Finisterre, losing two ships to the British, and then took shelter first in Ferrol and then Cadiz. Villeneuve, facing Napoleon's fury and the certainty of replacement, decided to take the British on. The Franco-Spanish fleet of thirty-three ships of the line sailed out on 19 October. On 21 October Villeneuve's and Nelson's fleets came to battle off Cape Trafalgar. Nelson was expert at communicating his ideas about tactics to his subordinate commanders, and the captains of the twenty-seven ships that sailed in two columns towards the French and Spanish knew what Nelson wanted of them. The basic plan was to concentrate raking fire (cannon shot that would pass from stem to stern of the ships that they hit) at two points on the enemy line, breaking the line and making it impossible for Villeneuve's fleet to function as a single unit. The deadly close-quarters battle lasted for more than five hours. Nelson was fatally wounded by a musket shot, but lived long enough to hear that the battle had been won. Seventeen French and Spanish ships were captured and two sunk. No British ships were lost, but many had suffered great damage. There were 1,679 casualties on the British side, of whom 437 died, but French and Spanish casualties may have numbered 8,000.

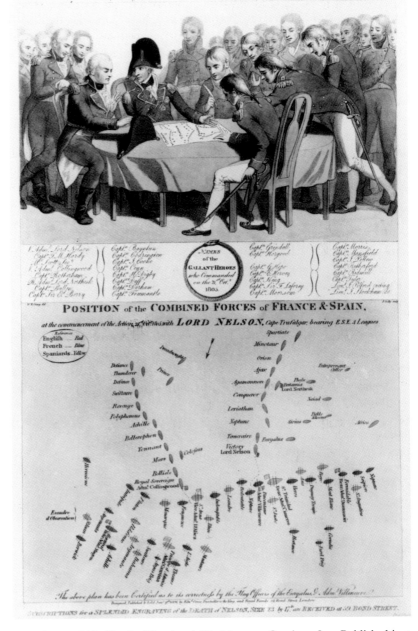

57 Nelson and his 'Band of Brothers', Trafalgar, 21 October 1805. Published just three months after Nelson's death, this engraving was part of a Nelson 'souvenir industry' that existed even before Trafalgar, providing the British public with images of the hero and his exploits in the struggle against France. Nelson's heroic death at Trafalgar sealed his enduring reputation as Britain's greatest admiral. The battle-plan shows the two columns of British ships advancing to break the Franco–Spanish line at Trafalgar.

Napoleon's invasion scheme was a serious one, but it is doubtful if his plan for wresting control of the English Channel from the Royal Navy was practicable. If Nelson had lost at Trafalgar matters might have been somewhat different, but any invasion force would have still had to attempt the crossing in the face of strong resistance from the smaller ships of the British fleet. It was a prospect that was to dismay Hitler's Wehrmacht 135 years later.

The sea war did not end with Nelson and Trafalgar. The French fleet survived, although Spanish seapower was crippled. Actions between small numbers of ships were much more common than major battles, but much of the work the Royal Navy undertook was hard and unspectacular. One of the most arduous duties was that of blockade, by which ships stayed on station for months in all weathers (until extreme conditions finally drove them home), attempting to prevent movement in and out of enemy ports. Another important if somewhat un-Nelsonian activity was the escort of convoys, a vital system of trade protection that was later all but forgotten, at the cost of many merchant ships in the First World War.

In 1812 the United States declared war on Britain. The Royal Navy had been impeding American trade with France, and stopping and searching American vessels, looking for British seamen and pressing Americans into service. The US Navy was small but well run, and possessed some very powerful frigates such as the *Constitution*, which presented the over-stretched Royal Navy with something of a challenge. The war in America, which saw land fighting in both the United States and Canada and small-scale actions between flotillas on the Great Lakes, came to an end in January 1815.

Napoleon was finally defeated in 1815. At the end of the war Britain was still the world's greatest seapower, and a string of overseas conquests, such as Malta, Ceylon, the Cape of Good Hope and Mauritius, were retained, providing the country with even more colonial naval bases and trading stations. The Royal Navy could not beat Napoleon on its own, but it did ensure that Britain was able to remain in the war against France and that French military successes were largely confined to the continent of Europe.[6]

Officers and men of the Royal Navy: the development of a professional navy

The English navy in Tudor and early Stuart times had never lacked for experienced seamen to run its ships. The problem was that, in a highly stratified society, seafarers did not rate highly in the pecking order. Ultimate control of fleets lay in the hands of the gentry or the aristocracy, people who did not necessarily know anything very much about seafaring or naval warfare. The turmoil of the Civil Wars and the Commonwealth changed things somewhat, filling the navy with professionals who were not courtiers (although they did have to display the kinds of political and religious reliability demanded by the regime).

The Restoration in 1660 saw the gradual reintroduction of officers who owed their positions to links with the court. But times were changing. Ideas of semiformal training were introduced for new officers. From the early 1660s it became possible for young gentlemen who wished to go to sea to enrol themselves with captains as a 'volunteer per order' (from 1661) or on seven-year apprenticeships (from 1662). The idea was that the gentlemen would learn the basics of seafaring in this way. Oral examinations for lieutenancies were introduced in 1677. In order to help maintain a professional core of officers, the half-pay system was introduced by which officers who were ashore between commissions received half their normal pay. Although indigent officers on half-pay were to feature in later fiction as sad figures (as in Jane Austen's work), half-pay helped to keep the sea officers together as a professional body. Admirals were the first to receive peacetime payment in 1668, and it was extended to all commissioned officers in 1693. The naval profession was finally beginning to develop, albeit slowly and imperfectly.

Control of the navy in the seventeenth and eighteenth centuries was split between two organizations. The old office of Lord High Admiral did not entirely lapse until 1828 (after being briefly held by the future William IV), but for much of the time from 1628 onwards (1628–38, 1645–8, 1652–60, 1673–1701 and 1709–1827) its authority was split between a group of Lords Commissioners of the Admiralty. The Admiralty had operational command of the fleet, but otherwise its remit was ill defined, and the navy was administered, built, paid, fed, armed and equipped by the Navy Board. It was a situation ripe for office warfare (see p. 150).[7]

The commissioned sea officers in the navy in the eighteenth and nineteenth centuries were generally from better-off social classes than those they commanded. In the eighteenth century, at least, only a tiny minority became officers after serving as common seamen. The navy attracted the sons of the middle classes, the gentry and aristocracy, and both the future kings William IV (r. 1830–7) and George VI (r. 1937–52) saw service in the Royal Navy. 'Naval families', in which it became a tradition for sons to follow their fathers into sea service, also became established in the eighteenth century.

Sea officers were commissioned by the Admiralty. They were generally a very cohesive body, with a strong (and often justified) sense of their professional competence, buoyed up by the many successes of the navy in the eighteenth and early nineteenth centuries. For a young man in naval service, the key rank to achieve was that of lieutenant. Once a man had achieved this rank, his future promotion was dependent on seniority; in other words, he would become an admiral if he lived long enough. Progression in society in this period was largely dependent on patronage and what would nowadays be called corruption. The navy was no exception to this: for example, in 1780 Admiral Rodney famously promoted his fifteen-year-old son to the rank of captain.

Warrant officers were the other group of officers aboard ship, and they were appointed by Navy Board warrant. They were basically the ship's specialists, outside the normal fighting command structure. The most important warrant officer (and one of the most important figures aboard ship) was the master, who had overall responsibility, below the commissioned captain, for sailing and navigating the ship. The other warrant officers – at varying levels of rank and social standing – comprised the chaplain, surgeon, purser, boatswain, carpenter, gunner, sailmaker, master-at-arms and schoolmaster (the last often an unhappy figure of uncertain status employed to teach midshipmen).

Although the officer corps existed as a body, there was no equivalent body of naval seamen. The navy drew on the same pool of experienced seamen as the merchant service, and the navy was not a very attractive option for most sailors. The pay of the naval sailor did not increase between 1653 and 1797, although it was probably not much worse than mercantile pay, and naval victuals may have been better. The main disincentives to naval service seem to have been the fierce discipline and the potentially interminable service. Although theoretically signed on to serve a particular captain on a particular ship, seamen inducted into the navy were generally sent on to another ship at the end of a commission. A man might serve a decade or more in the navy before legal discharge, if illness, disablement or death had not already removed him from the service. Even prize money, a lure for some, was very inequitably distributed, with by far the greater share going to the officers.

One of the best known, and most hated aspects of the eighteenth- and early nineteenth-century navy was the press-gang. Legal authorities of the time reckoned that the government's right to conscript men for sea service was implicit in various laws going back to the Middle Ages. As Brian Lavery remarks, there 'was no specific law which allowed impressment, but on the other hand, there was none which banned it.'[8]

Press-gangs had long existed, although in the eighteenth century their organization became more systematized, with the development of what came to be called the Impress Service. Press-gangs were used to recruit volunteers, but also took many men against their will. Their main targets were 'Seamen, Seafaring Men and Persons whose Occupations and Callings are to work in Vessels and Boats upon Rivers', according to a press-warrant of 1809. Although the press-gangs often swept up many landmen, they mostly let them go again as no captain would welcome having his ship filled with people who had never been to sea (although landmen were recruited into the navy through other means, with the ostensible aim of training them to be seamen). Impressment was deeply unpopular. Press-gangs took men from the streets, the taverns and from homecoming merchant ships, and they were to be found all round the coast: the Impress Service had gangs in nearly fifty British and Irish ports in 1795. Naval crews did include not insignificant numbers of volunteers as well, men who liked serving in the navy or had been attracted by a recruitment bounty, but most men seem to have ended up aboard through some means of compulsion. Local authorities were called upon to supply men as well; the Quota Acts of 1795, for example, specified the numbers of men that the counties and ports of Britain were to supply for the navy. It was claimed at the time that some tens of thousands of seamen were raised in this way. Impressment continued until the end of the Napoleonic War in 1815. Life for the 'Royal Tars of England' (as one typically effusive recruiting poster of 1803 put it) in the eighteenth and early nineteenth centuries was generally rather grim.

The term 'Jack Tar' as a generic description for seamen seems to have originated in the seventeenth century. A 1659 poem celebrating English victories over the Dutch refers to 'Jack-Sailor', and by the early eighteenth century 'honest Jack the Sailor' was a familiar literary figure. The linking of 'Jack' and 'Tar' came from the tarred waterproof clothing (tarpaulins) used by sailors. A common seventeenth-century term was 'tarpaulin', used for sailors in general, but also applied in relation to the post-Restoration navy to distinguish 'sea-bred' officers (i.e. experienced seamen who had risen from the ranks) from officers who owed their position to the fact that they were gentlemen. 'Jack Tar' became a popular figure, if often remote, distance doubtless lending enchantment.[9]

Officers had uniforms from 1748, but the ordinary sailor in the navy did not have an official uniform until 1857, more than a century later. Although the crews of certain ships might be fitted out in particular costumes, sailors were generally recognizable by their short coats and loose trousers which suited the practicalities of working on board ship.[10]

The navy grew enormously in size and strength during the eighteenth century. The numbers of ships are a measure of this, but so are the numbers of men. Manpower figures, of course, increased markedly during periods of war:

Table 5 Naval manpower 1702–1815[11]

Period	War or peace*	Maximum manpower**	Minimum manpower**
1702–13	War	50,000†	39,000
1714–38	Peace	21,000	7,000
1739–48	War	60,000	18,000
1748–55	Peace	34,000	10,000
1756–63	War	86,000	52,000
1764–75	Peace	27,000	13,000
1775–83	War	107,000	15,000
1784–92	Peace	39,000	14,000
1793–1802	War	129,000	70,000
1802–3	Peace	49,000	–
1803–15	War	142,000	49,000

* 'Peace' includes some short periods of war, such as the 1718–19 conflict with Spain.

** Figures rounded up or down to nearest 15000; based on numbers borne for pay.

† Maximum figure actually reached in 1714.

Our picture of the social history of the eighteenth-century Royal Navy has been dominated until recent years by a view that, in Nicholas Rodger's phrase, the navy was 'a sort of floating concentration camp', officered by brutes and sadists and crewed by the most degenerate men that Britain had to offer. Recent work, notably by Rodger himself, has shown that this picture was far from true, at least in the mid-eighteenth-century navy. Naval service could be harsh and dangerous, but

58 Sailors relaxing around a mess table aboard a British warship, early 19th century (by Pyne). Although the picture very much lives up to the 'Jolly Jack Tar' image (one man even has a wooden leg!), it gives a good idea of how warship sailors lived in their off-duty times.

crews were much more cohesive than one might suppose; officers seem quite often to have used persuasion and give-and-take to run their ships.

The naval mutinies of 1797 at Spithead and the Nore suggest that the situation had deteriorated by the end of the century, with a much greater class-consciousness among the seamen, a sense that the officers were a very separate 'them' to the sailors' 'us'. In those times, shortly after the French Revolution of 1789, such attitudes were not surprising. However, by the late 1790s the navy was far larger than it had ever been, the value of pay was falling, and the naval service was under great pressure. The 1797 mutinies were harshly suppressed, but it is also a fact that the Royal Navy did not suffer another such major outbreak during the French wars. If the threats of the lash or of being hanged from the yardarm were all that kept the fleet going, it is difficult to believe that the navy could have been as successful as it was.

The suppression of the 1797 mutinies involved the use of the navy's own soldiers, the Royal Marines. Soldiers had served on ships since ancient times, but in 1664 a special regiment, 'The Duke of Albany's Maritime Regiment of Foot' was raised for service in English warships. The regiment served in the Dutch Wars, but was disbanded in 1688. Several Marine regiments were raised in the War of the Spanish Succession, and took part in the capture and subsequent defence of Gibraltar in 1704/5. The Marines existed intermittently until the mid-eighteenth century, but the force was finally established under Admiralty command in 1755 (with 5,000 men). Marines were carried on board ships to act as infantry for amphibious operations and boarding actions, and to provide a kind of shipboard police force, backing-up the authority of the officers. Marines were involved in many of the naval actions and landing operations of the navy between the 1750s and 1815: by 1802, 30,000 Marines were in service. Marines were also used in the wars and smaller actions of the nineteenth century, from the bombardment of Algiers in 1816 to the defence of the foreign legations at Beijing during the Boxer uprising of 1900.[12]

Ships, tactics and ship-handling in the seventeenth and eighteenth centuries

Tactical developments of the mid-seventeenth century finally drew a line between ships powerful enough to stand in 'the line of battle' (generally ships of 50 guns or more, Fourth Rates and above) and those that were not. Just who invented line-of-

59 Line of battle: the Battle of Dogger Bank, North Sea, 5 August 1781. A British squadron (left) and a Dutch force (right), both escorting merchant convoys, bombard each other in line-ahead formation. Line-of-battle confrontations were seldom decisive. Although casualties were heavy on both sides, no ship was sunk during the battle. The British convoy was able to proceed while the Dutch one turned back, but the battle was an exhausting, bloody encounter that neither side could really call a victory.

battle tactics, and when they were invented, is still a matter of some debate. Earlier tactics favoured approaching an enemy fleet in line abreast, followed by a general mêlée in which ships sought out opponents of similar size. Put very crudely, the line of battle involved warships sailing in a line, one behind the other, towards an enemy, firing as their guns came to bear on the opposing vessels, and then turning away, perhaps to repeat the process. One of the aims of this tactic was to maximize the force of broadside firing, but it was also a means for an admiral to maintain control over his subordinate captains. The danger of captains breaking formation and haring off after lucrative prizes was well-recognized – Drake had done it with impunity in the Armada campaign of 1588 – and improving battle discipline served to make a fleet more effective. Instances of line-of-battle firing can be found earlier than the mid-seventeenth century, but it was the English who first made concerted use of the tactic in their battles with the Dutch in the early 1650s. The heavily-gunned English warships were ideal for this method of fighting. The great problem with these tactics was that they could make it difficult to get a decisive result in a battle.

The line-of-battle tactics called for a better means of controlling fleets, and it is no accident that the serious development of flag signalling systems dates from this period. The Commonwealth generals-at-sea, Blake, Deane and Monck, issued their first fighting instructions in 1653. Twenty years later the first printed set of sailing instructions was issued by the then Lord High Admiral, the Duke of York, and this included the use of flags for the transmission of orders.

Analysis of the fates of Royal Navy ships in service during three periods of intense warfare between 1688 and 1815 produces some interesting results:

Table 6 British ships captured, sunk or lost by accident in three war periods, 1688–1815[13]

Period	Total ships in service	Total captured in action	Total sunk in action	Total lost by accident
1688–1713	706 (100%)	89 (12.6%)	30 (4.2%)	27 (3.8%)
1739–63	722 (100%)	22 (3%)	5 (0.7%)	80 (11.1%)
1793–1815	2090 (100%)	103 (4.9%)	19 (0.9%)	327 (15.6%)

Very few of the casualties, from any cause, were First or Second Rates, a sign perhaps of their firepower, greater hull strength and superior handling, but also perhaps a sign that they were deployed less often than smaller vessels. It is apparent that the numbers of ships of the line lost in combat were very much lower than those of smaller ships. Line-of-battle tactics militated against battles between evenly matched fleets producing decisive results if neither side had a particular advantage. This continued to be so until the late eighteenth century, when commanders began more and more to attempt to break the enemy's line by sailing a column of ships through it. This maximized the firepower of the attackers and minimized that of the defenders, whose ships could be raked from stem to stern.

The shrinking relative proportions of ships lost in combat by the Royal Navy between 1688 and 1815 is a sign of its growing professionalism, and – at least in the later periods – a sign of the weaknesses of its opponents. The British lost many more ships in minor actions than in major battles, and most of these losses were by the traditional method of capture rather than destruction. With prize money to be gained from capturing a ship, there was a clear incentive not to send it to the bottom. One might argue that the growth in losses by wreck or accident in the mid- and late-eighteenth-century navy compared to those earlier in the century suggests that the navy's ship-handling was becoming less professional. However, is should be remembered that the wars of 1688–1713 were largely fought in north-western Europe and the Mediterranean. The wars of the mid-century and later involved global ship deployments, with greatly enhanced risks from storm and accident to ships operating so far from home. The fates of the *Cormorant* Class of 423-ton sloops are a case in point. Twenty-three vessels of this class were launched between 1794 and 1814, and four were lost by accident or wreck. Of these, one foundered on a voyage from Lisbon, but the other three went down in the Americas.[14]

A ship of the line had two or three gun-decks running continuously from stem to stern, with cannon firing through lidded gunports. Other guns were carried in the forecastle and on the quarterdeck. The broadside grew in importance, while the significance of bow or stern guns declined as the galley threat was long gone in most seas. The period from the mid-seventeenth to the early nineteenth century saw little in the way of radical technological progress, but over time warships became larger and more heavily armed, and rating systems had to be revised to take account of the changes. Contemporaries sometimes measured ships in terms of the total weight of the broadside that they could fire, and it is a good way of comparing changes in firepower. Compare, for example, these First Rates:

Table 7 Three First Rates launched between 1692 and 1814[15]

	Royal William	*Victory*	*Nelson*
Launched	1692	1765	1814
Tonnage	1568	2162	2601
Total no. of guns	100	100	120*
Total weight of shot in one broadside in lbs (kg)	864 (389)	1182 (531)	1442* (650)

* 22 of these guns were short-range carronades, with a total of 192 lb (88 kg) of the single broadside weight

Table 8 Minimum number of guns for a ship of the line, *c.* 1650–*c.* 1800[16]

c. 1650	30 guns
c. 1700	50 guns
c. 1750	64 guns
c. 1800	74/80 guns

The firepower of the *Nelson* of 1814 was roughly two-thirds greater than that of its counterpart of 120 years before. As described by Brian Lavery, the minimum rating for a ship able to stand in the line had to be raised over time (see Table 8).

The rigging of warships (and sea-going vessels in general) changed somewhat over this period. The fourth, bonaventure mast (stepped at or near the stern) was generally only found on large warships by the late sixteenth century, and it disappeared in the early decades of the seventeenth century. However, it was replaced by the first new mast to be developed for over two hundred years: the sprit topmast, mounted on the end of the bowsprit. The purpose of the sprit topmast sail was to assist the spritsail (carried below the bowsprit) in bringing the head of the ship round when tacking. Severely practical in intention, the sprit topmast nonetheless gave seventeenth-century warships an appropriately baroque appearance. The sprit topmast was eventually supplanted in the early 1700s by the jib, a sail attached to a stay (forward supporting rope) running from the topmost mast of the foremast assembly to the end of a bowsprit extension called a jib boom. The jib did much the same job as the sprit topmast and was nowhere near as vulnerable to damage. Attached to a stay, the jib was a form of staysail. Sails began to be rigged to the stays of other masts from the 1660s onwards, to improve the sailing qualities of ships. There were detailed changes in the forms of sails, and in other aspects of large warship rig between the seventeenth and early nineteenth centuries, but the ability to manoeuvre well, to be 'weatherly' (i.e., able to sail to windward without being pushed too far sideways) and to survive a battering in combat were always more important in a ship of the line than speed (most sailing warships could probably only touch about six knots).

The division of warships into different rates by gun power had its origins in the late Elizabethan period. The new pay scale of 1582 divided the fleet into six different rates according to tonnage (size was, of course, related to the number of guns a ship could carry).[17] This eventually translated into a rough order that rated ships by the number of their carriage-mounted guns. The first 100-gun ship under this system was the *Sovereign of the Seas*, built by Peter and Phineas Pett in 1637, the first warship also to have three flush-laid gundecks (i.e. running from stem to stern without a break). Built against the explicit advice of Trinity House (which regarded ships of this size as impractical), the *Sovereign* proved to be a formidable warship; undergoing two rebuilds, it remained in service until 1696, when it was destroyed by an accidental fire.

In the late 1640s, Parliament began rapidly expanding the navy. Ninety-seven

60 The *Sovereign of the Seas*, built 1637 (engraving by J. Payne). The first true three-decker in the English navy and, at the time of building, one of the most powerful warships in the world.

vessels of varying sizes were built between 1649 and 1659, nearly half (46) in the period 1649–53. Four three-deck First Rates were constructed in the 1650s, carrying between 64 and 80 guns, but the most important group consisted of 44 'frigates', vessels in the 500 ton-plus range. These were only two-deckers, but each carried 40 or more guns and they were the backbone of the English line of battle. By 1660, of the 254 ships in the English navy, over two-thirds (176) were Fourth Rates and above, able to stand in the line of battle. The English led the way with ships of the line, but their major competitors, the Dutch (in the 1650s) and the French (in the 1660s) set about creating their own line-of-battle fleets.

The concept of rating may tend to imply that ship-types were standardized in the seventeenth century. This was not the case, and there were variations in tonnage and gun power within every rate. The first real attempt to control the situation came in 1677 when Samuel Pepys (then First Secretary of the Admiralty and also a Member of Parliament) secured parliamentary approval for a major building programme comprising one First Rate (100 guns, 1,739 tons), nine Second Rates (90 guns, about 1,450 tons) and twenty Third Rates (70 guns, averaging about 1,100 tons). One of the aims of the programme was to increase the numbers of three-deckers as Pepys felt that England was falling behind in this respect. The programme was accompanied by the first 'Establishment of Men and Guns', which set down the crew sizes and numbers of types of guns to be carried by different ships.

In the late seventeenth and early eighteenth centuries, the English fleet was able to outbuild its rivals, and by the early 1700s England (from 1707, Great Britain) was unquestionably the greatest seapower in the world. However, the problem was that the warships in the English fleet were on the whole not very good. In a time when the theoretical knowledge of naval architecture was limited and design decisions could become political footballs, moves towards standardization created real problems. A major building programme of 1691 for twenty-seven ships produced vessels that were technically deficient or unsuitable for their purpose. In 1706 the first 'Establishment' was introduced for the Royal Navy, specifying the dimensions of different sizes of ship. There were five 'Establishments' between 1706 and 1745 but little real change, and their effect was to help fossilize design practices, a tendency increased by the rebuilding of old ships along the same lines and the replacing of lost ships with vessels of a similar size and type. Brian Lavery rightly describes the period from the early 1700s to the 1750s as 'the dark ages of British shipbuilding'.[18] The Navy Board, not the Admiralty, decided matters of design, and the Navy Board at this period was ruled by precedent and conservatism. It was fortunate for Britain that its potential enemies – France in particular – offered no significant naval challenge for many years.

This all began to change in the 1730s as the French fleet once again grew in size. French shipbuilders also developed in technical flair and expertise, revamping the old two-deck Third-Rate 74-gun type into a powerful, manoeuvrable vessel that was to become one of the standard warships for most of the last century of sailing warfare. The indifferent performance of the Royal Navy against French and Spanish ships in the war of 1739–48 showed that British warship design was lagging behind that of its enemies. Both France and Spain were ahead of Britain in building 74s, and the first true British 74s, the *Dublin* Class, did not begin to be launched until 1757. The 1750s saw a revolution in British ship design, as the Admiralty finally gained control of the process. In 1755 two progressive and innovative designers, Thomas Slade and William Bately, were appointed as joint Surveyors of the Navy. Of eighty-two 74-gun ships launched between 1757 and 1786, sixty-three were designed by Slade.

French ship design influenced that of Britain. The lines of some of the French ships captured between the 1740s and the early 1800s were used, in direct or modified form, for the design of more than two hundred British ships. This indicates something of the excellence of French design, but as some of the French designs were used on and off for decades, it also points up just how static the design of the wooden sailing ship was becoming. Advances could still be made, but these changes were mostly a matter of tinkering with existing designs and technology rather than developing something really new. One of the captured French ships was the 80-gun *Pompée*, taken at Toulon in 1793. After service in the fleet, in 1811 the *Pompée* became a prison hulk at Portsmouth, and it is believed that this vessel gave its name to the naval nickname for Portsmouth, 'Pompey'.

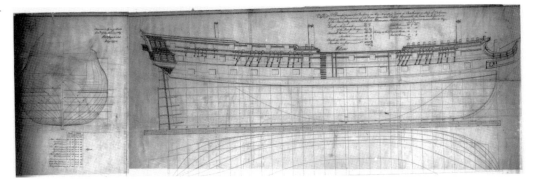

61 Lines and profile plan of the 74-gun ship HMS *Alfred*, launched 1778. The
techniques of ship design had reached an advanced stage by the second half of the
18th century, although science-based naval architecture did not develop until the
19th century. The lines drawn on these plans, shown in plan and elevation views, were
scaled-up by shipwrights to create the shape and structure of the finished hull. The plan
also shows the positions of decks and other internal features.

Because of poor performance, the three-decker fell out of favour in the
mid-eighteenth century. Likewise the numbers of First Rates constructed were
small. Only a dozen new First Rates were built between 1706 and 1786, but
between 1786 and 1830, twenty-one ships of this rate were constructed. One of
those built in the mid-eighteenth century was Slade's *Victory* (later Nelson's
flagship), launched at Chatham in May 1765. The *Victory* sailed as a two-decker as
well, and was often used as a flagship in an operational career that lasted nearly
sixty years.

Copper sheathing was routinely fitted to hulls from 1779, improving their
longevity – something very important with the long-range deployments that
were common in the Royal Navy. The warship designs of the latter part of the
eighteenth century gradually got larger, although the 74 pretty much reached its
maximum size in the 1790s. Three-deckers continued to increase in size, but came
up against a physical problem. The traditional framework of a wooden hull could
only be extended so far before both ends of the ship would tend to start drooping,
a phenomenon known as 'hogging', which put considerable strain on the hull and
could badly affect performance. The problem was alleviated to some degree by an
innovation introduced by Sir Robert Seppings (1767–1840), who was Surveyor of
the Navy from 1813 to 1832. He used diagonal wooden cross-braces to strengthen
the vertical frames of the hull, and made much greater use of knees (angle-brackets
that held beams and frames together) and other fixings made of iron. This made
hulls stronger, so it became possible to build them longer (although even these
innovations could not defeat the inherent weaknesses of wood, which make it
impossible to build a usable wooden hull much more than about 76 metres/250 feet
in length). Diagonal braces were first installed in a ship in 1810, but the technique
became more common in ships refitted or built after the end of the Napoleonic
War. Seppings also introduced much more rounded and strengthened bows and

sterns in warships. Bitter wartime experience had shown how vulnerable these areas could be.

However, it would be wrong to concentrate just on the line-of-battle ship. From medieval times onwards all navies had needed smaller, faster vessels for tasks for which larger warships were unsuited. Patrolling the seas against pirates was one of these tasks, as were reconnaissance and – particularly from the seventeenth century onwards – the defence of overseas colonies. These vessels were Fifth and Sixth Rates (or smaller). They were too small to survive in the line of battle, but were indispensable for any navy that aimed to be a credible fighting force. Such small warships had a variety of names over time, such as frigate, sloop or corvette, but a term often applied to them was that of cruiser, meaning a ship that cruised independently of the line of battle. Robert Gardiner has shown that cruisers never made up less than 40 per cent of the Royal Navy from at least the 1770s onwards, and were similarly prevalent in the French navy.

Fireships had proved their worth against the Armada in 1588, and they saw intermittent service in the navy until 1809. Purpose-built fireships were introduced in the seventeenth century, although these vessels often saw long service before being 'expended' in action. Out of nine *Tisiphone* Class fireships built in the 1780s, for example, only three ended their days by going up in smoke. The only truly new type of warship acquired by the navy in the age of sail was the 'bomb' or 'bomb vessel', which carried a large mortar and was used for shore bombardment. First developed by the French in 1685, the Royal Navy acquired its first bomb in 1687. By the mid-eighteenth century there were bomb vessels capable of firing a 193-lb (87.8 kg) shell a maximum distance of 2.3 miles (3.7 km). Bombs often had names related to fire in some way, such as the *Beelzebub* of 1813, perhaps the only serving Royal Navy vessel to be named after the Devil.

The navy also had many smaller types of warship and support vessel. One of these was the 10-gun brig *Beagle*, launched at Woolwich dockyard in 1820, which belonged to the most numerous class of sailing warships ever constructed. Converted into a survey ship in 1823, the *Beagle* was later the ship of Charles Darwin's epoch-making voyage. Other types included floating batteries, small gunboats, cutters, schooners and luggers. From the seventeenth century onwards, the navy used many purchased or hired merchant vessels, some as auxiliary warships (although few were powerful enough to serve in the line of battle after the mid-seventeenth century), but most as storeships or troop transports. Dockyards and other naval bases used considerable numbers of small craft for specialized purposes such as carrying water, ammunition or ballast.

Prize vessels were often an important element in English fleets, and the ships of the Royal Navy from the late seventeenth to the early nineteenth century included many ships of foreign origin (principally French). For example, the 'haul' during the French Revolutionary War of 1793–1802 included 143 First to Sixth Rates of French, Spanish, Dutch or Danish origin, plus about 180 smaller ships, including many French privateers.[19]

Naval gunnery techniques improved dramatically during the seventeenth and eighteenth centuries. The design of the standard naval cannon, a muzzle-loading

62 The quarterdeck of HMS *Queen Charlotte* during the bombardment of Algiers, 1816. The scene appears chaotic, but was probably fairly typical of the way gundecks looked during a battle. In fact, the gun crews are shown working their carronades with great concentration and discipline, and the wounded are being removed below deck with great speed. One of the sailors in the centre is of African origin, a sign of the multinational – and indeed multiracial – nature of Royal Navy crews at this time.

weapon on a four-wheeled truck carriage, did not change much over the period, but the firing rate of ships improved roughly sixfold, reaching a peak rate of about one shot per minute.

Aside from the seagoing mortar on the bomb vessel, the only other important naval weapon invented in the age of sail was the 'carronade', developed by the Carron Iron Company of Scotland in 1778. The carronade had a short barrel that could fire heavy shot over a short distance: the 32-pounder carronade, for example, had a maximum range of 1,087 yards (994 m), as opposed to the 2,900 yards (2,652 m) of the 32-pounder long gun. However, the chances of hitting anything intentionally at long range were small, and typical firing distances in battle were a few hundred yards or less. The carronade was widely used, but it was not a 'wonder weapon', as it could easily be outranged.

Despite developments in gunnery, boarding enemy ships remained a common tactic right up until the Napoleonic War, and warships always carried large amounts of small arms. Firearms became increasingly common over time, with the reliable flintlock pistol and musket being commonplace by the eighteenth century. Other hand weapons were also used, including the short naval boarding pike and a variety of swords, including cutlasses.[20]

The sea trade of Britain and Ireland, c.1600–c.1800

The slow change in the pattern and growth of English overseas trade accelerated considerably in the period between 1600 and the Civil War. The end of the Anglo-Spanish war in 1604 not only reopened many markets to English trade, it also left a lot of shipowners with large, armed merchantmen that had been built as privateers. Such ships were well suited to the dangers of long-distance trade and could carry sufficient goods to make such journeys worthwhile. London, ever the greatest port in the land, was at the centre of these changes, and by 1640 its sea trade had undergone an enormous structural shift. Between the early 1600s and 1640 the proportion of London's exports going to north-western Europe had fallen from over 90 per cent to 53 per cent. The other 47 per cent went to Iberia, the Atlantic islands, the Mediterranean and new markets such as the East Indies.

London, with its size, importance and wealth, was not a typical English port, for it was the home of the royal court, which demanded luxury. The city drew in luxury goods such as spices, silks, currants and tobacco, and the luxury trade was paid for by exporting bullion, but it did encourage the development of indigenous industry. London also grew as a centre for the re-export of imports, usually items from Asia or the American colonies, which went to the English provinces and, later, to other countries. The rise in these imports took place mainly between the mid- and late-seventeenth century. In 1640 re-exports made up about 6 per cent of the port's exports. By 1700 they constituted 38 per cent. The tonnage of shipping entering the port of London rose from just over 52,000 tons in 1600 to 254,000 by 1686, a near fivefold increase. The Navigation Acts of the mid-seventeenth century, which encouraged English shipping and excluded foreign vessels, served to 'anglicize' English sea trade as never before. In 1600 only about half of the shipping entering London was English; by the 1680s the proportion was over three-quarters.

Today the feeding of London is largely accomplished by the use of lorries. In the seventeenth century food supplies came in horse-drawn carts and in small cargo ships. London's continued growth meant that there was a ready market for foodstuffs and other goods shipped in the coastal trade from a host of smaller English ports. In 1724 Daniel Defoe shrewdly remarked that London 'sucks the vitals of trade in this island to itself'.

However, it was not just London or coastal shipping that benefited from the trade boom of the seventeenth century. A small number of regional centres also prospered, partly because of their geographical position and partly because of the general growth in trade. For example, Bristol's trade revived, particularly in the second half of the seventeenth century, due to the Newfoundland fish trade, sugar imports from the West Indies and, later, the slave trade. On the east coast, ports such as Newcastle and Hull, already prominent in the Baltic trade, grew as channels for local industrial or mineral exports. By the late 1690s annual Newcastle coal exports were at about 560,000 tons, four times the level of a century earlier. In the north-west, Liverpool rose from virtually nothing to become the region's

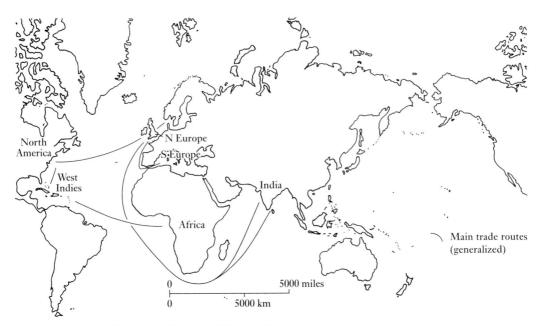

North America
N Europe
S Europe
West Indies
India
Africa

Main trade routes (generalized)

0   5000 miles
0   5000 km

63 The sea-trading net of Great Britain, *c.*1775.

leading port, based on the export of local cloth and (from the 1670s) salt. Like Bristol, the port also began to carve out a part of the slave trade. However, there were never more than ten or twelve of these regional giants. Most English ports of the period stayed small and poor.

The tonnage of the English merchant fleet grew five times between the 1580s and the 1680s, to 340,000 tons by 1686. Nearly half of this tonnage belonged to London, but some 56 per cent was owned in the non-metropolitan ports. London was also losing some trade to other places. In 1640, for example, London had 80 per cent of the tobacco trade; by the mid-1680s it had only about half, as provincial ports took an increasing share. London may still have been the biggest English seaport in 1700, but it was facing new rivals.

The Navigation Acts had a profound influence on the nature and development of English and later British trade in the seventeenth and eighteenth centuries. The first Navigation Act of 1651 expired in 1660 with the Restoration of Charles II, but it was reissued in a much more detailed form, much of which remained in force until the Act's repeal in 1849. The Act effectively restricted a large proportion of the trade with England, Wales and Ireland to the ships and crews of those countries, and it hit the activities of international traders like the Dutch (Scottish shipping was counted as foreign until after the Act of Union in 1707). Foreign ships and crews were again excluded from the coasting trade. Masters and at least three-quarters of the crews of English ships had to be English, a provision that was soon extended to cover seamen from the colonies.

From 1660 onwards prohibitive duties were laid on the export of coal from

England, the country's major bulk export in the seventeenth century. In the eighteenth century the use of British ships for the export of corn (the new bulk export) was encouraged by the payment of government bounties.

Nowadays there are concerns about international business corporations wielding political power. It is not a new problem. From its inception, the English East India Company (EIC) had a political and indeed military role. Dutch hostility in the Far East led the EIC to turn its attention to India. The Company established 'factories' (trading-posts) at Masulipatam (Coromandel coast, 1612) and Surat (Gujarat, western India, 1613), which gave it access to the western part of the Mogul Empire. Surat was an important trading and shipbuilding centre with links to the Persian Gulf, Red Sea and other parts of the East. The Portuguese, already established at Goa in India, attempted to drive the English out of Surat. They failed, and alienated the Mogul Emperor in the process. In

64 East Indiamen, late 17th/early 18th century, by Isaac Sailmaker. The red and white striped ensign identifies the vessels as belonging to the Honourable East India Company. East Indiamen were generally among the largest ships of the time.

1615 England sent its first ambassador to Persia, who worked to improve the EIC's position.

Although English relationships with the authorities in India and Persia were often not very good, the large, well-armed EIC vessels were able to achieve ascendancy over the Portuguese in the Indian Ocean. Only the Dutch could stand against them. The EIC had a policy of building large, defensible ships, known as 'East Indiamen', throughout its history. Out of seventy-six ships bought by the EIC between 1600 and 1640, forty-nine exceeded 300 tons, and in 1626 the Company declared that ships in the 300–700-ton range were the best for their purposes. From 1607 the EIC built its own ships, and acquired its own dockyards at Deptford and Blackwall for the purpose (Fig. 67).

The EIC did not have a satisfactory relationship with the English government until Cromwell virtually refounded it in 1657. Its activities in the first half of the seventeenth century were limited by war in the Far East and an intermittent lack of capital at home, although a new factory was established at Bombay in 1639 and in 1659 the Atlantic island of St Helena was acquired as a supply base.

British trade grew steadily in the eighteenth century. From the early 1700s to the 1780s, the ten-year average official values of imports, exports and re-exports rose about three times, to just over £30 million. In the 1790s the values rocketed to nearly £50 million, as the Industrial Revolution began to affect trade, pulling in ever greater amounts of raw materials and exporting more and more manufactured goods.

As in England, most sea trade in seventeenth- and eighteenth-century Scotland was centred on a handful of ports. These included Dundee and Leith on the east coast and Glasgow and Greenock on the west coast. Seventeenth-century Scotland's overseas trade was much smaller than that of England, but it ran along well-established routes, to France, the Low Countries, the Baltic and Scandinavia from the east coast ports, and to Ireland and France from the west coast. Scottish exports included fish, hides, wool and cloth; by the mid-seventeenth century, for example, the mainstay of Aberdeen's trade was plaiding (woollen cloth) and salmon, exported to Holland.

The Baltic provided Scotland with timber and 'naval stores', but it was also an important source of grain during major harvest crises (Ireland also fulfilled the same function). Scotland's economy remained essentially agricultural until the eighteenth century. It was only from the mid-seventeenth century, when the scale and reliability of Scotland's food production began to improve, leading to fewer terrible famines, that Scottish sea trade really began to develop.

The Scottish merchant communities were small but on the whole fairly enterprising and cohesive, facts that played a major part in the enormous growth of Scottish sea trade in the eighteenth century. Scots trade suffered some heavy blows during the wars of 1638–51 (Aberdeen, for example, was brutally sacked in 1644), but it managed to recover both from them and from the effects of English Commonwealth rule from 1652 to 1660. However, the Navigation Acts excluded Scottish shipping from legal trade with England and its colonies: Scottish merchants did not have the resources to break into transoceanic trade. Scotland's one major attempt to establish a colony, at Darien in Spanish territory on the Isthmus of Panama, was a total disaster. The colony of New Edinburgh was founded in 1698, but it soon collapsed through disease, lack of resources and deliberate English attempts to undermine the project (to avoid antagonizing Spain). Many of the colonists died and many in Scotland lost money. England became a convenient scapegoat for the failure of what had been, at best, a very risky venture.

Scotland and England had had an edgy and rather antagonistic relationship since the Union of the Crowns in 1603. The government of Queen Anne (r.1702–14) regularized the situation in 1707 by getting Scottish consent to the Act of Union. This made the two kingdoms part of the same country, Great Britain, and abolished the Scottish parliament. England's main motivation was to secure Scotland against Jacobite and French infiltration. One of the main benefits for the Scots was that it drew their country within the 'magic circle' of the Navigation Acts: Scots ships could now trade legally with the huge, lucrative and growing markets of the British Empire, what the historian T.M. Devine has strikingly described as 'the largest and richest common market in western Europe at the time'.

It took some decades for the benefits to manifest themselves, but the small, if well-educated and enterprising Scottish merchant community won out by being more agile, adept and aggressive than their competitors. Scotland's rise as a colonial trading nation became particularly focused on tobacco as an import, and cattle, fish and grain as exports. The victualling needs of the Royal Navy and the demands of London's ever-growing population provided ready markets for both Scots and Irish beef.

The Scottish capture of the British tobacco market was a great commercial achievement, although like many other aspects of British transatlantic trade in this period it was closely linked to the slave trade (p. 162). The tobacco trade was a game for a minority of rich players, known collectively as the 'tobacco lords'. However, the trade also pumped a good deal of money into indigenous Scottish industry, banking and agriculture. The tobacco lords lost a considerable amount of trade and money when America became independent in 1783, but such was the organization and cohesiveness of the Scottish merchant community that relatively few companies went to the wall, and they soon set about exploiting new markets in regions such as the West Indies.

Scotland's economy became closely linked to that of eighteenth-century England, but it was never overwhelmed by it. When Scotland was incorporated into Great Britain, it had already had a long history as a separate nation with a centralized government. Neither Wales nor Ireland had ever been unitary kingdoms before their conquest by the English, and this difference was to prove critical for their futures.

In Ireland the seventeenth century was characterized by a growing dependence on trade with England. Irish cattle, butter and wool became significant exports across the Irish Sea. Ireland became, in effect, an English colony dominated by Protestant landowners. Following on from the mid-seventeenth century, when land and wealth were expropriated from Catholic Irish people on a grand scale, legal and other measures were taken to decrease the wealth and power of the surviving Catholic aristocracy and gentry, to keep Catholics out of the professions, and to undermine the Roman Catholic Church (these measures were only gradually relaxed or repealed in the later eighteenth and nineteenth centuries). As is well known, military defeat and religious discrimination drove many Irishmen abroad to serve in the armies of France, Spain and other foreign powers – men described from at least the 1720s as the 'wild geese' – but substantial numbers of Irish seamen also served in foreign navies. Irish shipping was also deliberately excluded from direct trade with the English colonies under the Navigation Acts, and other moves were made to clamp down on Irish trade to prevent it from competing with that of England (for example, in 1699 it was made illegal to export Irish woollen goods abroad because it was competing successfully with English wool). However, some Irish trades began to grow rapidly. Irish linen, produced mainly in Ulster, conquered the huge British linen market in the eighteenth century, after import restrictions had been removed in 1696 and 1705. English prohibitions on Irish cattle, beef and butter imports were suspended in the 1750s, leading to considerable growth in the Irish provision trade, with the ports of Cork and Waterford in particular benefiting from the great appetite for beef of London and the Royal Navy. In 1779 trade with British colonies was finally made completely open to Irish shipping.

The downside of all this growth was that Irish trade became more and more dependent on England. England, as a nearby mass-market, had always been Ireland's primary trading partner, but the reorientation of Irish trade in the eighteenth century was more than just the result of geography and population. In 1700 about 45 per cent of the Irish export trade had gone to England, and about 55 per cent of Irish imports had come from there; by 1800 the respective figures were about 85 per cent and nearly 80 per cent.

The total tonnage of the Irish merchant shipping trading in Irish ports increased nearly threefold in the eighteenth century, from nearly 32,000 tons to almost 93,000, but the rate of increase of British-registered shipping was more than sixfold, to just over 502,000 tons. In proportional terms, the amount of Irish shipping operating in Irish trade was nearly halved in the eighteenth century. The Irish merchant fleet reached its peak in 1791 with 1,176 ships totalling 69,231 registered tons and 6,638 sailors, but most were coasters or fishing vessels. In 1789 there were only sixteen Irish vessels of more than 200 tons, nearly all of them based in Dublin or Cork. Coupled with higher interest rates and probably higher operating costs, there was not a great incentive to invest in shipping in Ireland or to develop significant related industries such as shipbuilding. Only a handful of Irish businesses undertook marine insurance and Irish shippers tended to rely on London for this service.[21]

The development of ports, *c*.1600–*c*.1800

The rising trade of the seventeenth and eighteenth centuries brought prosperity for a minority, but it strained the cargo-handling and storage resources of many ports and led to overcrowded quays, rivers and roadsteads: the first 'traffic jams' in British history. There was also a growing trend, evident in England, Wales, Scotland and Ireland, for the bulk of trade to become concentrated in a small number of ports. In England the picture was skewed by the dominance of London, but the period also saw the growing ability of a limited number of other English and Scottish ports to compete with the capital in certain trades. Glasgow, for example, became the largest tobacco importer in the eighteenth-century British Isles.

The late seventeenth and eighteenth centuries also saw the start of major harbour improvement schemes in many places. Merchants, landowners and others were keenly aware of the profits to be derived from a good harbour; conversely, they feared the 'decay of trade', as ships moved to more accessible ports. The improvement schemes took different forms, depending on local geography and the problems that it brought. At Exeter, a new cut was made by the river Exe in the 1690s to enable seagoing vessels to reach the city. At Littlehampton, in West Sussex, the wandering mouth of the river Arun was recut in the 1730s and successfully fixed in place by two wooden piers. Coupled with dredging and other works, this improved access to the main port on the river, at Arundel; ironically it also served to turn Littlehampton into a trade rival that overtook Arundel by the early 1800s. In other places, new or extended stone piers were built to turn a bay or open stretch of coast into a viable small port, such as Ilfracombe and many other places in Devon, Cornwall and Scotland. 'Harbours of refuge' were also constructed to allow shipping to shelter in bad weather, particularly on the exposed and dangerous east coast of England, that had relatively few harbours. This helped to lead to major works at Whitby, Scarborough, Ramsgate and elsewhere. Such works were generally authorized by Acts of Parliament, which created local harbour authorities empowered to fund construction and maintenance work from local tolls on shipping. Similarly funded developments took place at Lancaster (1750) and its new outport Glasson Dock (1780), but they were to be found in many parts of Britain. For example, besides Arundel, the Sussex ports of Rye, Newhaven and Shoreham all underwent redevelopment authorized by Parliamentary Acts between the 1720s and 1820s. In Scotland support for some harbour developments was provided by the Scottish Fisheries Board.

In other places, such as Whitehaven, Workington and Maryport on the Cumberland coast, local industrialist landowners took the initiative to develop ports in the seventeenth and eighteenth centuries. The coalmine-owning Lowthers were behind developments at Whitehaven between the 1630s and early 1800s, and the Senhouse family actually founded the town and port of Maryport in 1748/9.

In major ports the only long-term solution to overcrowding was to create dock systems. Such docks had to have gates, sluices and other equipment to keep ships within the dock afloat at the same level, whatever the state of the tide outside. Such

65 The Dublin Customs House, completed 1791. Despite opposition from Dublin merchants, James Gandon's massive, elegant building helped to shift the centre of economic activity in Dublin downriver to the east. Its scale and grandeur underlined the fact that, in the 18th century, Dublin was the second-largest city in the British Isles after London.

ideas were not new (a dock of this type was built for royal warships at Deptford in 1517), but their use for general trade was a novelty. The Howland Great Wet Dock at Rotherhithe on the Thames (completed 1700) was the first large commercial dock in Britain, but it was mainly used to repair and refit ships. Perhaps too far from the city to be a useful trading dock, it was leased for use by whalers in 1725 and eventually renamed the Greenland Dock.

Docks were very expensive, and ports only built them when they absolutely had to. The congestion on the Thames did not get bad enough to require docks until the late eighteenth century, but Liverpool, on the Mersey, was encountering problems by the early 1700s. The port lacked proper harbour facilities but had a good deal of space on land. To retain and develop the port's trade, docks were built, and Liverpool became the first port in Britain to combine a dock with its Legal Quays. The first dock was small (4 acres / 9.9 hectares), but fifteen more docks and basins were built at Liverpool over the next 120 years. The first large (9 acres / 22.2 hectares) commercial dock in the country was constructed at Hull in the late 1770s, and Hull also became the first port to create a dock company to run the enterprise. Docks followed in other places, such as Dublin (1790s) and Bristol (early 1800s), but in the end the greatest dock system to be created was that of London (see pp 215–17).

There were just over a hundred ports engaged in (legal) foreign trade in late eighteenth-century England, Scotland and Wales, but most of this trade was concentrated in fewer than one-fifth of them, such as London, Newcastle, Hull, Bristol and Liverpool in England, Swansea in Wales, and Leith and Glasgow in Scotland. In 1772, for example, out of about 325,000 tons of English foreign trade shipping, nearly 90 per cent was owned in ten major ports. In 1790, when the 35-mile Forth and Clyde Canal was completed, linking the east and west coasts of Scotland, 46 per cent of Scots tonnage was owned by ports on this axis: Glasgow, Greenock and Port Glasgow in the west, and Leith and Bo'ness in the east. Beyond the giant British ports and the middling harbours were hundreds of smaller havens engaged in coastal trade, fishing and smuggling.

Growing Irish dependence on English trade in the seventeenth century especially favoured Dublin, Cork and Belfast (see pp 158–9). Cork grew from a town of no more than 12,000 people in the 1670s to about 50,000 one hundred years later, largely on the basis of processing and exporting butter, meat, hides and tallow. As in Britain, the bulk of Irish Sea trade came to be centred on a handful of major ports. After Dublin, there were five other really significant Irish ports by the mid-eighteenth century, and these were (in order of importance), Cork, Belfast, Waterford, Drogheda and Dundalk. Despite the physical limitations of its harbour, Dublin was far and away Ireland's greatest port, a position in some ways analogous to that of London in Britain. Dublin rose to be the second city in the British Isles, the seat of the Irish parliament and administration, and (as aptly put by David Dickson) 'the national warehouse', with a population of nearly a quarter of a million by the 1820s. James Gandon's massive new Customs House (completed in 1791) reflected Dublin's pre-eminence both as a port and city. Built on reclaimed land on the north-eastern side of the city, away from the old customs house site, it also helped to shift the axis of Dublin's building redevelopment to the east. (Fig. 65)[22]

The slave trade

One consequence of the growth of English maritime trade in the second half of the seventeenth century was the growth of the English slave trade. The slave trade was one of the cruellest aspects of the European maritime imperialism and its story retains an enormous capacity to generate anger. Apart from John Hawkins' slaving voyages in the 1560s, the English were late arrivals in the trade, behind the Spanish, Portuguese and Dutch, but this was due to lack of opportunity rather than to any moral qualms. Britain became the most successful slave-trading nation in the world, and it is reckoned that between 1662 and 1807, when the trade was abolished, just over 3.4 million slaves were carried from West Africa to the Americas in ships belonging to Britain and her colonies. This was as many as all of the other European slave-trading nations put together.

For most of its history the slave trade functioned as a normal part of trans-oceanic trade, and until the latter part of the eighteenth century most British people regarded it in this way. Slaving was part of the infamous 'triangular trade', in which goods were carried from Britain to West Africa and exchanged there for slaves. The slaves were then taken to the American mainland or the Caribbean, where they were sold and the money was used to purchase colonial goods, such as tobacco, sugar and cotton, which were in heavy demand at home. Although slave trading carried considerable risks for investors, it offered, and often delivered,

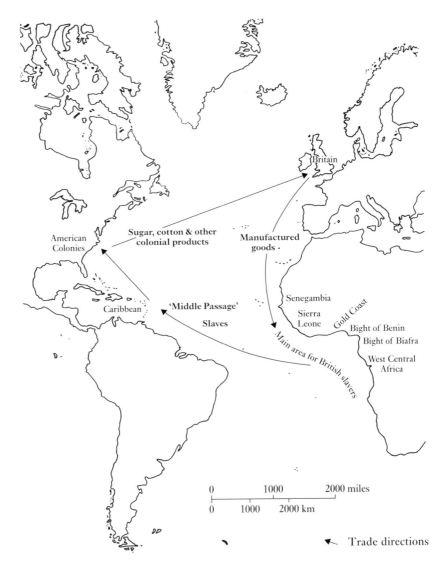

66 Map of the British slave trade, 1662–1807.

Britain

American Colonies

Sugar, cotton & other colonial products

Manufactured goods ·

Senegambia

Sierra Leone

Gold Coast

Bight of Benin

Bight of Biafra

West Central Africa

Caribbean

'Middle Passage'

Slaves

Main area for British slavers

0   1000   2000 miles

0   1000   2000 km

Trade directions

great profits. It has been estimated that between the 1750s and 1807, the profits of the British slave trade ran at an average of between 8 per cent and 10 per cent per year.

Slave-trading firms were normally formed by partnerships of merchants, sometimes as many as twelve or more in the biggest ports, although in smaller places such as Lancaster partnerships seldom numbered more than six or eight. The partnerships fitted-out the ships, crewed them and filled them with trade goods for Africa. The customers for these trade goods were mainly African merchants and rulers, for although transatlantic slave trading was run by Europeans, it could not have continued anywhere near as successfully as it did without the participation of local élites on the slaving coast, which ran from modern Senegal southwards to what is now Angola. The goods traded included cloth, knives and other weapons, gunpowder, spirits, tallow and even imports from the Far East, such as precious cloths, which were re-exported from Britain.

Slave ships came in many different forms, from craft as small as 20 tons to ships of several hundred tons. They were ordinary merchant vessels converted to carry slaves below decks, but usually carried much larger crews than would be needed with inanimate cargoes, in order to guard the slaves and also to offset the effects of disease among the sailors on the notoriously unhealthy West African coast. A 70-ton Lancaster ship was crewed by twenty men on five slaving voyages in the 1750s, but needed only thirteen on a direct voyage to Barbados in 1765. As a famous contemporary rhyme about the Bight of Benin put it:

> *Beware and take care of the Bight of Benin*
> *Of the one that comes out there are forty go in.*

Slave ships were notoriously overcrowded, as merchants and captains sought to pack as much potential human capital aboard as they could. Although this was recognized as potentially self-defeating – overcrowding caused more death and disease amongst the slaves and so reduced the eventual profit – it was still widely practised. The 100-ton *Cato* of Lancaster, for example, was reckoned to be able to carry 250 slaves, but in 1760 it landed 360 slaves in Jamaica, and the following year put 560 ashore in Barbados. Surgeons were not uncommon aboard slave ships to minister to the health of the crew and slaves, but any care for the slaves was strictly based on the need to maintain merchandise rather than any humanitarian consideration. That said, it is unlikely that even conscientious doctors could have done much to improve the health of slaves, given the prevailing conditions of packed holds, brutality, poor food and water, and unfamiliar tropical diseases.

The death rates aboard slave ships were very high. Between 1662 and 1807 about 450,000 slaves died aboard British ships in the Middle Passage between Africa and America, or just over 13 per cent of those taken from Africa. Out of 452 slaves shipped aboard the *Daniel and Henry* of Exeter in 1700, for example, 206 died. Later measures to reduce overcrowding lessened the death rate somewhat, but few slave ships crossed the Atlantic without fatalities.

The English slave trade was in the hands of successive monopoly companies from 1660 to 1698, but activity by individual 'interlopers' seems to have been considerable, to the extent that in the 1680s the Royal African Company began selling licences to private slavers. Government involvement was finally abandoned in 1712, and this rawest and roughest kind of trade was left entirely to the free market.

As with other forms of commerce, the level of activity in the slave trade rose and fell over the years. There were three major phases of expansion, from about 1650 to 1683, 1708 to 1725 and 1746 to 1771. These were interspersed with smaller rises and some major reductions in the amount of trading, usually caused by war. The trade was at its peak in the 1760s, when some 424,000 people were enslaved and transported.

London was the leading English slave-trading port in the early phases of the trade, as it was the largest and wealthiest port in England, and the home of the monopoly companies. Between 1699 and 1709, nearly 80 per cent of all English slaving voyages originated in London. However, two other English ports also became major centres of slave-trading activity. The first was Bristol, which in the 1730s briefly overtook London in terms of the number of its slave-ship sailings, but the lead was taken in the 1740s by Liverpool, which from about 1750 to 1807 was the main slave-trading port in the British Isles (in the 1790s, nearly three-quarters of all British slaving voyages left from this one port). The reasons for Liverpool's ascendancy are still not completely clear, although they may have been related to lower crew wage-rates in the north-west, comparative safety from wartime privateering and the proximity of the cloth trade, which produced goods that could be exported to Africa. That said, capital supplied by London merchants remained an important factor in the trade throughout its history.

The 'big three' ports were responsible for just under 92 per cent of the 11,615 slave-ship sailings from the British Isles between 1699 and 1807, but merchants and mariners in many ports around the British Isles took part in the slave trade at one time or another. The fourth-largest slaving port was Lancaster, from which over 150 slaving voyages departed between 1748 and the mid-1770s. Lancaster slave ships were typically smaller than those from the larger ports: the pockets of local investors were not as deep as those of their big-city counterparts. Smaller ships represented a reduced risk, were cheaper to crew and to fit out, and were able to enter shallower waters and rivers on the West African coast than larger vessels. Lancaster was largely knocked out of the slave trade after the 1775–83 American war, due in part to competition from Liverpool and in part to local merchants finding new markets. The local slave trade, while it lasted, made some Lancaster people rich and had an impact on the local economy. In 1774, for example, farms in the nearby Furness district were said to be growing beans to be used to feed slaves aboard ship. Exotic goods from the Americas came back to Lancaster as a result of the slave trade; the local cabinetmakers, Gillow's, made elegant furniture from American mahogany which had been bought using the profits from selling slaves.

Other ports also took part in the trade at different times, such as Deal in Kent, Poole, Weymouth and Lyme Regis in Dorset, Dartmouth, Exeter, Plymouth and Barnstaple in Devon, Falmouth in Cornwall and Whitehaven in Cumberland. Elsewhere in the British Isles, Glasgow was involved in slaving, as were some Irish ports, such as Dublin and Limerick.

Few of the Anglican or Nonconformist merchants engaged in the slave trade saw anything wrong with it. In religious terms it could be justified on the basis of making it possible to convert pagan Africans to Christianity, although other justifications were used, such as the specious claim that it helped Africa by relieving it of surplus population. It was, however, the Christian consciences of people such as the Member of Parliament William Wilberforce (1759–1833) that led to the long and ultimately successful campaign against the slave trade and slavery. It took Wilberforce nineteen years to secure the passage of a bill outlawing the slave trade in the British Empire, in one of the first great human rights campaigns in British history. The trade remained profitable to the end, and powerful vested interests in the City of London and Parliament worked against Wilberforce and his supporters. Slave trading was abolished in the British Empire from January 1808, although the institution of slavery itself survived in British colonies until 1834. The Royal Navy was subsequently used in attempts to suppress slave trading in the Atlantic and Indian Oceans.

The Africans who survived the Middle Passage had little to look forward to but a life of slavery and a probable early death. One of the reasons for the vitality of the slave trade was the fact that slave parents in the West Indies did not produce enough children to replace them, leading to a continuing demand for fresh slaves from Africa. This also helped to keep the British trade going for more than twenty years after the War of Independence largely closed the American markets to British slavers. The Africans, torn from their traditional societies and dumped in alien and hostile environments, could have succumbed to these dehumanizing circumstances. Some did, but both in America and in the Caribbean the slaves succeeded, against the odds, in creating their own new cultures, incorporating both African and European elements. As the historian Philip D. Morgan has put it: 'drawing upon some shared principles and passing through the fires of enslavement, blacks everywhere forged a new culture'.

The large-scale shipment of cheap labour in British ships did not stop with the slave trade. In the late nineteenth century Chinese 'coolie labourers', although nominally free and paid meagre wages, were shipped in bad conditions and in very large numbers to parts of the British Empire in Asia, the Pacific and elsewhere. Even as late as 1918, some 100,000 Chinese labourers were to be found working for the British army in France.[23]

Piracy and privateering

Writing in his discourse *Of the Beginnings, Practices and Suppression of Pirates* of about 1616, the naval officer and pardoned former pirate, Sir Henry Mainwaring, gave his own opinion of why ordinary sailors turned to piracy: 'the common sort of seamen are so generally necessitous and discontented'.[24]

Called by David Cordingly 'the great age of piracy',[25] the period from the 1650s to the 1720s spawned some famous pirate figures. These included Sir Henry Morgan (*c.*1635–88), Captain William Kidd (*c.*1645–1701) and Edward Teach, alias 'Blackbeard' (d. 1718), on whom the character of Long John Silver in Robert Louis Stevenson's *Treasure Island* (1883) was based. *Treasure Island* drew on a lurid publication of the 1720s entitled *The General History of the Robberies and Murders of the Most Notorious Pyrates*, written by an otherwise unknown 'Captain Johnson' (a theory that he was Daniel Defoe is now thought to have little foundation). Thanks to Stevenson, and perhaps Johnson also, the tricorn-hatted pirate, with or without wooden leg and parrot, became a stock figure in fiction, film and humour.

Direct analysis of the motives that drove most men to be pirates is not possible because of lack of evidence. However, it seems likely that the main factors were poverty and discontent, as laid out by Mainwaring, coupled with greed. It was becoming less easy to be a pirate in European waters by the second half of the seventeenth century. Growing state power and the greater size and efficiency of state navies made it a much more difficult proposition, at least in northern Europe. The geographical focus of European piracy shifted out into the Atlantic, to the coast of Africa and to the Caribbean. English and other European pirates had operated in the region in the sixteenth century, and in the seventeenth century they acquired a new name, 'buccaneer', which derived originally from *boucaniers*, illegal French hunters on Hispaniola.

Limited control by European governments in the region made it possible for pirate ports to develop. For example, the English took Jamaica from the Spanish in 1655. The town of Port Royal was established there, and between 1657 and 1680 became the base for numerous pirates, encouraged by corrupt local governors and decidedly lax interpretations of the meaning of privateering. The chief victims of English piracy in the region were the Spanish, as Spain was the main imperial power: during the twenty and more years of Port Royal's time as a pirate base many Spanish ships and settlements were attacked, including twenty-two major towns. Ironically, the piracy operating from Port Royal was suppressed by Sir Henry Morgan, a former pirate who had gained immense wealth from his activities and had bought himself a sort of respectability. Perhaps the closest modern parallels to people like Morgan are South American drugs barons; equivalent to him in violence and ruthlessness, even drug lords do not sack entire cities, which is what Morgan did in 1671 when he led an assault on the great Spanish treasure port of Panama, terrorizing, raping and killing many of its citizens. Morgan burnt the city to the ground, but the raid yielded little in the way of booty. This happened when England and Spain were at peace; Morgan was recalled to England to appease the Spanish but never prosecuted, and from 1674 to 1682 he served as lieutenant-governor of Jamaica.

Morgan operated on the grand scale, but there were many 'little Morgans' in the region who were just as brutal and just as unconstrained by conscience. Piracy has acquired a false glamour, thanks in part to *Treasure Island*, but the reality was often squalid and vicious. However, one of the attractions of the pirate's life was that it was much freer than that to be found in the warships or merchantmen of any nation of the period. Pirate ships were typically run on democratic lines, with major decisions taken in common and crew agreements that set standards of shipboard behaviour. On some ships, at least, these agreements decreed fair shares of booty, and outlawed gambling and bringing boys or women aboard. The clear intention behind such rules was clearly to avoid violent quarrels that could split a ship's company. If, in the contemporary phrase, the pirate was 'the enemy of human kind', the pirate at least knew that he had to be able to rely on his shipmates. The only equivalents to such shipborne democracies in the seventeenth or eighteenth centuries were short-lived millenarian communities such as appeared during the English Revolution. However, pirate democracies were based upon plunder, and concepts of fair dealing usually stopped short when it came to their victims.

As pointed out by Cordingly, the 1536 Act that had first outlawed piracy became out of date in the seventeenth century. The Act called for pirates to be tried before the Lord High Admiral and common law judges in London, something feasible when the men were apprehended in English waters, but utterly useless if the pirates were operating thousands of miles away. An Act of 1700 made it legal for vice-admiralty courts (local maritime courts which existed both in England and its overseas territories) to try to execute pirates. When the British government finally determined on the suppression of piracy, it first tried issuing royal pardons in 1717 to any pirates who would give themselves up, which had some effect in North America and the Caribbean. Rewards were then offered for the capture of any remaining pirates, and the Royal Navy was sent to hunt them off Africa and in the Spanish Main. The campaign was successful. Even the fearsome Blackbeard ended up with his head dangling from the bowsprit of a naval vessel. By the mid-1720s most pirates had been captured and many had gone to the gallows.

European piracy survived until the early nineteenth century, although on a much reduced scale as more and more of the sea came under the control of centralized states. The Royal Navy and other European navies took part in the suppression of North African piracy with the bombardment of Algiers in 1816, and later suppressed much of the piracy rampant in the South China Sea and other parts of the Far East.

However, piracy has not gone away. Since 1984 the International Maritime Organization of the United Nations has logged over 2,500 instances of piracy, mainly in the Far East, Africa and South America. Most of this is in the form of straightforward robbery from ships in harbour, but it often involves the use of violence and the victims have included British seafarers and ships. Modern piracy, like its ancient counterpart, is generally conducted for gain, but some attacks have had political motives. The pirate is still with us.[26]

Shipbuilding and the development of the merchant ship, c.1620–c.1800

In the 1620s the typical English merchant ship was large, well armed and carried a considerable number of crew. It was a type well suited to the dangers of long-distance trade, but it was costly to run and not such a good proposition on shorter routes across the Channel, the North Sea and to the Baltic.

The Dutch by the early 1600s possessed a type of ship called a *fluit*, known to the English as a 'flyboat'. Modern container ships are sometimes criticized for their graceless design, but in essence an efficient cargo vessel is a floating box designed to carry as many boxes or other containers as possible. The flyboat was such a ship, with a rounded, flat-bottomed hull that maximized cargo stowage. The type also carried relatively little sail and few guns, so needed fewer men per ton than contemporary English ships. English merchants and pamphleteers of the seventeenth century were keenly aware of the advantages of Dutch ships, and frequently complained about it. Despite the moans of merchants and shippers, English shipyards did little or nothing to change their practices and to produce bulk-carriers similar to the Dutch types. Concentrated in the London area and earning a reasonable living from the long-distance trades, they had little incentive

67 *East Indiaman off Deptford* by Isaac Sailmaker, 1721. The slipways, buildings and general clutter were typical of many wooden shipyards over the centuries.

to change. The industry was to suffer for its conservatism and complacency.

Although the wars between the 1650s and the 1690s saw the capture of many English merchant ships, the English also captured many foreign ships. In terms of numbers the balance may have been about even, with about 2,400 foreign ships taken in the Dutch and Spanish wars between 1652 and 1674, and between 1,500 and 2,300 English ships lost. The foreign vessels captured included many Dutch flyboats, which were taken up by English shipowners and proved to be a good deal cheaper to sail than traditional English types. It has been estimated that by 1675 as much as half the English merchant marine may have been foreign-built. Orders for new ships fell; the London shipyards survived, but the Act to Encourage the Building of Ships in England of 1685 named nine provincial ports in which there 'hath been observed a more than ordinary decay in building ships'. Two were in the north – Newcastle and Hull – but the other seven were in Essex, Suffolk or Norfolk, and included the former shipbuilding centre of Ipswich. By the 1680s and the 1690s, when most of the prize ships of the earlier wars would have been wearing out, English shipyards were building their own versions of flyboats.

The north-eastern yards took over the bulk of the shipbuilding trade from the East Anglian yards. Although London was still the largest single shipbuilding port in the late eighteenth century, the north-eastern ports, from Hull to Newcastle, made up the biggest shipbuilding region. Between 1787 and 1799, London constructed 576 vessels totalling 129,557 tons, but Hull, Whitby, Sunderland and Newcastle between them built 1,429 ships totalling 261,664 tons. By this stage Liverpool had also emerged as a major shipbuilding port (322 ships, 48,955 tons). The Thames shipbuilders retained the monopoly of building East Indiamen, and large ships for the Levant trade (and some for the West Indies trade) were still built on the Thames, but most of the construction of large bulk traders transferred to the north-east.

The rise of Whitby as a shipbuilding centre was phenomenal: by the late eighteenth century the average size of Whitby-built ships, 246 tons, was the largest in England, 20–25 tons greater than its nearest rivals. Whitby harbour had been enlarged and improved in the early decades of the eighteenth century, making it possible to build very large ships (Cook's *Endeavour* of 1768 had been built at Whitby as a 369-ton collier), and the port acquired its first dry dock in 1734. The port was very important in the north-eastern coal trade, and in traffic with Norway and the Baltic, with a fleet of 120 ships in 1733, most of them colliers.

There were only two shipwrights' guilds in seventeenth- and eighteenth-century England, one at London and the other at Newcastle. As with other guilds, they regulated wage rates, standards of work, entry to the trade and other matters. The Newcastle guild fought occasional battles to maintain its supremacy in the seventeenth century, and reached a peak of about two hundred members in the early 1700s. However, as the north-east's shipbuilding trade expanded, it gradually lost its ability to restrict local shipbuilding to the Tyne or to control what went on there. Perhaps because of this, Tyne shipbuilding began to develop as never before, and by the 1780s there were also six yards operating on the Wear.[27]

The English shipbuilding industry started to get competition from an unusual quarter in the seventeenth and eighteenth centuries. England's American colonies came within the orbit of the Navigation Acts, so that American-built ships legally qualified as English. Timber and other shipbuilding materials were abundant in America and the colonies began to develop their own merchant marine. It is reckoned that about half of the 'English' ships trading between England and English America by the 1680s were owned by colonists. During the wars of 1689 to 1713 American yards began to pick up more and more orders from English owners, probably because the cheaper American materials meant cheaper ships than could be purchased in England. Although London shipwrights complained loudly about American competition in 1724, the proportion of the British merchant marine built in America grew steadily in the eighteenth century. It has been estimated that by 1760 about one British merchantman in four was American-built (a proportion said to have risen to one in three by the 1770s). The loss of the American colonies in the War of Independence may have been a bitter blow to British power and prestige, but it was good news for the British shipbuilding industry, removing a potent and dangerous competitor from the protective ring of the Navigation Acts.

The wars of the eighteenth century brought considerable numbers of merchant-men as prizes. Between 1702 and 1713, 2,203 ships were captured. A total of 1,499 ships were taken between 1739 and 1748, and the Seven Years War yielded 1,855 prizes. While perhaps not as devastating to the native shipbuilding industry as the Dutch Wars, these prizes must have depressed demand for British-built ships.

It is apparent that between the late seventeenth and mid-eighteenth centuries British ships in most trades became very much more efficient in terms of their manning, which appears to have been due to major technical improvements (although Davis remarked that not enough research had been done on merchant ships of the period to make it clear). This shows up in the average numbers of tons of ship per mariner, which rose considerably in most trades. On most routes to

● Major shipbuilding ports (in order of output)

Shipbuilding regions
No. of ships built *Total tonnage*

North-east coast
249 *40926*

Newcastle 2
Sunderland 7

Whitby 3

Whitehaven 8

North-west coast
116 *14945* Hull 4

Liverpool 5

East Anglia
136 *7787*

Gt Yarmouth 6

London 1
119 *16732*

Bristol 9

Bristol Channel and Wales
145 *8240*

South coast
341 *15740*

0   100   200 miles

0   100   200 km

north-western Europe average British crew sizes dropped by between 20 per cent and 30 per cent, whilst on the southerly or transatlantic voyages the drop was between 30 per cent and 40 per cent. Fewer men aboard meant less of a wage bill, and this made it possible to drop freight rates. The effect that these changes may have had on working conditions for sailors is quite another matter; no matter what technical changes were introduced, the eighteenth-century sailing ship was still a machine that was worked by muscle-power.

As the volume of international trade grew towards the mid-eighteenth century, there were more opportunities for using larger ships as there was much less danger of a ship sailing without a full cargo. Larger ships were also becoming cheaper to run than smaller ones as their manning rates were lower. In the 1760s a merchant ship of, say, 250 tons sailing to St Petersburg and the eastern Baltic needed only a crew of eleven or twelve (one man per 21.9 tons on average). A contemporary vessel of 125 tons on the same route needed about nine crewmen (one man per 13.3 tons). The wages and feeding costs of a sailor in the larger ship could be used to shift about 65 per cent more cargo than the equivalent costs for a man in a smaller vessel.

The development of bluff-bowed, full-bodied hulls with flat bottoms, originating it would seem with the old Dutch flyboats, revolutionized carrying capacity in those trades where speed was not an issue. One type built by the English in the eighteenth century was the 'cat', which in itself derived from a Dutch type the '*Katschip*', which was similar to the *fluit*. Cats were three-masted bark-rigged vessels, and Cook's *Endeavour* of 1768 was defined as a cat-bark. Ralph Davis suggested that the development of new sails, such as jib and staysails, improved the windward handling capacities of vessels, and at the same time made it possible to reduce crews by breaking the sail-plan down into smaller units. Voyages were made faster and safer.

Crew reductions were also made possible by the increasing size of two-masted vessels. Between 1680 and 1720, the dividing line between two- and three-masted ships generally lay between 50 and 60 tons. By the 1730s it was around 80 to 90 tons, and by the 1760s it was between 140 and 150 tons. Two-masters were usually called brigs or snows in the eighteenth century: brigs were generally coastal and North Sea vessels, while snows appeared more often on transoceanic routes. By eliminating the third mast, crew size could be reduced. The change may well have been led by the shipbuilders of the north-east, and by the late eighteenth century the practice of differentiating ships by rig was growing. By the 1770s all ships over 300 tons and most over 200 tons were three-masted, although by this time a distinction was being made between 'ship-rigged' three-masters with a square sail on every mast (plus a lateen or gaff on the mizzen) and 'barques' which had no square sail on the mizzen. After the mid-eighteenth century the size of merchant ships began to increase again: although great ships of 400 tons plus were generally confined to the East India, Baltic and Russian trades, vessels of 300–400 tons were common on the transatlantic routes. In the 1770s vessels in the 200–350-ton range were the mainstays of the transatlantic, Baltic, Norway and coal trades.

London was still far and away the largest port in the kingdom and led the way when it came to large ships. In 1788 200 ships of 360 tons or more were registered in London. However, most ships were of much smaller size. In 1788 there were 9,355 ships registered in English ports, and of these, 7,756 (83 per cent) were of less than 200 tons. There were many coastal or short-range international trades that could only be worked economically by smaller ships, and many ports, beaches and estuaries into which the giant trading ships could not fit. Two-masters predominated among these smaller types, and smaller sea-going ships were produced all around the coast.[28]

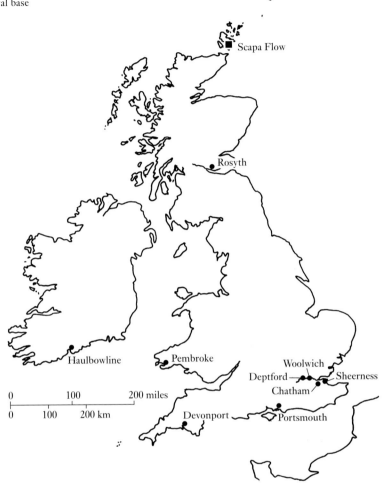

69 Royal dockyards in the British Isles, 1689–1914.

● Dockyard
■ Other naval base

The royal dockyards and shipbuilding for the Royal Navy, 1689–1815

The royal dockyards developed considerably in the seventeenth and eighteenth centuries. To the existing yards of Deptford, Woolwich, Chatham and Plymouth were added Harwich in Essex (seventeenth century), Sheerness, at the mouth of the Medway, in Kent (early 1670s) and Plymouth Dock (1690). Harwich's position on the east coast meant that it achieved some importance in the Dutch Wars, but its use declined thereafter and it was closed by the end of the seventeenth century. Sheerness closed in 1960. Plymouth Dock, renamed Devonport in 1823, is still one of the navy's principal bases.

Chatham was the principal naval base in the seventeenth century, but the south coast dockyards of Portsmouth and Plymouth became more significant in the

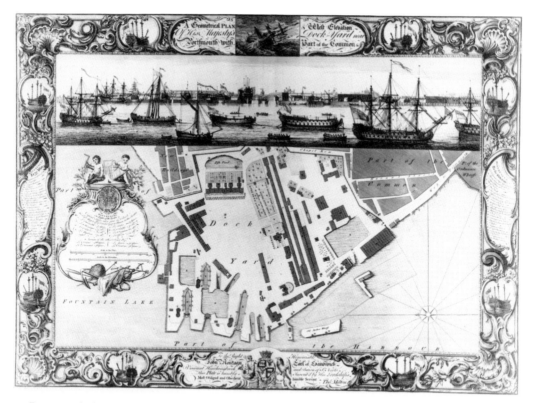

70 Portsmouth dockyard, plan and view by T. Milton, 1754. Dockyards were the largest and most complex industrial sites in the 18th-century world.

eighteenth century because of the threat from France. Plymouth had been used by the navy before as a port of call and supply base, but in 1689 the Assistant Surveyor of the navy, Edmund Dummer, recommended that a new dockyard should be sited there. Construction began in 1692, and by 1700 the dockyard had a large wet dock and dry dock, as well as a ropery and a comprehensive range of storehouses and workshops. This huge and difficult building programme cost over £67,000. It was, proportionately, the largest single investment that the English government had ever made in the west of England.

As the navy's commitments grew in the eighteenth century, new base facilities were opened in the West Indies (Jamaica and Antigua), Canada (Halifax, Nova Scotia) and the Mediterranean (Gibraltar and Port Mahon, Minorca). In the early nineteenth century dockyards were also built in Malta (then newly-conquered), Bermuda, and Pembroke in west Wales. By 1815 the Royal Navy had the largest network of naval bases in world history.

Besides docks (both wet and dry docks, although not all yards were big enough to have dry docks), dockyards typically contained storehouses for ships' gear, building slips for the construction of vessels, roperies for manufacturing cordage, other workshops such as smithies, and accommodation for dockyard officers.

Major dockyards were run by commissioners, although smaller concerns were often the responsibility of a master shipwright. The major dockyards were the greatest industrial concerns anywhere in the eighteenth-century world. The numbers of men employed at Portsmouth, for example, seldom fell below 1,000, and in 1718 reached a peak of 1,750. The yards employed a great range of trades, including shipwrights, caulkers, house carpenters, joiners, sailmakers, ropemakers, riggers and others.

Steam power was first introduced into the royal dockyards in 1799, when a steam engine was installed to work some pumps at Portsmouth. This innovation was introduced by the Inspector-General of Naval Works, Samuel Bentham (1757–1831; appointed in 1796, he was the only holder of this post), and it was he who supported the engineer Marc Isambard Brunel (father of the famous Isambard Kingdom Brunel) in his plan to build a steam-powered factory to mass-produce pulley-blocks. Blocks were fundamental to the operation of a ship's rigging and the sailing navy used them in huge quantities – an estimated 100,000 per year. The ability to produce blocks faster and more cheaply than the time-consuming hand method was enticing, and it was claimed that ten unskilled men in the mills could replace 110 skilled blockmakers. The block mills were built between 1802 and 1806. Within three years of operation they had recovered their construction costs through savings in production, and by 1808, 130,000 blocks a year were being made. So well built was the machinery that some of it was still used until the mid-twentieth century.[29]

The Royal Navy's demand for ships in wartime could never be satisfied by the royal dockyards alone for they simply did not have the capacity, so the civilian shipbuilding industry made a huge contribution. Analysis of the numbers and tonnages of ships launched for the Royal Navy during two periods dominated by prolonged warfare, 1690–1713 and 1789–1815, gives some idea of the importance of civilian yards in keeping the navy supplied with ships (see Tables 9 and 10).[30]

The two periods offer some striking changes. The vastly increased global demands made on the navy in the wars of 1793–1815 are immediately apparent in the fact that the tonnage and number of ships built in the later period is more than

Table 9 Ships built and launched for the Royal Navy by royal dockyards and private yards, 1690–1713 and 1789–1815

	1690–1713 Total tonnage	No of ships	1789–1815 Total tonnage	No of ships
Royal dockyards	138,138	225	158,269	169
Private yards	95,816	171	333,166	670
Totals	233,954	396	491,435	839

County/place	1690–1713 Total tonnage	No of ships	1789–1815 Total tonnage	No of ships
London & Thames	49,417	95	118,943	190
Cheshire	–	–	1,708	5
Cornwall	–	–	1,146	3
Devon	–	–	29,006	73
Dorset	–	–	5,358	19
Co Durham	–	–	354	2
Essex	2,364	3	11,358	20
Gloucestershire	896	1	365	1
Hampshire	13,481	17	47,180	74
Kent	–	–	66,617	125
Lancashire	–	–	944	1
Norfolk	–	–	10,885	37
Northumberland	–	–	9,566	3
Scotland	–	–	354	2
Suffolk	1,742	5	8,786	27
Sussex	4,955	17	3,464	8
Yorkshire	3,837	6	7,589	12
Ireland	67	1	–	–
Bermuda	–	–	7,026	43
New England	1,010	2	–	–
Uncertain	–	–	2,517	5

double that for the earlier era of conflict. Interestingly, the total tonnage built by the royal yards in the two periods was only about 14 per cent greater, although the average tonnage of the ships completed was about 52 per cent higher. Ten royal dockyards were in use in the later period as opposed to six in the earlier period, and the main yards were (in order of production totals) Deptford, Woolwich, Portsmouth, Chatham and Plymouth. The really striking difference is in the contribution of the private yards, which in terms of tonnage was nearly three and a half times greater. Also, the geographical range of yards used was much increased. Outside of London and the Thames region, only six English counties feature in the earlier period, as opposed to sixteen a century later, a reflection of the increased demands of the navy, but also indicating considerable net growth in the size of the English shipbuilding industry itself (approximately 110 private yards were involved in building for the navy over this period).

It is not easy to estimate the effect of this government spending on warship-building in private yards. One might think that it must have put a good deal of money into local economies, and that conversely periods like that of 1710–41, when the Admiralty stopped awarding private contracts, must have been a major blow. The county of Hampshire built 211 warships for the navy between 1650 and 1814 (most of them at Southampton or on the Hamble or Beaulieu rivers), but the effect of this on the county's economy seems to have been limited, for there was no great slump when the Napoleonic War ended and naval orders ceased.[31] However, it may have been that the impact of naval shipbuilding was greater in the really big centres, such as the Thames and Kent.

The development of naval architecture

Although written specifications for building ships were known in England in the Middle Ages, the use of plans was slow to catch on, even in the construction of ships for the navy. In merchant shipbuilding, plans were only patchily employed until the nineteenth century. Models were used by shipwrights, but aside from a few outstanding practitioners such as Matthew Baker, the Pett family and Anthony Deane, few English shipwrights in the sixteenth and seventeenth centuries seem to have taken advantage of mathematics and geometry in ship design. In addition, even mathematical ship design was more a matter of putting a geometrical gloss on things discovered empirically; there was as yet no science of hydrodynamics to give naval architecture its theoretical base.

In any event, shipbuilding does not appear to have attracted many intellectual high-flyers. According William Sutherland, author of *The Shipbuilder's Assistant* (1711), 'the proper business of a shipwright is counted a very vulgar Imploy; and which a Man of very indifferent Qualifications may be Master of'. Sutherland cited a story told to him by a master shipwright of a gentleman who said that he 'had a Blockhead of a Son incapable to attain any other trade' apart from that of ship-wright! The state of theoretical knowledge improved in the second half of the eighteenth century, but it was not until the nineteenth century that it really began to be anything much like a science. The Royal Navy opened a School of Naval Architecture at Portsmouth in 1811, but as late as the 1830s it was still relying on textbooks written by the great Swedish shipbuilder Frederik af Chapman in the 1760s.[32]

Navigation and nautical science

Into the eighteenth century the basic tools of marine navigation were the compass, the lead-line, the sandglass and the chart. There were also instruments for finding latitude by measuring the height (angle) of heavenly bodies, such as the sun, above the horizon. Early instruments for this were the astrolabe and the cross-staff, but in the seventeenth century, in English service at least, these were replaced by a simpler device, Davis's quadrant or backstaff, said to have been invented by the English seaman, John Davis, in the 1590s. Davis's instrument was later replaced by Hadley's quadrant (invented 1731), which in turn was supplanted by the sextant (invented 1757). Both Hadley's quadrant and the sextant were

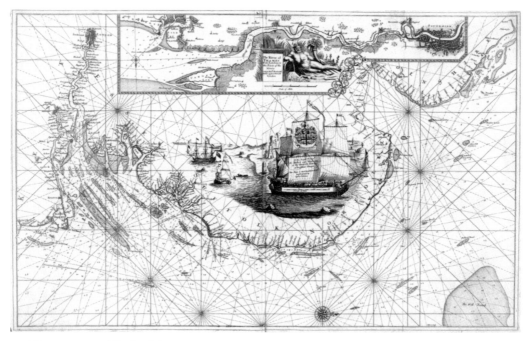

71 The east coast of England from Dover to the Humber, from Captain Greenvile Collins' *Great Britain's Coasting Pilot*, 1693. Collins' went though numerous editions, and became the standard chart-atlas for Britain in the 18th century.

developed in England and both improved the accuracy and range of celestial navigation.

Methods for finding latitude at sea had been known since the fifteenth century, and enabled sailors to work out how far north or south they were on the globe. However, such knowledge was of limited use when they could not tell with any accuracy just how far east or west they were until a known coastline hove in sight. To know their easterly or westerly position they had to find out longitude, and this eluded both astronomers and others until the eighteenth century.

When Charles II established the first Royal Observatory at Greenwich in 1675, it was with the aim of improving astronomical knowledge for seamen and especially of determining longitude. The long-term work of successive Astronomers Royal culminated in 1767 in the production of the first of an annual series of *Nautical Almanacs*, which made it possible to determine longitude by working out lunar distances – in effect, using the moon as a clock. Although the lunar tables were superficially made out of date by the invention of the marine chronometer, they continued in use on many ships into the nineteenth century, partly at least because of the high cost of chronometers.

The story of John Harrison's development of the first accurate marine chronometers has recently been dramatically told in Dava Sobel's best-seller *Longitude*. Queen Anne's government set up what came to be called the Board of Longitude in 1714, with the aim of finding a reliable method of determining longitude. A prize of £20,000 was offered for the development of a marine chronometer so accurate that it would maintain Greenwich time for the duration of a voyage. It was recognized that, by dividing the 360-degree circle of the globe into twenty-four 15-degree sections, each representing an hour of the day, it would be possible to determine local longitude by finding the difference between local time and Greenwich time. John Harrison (1693–1776), a Lincolnshire clockmaker, took up the challenge. Between 1735 and 1760 he completed four chronometers, of decreasing size, which eventually made it possible to determine shipboard longitude. Making clocks that would run accurately and consistently in the highly unstable environment of a ship was an extraordinary achievement, but Harrison had to wait until 1773 to get the balance of his prize and the full public recognition that this brilliant man was due.

English seafarers had used charts from at least the 1530s, if not before. One of the great landmarks in sixteenth-century chart-making was the huge chart-atlas produced in 1584–5 by the Dutch navigator Lucas Janszoon Waghenaer, *Spieghel der Zeevaerdt*, translated into English as *The Mariners Mirrour* in 1588 (see Figs 36 and 43). 'Waggoner' was used in Britain as a term to denote any chart-atlas until at least the early nineteenth century. The first comprehensive survey of the coasts of the British Isles was not made until nearly a century later, when in 1681 Samuel Pepys commissioned Captain Greenvile Collins to carry one out. His work was published in 1693 as *Great Britain's Coasting Pilot*, and, through numerous updated editions, became the standard chart-atlas for eighteenth-century Britain. Although Collins had been appointed as 'Hydrographer to the King', the Royal Navy did not have a hydrographic department until 1795, and the first Admiralty chart was not published until 1801.

Despite inventions such as Harrison's chronometers, it is apparent that the navigational equipment of most merchant ships in the seventeenth and eighteenth centuries remained rudimentary, with the compass and lead-line playing a central role in getting a ship from port A to port B. Charts and other navigational instruments were used, but seamen also relied on a great deal of knowledge gained from practical experience, at least for short-range journeys in Europe.

Improving navigation on board ship was one way of making seafaring safer; another way was to build more lighthouses. All lighthouses in the British Isles were sited on the coast until the construction of Winstanley's lighthouse on the dangerous Eddystone Rocks off Plymouth in 1699. The lighthouse disappeared in the 'Great Storm' of 1703, along with its inventor, but it was soon replaced by another light, the value of marking major shipping hazards out at sea having been proved. The construction of such lights was a major engineering feat. Other rock lighthouses followed in other locations, and lightships were also introduced in a few places from the 1730s onwards.

Scotland lacked a body like Trinity House to take responsibility for lighthouses. Some lights were constructed in the seventeenth century – on the Island of May at the entrance to the Firth of Forth (1636) and at Dundee (1687) – but few, if any, other lights seem to have existed at this period. Scottish lighthouse development was given a great boost in 1786 by the establishment of the Northern Lighthouse

Trust (later the Commissioners of the Northern Lighthouses), which began a rapid programme of lighthouse construction, freed of the need to get an Act of Parliament to authorize construction. By contrast, all lighthouses in Ireland effectively became Crown property in 1717, and the Dublin port authorities gradually took over responsibility for their management. A corporation was set up in 1786 to manage Irish lighthouses, to be succeeded in 1867 by the Commission for Irish Lights, which is still the authority.[33]

Fishing in Britain

The English commercial fishing trade was at rather a low ebb in the sixteenth and seventeenth centuries, unable to compete with the Dutch and others in the North Sea, and attempts to exclude foreign fishermen failed. The Dutch were England's major fishing competitors, and they kept a technological edge in fishing vessels and fish preservation for much of this time. During the Anglo–Dutch Wars, English efforts were aimed at hampering and if possible destroying Dutch sea trade and fisheries, which had a far greater importance to a small nation such as the Netherlands than it did for England.

The Iceland fishing trade saw a revival in the early 1600s, but was hit by royal taxes in the 1630s and then by the Civil War. Rising taxes on salt helped to kill the fishery off by 1700. The English Newfoundland fishery prospered until the 1790s, when it was effectively ended by the Anglo-French war. By the time peace came in 1815 the Newfoundlanders had taken over most of the Grand Banks fishing.

The English learned whaling from the Basques in the early seventeenth century. The Muscovy Company's subsidiary, the Greenland Company, hired Basque whalers to teach the techniques of catching whales to English sailors. However, the whale-catching enterprise that the Greenland Company set up did not prosper. Greenland whaling was one of the activities of the South Sea Company, which collapsed disastrously in 1720 (the 'South Sea Bubble'), and the only one to survive the ruin of its inflated schemes to trade with the Pacific. Attempts by the government to subsidize whaling (with a bounty on the construction of whalers of more than 200 tons) did produce a small upsurge in the trade in the mid-eighteenth century, which then again declined. The Board of Trade began to give greater support to whaling, both in the Arctic, the North Atlantic and in the southern oceans from the 1780s. The settlement of Australia opened up a new region for whaling, although the whalers soon earned themselves an unenviable reputation for brutality to native peoples in Australia and New Zealand.

Scottish fishing, especially on the west coast, probably began to revive rather earlier than the English industry, aided by Scottish business acumen. However, even this was a tale of failed initiatives and lost opportunities. The most important early government Act as regards the Scottish fishing industry was the creation of a Fisheries Board for Scotland in 1808, with a body of fishery officers who maintained strict quality control over the herrings sold. This vastly improved the reputation of Scottish catches. The quality-controlled fish found a ready market and the Scottish herring industry expanded rapidly.

The English commercial fishing industry in the eighteenth century expanded more slowly than that of Scotland, probably in part because the English were not then great fish-eaters. Something like 90 per cent of the fish brought back from Newfoundland was re-exported to Catholic Europe. The navy also adversely affected the fishing industry by routinely pressing fishermen into its ranks. However, the fishing industry in England and Wales was not static, and by 1786 there were 1,584 fishing boats in the two countries, the figure having risen by almost 15 per cent since 1772. One of the big problems for fishing in Great Britain and Ireland was the salt tax, which reached punitive levels by the late eighteenth century; its abolition in 1825 was a stimulus to the industry.

Drifting is a technique that uses a net close to the surface to catch shoals of pelagic fish, such as herring, that live close to the surface. Trawling is fishing with a net that runs along the bottom of the sea and it is used to catch demersal fish, such as cod, that live on the sea bed. In the early eighteenth century trawling was largely confined to southern England, and only gradually spread up the east and west coasts, probably driven by problems of food supply during the 1793–1815 wars. Fishing fleets had always moved around the coast in pursuit of new fishing grounds, and fishermen moved to settle in new places. The locals did not always welcome them, but this was one of the most important means by which new fishing techniques were communicated.[34]

Colonization and exploration

The seventeenth century saw little in the way of major voyages of exploration by the English or by anyone else. Long-distance voyages to the Americas and the Far East became common, if far from risk-free, and the period saw the consolidation and exploitation of known sea routes rather than any strikingly new enterprises. The search for north-east or north-west passages to the Pacific was finally given up in the 1630s, but the Pacific became the main arena for voyages of exploration in the eighteenth century.

The Americas

English attempts at the colonization of America had their first successes in the first decade of the seventeenth century. Although the story of the early colonization of America tends to be dominated by the Pilgrim Fathers and their flight from religious persecution, these earlier attempts were the work of companies looking to make a profit from the venture. The Virginia Company of London established Jamestown in Virginia in 1607, and in the same year the Virginia Company of Plymouth planted a small colony at Sagadahoc, Maine. The Sagahadoc settlement failed within two years, and Jamestown came close to collapse through internal disputes, attacks by native Americans and uncertain support from home. The London Virginia Company went bust in 1624, but Jamestown itself was saved by the development of tobacco as a crop, which rapidly became a significant export.

The voyage of the *Mayflower* in 1620 landed a small group of families, mainly

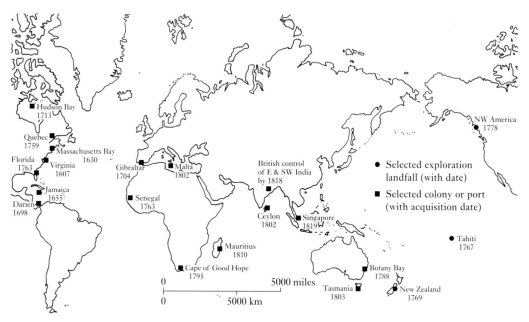

72 Exploration and empire 1606–1819.

Puritans, at a place that they named Plymouth in what is now Massachusetts. Led by William Bradford, they aimed to establish a community run along religious lines in what they saw as a wilderness. Puritan London merchants, who saw godly living and profit as going hand in hand, established a second colony in Massachusetts Bay in 1630. It was the most successful of the early colonies, attracting 13,000 settlers in its first decade. By mid-century the New England colonies had 23,000 inhabitants.

The arrival of Europeans in North America was disastrous for the native Americans. Although military pressure and land-grabbing served to push them to the margins, their biggest problem came in the form of unfamiliar diseases such as influenza and smallpox, brought in unwittingly by the settlers. It has been estimated that the native population of eastern North America was about half a million in 1600. By 1700, while the colonial population had risen to about 260,000, the indigenous population had been reduced by roughly half.

The southern colonies, such as Virginia, came to rely on tobacco and other single crops. Cold, wooded and rocky, New England had at first seemed an unlikely place to make much money, but it rapidly developed a diversified economy that came to play a central role in the English Atlantic economy. Timber and other materials for shipbuilding were abundant. By 1660 New England was virtually self-sufficient as regards ship construction and went on to take an increasingly large slice of the British shipping market. Fishing developed rapidly, as did trade with the West Indies, supplying provisions that fed the English settlers there and their slaves (much of the arable land in the West Indies was given over to sugar cane production).

Small English colonies had been established in the West Indies in the 1620s and 1630s, on small islands such as Barbados and Antigua. The conquest of Jamaica in the mid-1650s was a major addition to England's Caribbean empire, but the English population of the region was already growing rapidly through immigration. It is reckoned that over half of the immigrants from the British Isles to the West Indies and North America south of New England in the seventeenth century were indentured servants. These were people who worked for an agreed number of years in America in return for the cost of the voyage and their settlement there. It was not slavery as such, for slavery is usually endless, but it was an option that was probably only for the very desperate or the very hopeful. However, by the mid-seventeenth century, the economies of the West Indies and North America were coming to rely, in one way or another, on the slave trade with Africa.

The Pacific

In the eighteenth century settlement was often preceded by exploration. Anson's circumnavigation of 1740–4 began as an expedition of war, but Captain Samuel Wallis's circumnavigation in HMS *Dolphin* of 1766–8 was peaceful, and resulted in the European discovery of the island of Tahiti. The search for an unknown great southern continent (*Terra Australis Incognita*) helped to drive much exploratory effort and Australasia was visited intermittently by European seafarers from 1642 onwards.

Scientific curiosity became a major element in these voyages, although mixed with the perceived need to discover and annex new lands. The most famous British voyages of the eighteenth century were those of Captain James Cook (1728–79). Cook's three voyages (1768–71, 1772–5 and 1776–80) made the geography of the Pacific far clearer than it had ever been, and opened the way for European settlement in Australia, New Zealand and other parts of the region. Cook was the son of a Yorkshire labourer who learned his profession as a seaman in the coal trade. He joined the navy in 1755 and rose rapidly to become a sailing master and later a commissioned officer. He gained considerable experience in marine surveying off the coast of Canada, and came to the notice of the Royal Society because of observations that he had made of a solar eclipse. Cook was sent south in 1768 in command of HMS *Endeavour*, a Whitby-built collier purchased on his advice. His orders were to sail to Tahiti to record a transit of the planet Venus across the sun, and then to search for the *Terra Australis*. On this first voyage Cook charted the coasts of New Zealand, explored the east coast of Australia (landing at Botany Bay in 1770) and confirmed that Australia was separate from New Guinea by sailing through the Torres Strait. The second voyage showed that no great habitable southern continent existed south of Australia and New Zealand, and Cook and his men became the first seafarers to cross the Antarctic Circle. The third voyage involved a search for a north-west passage from the Pacific side, and included a voyage up the coast of what is now western Canada and Alaska, as well as the first European landing on Hawaii. It was on Hawaii, in February 1779, that Cook was tragically killed in a skirmish with the Hawaiians. Cook's voyages made a very great number of geographical, scientific and ethnographic discoveries. He was accompanied on the first voyage by the botanist Joseph Banks; it was as a result of his discoveries with Cook that Banks became one of the leading scientific figures in late Georgian Britain.

British exploration of the Pacific was carried on by Captain George Vancouver (1758–98), among others, who had served with Cook and explored the north-west coast of America. However, where exploration led, colonization often followed. Cook had named and claimed the Australian territory of New South Wales for Britain in 1770, and in the 1780s the British government decided to establish a penal colony and a British base there. Transportation of convicts was not a new policy, and at least 50,000 had been sent to America before the War of Independence. The 'first fleet' of eleven ships arrived at Botany Bay in January 1788, with 736 convicts and a military garrison. Botany Bay had been selected on the advice of Banks, who believed it to be very fertile, but this proved not to be the case. The fleet moved to Port Jackson (now Sydney Harbour) and set up the first permanent British settlement in Australia. Non-convict settlers soon followed, but some 160,000 convicts were to be transported to Australia before the practice was ended in 1868. The circumnavigation of Australia was completed in 1803 by Matthew Flinders, and British settlement gradually expanded along the coast.

European contacts with New Zealand began in the late eighteenth century, with Cook and others, but they were followed by European and American whalers and timber-traders, whose lawless and often brutal behaviour antagonized the Maoris. More peaceful trade, settlement and missionaries followed in the 1810–40 period, but the impact of European settlement on the Maori people was similar in some ways to what happened in seventeenth-century America; diseases that were new to the Maoris came with the settlers and by the 1830s, the Maori population may have shrunk by as much as 30 per cent.

India

The English presence in India in the seventeenth century was limited to trade, in which silk, cotton, spices, pepper and other exotic goods played a large part. By 1700 the EIC was England's largest corporation, running a fleet of large vessels with between twenty and thirty sailings to the East (mostly India) per year, with its main Indian base at Madras. The Dutch and French (from the 1720s) were active in the region, and the British and French East India Companies went to war in the 1740s and 1750s when their home nations did. In 1761 the British finally defeated the French, who ceased to be major players in India. The transference of European conflicts to India seems to have played a part in the East India Company moving from a policy of relatively peaceful trading to one of military aggression and conquest. Robert Clive's victory at Plassey in 1757 secured control of a large part of northern and north-eastern India for the Company, and other territories followed. By the early 1800s the Company (brought under British government control in the 1770s and 1780s) ruled the eastern seaboard of India, as well as Ceylon (Sri Lanka). In the wars of 1793–1815, the Royal Navy eliminated the

French and most other colonial rivals in the Far East, laying the foundations for the development of the British Empire in the region during the nineteenth century. The East India Company's establishment of Singapore in 1819, at the southern end of the major shipping route through the Straits of Malacca between Malaya and Sumatra, was just one of the major maritime trading developments made possible by this new British hegemony.

The EIC went on to become the main instrument of British power in the Far East until the first half of the nineteenth century, creating its own army and navy. The Company had monopolies on British trade with India until 1813 and with China until 1833. It was only in 1858, in the wake of the Indian Mutiny, that it was abolished and English possessions in India came under the direct rule of the British government.[35]

Merchants and shipowners, 1600–1800

'Fractional shipowning' (several partners owning a vessel) was commonplace in the seventeenth and eighteenth centuries. Various means were used to divide up the ownership, usually based around multiples of four. This went up to sixty-fourths, which were fixed as the standard ownership units by the 1854 Merchant Shipping Act. Management of a ship might devolve upon one or two partners, or sometimes

73 The *Cadiz Merchant*, 1682, by Edward Barlow (1642–*c*.1703). A large merchantman of the period, depicted by the sailor and later writer, Edward Barlow. As a youth, Barlow had run away to sea to escape rural boredom and to see the world (see p. 190).

the ship's master. By the eighteenth century such managers were coming to be called 'ship's husbands', and this marked the beginning of the divide between trader and shipowner.

One of the original reasons for fractional ownership was to spread risk: not just the risk of shipwreck, but the risk of not making a profit. Ralph Davis cites an example of Richard Lascelles, who 'covered his bets' in the mid-eighteenth century by having interests in twenty-two ships, his total shares amounting to the equivalent of two ships. This system of ownership was also a way of raising capital. As the development of marine insurance in the eighteenth century began to reduce the financial risks associated with seafaring, shipping partnerships became a way of merchants exploiting their existing trading connections by using ships in which they had an interest. In Davis' phrase, the mercantile community of the seventeenth and eighteenth centuries 'was in effect bound together in a network of back-scratching'.[36]

These shipowning partnerships were not usually formed by shipowners wishing to move their own cargoes. It appears that until the late eighteenth century most merchants sent their cargoes in other people's ships, either by chartering the vessel or by hiring stowage space. A partnership would aim for the highest possible freight rates, and this would make the movement of one's own cargoes by the partnership uneconomic. The two exceptions to this were the coastal coal trade, where it was the shipping community that banded together to provide the service (buying the coal), and the slave trade. Slave-trading required that a ship's master should move his fragile human cargo as quickly as possible and with as few deaths as could be managed (for commercial rather than humanitarian reasons). This meant that it was to the advantage of the trading partnership to have a close working relationship with the ship's master.

The structure of shipowning is not at all clear before the start of registration in 1786, but Davis found the following in an analysis of bills of sale for fifty-three ships from the late seventeenth century (see Table 11).

In London, shipowning was dominated by mercantile interests; even the women listed may have been the widows or other relatives of merchants. In the provinces

---

Table 11 Participants in shipowning, late seventeenth century[37]

Merchant community	174	(51.5%)
'Maritime community' (seamen, sea traders, victuallers)	102	(30.1%)
Miscellaneous tradesmen	25	(7.4%)
Gentry, minor aristocracy	24	(7.1%)
Women	12	(3.6%)
Yeomen	1	(0.3%)
Total	338	(100.0%)

---

shipowning was much more broadly based, with shopkeepers and other tradesmen becoming part-owners of vessels. Shipowning was more attractive than other partnerships because, despite its manifest risks, profits could be high from successful voyages and they would be shared amongst the partners. Also, in land-based partnerships, a partner risked losing all his property if the venture collapsed and there were debtors to be paid. This problem was not resolved until the Limited Liability Acts of the 1850s and 1860s. Shipowning was different. Governed by Admiralty Law, it had its own form of limited liability which meant that, if a ship sank, the partners lost only their investment in the ship, not the shirts from their backs. The situation could be very different for the sailors that they employed, of course.

The shipping business in the seventeenth and eighteenth century, like all other forms of trade, relied on face-to-face contact. In London business tended to be conducted at the Royal Exchange. Founded in the sixteenth century, the Exchange was destroyed in the Great Fire of 1666; although later rebuilt, in the interim the taverns and the new coffee houses of London became venues for conducting business. Particular coffee houses became known as centres for specific trades. Edward Lloyd was a Welsh coffee-house owner who opened a business at Tower Street in London. In 1692 he shifted his premises to Lombard Street, close to the rebuilt Royal Exchange and the Bank of England. The coffee house became a centre for marine insurance underwriters. As their business relied on accurate information, Lloyd's also became a place where people went to hear the latest shipping news, which was read out continuously by one of Lloyd's servants from a kind of pulpit, a sort of human tickertape machine.

In 1696 Lloyd began issuing shipping and trade information in printed form. His short-lived newsletter *Lloyd's News* had to close because it contained a reference to Parliamentary proceedings (then illegal), so he reverted to producing shipping lists. For example, his list of 5 October 1702 for ships trading to East India and China gives fifty-eight vessels which had sailed to those regions since 1698, and nineteen which had returned since December 1701. The type of information was very limited. For instance, the reader is told that the *Rook Galley*, owned by the English East India Company, had sailed for Surat on 16 August 1699. A vessel of 250 tons with twenty guns and fifty men, it was commanded by George Simons. The *List* also communicated information about shipping casualties, such as 'The *Anne*, [Captain] Adam Spencer, was blown up May the 4th, near the Isle of Wight, returning Home'. Lloyd's continued as an organization after Edward Lloyd's death in about 1726, and in 1734 it revived *Lloyd's List* as a newspaper for shipping and trade information. Still published today, it is one of the oldest news-papers in the world.[38]

In 1760 a group of underwriters formed an association to establish some means of covering their own risks by setting up a scheme for classifying ships according to their condition. This resulted in the publication in 1764-5 of the first *Lloyd's Register of Shipping*, which listed merchant ships according to their present and former names, master, home port, trade, tonnage, armament, crew size, place and date of build, hull condition and equipment state (the last-named denoted by classification letters and later numbers also, which covered a range from good to bad; the 'A1' – very good – classification was introduced in 1775). As well as being invaluable to underwriters who now had a much better means of judging insurance risks, the *Register* (published annually), became an invaluable reference source for merchants, prospective owners and others engaged in the shipping business, and remains so today. Lloyd's Register and the insurance arm later became separate organizations. In the second half of the nineteenth century, Lloyd's international influence extended markedly, with the setting-up of branch offices abroad that conducted technical surveys of ships; by the 1870s, Lloyd's had more than sixty surveyors operating abroad.[39]

National ship registration lagged behind the commercial documentation. Forms of local ship registration had been proposed and implemented in the seventeenth century (and even enacted in a limited form in 1696), but it was not until 1786 that full ship registration became obligatory in Britain for all decked ships of more than 15 tons burden. Registration remained the responsibility of customs officers from 1701 to 1994. Although registration recorded technical data about a ship, it also provided a legal record of ownership that helped to prevent fraud. It was not unknown for shares in a vessel to be deliberately over-sold. By the late eighteenth century British shipping was better documented than it had ever been, making it easier and safer (financially, at least) to take part in the shipping business. Insurance rates fell in the eighteenth century as the organization of the marine insurance sector improved, increasing the attractiveness of shipping as an investment. However, for ordinary sailors the shipping business mostly remained 'a mere lottery'.

The life of seafarers, 1600–1800

Shipwreck has always been one of the greatest dangers for the seafarer. It has been estimated that in the eighteenth century between about 3 and 5 per cent of ships were lost each year. This may not sound a great deal, but if one took an average group of a hundred ships of the period and assumed this sort of loss rate, it would mean that over a decade more than one-quarter would have gone down. Most sailors must have experienced at least one wreck, and probably several, in the course of their working lives. Not all wrecks were fatal, although it seems from early nineteenth-century figures that about one in four involved some deaths, and one in eight resulted in the loss of most or all of the crew.[40]

One might think that working in such a dangerous environment might turn a person's mind towards religion, but British sailors, at least in the eighteenth century, were notoriously irreligious. Although the evidence is limited, there are few signs of this in the Middle Ages and the sixteenth century. It may be, as Marcus Rediker has suggested, that a crucial change of some sort took place in the seventeenth century. Certainly, by the 1700s, seamen were almost proverbially anti-religious. The causes of this are difficult to determine, but it may have had its roots in the isolation of shipboard life, far from church authorities, where a man who made his piety plain would often end up being abused by his shipmates until,

74 *This Encouraged, England must Flourish*: English seamen, from *England's Safety*, patriotic pamphlet by Captain George St Loo, 1693. The sailors are wearing canvas aprons, skirted jackets and thrum caps (warm caps made of rough wool). The man on the right holds a backstaff, and a mariner's compass is at the feet of each sailor. The anchor is surrounded by (clockwise from top left): a seaman's fid (for ropework), a shipwright's maul or hammer, a sounding lead and line (for measuring depth) and a buoy (for marking the position of an anchor).

England's *Safety*: Or, a *Bridle to the* French *King, &c.* 2

This Encouraged, *England* muſt Flouriſh.

London: Printed for *Will. Miller*, at the Gilded Acorn in St. *Paul's*

at least outwardly, he dropped his beliefs. Another potent cause may have been the closeness of death in the sailor's working day, breeding a sort of fatalism, as well as a determination to survive by one's own efforts. Seamen encountered mortality through accident more than any other kind of worker and this seems to have left its mark. In 1682 the Reverend John Flavell, in a sermon entitled *Navigation Spiritualized: or a New Compass for sea-men*, wrote of what he regarded as the common failings of seamen: 'the horrible and detestable sin of drunkenness, swearing, uncleanness, forgetfulness of mercies, violation of promises and aetheistical contempt of death.'[41]

The seaman's life was a hard one. Figure 75 shows the minimum monthly pay-rates of English merchant seamen between 1604 and 1775. The great upward spikes in the graph all relate to periods of international war, when seamen were at a premium because the Royal Navy took so many. Seamen must have lost out as regards pay in the seventeenth and eighteenth centuries: the minimum monthly peacetime pay in 1604 was 17 shillings, but in 1775 was 25 shillings, only 47 per cent higher; although the prices of staples such as bread fluctuated over the period and wages in some other trades were fairly static, the seaman suffered in the inflation of the period. In real terms, the 1775 wage may have been only three-quarters the value of the 1604 pay. An Oxfordshire farmworker of 1770 only had to work twenty-two days in a month to equal the monthly pay of the common seaman of his day. The farmworker normally worked a six-day week, while the seaman had to work every day. Edward Barlow, who ran away from a life of agricultural labour in the late seventeenth century to go to sea, lured by a curiosity to see the world, remarked 'all days were alike to us, and many times it fell that we had more work on a Sabbath day than we did on other days'.[42]

Most seamen were paid by the month; some were paid in advance for long voyages and by stages thereafter at ports of call. Fixed lump-sum payments were also used in the more predictable short-range trades, but the ancient system of shares (the crew sharing in the profits of a voyage) only survived by this stage in

Table 12 Age-ranges of Anglo-American seamen and officers, 1700–50[45]

Age	Common seamen*	Officer/skilled worker
15–19	21 (10.6%)	–
20–29	118 (59.6%)	39 (43.3%)
30–39	37 (18.7%)	36 (40.0%)
40–49	18 (9.1%)	11 (12.2%)
50+	4 (2.0%)	4 (4.4%)
Total	198 (100.0%)	90 (100.0%)

* 'foremastmen'

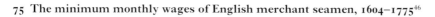

75 The minimum monthly wages of English merchant seamen, 1604–1775[46]

fishing, whaling, privateering and piracy. In the case of wreck, any salvage was to be sold off to pay the crew's wages, a feature of the law that was useful to the sailor and owner alike, for it encouraged seamen to save what they could from a wreck. Seamen were also subject to penalties for desertion, mutiny, pilfering and other such acts, and an Act of 1729 reinforced such penalties and made written employment contracts mandatory.[43]

The food consumed by merchant seamen of the seventeenth and eighteenth centuries (or of the nineteenth century, for that matter), was little different from that encountered by their forebears (see pp 102–3). Their medical care was probably not much better. Although surgeons sailed on ships from the sixteenth century, their presence on merchant vessels did not become obligatory until very late on. Acts of Parliament required that surgeons be carried on Arctic whalers from 1786, on slave ships from 1789 and on emigrant ships from 1803.[44]

The age-ranges of seamen in the first half of the eighteenth century were also rather similar to those from the sixteenth century (see p. 98).

The development of nautical education, 1600–1800

Most seamen in this period learnt their trade either through first-hand experience on the job or through formal apprenticeships, with boys generally going to sea between the ages of twelve and sixteen. Merchant sailors tended to come from London or the coastal counties, making it quite likely that they came from seafaring families. Literacy rates – as least as far as they can be judged on the ability to sign one's name – were quite high among sailors in the first half of the eighteenth century. Research by Marcus Rediker suggests that literacy rates were about 95 per cent among ships' officers and skilled workers (with all masters and mates literate), and about 69 per cent among other seamen, including common sailors. Anyone wanting to rise in the shipboard world had to be able to read, write and add up.[47]

The education of potential officers included some schooling in mathematics and navigation, although until the late seventeenth century most of this seems to have been received from private tutors rather than in grammar schools. Charles II established a navigation school at Christ's Hospital in London in 1673, which produced its first fifteen graduates in 1675. The number of schools offering mathematical and navigational training began to multiply in the early eighteenth century. These included the highly successful Royal Hospital School at Greenwich (founded 1716), which began as a naval orphanage and went on to train many boys for the sea. Navigational schooling also began to develop in Scotland in the late seventeenth century. The people trained at these schools included seamen wishing to develop their knowledge, as well as boys.[48]

A Royal Naval College was established at Portsmouth in 1729 with the aim of training officers, but most future naval officers started as volunteers or 'servants' under the tutelage of a particular captain. It took three years' sea service to qualify as a midshipman and six to become a lieutenant; despite the fact that some did part of their 'sea time' on paper only (carried on the ship's books of a relative or family friend), this system did produce a large number of competent officers.[49]

From the mid-eighteenth century there was an organization devoted to sending the poor to sea. The Marine Society was founded in 1756 by the philanthropist Jonas Hanway with the twin aims of rescuing poor boys from destitution and providing manpower for the Royal and merchant navies. The society provided clothes and other items to boys who were willing to go to sea to learn the sailor's trade, and made arrangements for them to be berthed on warships under humane conditions. Steps were also taken to ensure that as many Marine Society entrants as possible would be taken up by the merchant service once they had been discharged from the navy. Although it was not a miracle answer to the navy's manning problems, it did provide it with thousands of sailors. The society placed 10,625 boys in the navy during the 1756–63 war, and another 22,973 during the wars of 1793–1815. One might argue that putting poor boys in the navy during a war was hardly doing them a kindness. However, it does seem to have been seen as act of charity at the time, for it took many away from degrading poverty and offered them the chance to learn a trade.[50]

Women and the sea, 1600–1900

Although the sailing of ships has been a largely male domain until the last few decades, women have played a major part in maritime history. Sailors' wives and prostitutes are the two kinds of women most obviously associated with seafarers. The nature of work at sea meant that men were away from their wives and families for long periods, and that women in effect often became heads of households. Did this result in their attaining greater independence and status than their inland sisters? There are some indications that it did. In 1796, for example, just over a quarter of the licensed victuallers in the port of Liverpool were female. In some seaport towns in the nineteenth century the sailor's wife may have slipped easily into the role of seaside landlady. At Littlehampton in West Sussex in 1899, then a declining port but a rising seaside resort, about 50 per cent of the town's two hundred or more boarding houses were run by women. A great deal of research would be needed to substantiate this; the most that can be said at present is that the seaman's conditions of work must have meant that his wife was thrown upon her own resources and that of her community to make ends meet and keep her family together.[51]

The lot of a seaman's widow could certainly be hard. In 1872 Charlotte Belchamber of Littlehampton was left to look after a family of four children when her husband William drowned along with his crew in the wreck of the collier *Russell*. The family were not wealthy – being a sea captain was not necessarily a high-status job in the nineteenth century – and lived in a two-up, two-down terraced cottage. It is apparent that Mrs Belchamber must have had to take in washing in order to earn a living, for the 1881 census describes her as a 'washerwoman'.[52]

Prostitutes have always existed in seaports, catering to the physical needs and fantasies of seafarers and others. Getting accurate numbers for prostitutes is difficult, partly because the trade was illegal and of very low status (if highly popular with many men), and partly because it was not necessarily something that women undertook on a regular basis. Particular areas in ports were known for their large concentrations of brothels. In sixteenth-century London it was Southwark, whereas in 1857 a large number of London's (estimated) 2,825 brothels and 8,600 prostitutes were to be found near the Ratcliffe Highway in East London, close to the docks. Prostitution was ever a grim trade and it is probable that most women resorted to it because they had little other option. A minority succeeded in the business to become famous madams, such as Damaris Page who ran a number of London brothels in the 1650s and 1660s and died rich. In eighteenth-century London, as David Cordingly relates, there were even annually produced guide-books describing where the best prostitutes were to be found and listing their accomplishments!

Venereal disease was a perennial problem among seafarers; in 1863 the rate of VD was running at about one man in fifteen in the Royal Navy. The government introduced the Contagious Diseases Acts between 1866 and 1869, which regulated prostitution around naval bases and army garrisons. The venereal infection rate in the navy had been halved by 1874 as a result of the Acts, but the legislation was highly controversial. Regulation involved subjecting women to degrading and unpleasant examinations, and was seen by some as tantamount to state acceptance of prostitution. The repeal of the Acts in 1886 was achieved by a vigorous campaign led by the women's rights activist Josephine Butler. The naval VD rate rapidly increased again, and decades were to pass before health education and the prevalence of condoms got it under control.[53]

Women were sometimes clandestinely taken to sea on warships and other vessels, despite the fact that in the Royal Navy the practice was against the rules from at least 1731 and was frowned on by most senior officers. However, in the eighteenth century it became common for the wives of non-commissioned Royal Navy officers, such as gunners and carpenters, to accompany them to sea. Unlike commissioned officers, these men stayed with their ships for long periods. In the nineteenth century it was also common for the masters of merchant ships to take their wives along on voyages.

The historian Suzanne Stark found more than twenty documented instances from the period between the late seventeenth century and the early nineteenth century of women disguising themselves as men and serving either in the Royal Navy or the Marines. It is impossible to ascertain the full extent of this practice, made all the more remarkable by the way that these women were able to conceal their gender in the close confines of a ship. Anne Chamberlyne, 'aspiring to great achievements unusual to her sex and age', is said to have served at the age of twenty-three aboard a fireship at the battle of Beachy Head in 1690; Hannah Snell, after a brief time in the army, served as a marine between 1747 and 1750 and was wounded in combat in India.[54] However, such extraordinary and brave women, who stepped far outside the bounds of contemporary gender roles, appear to have been a very small minority.

CHAPTER SIX

Pax Britannica, 1815–1914

The Royal Navy: peace, the Empire and gunboat diplomacy

For much of the period from 1815 to 1914, the Royal Navy's combat activity was limited to one form or another of 'gunboat diplomacy' (the use or threat of limited naval force to achieve a political objective). However, sail-driven ships of the Royal Navy did fight two more major actions after the Napoleonic War. In 1816 an Anglo-Dutch fleet conducted a fierce bombardment of Algiers, with the largely successful aim of stopping Algerine piracy and freeing European captives. The second battle came in 1827 when a joint British, French and Russian force destroyed over thirty-five vessels in a Turkish fleet at Navarino Bay in Greece. The allied force had been ordered to prevent the Turks from attempting to restore their rule in newly independent Greece. The Turks fired first, but may well have been deliberately provoked. It was the last occasion on which two major entirely sail-driven fleets fought.

The only large-scale conflict in which the navy participated in the nineteenth century was the Crimean War (1853–6). Britain and France supported Turkey against Russian expansionism. Although the war is chiefly remembered as a land conflict, both the British and French relied on seapower to bring their troops into action against the Russians. Russia had a sizeable navy of about 130 ships, an extensive and well-manned coastal defence system, and some modern ships and weapons. Turkey declared war on Russia in October 1853; the British and French allied themselves with Turkey and declared war in March 1854. The Russian fleet, split into two main squadrons, one in the Black Sea and one in the Baltic, was superior to the Turkish navy, but the British and French, who had more large, modern warships, overmatched it. The Russian fleet retreated to defended ports where it remained for much of the war. The allied British and French fleets landed 62,000 men near Sebastopol in the Crimea in September 1854. The British contingent numbered some 150 transports, escorted by 13 Royal Navy warships, along with 40 French warships and 11 Turkish vessels (the French and the Turks had no transports available and carried their soldiers on the warships).

The allied fleets were used for the bombardment of Sebastopol and other Russian ports and fortifications. Sebastopol fell in September 1855 after a long and bloody siege. The Black Sea fleet of more than forty warships was virtually wiped out in harbour, either destroyed by allied fire or deliberately scuttled. The first ironclad warships (vessels with iron armour protection) – floating batteries – were employed by the French in the war, and the Russians made the first use of floating sea mines. These so-called 'infernal machines' carried too little explosive to do much damage, but they were to remain a significant and increasingly dangerous feature of naval warfare.

The other main Royal Navy assault against the Russians was in the Baltic, although minor operations were also conducted in the White Sea and the Pacific. All were marked by ineptitude, for, like the army, the navy had too many senior commanders who had seen their best days in the war against Napoleon, forty years before. However, the Crimean War did demonstrate the latent power of the Royal and merchant navies, in their ability to move a large expeditionary army from Britain to the Black Sea.

Even more than in previous centuries, British naval forces, whether the Royal Navy or ships of the East India Company, were used in the nineteenth century as an instrument of diplomatic and commercial power. Britain fought two so-called 'Opium Wars' with China (1839–42 and 1856–60). The first was sparked by Chinese attempts to stop the import of opium (grown in British India) into China, but both were really about Britain and other European powers having their way in China. The British seized Hong Kong in 1839, and their possession of this prime trading port was recognized by the Chinese in the treaty of Nanking, which ended the first war. The second war, which started when China was already weakened by major civil conflict, saw the British and the French take the port of Canton and even penetrate as far inland as Peking (Beijing), destroying the Imperial Summer Palace. Chinese junks and military forces were no match for British naval firepower. For example, during the Second Opium War, nine British gunboats and their landing parties captured seventy armed Chinese war junks in Fatshan Creek near Canton. The Opium Wars led to the opening of more Chinese ports to British trade.

Britain used naval bombardments on other occasions and in other places to get its way. In 1840 the bombardments of Beirut and Acre forced newly-independent Egypt to give up Crete and northern Syria; in 1864 the shelling of the port of Kagoshima forced Japan to accept foreign traders back; in 1882 the bombardment of Alexandria was the prelude to the military occupation of Egypt, to ensure British control over the strategically-vital Suez Canal. Naval force was not always used in the pursuit of narrow economic and political objectives – for example, the Royal Navy provided cover for the landing in Sicily of Garibaldi and his Italian army of liberation – but Britain's gunboat diplomacy flourished in the nineteenth century and after (see p. 239).[1]

Although the nineteenth century was described as the century of the 'Pax Britannica', with Britain 'ruling the waves', the British were not always persuaded of the security given them by their fleet. There were intermittent fears of war with France that were not really dispelled until the development of the Entente Cordiale in 1904; in the 1850s, by contrast, despite the Anglo-French alliance in the Crimean War, fears of French invasion prompted the building of more coastal fortifications and a craze for volunteer soldiering, along with the development of the first British ironclad warship, HMS *Warrior* (Fig. 80).

However, for long periods Britain was supremely over-confident of its naval superiority. In 1884 the *Pall Mall Gazette*'s revelation that the French fleet was

76 Gunboat diplomacy and war: Royal Navy operations, 1815–1914.

Selected major RN operations

● Punitive shore bombardment

■ War operations

✕ Battle

approaching parity – at least on paper – with the Royal Navy, led to public pressure on the government to spend more money on the navy and build more ships. There were fears, too, of Russia and of the growth of the Russian fleet. In 1889 the Naval Defence Act was passed, which introduced a policy by which the Royal Navy was to be as strong as the next two naval powers put together. The Act ushered in a £21.5 million shipbuilding programme, in which seventy vessels, including eight *Royal Sovereign*-Class battleships, were constructed. These 14,150-ton ships each carried four 13.5-inch (34.29-cm) guns and a secondary armament of quick-firing guns designed to deal with fast torpedo vessels. They were followed in the mid-1890s by the even larger *Majestic* Class, and the row over their high cost led to the resignation of the Prime Minister, William Gladstone, in 1894. The French, Russians and later the Germans were also building new ships. A naval arms race was in full swing years before the launch of the *Dreadnought* in 1906 put matters into an altogether higher gear.

As had happened in the sixteenth century when England's main adversary changed from France to Spain, in the nineteenth century Britain's number one potential enemy changed from France to Germany. The imperial ambitions of Kaiser Wilhelm II's Germany included the building of a powerful High Seas Fleet that the British would not be able or wish to confront and which would enable German to extend its influence on a global scale. In 1898 the German Naval Law laid out an ambitious programme of warship building that would give Germany a fleet capable of seriously challenging the Royal Navy.[2]

The royal dockyards

As in the eighteenth century, the royal dockyards remained among the greatest industrial installations in Britain. A few new royal dockyards were established in the British Isles. Pembroke was officially opened in 1815, the largest naval installation ever constructed in Wales. It underwent further expansion in the 1830s, with a dry dock and other facilities, and in 1890 was employing over 2,000 workers, many of them living in the adjacent community. The navy also constructed a new facility in Ireland at Haulbowline Island in Cork harbour. Although work on this began in the 1860s (largely with convict labour), it was not completely ready until 1894. Like Pembroke in Wales, the Haulbowline yard was the largest-ever naval investment in Ireland, with a large wet dock and a dry dock that could accommodate a major warship.

Dockyard locations were not merely a matter of navigational convenience: they were a part of naval strategy. Pembroke and Haulbowline provided facilities for ships operating in the Atlantic; the development of Rosyth on the east coast of Scotland in the 1900s was in the context of the growing naval threat from Germany. Begun in 1909, Rosyth was not ready for the Grand Fleet (the main British war fleet) until some time after the outbreak of war in 1914. It was a vast base, equipped with three dry docks able to take *Dreadnought*-Class battleships, and had a great deal of space for ships in its main and tidal basins.

Some of the existing yards underwent great change and expansion in the nineteenth-century. Most ships were built on slipways, and covered slips began to be introduced in the latter years of the Napoleonic War, probably based on a Swedish example. The huge roofs made shipbuilding easier because they reduced the effect of the weather on the process, and helped to slow the growth of rot on the slipways themselves. New building techniques also began to appear in the dockyards, such as iron-framed buildings like Portsmouth's magnificent No. 6 Boathouse of about 1844. The Block Mills at Portsmouth (see p. 175) were not the only examples of the early applications of steam power. A steam-powered sawmill, which could cope with timbers up to 70 feet (21m) in length, was working at Chatham by 1814, although the use of steam in the dockyards was somewhat intermittent in the early decades of the nineteenth century.

Sheerness was modernized after the Napoleonic wars, with three dry docks, and reopened in 1823. The first successful steam vessel completed by a royal dockyard was launched at Deptford in 1822, although it was not until the 1840s that the dockyards began to develop in-house expertise in the construction of engines, first at Woolwich (1843), but later also at Portsmouth and Malta (both opened in 1848) and at Devonport (Keyham yard, 1853). All of these projects involved the extension of the yards and the construction of new docks.

The royal dockyards did not launch their first ironclad until 1863, when the massive HMS *Achilles* (9,820 tons) went down the slipway at Chatham (the navy's first ironclad, the *Warrior* of 1860, was built in a private yard). Shipwrights schooled in wooden ship construction had to learn new iron-working techniques or face redundancy, and by and large they did. Deptford and Woolwich dockyards closed in 1869; their restricted sites were not really suited to the production of the new and very large iron-hulled ships, and the government had decided to concentrate naval shipbuilding in particular dockyards.

The new iron construction techniques meant the introduction of new machinery and the enlargement of many docks to accommodate bigger ships. Chatham was enlarged to four times its original size between 1862 and 1885; Portsmouth grew to two and half times its size between 1867 and 1876. A good deal of the construction work, as at Haulbowline, was conducted by convict labour. Devonport and the nearby Keyham yard were expanded in the 1890s and 1900s. In terms of relative importance Portsmouth was the most significant late nineteenth-century dockyard, followed by Chatham, Devonport and Pembroke, all of which were building ships for the navy (see Table 13). By this stage Sheerness had been reduced to a repair and maintenance yard. The four main British yards alone employed over 20,000 people in 1890, and in 1900 the total home dockyard force exceeded 32,000.

Table 13 Major royal dockyard workforces, 1890[3]

Dockyard	No. of workers
Portsmouth	7,615
Chatham	5,670
Devonport & Keyham	5,206
Pembroke	2,092

Malta was the most important overseas yard, given the island's central location in the Mediterranean and the increased strategic significance of that sea for Britain after the opening of the Suez Canal in 1869. The Malta dockyard underwent considerable improvement from the mid-1890s, and Bermuda saw some redevelopment in the late nineteenth century, but some other overseas yards were either closed or downgraded. Antigua was reduced to a coaling station in 1889 and Port Royal, Jamaica, was shut in 1907.

The early twentieth century saw Portsmouth and Devonport become the foremost building yards, concentrating on large warships such as the dreadnoughts. Chatham, which did not have the space or facilities for such vessels, began to develop expertise in the construction of submarines.[4]

Warships

The Royal Navy was the leading world naval force both in 1815 and 1914, even if by the latter date that pre-eminence was coming under very real threat. In the years between the ships and weapons used by the navy and its competitors underwent enormous change.

Warship development in the nineteenth and twentieth centuries saw the science and technology of the Industrial Revolution used to make naval warfare even more destructive. It also served to make navies much more expensive. Although there were strong elements of conservatism in the Royal Navy (some seamen officers, for example, regarded the later commissioned engineer officers as grubby upstarts who did not really belong in the officers' wardroom), there were also good reasons why the adoption of some technologies was so slow.

The Royal Navy experimented unsuccessfully with its first paddle steamer in 1816.[5] Early marine engines were often unreliable, paddles were vulnerable to storm and battle damage, and paddle-boxes took up broadside space that could have been used for guns. For these reasons, naval paddle steamers were seldom more than auxiliaries. The development of the screw propeller in the 1840s changed the prospects for steam navies. The screw made more efficient use of the engine power, was not vulnerable to shellfire and did not take up gunnery space. The navy's first screw-driven warships were small, but in 1847 the 1,741-ton *Ajax* was converted to screw propulsion, the first line-of-battle ship to have the new motive force. The navy used large sailing warships for the last time in the Crimean War, although steam-driven warships remained encumbered by masses of mostly useless rigging until the 1880s. One development associated with the rise of steam power was that of 'coaling stations', bases dotted across the globe that were kept supplied with coal to keep the navy fuelled.

Marine steam engines improved considerably in performance and reliability in the second half of the nineteenth century. The highest point of 'conventional' marine steam engine development was the triple-expansion engine, which was

77 An early steam warship: HMS *Terrible*, built 1845. The 3,189-ton *Terrible* was the largest of the early paddle-driven frigates in the Royal Navy, and was used in the Crimean War. However, the inadequacies of paddle power for warships were soon recognized, and they were eventually replaced by superior propeller-driven warships.

78 HMS *Dreadnought*, completed 1906. Like the *Warrior* more than forty years earlier, the *Dreadnought* was an epoch-making ship which made previous warships obsolescent or obsolete. As the poet Thomas Hardy put it in his poem *Channel Firing*, these new vessels served to 'make red war yet redder'.

more efficient than earlier types and had lower coal consumption. Experiments were carried out with the engine in the 1870s, but the first large ship to use it was the 2,000-ton merchantman *Aberdeen* of 1881. Triple-expansion engines began to appear in Royal Navy ships of the 1880s, but the Naval Defence Act of 1889, which authorized the construction of a massive new fleet of seventy vessels, provided for all new ships to have the modern engine.

The British engineer Charles Parsons revolutionized marine propulsion in the 1890s with the development of his steam turbine, which had a very much higher power to size/weight ratio than any preceding engine type. Work began on the first small, turbine-driven British naval vessel in 1899, which proved both the engine's reliability and economy. In 1905 the decision was made to equip the new *Dreadnought* (completed 1906) with turbines. It was a risky decision with such new technology, but Admiral 'Jacky' Fisher (1841–1920; First Sea Lord, 1904–15) was looking for speed in his new ships. Placing turbines in the *Dreadnought* is said to have saved over £100,000 in costs and 1,000 tons displacement, giving the ship 23,000 shaft horsepower (shp) and a speed of 21 knots. Power output in turbines increased rapidly, so much so that the battlecruiser *Lion* of 1912 had engines that produced 70,000 shp. The turbine had a major impact on British warship development, eventually replacing the older types, although in merchant shipping it was used principally in fast liners.

Naval guns became larger, more destructive and accurate in the nineteenth century, but as late as the early 1900s the effective range of naval guns was still reckoned to be no more than about 3,000 to 4,000 yards (2,743–3,657 m) – not much more than a century earlier (see pp 152–3). Traditional cast-iron solid shot began to give way to explosive shells from the 1820s. The Royal Navy briefly tried out breech-loaders (which were quicker to reload than the old muzzle-loaders) in the 1850s, but found them not to be reliable, and replaced them with rifled muzzle-loaders (the rifling made the gun more accurate). Effective breech-loaders only

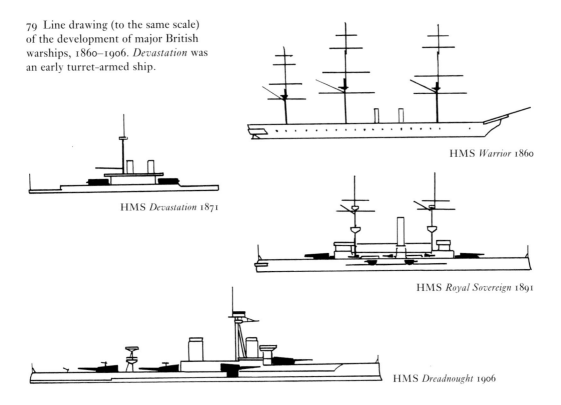

79 Line drawing (to the same scale) of the development of major British warships, 1860–1906. *Devastation* was an early turret-armed ship.

HMS *Warrior* 1860

HMS *Devastation* 1871

HMS *Royal Sovereign* 1891

HMS *Dreadnought* 1906

came into service in the 1880s. The technology of making gun barrels improved in the second half of the nineteenth century, making larger guns feasible, and gun propellants also changed. The old black powder (gunpowder) was gradually supplanted by more complex compounds that burned more slowly, making it easier to predict where a shot would land. Guns still dominated sea warfare, although experience from the American Civil War of the 1860s and the 1866 battle of Lissa introduced a somewhat suicidal vogue for ramming tactics and the provision of ram bows on warships.

Broadside-mounted guns on wheeled carriages were the norm on warships until the second half of the nineteenth century. A bewildering array of experiments was conducted by various nations into mounting guns on revolving turrets to improve their field of fire. It was not until the 1880s, however, that the Royal Navy adopted what became the standard design solution, with HMS *Collingwood* of 1887. This design was the barbette, which consisted of an armoured tower inside the hull, protecting the ammunition hoists, topped by a revolving armoured gun turret.

Armour was another area of warship development with a complicated history. Ordinary iron hulls produced more – and deadlier – splinters when hit with shot than wooden hulls, so iron *per se* was not much of a defence. The notion of 'iron-clads' gathered pace in the 1850s, and in 1859 the French navy launched *La Gloire*, the first sea-going ironclad in the world: a wooden-hulled ship with armoured sides that was invulnerable to most contemporary weaponry. As this happened during one of the periodic French war-scares in Britain, the Royal Navy was stung into making a response. The *Warrior* of 1860 was more than a match for *La Gloire*. Like its French contemporary, it was a broadside-firing frigate with both sails and screw propulsion, but the *Warrior* was bigger, carried more guns and had an armoured hull made of iron. The arrival of sea-going ironclads changed the nature of navies: henceforth, any navy that did not want to risk being wiped out had to invest in even costlier armoured warships and better guns.

Iron was in some ways a problematical material for ships' hulls, particularly as it attracted marine growths in enormous quantities on long voyages, which affected the ship's performance. Ingenious iron-framed hulls with wooden planking and copper plating, known as composites, were introduced. However, new steel-making processes in the 1850s and 1860s eventually made the production of steel in large quantities an economic proposition, and steel rapidly supplanted iron in naval shipbuilding as it was lighter and stronger. Naval architecture and the science of hydrodynamics developed considerably in the second half of the nineteenth century, with innovations such as tank-testing making it much easier to predict how a given hull form would perform at sea.

In the late nineteenth and early twentieth centuries other new technologies transformed the warship. Improved optics made range-finders possible, primitive mechanical computers were introduced for fire control, and electric power led to the introduction of a host of new devices, including searchlights, wireless and director towers. The tower put all the main guns under the control of one officer, and greatly increased accuracy. By 1914 ranges of up to 14,000 yards (12,800 m) were possible, and the likelihood of hits was made much greater.

80 HMS *Warrior*, the Royal Navy's first ironclad, in service from 1862. The development of ironclad warships in the 1850s and 1860s sparked a naval arms race that in some ways still continues. The *Warrior* ended its service days as a floating oil jetty at Pembroke, but after a massive restoration programme, the ship went on permanent display at Portsmouth in the 1980s.

81 The ironclad HMS *Achilles* under construction at Chatham dockyard, 1863. The *Achilles* was even more powerful than the *Warrior*, carrying twenty 100-pounder guns.

Other developments made naval warfare more destructive. Self-propelled torpedoes were adopted by the Royal Navy in the 1870s. A new class of warship, the small, fast 'torpedo boat', appeared; its nemesis, the 'torpedo-boat destroyer' (soon called just 'destroyer'), was developed in the 1880s, and went on to become a major new type of escort vessel. Another new type was the submarine, which became a practical weapon of war in the late nineteenth century. The Royal Navy acquired its first submarine in 1901, with the construction by Vickers of a submarine boat to a design by the American engineer, John Holland. British designs were rapidly produced, although planning and design flaws at first hampered submarine development, and by 1914 the navy had a number of different classes of boat, of which the C, D and E classes were to be the most prominent.[6]

Officers and men in the Royal Navy, 1815–1914

The post-1815 navy was a much-reduced force, but still committed to operating on a global scale. However, the navy was slow to change. Even the press-gang, a wartime necessity, still existed in theory. The navy had difficulties recruiting men in peace time; various expedients were tried, but in 1853 the Continuous Service Act was introduced with the aim of making naval service more of a career for ordinary seamen and less of a form of prison sentence. The Act increased pay and made it possible for eighteen-year-olds to sign on for periods of ten years, with the option of re-engagement before entering the reserve service. Long-service pensions were introduced, as well as the ranks of chief petty officer and leading seaman, which gave men from the lower deck greater opportunity for advancement. In the wake of the Crimean War, which had seen real problems in manning ships, other conditions of service were improved, the standard of the victualling was raised and official naval uniforms for seamen were introduced for the first time in 1857. The Naval Discipline Act of 1860 regularized discipline for the first time, making it less brutal and arbitrary, although flogging with a cat-o'-nine-tails was not suspended as a punishment until the 1870s and corporal punishment was not ended until 1907.

Table 14 The manpower of the Royal Navy, 1830–1913[7]

Date	No. of men*	
1830	30,000	
1840	35,000	
1850	39,000	
1854	62,000 }	Crimean War
1856	68,000 }	
1860	79,000	French war scare
1870	60,000	
1880	58,000	
1890	67,000	
1900	113,000	Boer War
1910	131,000 }	German war scare
1913	146,000 }	

* Figures rounded up or down to nearest 1,000.

Naval accommodation began to improve in the late nineteenth century; previously sailors in port had either slept aboard their ships or in old warships turned into accommodation vessels. The first naval shore barracks were opened in 1890 at Devonport, followed by others, although sailors in barracks still had to sleep in the traditional hammock. Training for the common sailor in the Royal Navy also improved, partly in reaction to the changing times – the introduction of state education in the 1870s raised the general educational levels of recruits – but it was also a reflection of the increasing technical complexity of warships. By the late nineteenth century the days when all an able seaman had to be able to do was to 'hand, reef and steer' were long gone.

Changing times also affected the officer corps. Poor performance in the Crimean War by elderly flag officers led to a round of compulsory retirements that helped to free up the seniority-based promotion system. More attention was also given to the education of naval officers. The hulked warship *Britannia* was commissioned for the training of officer cadets in 1859, and was moved to Dartmouth in 1863, where the hulk was later replaced by the Britannia Royal Naval College as a shore station. The training of officers above the rank of midshipman was improved in 1873 with the opening of the Royal Naval College at Greenwich in the buildings of the old Royal Hospital. The college provided advanced training in technical and scientific subjects, as well as in topics such as naval history and languages. It continued to provide advanced education for naval officers until it was closed in the 1990s and its training facilities were merged with others in the services.

Naval officer training was shaken up considerably in 1902 by the introduction of a common entry and training scheme for officers, instituted by Admiral Fisher when Second Sea Lord (in this position he had special responsibility for personnel). Fisher was a radical, modernizing figure impatient with the aristocratic ways of the traditional officer corps. The common entry scheme was aimed at making officers who could serve alike as seamen officers or engineers, and although it failed in this regard, the broad naval education that it fostered did produce large numbers of technically competent men who helped to make the Royal Navy such a formidable force in the First World War. Fisher was also responsible for the changes made to the training and conditions of ordinary seamen and stokers, which encouraged recruitment and re-enlistment and were vital to the manning of the rapidly growing fleet.[8]

Merchant seamen, 1800–1900

The legislation affecting British merchant seamen and shipping changed considerably in the nineteenth century. Measures for the registration of seamen were developed originally as a means of finding out what men might be available for war service, but an attempt to set up a standing register of seamen in 1696 did not succeed. Ship registration became obligatory under the Shipping and Navigation Act of 1786, but there was no proper registration system for sailors until the 1835 Merchant Seamen Act established the General Register Office of Seamen, and ship masters were obliged to file crew agreements and lists with the office. The 1854 Merchant Shipping Act transferred responsibility for both registers from the Board of Customs to the Board of Trade.

The Seamen's Fund, set up in 1747 by the Act for the Relief of Maimed and Disabled Seamen, was to use sixpences from all seamen (1 shilling per month from 1834) to help fund welfare for Royal Navy sailors. The fund was wound up in 1851 and new provision was made for the payment of pensions to merchant seamen or their widows and children. Long-service seamen received additional pension arrangements in 1911, with the establishment of the old-age pension, and they continue to do so today.

The merchant seaman's progression, from apprentice, to ordinary seaman, and then to able seaman, was well established by the nineteenth century; the period also saw the first real effort to ensure that ships were run by competent officers.

82 The crew of the Littlehampton brig *Ebenezer* at Lowestoft, 1908. The ship's captain, Louis Henry Robinson (in the trilby), was one of several seafaring sons of the Robinson Line's sole owner, the redoubtable Joseph Robinson (1820–1917). Coasters like the *Ebenezer*, and even overseas trading ships, were often crewed by men and boys from the ship's home port.

Voluntary examinations for masters and mates in foreign trade were introduced in 1845, the examinations being conducted by Trinity House and local marine authorities. Compulsory exams were introduced from 1850 onwards, and also from 1850 masters had to keep official logs of voyages. Exams for masters and mates in the home trade (i.e., fishing and coasting) followed in 1854. A master or mate's 'ticket', as a certificate of technical competence, became a requisite for command. Engineers' tickets followed rather later, in 1862, and those for ships' cooks not until 1908.

Discipline could be harsh in merchant ships and desertion was common. Pay was perhaps relatively better than might be found for similar levels of work on land, but the work was casual and unemployment was frequent. The food on offer to merchant seamen in the nineteenth century was little different in kind from that of three hundred years before (see Table 15).

Everything bar the coffee, sugar and tea would have been a regular part of the Tudor seaman's diet, and the quantities of other foods were not much different. The *Marmora* was a coaster, so the food may have been fairly fresh, rather than salted, but even in the 1860s salted food was common on long voyages. The master of *Marmora* may have been a decent man to sail under: at least he recorded on the

Table 15 Diet of the crew of the *Marmora* of South Shields, 1865

Daily	Sun/Mon/Wed Thurs/Sat	Tues/Fri	Saturday	Weekly* Monthly**
1 lb (450 g) bread	1 lb (450 g) beef	1 lb (450 g) pork	½ lb (226 g) rice	1 lb (450 g) butter*
½ lb (226 g) flour		¼ pint (0.14 l) peas		1½ lb (670 g) coffee**
				4 lb (1.8 kg) sugar**
				¼ lb (110 g) tea**

crew agreement what the men were supposed to eat. Others did not bother, or merely scrawled 'Sufficient' on the form.

Going to sea did not just bring hardship and misery: it also brought new experiences to men who might otherwise have strayed no further than their home parishes. Captain Robert Thomas (1843–1903) came from a poor and ill-educated Welsh-speaking background in a small north Wales village. When he went to sea as a teenager his English was, by his own admission, 'very backward & Welshy'; his first voyage also saw his first experience of having a haircut from a barber, during a stopover in Cardiff. He went on to become a ship's captain and wrote a vivid account of his life in English. Robert, like tens of thousands of others, came to know places that were just exotic names to most British people of their time, such as Constantinople, Ceylon and Montevideo. In Montevideo, having jumped ship, this pious Methodist lad worked for a short while as a servant in the 'London Hotel', a place that sounds to have been some kind of brothel. Robert remembered with some bitterness the ill treatment he had had from others – particularly shipowners – but he also never forgot kindnesses, like the Royal Navy seaman who stood him and another ship's boy a meal when they were wandering hungry in the streets of Montevideo: 'An English sailor can never see another hungry if he can help him.' He contrasted life in English ships with the cowed nature of the crew of an American ship, 'where discipline is kept and carried on by kicks & cuffs which was quite common in those days, especially on American Ships', the men having 'no life in them after work as we used to have in English ships, skylarking, etc'. A man with a great hunger for knowledge and a deep affection for his family, whom he missed terribly when at sea (and for whom the reminiscences were written), Captain Thomas died aboard his ship at San Francisco in 1903.[10]

The Victorian age saw numerous public campaigns against social evils. One of these evils was the lot of the seaman, rooted as it was in the age-old determination of many shipowners to drive down freight rates to win more cargoes. This resulted in the overloading of ships, under-manning to save on wages, and the continued use of old, badly built or poorly maintained ships which were death-traps). Some unscrupulous – indeed, murderous – owners relied on insurance to recoup money from a ship that went down. Masters and men were certainly pressured into taking ships out against their better judgement. In 1867 Captain Lean of the *Utopia* resigned because the ship's Liverpool owners ignored his protests against overloading the ship for a voyage to India. His successor, Captain Dickie, was strong-armed into sailing by a letter from the owner's agent, 'if…you do not go in the vessel, I will take care you never get any employment in a ship out of Liverpool….' The ship foundered three days out from Liverpool, although fortunately the crew got away in time. Seamen could be, and were, sent to jail for breach of contract if they refused to take a ship out after they had signed the crew articles.

The Board of Trade reported that more than half the shipping casualties in the 1862–8 period was due to 'unseaworthy or ill-found vessels of the collier class' in the coastal trade. The terrifying experience of a stormy voyage from London to Redcar in 1864 focused the attention of businessman and later MP Samuel Plimsoll (1824–98) on the plight of the sailor in 'coffin ships'. Plimsoll conducted extensive investigations into the state of shipping, and started a campaign to introduce the compulsory inspection of all ships not classed by Lloyds, to institute a maximum load line, and to prevent shipowners from insuring more than two-thirds of their property in any one ship. It must be said that the 'coffin-ship' owners were in a minority, and that many owners, including big firms such as Cunard, wanted better regulation. Plimsoll's book *Our Seamen*, published in 1873 in book and pamphlet form, helped to stir up widespread support for his aims. A blistering national campaign forced Disraeli's government to introduce load-line regulations in 1876. However, until 1890, when the Board of Trade took over the responsibility, it was the duty of the shipowner to mark the 'Plimsoll line', as it came to be called (incidentally, the plimsoll beach-shoe was not invented by Plimsoll, merely named after him as an advertising gimmick). Plimsoll's high-profile activities were only a part of the movement to improve the sailor's lot. Both local and national relief societies were set up in nineteenth-century Britain, such as the British and Foreign Sailors' Society, to provide decent shore accommodation and other welfare for sailors.

Although trade unions had been legal since 1825, and local seamen's unions did exist, the first national union for seamen, the National Amalgamated Sailors' and Firemen's Union (firemen in the sense of engine stokers), was not formed until 1887 (it was formed by J. Havelock Wilson, a Sunderland merchant seaman). The union was re-formed as the National Sailors' and Firemen's Union (NSFU) in 1893. Trade unionism rapidly had an effect. Shipowners formed the Shipping Federation in 1890 to oppose them, and in 1891 they attempted to break a seamen's strike in the Bristol Channel by bringing sixty-two sailors from Newcastle to Cardiff. Most of the sailors were persuaded peacefully not to strike-break by Havelock Wilson, pickets and others, but Wilson was jailed for six weeks for unlawful assembly and riot.[11]

Royal National Lifeboat Institution

The National Institution for the Preservation of Life from Shipwreck (later the Royal National Lifeboat Institution or RNLI) was founded in 1824 by Sir William Hillary. Organized life-saving at sea already had a long history, and the first purpose-built lifeboat designs had emerged in the eighteenth century. By 1824 there were about thirty-nine individually-run lifeboat stations in existence, but the institution was able to bring a coherent structure to life-saving in Britain and Ireland, as well as centralized funding. Some £10,000 was raised in donations in its first year, and a dozen new lifeboats were deployed. However, the organization went through some parlous times until 1851, when the Duke of Northumberland became President and set about revitalizing its funding and activities. An annual government grant helped keep it going from 1854, when it was renamed the Royal National Institution for the Preservation of Life from Shipwreck, to 1869, when it reverted entirely to voluntary funding.

The RNLI was gradually able to create a chain of lifeboat stations around the coast manned by volunteer sailors and fishermen. The extraordinary courage of lifeboatmen, past and present, is well known, and some rescuers have died attempting to save others. For example, in the RNLI's worst year, 1886, the Southport and St Anne's lifeboats were launched in a gale to rescue the crew of a ship that had run aground off the Lancashire coast. Both lifeboats were wrecked and twenty-seven lifeboatmen were drowned, devastating their communities.

All lifeboats were driven by sail and oar until the 1890s, when a small number of steam lifeboats were built. The first petrol-engined lifeboat was not launched until

83 The Beach-Class Aldeburgh (Suffolk) lifeboat *Alfred and Patience Gottwold* on its christening day in 1959. The lifeboat station was established at Aldeburgh in 1851, replacing one of 1826 at nearby Sizewell.

84 The Mersey-Class Aldeburgh lifeboat *Freddie Cooper* just off Aldeburgh beach on
14 December 1995. The photograph conveys some of the conditions in which RNLI
lifeboatmen – all volunteers – risk their lives to carry out rescues.

1908, and complete motorization took some decades to achieve. Air-sea rescue
helicopters, provided by the Royal Navy or RAF, were introduced from the 1940s
to supplement the work of the RNLI. The postwar growth in sailing, motorboats
and other water-based sports led the RNLI to supplement its existing bases with
new stations housing inflatable inshore rescue boats, designed for speedy rescues
close to the coast. The RNLI currently has 224 stations around the coasts of
Britain and Ireland (including Eire), and since 1824 its lifeboatmen have saved over
135,000 lives. Indeed, the writing of this book has been punctuated by the firing of
the maroons to summon the local lifeboatmen to another rescue.[12]

International trade, 1815–1914

The industrialization and urbanization of Britain continued apace from the late
eighteenth century and into the nineteenth: at some point in the 1840s, the
urban/rural balance tipped, and for the first time in history more people were
living in towns and cities than in the countryside. The population of England,
Wales and Scotland rose dramatically, from about 10.75 million in 1800 to 37.5
million a century later. These people had to be fed; the industries and trades on
which many of them relied had to be kept supplied with raw materials; and a large
proportion of the goods made by those industries had to be exported. Britain
came to rely on sea trade as never before. For example, although grain imports
(particularly in Scotland) had often been used to make up food shortages caused by
harvest crises, from the 1770s the large-scale import of grain into Britain became
routine. British agriculture was finding it difficult to keep up with home demand.

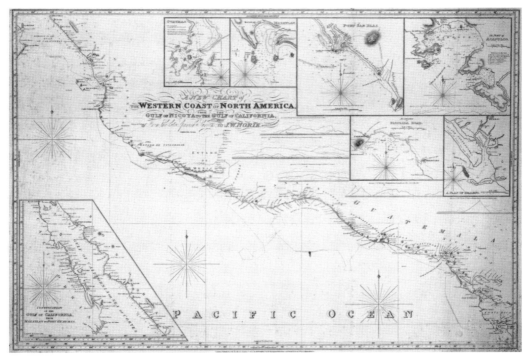

85 Chart of the western coast of North America, by John William Norie, 1846. Norie was one of the leading British commercial chartmakers, producing 'blueback' charts for merchant shipping (the charts had blue backing paper).

This reliance on sea trade was both a source of strength, feeding industries with materials that were not available at home, but, as the two world wars were to show, it could also be a source of danger (see pp 235–7 and 244–7).

The Industrial Revolution drove Britain's overseas trade in the nineteenth century, and also drove the development of Britain's merchant shipping industry. Britain had plentiful supplies of coal and iron, some of the basic raw materials for industrial development, but large amounts of other raw materials had to be imported. By 1913, aside from coal, Britain was importing seven-eighths of the raw materials that it used. Typically, Britain also exported large amounts of manufactured goods: describing the country as 'the workshop of the world' was no idle phrase, for by mid-century Britain was producing 40 per cent of the world's manufactured items. Even as late as the eve of the First World War, one-quarter of the world's seaborne trade passed through British ports.

The volume of Britain's exports in 1914 was about thirty-two times greater than it had been in 1815; for imports over this period the figure was roughly thirty-six times greater. After a post-Napoleonic War depression, British export trade rose rapidly between the 1820s and the 1870s, then began to slow down because of an international depression, growing competition from the industries of Germany and the United States, and the growth of international protectionism.

As has been remarked by various historians, from the point of view of the

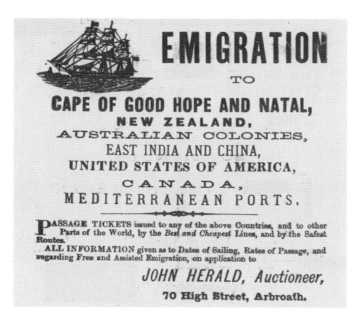

86 Emigration poster, Arbroath, Scotland, 1882. Huge numbers of people emigrated from and immigrated to Britain in the 19th and 20th centuries. Although they are not always recognized in quite the same ways as the Irish diaspora, the Scots, English and Welsh had their own diasporas.

87 Taking the air: artist's impression of life for a first-class liner passenger, 1912. The development of the reliable steam-driven passenger liner in the 19th century made it possible to promote sea travel, whether for business or pleasure, as something to be enjoyed – for those with enough money to do so. This drawing is from an advertising brochure showing the first-class promenade deck of the SS *Titanic*. When the *Titanic* sank in the early hours of 15 April 1912, after hitting an iceberg, the ship only had enough lifeboats for about half of those on board. Nearly 1,500 perished, including many of the crew and disproportionate numbers of the third-class passengers.

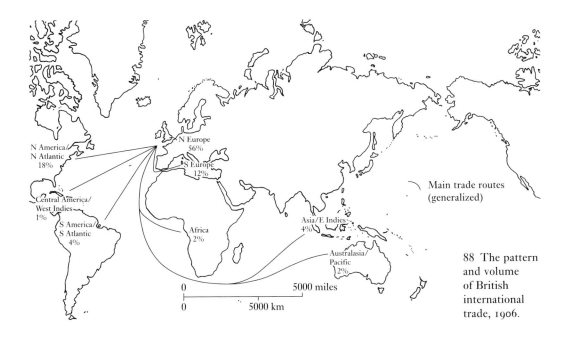

N America/
N Atlantic
18%

N Europe
56%

S Europe
12%

Central America/
West Indies
1%

S America/
S Atlantic
4%

Africa
2%

Asia/E. Indies
4%

Australasia/
Pacific
2%

Main trade routes
(generalized)

0   5000 miles

0   5000 km

88 The pattern
and volume
of British
international
trade, 1906.

89 Travelling steerage, 1904. The steerage-class dining-room of the *Baltic*, built by
Harland & Wolff in 1904. The room could accommodate more than 1,000 passengers
('steerage' was the least comfortable part of a ship, over the propellers). Many European
emigrants to America will have travelled in such spartan conditions, a sharp contrast to
the luxury available to first-class passengers.

shipping industry it is the volume of trade that matters, not its value. Fig. 88 shows how the volumes and values of British trade imports matched up in the early 1900s. Although a significant parts of the import trade arrived in foreign shipping, Britain still had the world's largest merchant fleet in this period, and the pattern of trade gives a fairly good idea of the employment of British ships. From the point of view of actual cargo shipments, European trade made up about two-thirds of the total cargo moved, and North America just under one-sixth. Imports from the rest of the world made up just under 14 per cent of the remainder by volume, but just over 37 per cent of the value, represented by valuable commodities such as rubber.

The nature of Britain's export trade changed through the nineteenth century. The proportion of manufactured goods in British exports declined considerably in the second half of the century. However, the demand for coal in industrializing nations with little or nothing in the way of their own coal reserves helped to turn Britain into a major exporter of coal, rising from about 4 per cent of the total exports by value in the 1870s to 10 per cent by 1910. This internationalized the British seaborne coal trade in a way that had not been seen before, and between the 1870s and 1914 turned Cardiff from a middling provincial port into what has been called a 'coal metropolis', the largest coal port in the world. Cardiff exported 13.5 million tons of goods in 1913, of which 10.5 million tons consisted of coal.

The sheer volume of imports climbed rapidly in the late nineteenth century, fuelled by economic growth and population rise. To take a few examples: tea imports doubled between the early 1870s and the eve of the First World War (351 million pounds of tea – over 159,000 tons – brewed a lot of pots); wood imports, used in house building and a host of other areas, rose by 82 per cent; oil, used mostly to light lamps in the 1870s, was a motor fuel by 1914, imports over the period rising from 12 million gallons to 403 million gallons.[13]

Irish sea trade

Ireland was to remain heavily dependent on trade with Britain well into the twentieth century, even after the establishment of the Republic in the 1920s. In the early nineteenth century Dublin and Belfast had linen as their main export, with Cork and Waterford concentrating on foodstuffs, such as meat, butter and corn. The Irish provision trade had grown considerably in the years before the Great Famine of 1845–9. The Famine devastated the trade, which was, as Ruth Dudley Edwards points out, already a terrible paradox in a country where hunger was commonplace.

The Great Famine was caused by the widespread destruction of the potato crop by disease. Potato was a staple of the diet of many Irish people, and something like one million people – about one person in every eight – died from hunger or its attendant diseases. Famine and consequent mass emigration reduced the Irish population from 8.2 million in 1841 to 6.5 million in 1851. Government response to the crisis was patchy and inept, and the Famine left a legacy of great bitterness. Emigration itself had its risks: many emigrants were exploited by unscrupulous shipping agents and the early emigrant ships were notorious for their poor

90 *The Emigrant Ship Leaving Belfast, 1852*, by John Glen Wilson. The huge wave of emigration from Ireland that followed on from the Famine of the 1840s created what has since been called the Irish Diaspora, which took Irish people to Britain, North America, Australia and many other places. The initial emigration was prompted by human disaster on a vast scale.

condition. Twenty per cent of Cork emigrants to Quebec, for example, either died at sea or soon after arrival.

After the Famine, cattle and corn exports became more important. Livestock-rearing and cattle exports became a vital part of Irish agriculture. The linen trade went from strength to strength in the nineteenth century, although America, rather than Britain, became the main destination for Irish linens. It was only changes in fashion from the 1920s onwards that dealt a mortal blow to the linen industry. Otherwise, agricultural produce continued to dominate Irish exports: they were not overtaken in value by industrial products until the 1970s.[14]

Ports and trade

London was far and away the largest port. Before the building of the first of the great London dock systems in the early 1800s, the amount of river frontage available for cargo-handling was limited. Most sea traffic went to the Pool of London, a stretch of the Thames between London Bridge and the first major bend in the river to the east. Most of the wharfage, both the legal wharves between the Bridge and the Tower, and the tolerated 'sufferance' wharves east of the Tower, were on the north bank, but the total wharfage length on both sides of the river was only about one mile.

By 1797 nearly 13,500 vessels were arriving in the port of London each year, and either mooring at the wharves if they could or unloading out in the river if they could not. The level of congestion had grown enormously, made worse by the flotillas of river craft that plied the Thames, and cargoes were very vulnerable to theft.

In the 1790s the West India merchants began campaigning for the construction of walled docks outside the city boundaries, to create extra cargo-handling space and better security for the goods. The first docks opened between 1802 and 1806, and added enormously to the amount of cargo-handling space available for ships

91 Detail from the Rhinebeck Panorama, an aerial view of the upper Pool of London, *c.* 1810. Probably painted as the artwork for a moving panorama of London (a precursor of the cinema) amongst many other things, the Panorama shows the sort of shipping congestion that made dock-building essential.

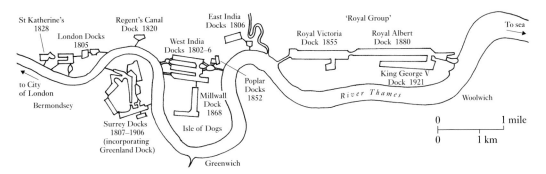

92 The growth of the London dock system, 19th and 20th centuries (after NELP 1986, p. 17).

reaching London: the West India Docks alone had over two miles of quayside. Protected by high walls and (in some cases) their own police forces, the docks contained large bonded warehouses and proved to be great commercial successes. Cargo-handling was cheaper and theft was much reduced.

The dock companies began with trading monopolies, which were much resented, but such was their success that other groups were encouraged to develop new docks. The system was expanded considerably in the nineteenth century, with the last major addition in the 1920s. To meet competition, the dock companies amalgamated during the nineteenth century, and were eventually subsumed in the Port of London Authority, created in 1909.

93 *West India Dock, London, 1830*; lithograph by William Parrott. Human muscle-power remained an essential part of cargo-handling well into the 20th century, as many cargoes were made up of small boxes, sacks or other units.

A vital counterpoint to the redevelopment of ports in the eighteenth century was the construction of canals, which gave coal and mineral-fields, and manufacturing areas, waterborne access to each other and to ports. Some seaports were actually created by canals, such as the Sharpness docks, which were built at one end of the Gloucester and Berkeley Canal (opened in 1827), and allowed shipping easier access to Gloucester. The canals were a major engine of economic growth until competition from the railways in the nineteenth century led them to decline.

The development of steamships in the nineteenth century put pressure on existing dock systems. Iron and later steel ships grew to be much larger than the average run of sailing ships (see p. 231) and many docks were not large enough to accommodate them. Either existing facilities had to be enlarged or new dock areas had to be created to serve them. Given the vast expense involved, only a small number of places could afford to invest on this scale. As the historian Gordon Jackson remarked, steamships 'helped to tie the country's trade to a very small number of ports' that had good docks and internal communications links. Steam power affected docks in other ways: the national railway network was established by the 1840s (if not yet completed), and this made it far easier to move raw materials, goods and people in and out of ports. Cardiff, for example, became the leading Welsh coal port in the 1840s because the largest local landowner, the Marquis of Bute, ensured that the new railway from the mining valleys went to his new West Bute Dock at Cardiff. Cardiff's rise to become a 'coal metropolis' (see p. 232) would have been inconceivable without the railway. In other places, railway companies

94 The South West India Dock, London, late 1880s. The dock is crammed with large iron and steel barque-rigged ships, which represented almost the last flowering of the merchant sailing ship.

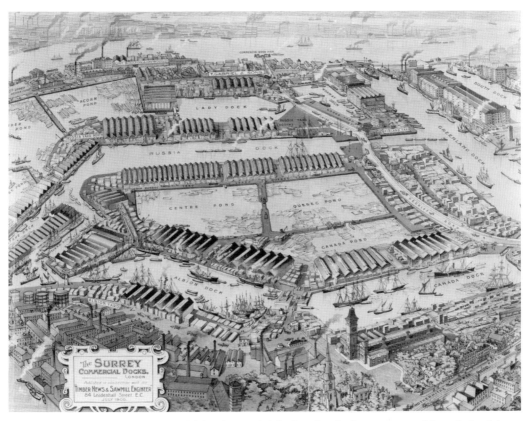

95 Surrey Commercial Docks, 1906. The London docks were powerful symbols of the port's prosperity.

developed ports themselves: the London, Brighton and South Coast Railway began running Newhaven–Dieppe steam ferries in the mid-nineteenth century and tripled annual passenger numbers between the 1880s and the early 1900s to 212,000, after major investment in the harbour and ferries.

The railway also helped to lead to the revitalization of Southampton. Its position on the Channel coast and its relatively quick rail link to London (opened 1840), led to dock development and attracted long-distance passenger and mail lines such as P & O. Southampton went through some ups and downs with its oceanic trade, but finally emerged in the 1890s as a major transoceanic passenger port.

Investment in port development in Britain kept pace with the rising tonnage using British ports from the 1870s to the early 1900s, if not somewhat ahead of it. As well as growing levels of international imports, the British coal trade continued to develop, boosting the trade of ports in south Wales, north-eastern England, Scotland and other parts of the UK. The coal was shipped abroad (export tonnages rise about tenfold between 1860 and 1914), but also around the coast, causing the volume of coastal shipping to grow just at the time when one might have expected it to succumb to competition from railways.

The major ports underwent considerable expansion during this period. Between the late 1850s and 1914, the dock area in Liverpool and Birkenhead grew by more than 20 per cent, and there was substantial modernization of the older docks. Liverpool became a port not just for bulk trades, but also for transatlantic liner traffic, able to take the great new ocean liners being constructed in the late nineteenth and early twentieth centuries. In terms of shipping tonnage leaving British ports for foreign destinations, the leading ports between the 1870s and 1914 were London and Liverpool (more or less equal throughout the period), followed by Newcastle and Cardiff (the latter was in third place by 1914). By 1914 Southampton had risen to fifth place in tonnage terms. The massive investment in British port infrastructure in the nineteenth century was to help 'carry' some ports through the wars, slumps and other crises of the first half of the twentieth century. It was the changes of the second half of that century that were to kill many of them off (see pp 269–71).[15]

Fishing in Britain and Ireland

The English herring industry grew in the nineteenth century, but Scotland had by far the largest share of the British industry; Scottish landings of herring always exceeded those of England, sometimes by as much as two-thirds. Productivity generally improved, and the British herring industry became a European leader. Cotton drift nets began to replace the older hempen variety in the 1860s, making it possible for boats to carry more nets and so increase productivity. Gaff rig began to replace the older lug rig in the second half of the nineteenth century as it made a vessel more manoeuvrable and could be worked by fewer men, and steam drifters started to replace sailing vessels in the late 1890s. On the east coast, a spring herring-fishing season was introduced to complement the traditional autumn season. A large shoreside herring curing and processing industry grew up, dominated by 'fisher lasses'. Although the English herring industry did not overtake that of Scotland, it saw a great rise in productivity in the early 1900s because it was less hidebound by established rules and interests than that in Scotland: by 1914, English catches of herring were up to 81 per cent of those in Scotland.

The railway boom of the mid-nineteenth century was particularly good for trawling, as white fish like cod had always been something of a luxury food. The railway opened up major inland cities for large fish sales in a way that had never been possible before because perishable loads of fish could not be moved very far by horse and cart. The fishing ports of Hull and Grimsby were essentially creations of the railway. Although Hull was already an important seaport, it had only a few fishing boats in 1840, as did Grimsby. The railway opened up markets for these ports in mushrooming industrial cities like Manchester, and by the 1880s the Humber had nearly a thousand trawling smacks. In 1883 the Hull fish trade employed something like 20,000 people. Amongst other things, the inland fish and chip shop, or 'chippie', would have been inconceivable without the railway.

98 Fishwives gutting herrings at Arbroath, *c.* 1890. Commercial fishing has always employed many people ashore as well as afloat. Fishwives were to be found in many harbours around Britain and Ireland, gutting fish in preparation for their curing or sale. It was a hard, dirty job; some fishwives also sold fish, and their rough, aggressive language was proverbial by at least the 17th century.

Fishing had always been a harsh trade, but the need to expand to meet growing demand in the nineteenth century made it harsher still. The rapid growth of the trawling industry created manpower problems that were generally solved by taking boys from reformatories and workhouses, and signing them on as apprentices. This created a large, if rather unstable, workforce. Conditions ashore and afloat were rough and many boys deserted. However, even before the passing of the 1894 Merchant Shipping Act, signing a crew agreement for a fishing boat meant that desertion was punishable by imprisonment. By 1881 more than one Grimsby apprentice in five had done a spell in jail.

Trawling underwent a variety of technological changes. Trawlers got larger in the mid-nineteenth century, and were able to use larger nets, which in turn made them more efficient. Ice, imported from Norway, was first used to keep catches fresh in the late 1840s (over thirty years before refrigeration made possible the shipment of meat from Australia). The first steam fishing boat appeared in about 1877, but the mechanization of trawlers did not really take hold until the 1885–1900 period, during which time most of the big ports replaced their sailing trawlers with steam-driven ones. The steam-engine made it feasible to exploit distant fishing grounds off Iceland and Newfoundland.

The long-distance trawling industry, from the nineteenth century to its collapse

99 Whalers scraping walrus skins aboard the SS *Eclipse* of Peterhead, 1888. The killing of whales as a moral and ecological matter only became a serious issue in the second half of the 20th century, but the depletion of whale numbers has a long history. The men of the *Eclipse* had hunted walruses in this instance because their normal prey, the Greenland Right Whale, was getting harder to find.

in the 1970s, was noted for aggressive management and bad labour relations. Fishermen could still go to jail for missing a boat, work was casual and they were forced to accept a pay system that based remuneration partly on the level of the catch, which led to overwork and a variety of other evils. Trawlermen did not get full employment rights, including redundancy pay, until 2000.[16]

The herring fishery was encouraged in Ireland in the eighteenth century by a variety of bounties, but these came to an end in 1829, along with the Irish Fisheries Board, and the Irish fishing industry was plunged into a crisis. In 1836 there were said to be some 54,000 fishermen in Ireland, but all bar about 9,000–10,000 of these seem to have been part-timers who combined fishing with some other job, such as farming. Extensive fish supplies were simply not available to alleviate the Great Famine, for Ireland did not have proper fishing or fish-processing industries. Few of the smaller harbours had proper piers or fish-curing facilities, and most fishermen could not afford to invest in fishing boats of any size. Fishermen from across the Irish Sea and elsewhere regularly fished off the Irish coast in large numbers, perhaps reducing the amounts of fish that might have been taken by native Irish fishermen. Various schemes were tried to set up fishing companies in Ireland between the 1810s and 1840s, but all failed.

Ireland's fishing industry appears to have declined further in the second half of the nineteenth century, with total employment (presumably including part-timers) falling from above 60,000 in the mid-century to about 26,000 in 1896 and 16,000 in 1919. Not every sector of the industry declined, for the Irish Sea herring industry was revived in the 1860s using boats from different parts of the British Isles, and was directed at the English market. These developments, which included the construction of fish-curing centres, affected a number of east coast ports. A mackerel industry was established at Kinsale in the 1880s on a similar basis. Ireland managed to be a very small-scale net exporter of fish in the early 1900s, although the industry was technically backwards. Even the east coast fishery did not begin to be motorized until the 1920s and 1930s.[17].

British shipbuilding and the development of the merchant ship

The British merchant fleet in 1815 consisted of 21,869 vessels with a total tonnage of 2,478,000 tons and an average tonnage of 113 tons. Nearly a century later, in 1913, the fleet was numerically smaller, with 20,938 ships, but the total tonnage was 11,273,000 tons, and the average tonnage was now 538 tons, 4.76 times greater. While the 'average ship' is a purely theoretical concept, the changing figures do show that in the intervening period the general run of ships had grown significantly larger. One of the major reasons for this was that wooden shipbuilding had been more or less abandoned in favour of first iron, and then steel, ship construction. As Crouzet points out, the growth in the size of the merchant fleet was in part a reaction to expanding international trade, but in part caused by changing technology. Steam power made ships faster, and ultimately also made the shipping of cargo more predictable because it was not dependent on the wind. Wooden ships could not be built beyond a certain size (see p. 151) before the inherent weakness of the material would cause the structure to fail. As iron and steel were much stronger, the practical limits on size were effectively removed, and this made possible the giant oil tankers and aircraft carriers of the twentieth century. The capability for building much larger ships in the nineteenth century made the long-distance carriage of certain bulk cargoes such as coal economic. In these ways steam engines and metal hulls served to reduce costs and freight rates, and increase profits.

Notions of what nineteenth-century merchant ships were like tend to be dominated by two famous surviving examples, Brunel's steamship *Great Britain* (1843) and the sail-driven *Cutty Sark* (1869). The *Cutty Sark* was a clipper, part of a fairly short-lived phenomenon, the fast merchant sailing ship. Such vessels were first developed in America and to begin with were used to move illicit opium into China and bring illicit slaves across the Atlantic, trades where speed was imperative. From 1837 to 1869 a series of 'Blackwall frigates' was built in Britain after the expiry of the East India Company's monopoly on eastern trade in 1833. These were large, fast sailing ships used on Indian trade via the Cape of Good Hope. British clippers like the *Cutty Sark* were built in the 1850s and 1860s to carry Chinese tea as quickly as possible to Britain. The opening of the Suez Canal in 1869 and the rise of the steamship soon made them obsolete.

The typical sailing merchant ship of the first half of the nineteenth century was far removed from the romantic clipper or Blackwall frigate (which never existed in very large numbers). The introduction of central government ship registration in 1786 was accompanied by new tonnage calculation rules that made the arbitrary assumption that the depth of a ship's hull was equal to half its beam. Tonnage figures were used to calculate many of the harbour dues charged on ships, and this meant that ships were built with narrow, deep hulls and rounded bows that could maximize cargo space for a given notional tonnage. Such ships were slow and did not sail very well. Changes to tonnage calculation methods were made in the 1830s, which encouraged the construction of shallower and wider vessels, but such types did not become common until the 1860s.

British merchant ship construction, and the merchant fleet itself, went into something of a decline between 1815 and the late 1830s because of competition from the United States and Scandinavia. Britain had to import most of its shipbuilding timber by this time, whereas these competitors had plentiful timber

100 The brig *Mitchelgrove* (second from left) and the snow *Emma* (right) of Littlehampton, Sussex, 1866. Built in 1815 and 1866 respectively, the two ships typify some of the changes in wooden merchant ship design. The *Mitchelgrove* was a deep-hulled brig of a type common in many trades, including the coal trade. By contrast, the *Emma* was designed to operate in the shallow waters of the river Plate in South America: its hull shape was finer, and it was not as deep-hulled as the *Mitchelgrove* (the terms 'brig' and 'snow' referred to rig configuration). (Description after Greenhill 1980, 21)

101 A shipyard on the Wear, north-eastern England, early 1870s. The frames of a wooden ship under construction are in the foreground, surrounded by scaffolding. Such a sight was probably typical of most shipbuilding scenes from the Middle Ages to the 19th century.

supplies to hand and so could build cheaper ships. One of the results was that for decades American shipping dominated trade between the USA and the British Isles.

Although it now seems that the 'triumph of the steamship' (Crouzet) was inevitable, it did not look that way to begin with. British-registered steam tonnage did not exceed that of sailing ships until after 1880, although port records make it clear that by 1876 sail-driven tonnage entering British ports (11.3 million tons) had just been overtaken by that of steam tonnage (13.3 million tons). Thereafter the balance swung rapidly: steam tonnage entries were double those of sail by 1881 and six times greater ten years on. By 1913 only about 7 per cent of British merchant tonnage still proceeded under sail.

Steam power excited extreme prejudices in many a sailor's heart ('Sail's a lady; steam's just a bundle of iron'), but this was not the main reason for its faltering start. Early steam engines were unreliable and, although these problems were eventually solved, paddle-engines did not produce a great deal of power in return for the amount of coal shovelled into them. In addition, the paddles were vulnerable to damage, coal-bunkers took up cargo-space, and steam-powered voyages became more expensive the longer they took (even remote coaling stations did not really reduce costs as their coal became more expensive the further it was shipped). However, steamers proved to be of considerable use on ferry routes and on short sea trade routes, where speed and the ability to run to regular timetables were important and coaling costs were not prohibitive. Described as 'the first modern ship' (Corlett), Brunel's *Great Britain* was a massive 3,443-ton vessel (registered tonnage) with a screw propeller, an iron hull and six masts (some decades were to pass before merchant vessels were routinely built without auxiliary sail power). Designed by one of the great engineering geniuses of the nineteenth century, the *Great Britain* was a trailblazer, but it was not until 1868 that the tonnage of new iron ships launched in Britain equalled that of new wooden vessels, and only surpassed it in the early 1870s. As in warships, steel began to replace iron in merchant shipbuilding from the 1880s onwards.

The development of the screw in the mid-nineteenth century improved power output, but it was the introduction of iron hulls that eventually allowed steamships to overtake sailing ships. Iron hulls were not only stronger and more durable than wooden ones, they were lighter and less expensive for the equivalent tonnage in wood. As they could be built in much larger sizes they gave sufficient space for engines and coal-bunkers, but also the potential for vastly increased cargo space.

Iron, and later steel, sailing ships were soon eclipsed by steam vessels. Britain was a world leader in steam engine manufacture and designers worked to produce new engine types that would maximize power output and reduce fuel consumption. The coupling of high-pressure boilers with the compound engine (1860s) and

102 The P & O steamer SS *Hindostan* leaving Southampton, 24 September 1842. This was the inauguration of the Indian Mail Service: steam power made commercial sea trade much more predictable.

103 The SS *Rossetti*, a cargo steamer of the 1890s. Shown here in the river Avon near Bristol, the *Rossetti* was a steel-hulled vessel of 2,080 tons gross, built at Sunderland and owned by a London firm. Vessels of this type supplanted sailing ships; the masts here have become cargo-handling derricks.

the introduction of the triple-expansion engine (first used in a cargo-steamer in 1874) helped to make steam power an even better economic proposition.

Britain's great supplies of iron ore and coal conferred enormous advantages on the country in the Industrial Revolution; mineral extraction centres and manufacturing centres were not far removed from each other, reducing transport costs. One result was that Britain could produce many metal items, including ships, more cheaply than its competitors, such as the Germans. Big yards did exist in various places, such as Harland & Wolff in Belfast (building in iron from the 1850s), but the Clyde and the north-east of England, close to mineral supplies, became the great centres of British shipbuilding. Shipyards used to building in wood had to adapt or die. Other major shipbuilding centres, such as London, declined because they were too far from the coal and the iron ore to be economic.

The economies of scale occasioned by the sheer size of the British shipbuilding industry meant that it could get steel at lower prices than its foreign rivals. The steam engine and the metal hull helped to ensure British maritime supremacy in

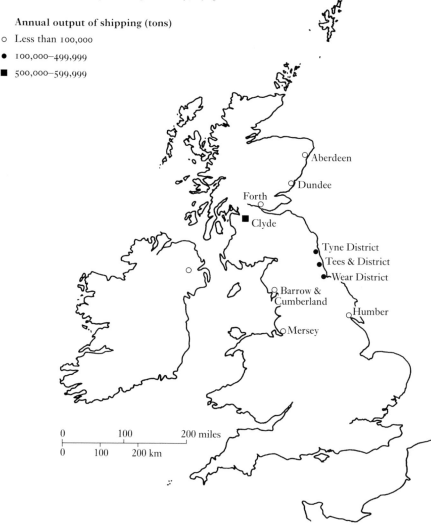

Annual output of shipping (tons)

○ Less than 100,000

● 100,000–499,999

■ 500,000–599,999

Aberdeen

Dundee

Forth

Clyde

Tyne District

Tees & District

Wear District

Barrow &
Cumberland

Humber

Mersey

0	100	200 miles
0	100	200 km

the second half of the nineteenth century. The British share of world merchant shipbuilding fell from 79 per cent in the first half of the 1890s to 61 per cent in 1913, as foreign shipyards developed, but Britain was still the number one merchant shipbuilder. British workforces and management were highly skilled, with productivity nearly double that of their closest rivals, the Americans, although British yards on the whole were not as technologically advanced as those in some other countries.

Britain was also a major builder of warships, and had about one-third of the world warship market in 1913. The growing technical complexity of warships, and armaments in general, led British governments to encourage the development of private armaments firms to provide the country with greater arms manufacturing

105 Launch of the ocean liner *Celtic* at Harland & Wolff's Belfast yard in 1901. At 20,904 gross tons, the *Celtic* was at this time the largest ship in the world. The *Celtic* was one of sixty-one ships built by the Belfast firm for the Oceanic Steam Navigation Company between 1870 and 1931 – a firm better known as the White Star Line.

106 C.H. Bailey's Commercial Drydock, Barry, South Wales, early 20th century. Bailey's and many other maritime businesses thrived on the massive export of coal from Cardiff and other ports in South Wales.

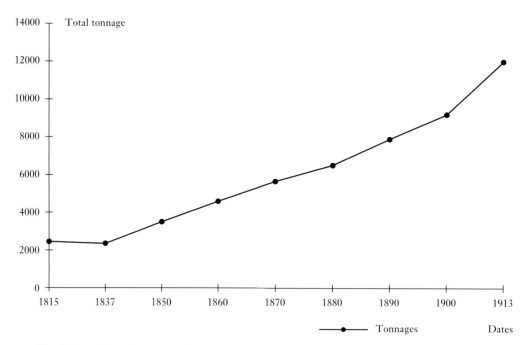

107 The UK-registered merchant fleet 1815–1913.

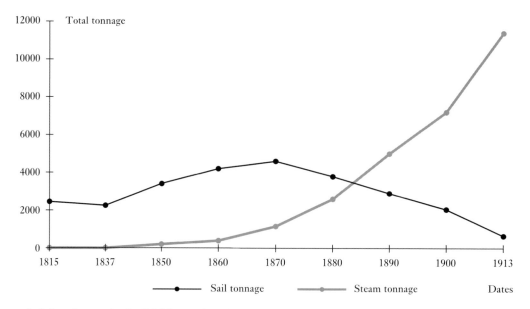

108 Sail and steam in the British merchant fleet, 1815–1913.

capacity in case of war and to reduce the spiralling costs of its own dockyards and ordnance factories. Metal-working cities such as Sheffield became linked to the navy in ways that they had never been before by making guns and armour-plate.

The British merchant fleet was still the largest in the world in 1913, with 34 per cent of total ocean-going tonnage, and a very substantial part of the world's trade moved in British-owned or British-built vessels. Even Britain's greatest maritime rival, Germany, only had 9 per cent of total tonnage, and the US merchant fleet had never really recovered from the American Civil War of the 1860s.[20]

The shipping industry

The nineteenth century saw an increasing division between merchants and shipowners. In the late eighteenth and early nineteenth centuries it was common for shipowners to be traders, or vice-versa. For example, the Henley family of Wapping, on the Thames, who operated as shipowners in this period, were mostly the sole owners of their vessels and had a fleet of nine in 1801. They traded with the Baltic, other parts of Europe and North and South America, carrying other people's cargoes, but they also bought Tyne coal, which they then shipped to London and sold. The largest ship they owned was of 466 tons, but most were between 225 and 397 tons, not small by contemporary standards, but miniscule when compared with ocean-going ships of a century later. For example, in 1911 even a two-ship firm such as the Duffryn Steamship Company of Cardiff owned vessels that were, respectively, of 2,085 and 4,158 tons gross.[21]

A great deal of capital was required to build steamships, and a large amount of revenue to keep them running. This favoured the development of large shipping companies with enough money to build and maintain fleets. By 1900 about one-third of British tonnage was owned by twenty-four major firms. The development of at least some of the big companies was not just a matter of mercantile enterprise. Britain's first major steamship companies, P & O (Peninsular and Oriental Steam Navigation Company), Cunard and Royal Mail, were all founded between 1837 and 1840 on the basis of successful tenders for British government overseas mail contracts. Although the lines subsequently expanded beyond the carriage of mail, the contracts did operate as a form of government subsidy, helping to keep them afloat in both senses of the term. The increasing reliability of steamships made possible the development of regular shipping routes, or lines, that ran to timetables. Shipping lines had existed in the days of sail and sailing-ship lines continued to exist in some countries into the twentieth century, but steamers were generally faster and more predictable.

Despite the dominance of the big companies, most nineteenth-century shipping concerns were much smaller, many comprising just one or two vessels. These vessels were often tramp steamers, merchant ships that did not sail on fixed routes but moved from port to port, picking up cargoes when they could, or sailing in ballast only (i.e., without cargo but with enough ballast for stability) when they could not. About 60 per cent of British shipping consisted of tramp steamers in 1913, and of this about 40 per cent was used to move coal. The coal trade turned the port of Cardiff into one of the greatest tramping ports of the world by the early 1900s. The development of the Bute Docks and later port facilities from the mid-nineteenth century onwards made Cardiff the main port for the output of the vast south Wales coalfields. Cardiff was transformed from a place with just 68 ships totalling 13,950 tons in 1860 to 367 ships of about 1.3 million deadweight tons (tonnage measured as actual carrying capacity) by 1910.

The development of legal limited liability in the 1850s and 1860s encouraged investment in all sorts of areas, including shipping (although it had had its own form of this for centuries), and some ships acquired literally hundreds of investors. Even some household servants, scarcely the wealthiest people in the country, are known to have put money into shipping shares. This sort of situation created shipping managers who did not own the vessels they managed, but drew fees for what they did. Most were competent and honest, but some were not and ran off with investors' money.

However, despite the development of shipping managers, shipowning families still survived and some traded their own cargoes. The Duffryn Steamship Company was run by George A. Harrison and his sons; renamed the Town Line in 1914, it rose to become one of the successful Cardiff shipping companies by 1920s. The Harrisons also owned mines, and their advertisements boasted that they shipped:

> *Our Own Coals,*
> *In Our Own Waggons,*
> *Sent by Our Own Steamers.*

Shipowning, both past and present, has not always had a very savoury reputation. Crews have been employed for scandalously low wages, rust-bucket ships run until they fall apart or sink, and, more recently, the prevalence of flags of convenience with more 'relaxed' (i.e., ineffective) inspection regimes, have all combined to cast a pall over the shipping industry. This is not to say that all, or even most, owners, past or present, have been ruthless, callous or negligent. However, there is no doubt that some of them were.

In the nineteenth century a minority of Cardiff owners were strongly suspected of sinking their own ships in order to be able to claim on insurance. Even overtly Christian shipowners might be no better. The Methodist shipowners of north Wales in the mid-nineteenth century had a strong reputation for religious zeal, business acumen, and, to their seamen 'incredible meanness, not to say harsh self-interest'. Mesach Roberts, a Bangor (north Wales) chemist, was also a Poor Law Guardian and was said to use the local ragged schools to supply cheap labour for his ships. Captain Robert Thomas, who went to sea in the employ of one such owner in the late 1850s (see p. 207), later reflected that 'I sometimes wonder if God will hold such men guiltless that lived on men and boys' labour at the expense of their body and soul.'[22]

CHAPTER SEVEN

Flagging-out, 1914–2001

The Royal Navy and the First and Second World Wars, 1914–45

It was not inevitable that Britain, France and Russia would go to war with Germany, Austria-Hungary and Turkey in 1914. The previous thirty years and more had seen various combinations of great powers coming close to conflict. However, there was widespread suspicion and some fear of the expansionist aims of Germany, led by the bombastic figure of Kaiser Wilhelm II, and the alliances that would drag nations into a world war were in place by 1914. A costly and destabilizing naval arms race began as Britain and Germany built large numbers of dreadnought-type battleships, the most powerful vessels afloat.

The assassination of the Archduke Ferdinand of Austria-Hungary in Sarajevo on 28 June 1914 was the trigger for the conflict. Britain's entry into the war came on 4 August 1914. Germany had declared war on France the day before, and, as its war plans required, had invaded Belgium in order to attack the French army from behind. Britain was bound by a treaty obligation of 1839 to uphold Belgian neutrality. The coast of the Low Countries had been seen as presenting a good base for an invading force from the sixteenth century onwards, and it was perceived to be in Britain's interests that it was not held by a great power.

The British Expeditionary Force sailed for France, and within a few months what had begun as a war of movement turned into trench warfare, a sort of vast siege that lasted for the best part of four years and consumed millions of lives. It had been expected by many that the outbreak of war would lead to a shattering Trafalgar-like battle between the British Grand Fleet and the German High Seas Fleet. On the British side there was an assumption, born of long-term naval superiority and the Nelson myth, that the Royal Navy would emerge triumphant. The commander of the Grand Fleet, Admiral Sir John Jellicoe (1859–1935), was less sure. The Grand Fleet was anchored in its new base at Scapa Flow, a huge sheltered anchorage in the Orkney Islands, poised to take on the High Seas Fleet should it emerge in force into the North Sea. One of the navy's first duties in the war was to blockade Germany, keeping the High Seas Fleet in check and strangling German sea trade by controlling the exits from the North Sea. The blockade proved very effective: the German war economy was badly hit as the flow of food and raw materials from overseas was cut off. Although the Royal Navy's blockade of Germany did not involve direct attacks on civilians in the way that the later German U-boat campaign did, it did bring suffering, malnutrition and death to many German civilians. Even a 'passive' weapon can kill.

The Royal Navy and its imperial allies had rapidly eliminated most German

109 The First World War at sea in north-western Europe.

- ● British naval base
- ■ German naval, base
- U German U-boat base
- X Battle
- ⬚ German coastal bombardment

Scapa Flow

Invergordon

Rosyth

X Jutland

X Dogger Bank

Kiel ■

Hull

Wilhelmshaven

Berehaven

Queenstown

Milford Haven

Harwich

Chatham Dover

Portsmouth

Devonport

| 0 | | 100 | | 200 | | 300 miles |
| 0 | 100 | 200 | 300 km | | | |

surface ships of any significance outside Europe within a few months of the out-break of war. However, the German surface fleet in Europe was not confined to port. In December 1914 German warships bombarded Scarborough, Whitby and Hartlepool on the east coast, causing considerable loss of civilian life, and escaped retaliation from the Royal Navy. In January 1915 a German squadron was inter-cepted near Dogger Bank in the North Sea by British ships, but a misinterpreted signal from the British commander, Rear-Admiral Beatty, led to the escape of most of the German ships, apart from the cruiser *Blucher* which was sunk with the loss of hundreds of men.

The largest naval battle of the war was fought on 31 May and 1 June 1916, some distance off the Danish Jutland coast. The aim of the German fleet was to bring the Grand Fleet to battle and to defeat it. Had the Germans succeeded, the High Seas Fleet might have been able to isolate Britain and bring about its surrender. The battle cost the lives of over 8,000 sailors and sank 25 ships (about 6,000 men and 14 ships on the British side and about 2,500 men and 11 ships on the German). The

110 The battlecruiser HMS *Queen Mary* blows up during the battle of Jutland, 4:26 pm, 31 May 1916. German gunnery was more accurate than that of the British, and a 12-inch shell from the German warship *Derfflinger* set off an explosion in one of the battlecruiser's poorly-protected magazines. This huge cloud of smoke marked the deaths of 1,266 men: only 20 survived.

Germans declared it a victory and, on the face of it, they were right. Not only were British casualties much heavier, three of the British ships sunk were modern battlecruisers. The battle revealed poor design in some British ships of armour and of shell magazines, and some British shells failed to penetrate German armour. However, the battle was a strategic victory for the Royal Navy, as the Germans did not break the Grand Fleet and the battered High Seas Fleet retired to port. German surface forces were later to mount raids in the North Sea and Channel, but they never again attempted a large-scale challenge to the Royal Navy. The blockade held.

The largest single British naval surface operation outside the North Sea and English Channel was the assault on the Turkish-held Dardanelles, between February 1915 and January 1916. Mounted to aid Russia, the campaign was aimed at destroying land defences on the Gallipoli peninsula so that British and French ships could break through the narrow Dardanelles and capture Constantinople. The plan failed: the bloody Gallipoli campaign (promoted by Winston Churchill as First Sea Lord) cost half a million casualties on both sides (including many Australian and New Zealand troops) and the Royal Navy lost five major warships.[1]

The Royal Navy by itself could not win the war against Germany. However, the U-boat arm of the German fleet came close to winning the war against Britain. The first submarine attack of the First World War took place on 8 October 1914, when U17 sank the British steamer *Glitra* off the coast of Norway. The U-boat commander behaved humanely, giving the crew time to abandon ship before the sinking and even towing their lifeboat for a short distance towards Norway.

However, it was not long before the ruthless logic of submarine war began to change the nature in which it was waged. Surfacing and giving warnings, or giving people time to escape, put the attacking submarine at risk. Commerce raiding had been a feature of sea warfare since the Middle Ages, but the object was generally to capture an opponent's merchant shipping rather than sink it. Submarines could not capture; for the most part, they could only sink, for they could not spare sufficient men to crew captured ships. It was part of the nature of a new form of warfare that was to have profound military, economic and political consequences.

It took the Germans some months from the start of the war to decide to use submarines in an unrestricted offensive against British sea trade, because this was contrary to international law. However, on 4 February 1915 the Germans declared the waters around the British Isles to be a war zone, with merchant ships – Allied and neutral alike – subject to attack. In the face of protests from neutrals, particularly from the United States, the Germans declared that obviously neutral ships would be safe.

The early German submarine attacks often took place on the surface, using a deck gun or even explosive charges placed by a boarding party to sink a vessel. These tactics were designed to conserve torpedoes. Mine-laying submarines were also developed to release mines in seaways frequently used by enemy shipping. Between March and September 1915 the U-boats sank 480 merchant vessels in British waters, including the 30,000-ton Cunard liner *Lusitania*, which went down off the Irish coast in May with 1,201 men, women and children, of whom 128 were American. The international outrage and diplomatic shockwaves that followed the attack led the German government to modify their campaign orders yet again, exempting large liners from attack. Unrestricted submarine warfare was called off in September 1915 and, apart from a brief revival in spring 1916, was not resumed until February 1917. The campaign had done some damage to British merchant ships and to the neutral shipping that the country relied on for vital imports of foodstuffs and raw materials, but the effect was not, as yet, potentially catastrophic.

The German high command rightly regarded Britain as the powerhouse of the Allied war effort, and deduced that if the country's sea trade could be sufficiently damaged, the import-dependent nation would have to surrender, with France, Italy and the other allies soon following suit. They came close to achieving their aim. As an island Britain was more vulnerable to the effects of blockade than continental Germany. In terms of its energy value, roughly 60 per cent of the food consumed in Britain by 1914 came from overseas. The slowing down or interruption of this supply could have led to malnutrition or even starvation, to say nothing of the effect that interruptions in the supply of vital industrial materials would have on the war effort.[2]

The anti-submarine measures employed by the Royal Navy were at first not very effective, relying on crude weapons, anti-submarine patrols and Q-ships (warships disguised as merchantmen). Depth charges, minefields, sea barrages and primitive hydrophones were also used with slight success to fight the U-boats, but in the end the U-boat threat was countered more by organizational than technological

111 A British convoy sighted at sunset by the German U-boat *U35*, 1914–18.
An ominous fact underlies this seemingly peaceful scene: German submarines favoured
night attacks on the surface, where their speed was greater and the chances of detection
were reduced. *U35* operated in the Mediterranean from 1915 to 1918.

changes. Part of the problem lay in the fact that until the spring of 1917 the
Admiralty was not really aware of the sheer scale of shipping losses. The idea of
sailing ships in convoy for mutual protection went back to the Middle Ages, and
had operated very efficiently during the wars of 1793–1815, but it had fallen out of
favour in the intervening period. Convoys had been introduced on the short sea
crossing to Holland in 1916, and were introduced for coal ships sailing to France
early in 1917, but even at this time the Admiralty was still very resistant to the idea
of the general use of convoys. Objections included the notion that a convoy was a
large, slow target that would present U-boats with enormous opportunities for
creating mayhem, and it was also thought that merchant ships would not be able to
keep station in convoys. Convoys were indeed large, slow targets, but U-boats had
to find them first. In a vast area such as the Atlantic Ocean it was as difficult for a
submarine to find a convoy as it was to find a single ship. Statistical misreading
made the Admiralty think that there were many more merchant ships than it
could convoy. Conversely, the figures did not appear to show quite how bad the
situation was.

Once the error had been spotted, the real rate of destruction was found to be
truly appalling. Between January and April 1917 2.3 million tons of Allied shipping
was sunk (860,000 tons in April, the worst month of the war), just over half of it
British. Anti-submarine warfare was proving largely ineffective. By late 1916 the

Allies were losing an average of 65 merchant ships for every U-boat sunk, a figure that rose to 167 ships to one submarine in April. The disastrous events of April 1917 decided the Admiralty in favour of the convoy system. However, convoys did not bring immediate relief, and it took some months for the situation first to stabilize and then to improve. Even so the U-boats remained a threat: something in the order of 2.75 million tons of world shipping was sunk in 1918. Unrestricted submarine warfare had proved to be the most devastating naval strategy ever devised.

Britain relied on its own and other merchant fleets to keep it in the war. The merchantmen in turn relied on the Royal Navy, which could have lost the war for Britain. If either the High Seas Fleet or the U-boats had won, there would have been a total blockade of the British Isles, followed by ignominious surrender, and Germany would soon have won the war in the West. The fact that the German surface fleet was contained, and the U-boat threat was eventually controlled, was due largely to the Royal Navy.

The First World War saw the first use of air power at sea, although it was effective mainly in patrol and reconnaissance roles rather than in direct combat. The Royal Naval Air Service (RNAS) was formed in 1914, and by 1918 had a force of 67,000 men, 3,000 aeroplanes and just over 100 airships. Successful experiments were also carried out with aircraft carriers during the war. The RNAS was merged with the Royal Flying Corps in 1918 to form the Royal Air Force (RAF). The naval part of the RAF (called the Fleet Air Arm – FAA – from 1924) did not return to Admiralty control until 1937. The navy believed, with some justice, that the RAF did not rate naval concerns very highly, and that this accounted for the many slow and obsolescent types that the FAA possessed at the outbreak of war in 1939.

The High Seas Fleet sailed into Scapa Flow at the end of the war, to be scuttled by its own sailors in 1919. The U-boats were interned and later scrapped or sunk. The Versailles Peace Treaty of 1919 decreed that Germany would have no submarines and a fleet only capable of coast defence. This and other more punitive provisions of the Treaty helped to sow the seeds of German resentment that would later be exploited by the Nazis.

The inter-war period was not one of inactivity for the Royal Navy. Its first major post-war operation was against Russia (involving, at its height, eighty-eight warships). The Bolshevik Revolution of 1917 was followed by a bloody civil war in which the Tsarist Whites fought the Bolshevik Reds. The Reds pushed westwards into the Baltic republics of Estonia, Latvia and Lithuania, and eventually into Poland (where they were defeated). British naval and military intervention in the Baltic in 1919 helped to secure the independence of the Baltic republics, but in the Baltic and Arctic Russia (Archangel) it failed to inflict lasting defeat on the Bolsheviks.[3]

The founding of the League of Nations in 1919 was just one of a number of measures taken in the inter-war period to limit conflict. The 1922 Washington Naval Treaty set limits on the size, numbers and armaments of warships that the great powers could possess, and succeeded in putting the brakes on a growing post-war naval arms race. The London Naval Treaty of 1930 extended restrictions

112 The Grand Fleet at Scapa Flow, Orkney, 1914–18. This huge, elaborately defended anchorage was a major fleet base in both world wars.

on warship building and development until 1936. However, by the late 1930s international warship building and development were in full swing once again.[4]

Royal Navy warships were used on many occasions between 1919 and the outbreak of war in September 1939 in attempts to effect one form or other of gunboat diplomacy. These ranged from the evacuation of British nationals from Georgia before it fell to the Bolsheviks in 1920, breaking a dock strike in China in 1926, and sending five warships to Egypt in 1928 to 'persuade' the Egyptian parliament to drop a bill that the British did not like. More laudably, the Royal Navy was used to protect food shipments into Republican Spain during the 1936–9 Spanish Civil War, and also took part in the evacuation of refugees.[5]

Nazi expansionism led to the Second World War: the German invasion of Poland in 1939 went too far even for the appeasement-minded governments of Britain and France. The first nine months of the war, from September 1939 to May 1940, were known as 'the Phoney War', because little military action took place in Western Europe. However, the Royal and Merchant Navies were at war from first to last.

The Royal Navy was much stronger than the German Kriegsmarine, but it had a very much larger remit – to defend Britain and the British Empire – whereas the German navy was suited mainly to commerce raiding and for action in European waters. However, Germany did possess some powerful modern battleships and a small but growing force of U-boats. Learning from the Great War, the Royal Navy instituted convoys from the outset, although early on there were some ineffectual but occasionally disastrous U-boat hunting patrols. The first major casualty came

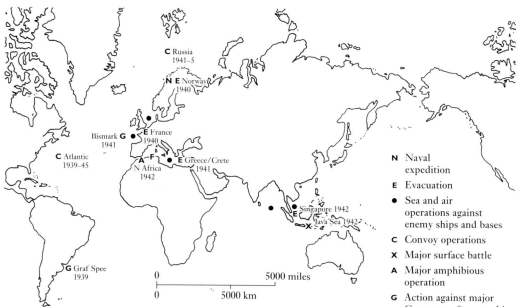

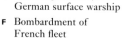

113 The Second World War at sea: 1939–42.

N Naval
   expedition

E Evacuation

• Sea and air
   operations against
   enemy ships and bases

C Convoy operations

X Major surface battle

A Major amphibious
   operation

G Action against major
   German surface warship

F Bombardment of
   French fleet

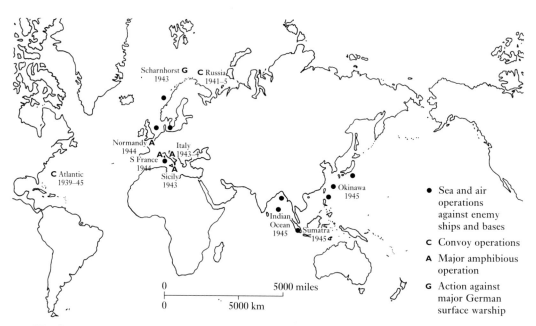

114 The Second World War at sea: 1943–5.

• Sea and air
   operations
   against enemy
   ships and bases

C Convoy operations

A Major amphibious
   operation

G Action against
   major German
   surface warship

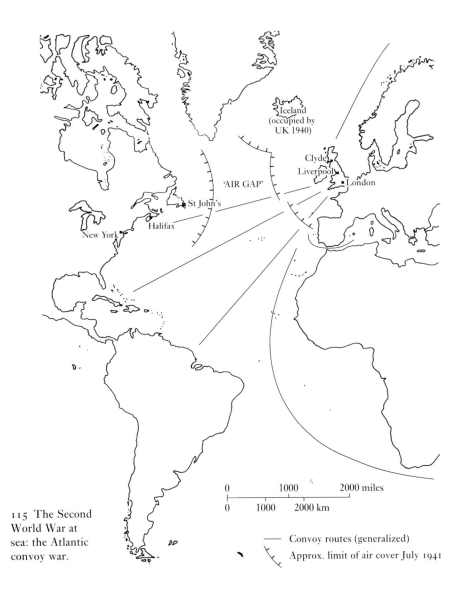

115 The Second
World War at
sea: the Atlantic
convoy war.

0   1000   2000 miles
0   1000   2000 km

—— Convoy routes (generalized)

Approx. limit of air cover July 1941

in October 1939 when U47 managed to penetrate the protected anchorage at Scapa
Flow and sink HMS *Royal Oak*, with great loss of life. Two months later, the
German commerce-raiding 'pocket battleship', *Admiral Graf Spee*, was hunted to
destruction by three British cruisers in the South Atlantic.

In April 1940 Germany invaded Norway in order to secure the shipment of
Swedish iron ore from the north Norwegian port of Narvik. British and French
forces totalling 25,000 men were sent to resist the invasion, including a strong
Royal Navy force. The Germans were able to conquer Norway and the last Allied
troops were withdrawn in June, but the Norwegian campaign was a disaster for the
Kriegsmarine, which lost three cruisers, ten destroyers and a U-boat, most of them
destroyed by the Royal Navy. All of the destroyers were sunk in April in the two

battles of Narvik Fjord. However, the Royal Navy did not come away unscathed: the Germans had air superiority over Norway, and the campaign gave the navy a hard lesson in what it was like to operate in an area where the enemy controlled the skies. The Royal Navy lost one aircraft carrier (HMS *Glorious*) and six destroyers.

By the time that the Norwegian campaign was coming to an end, Britain was faced by a very immediate danger. In May 1940 the Germans invaded the Low Countries and France, and rapidly pushed the Allied armies back towards the sea. In May and June the Royal and Merchant Navies evacuated over 560,000 British, French and other soldiers from Dunkirk and the west and south coasts of France, as part of Operations 'Dynamo' and 'Aerial'. However, casualties among the rescuers were heavy. The Royal Navy alone suffered 7,000 killed in Operation 'Dynamo' at Dunkirk; few, if any, single wartime naval battles were as costly.[6]

The defeat in France was a military disaster of the first magnitude, but the successful evacuations helped to keep Britain in the war. Winston Churchill (who had become Prime Minister in May 1940) was desperate to keep the powerful and modern French fleet out of German hands. French ships in British-controlled ports were seized, but the Admiral of France's Mediterranean fleet, stationed at Oran in Algeria, refused to accede to British demands and nearly 1,300 French sailors died in the ensuing British bombardment. It was an action of great ruthlessness and caused enormous bitterness in France.

The fall of France put the French Channel and Atlantic ports in German hands (the south of France remained under Vichy French control until 1942), providing forward bases for the German fleet, including its submarines. It also laid Britain open to the threat of invasion. Doubts have been raised about how 'serious' Hitler was about his invasion plan, Operation 'Sealion'. If the German Luftwaffe had broken the RAF in 1940 in the Battle of Britain, the invasion might well have gone ahead. The Royal Navy would still have been a significant obstacle, but it could have been massacred if it had had to operate in the English Channel without air cover and within easy range of German airfields in France.

In the Mediterranean, the Royal Navy's principal enemy from June 1940 was the Italian fleet. There was land fighting in North Africa between British and Italian forces, but in October 1940 Italy invaded Greece. Britain gave support to Greece and established a base on the island of Crete, but supply lines from North Africa and Malta were threatened by the Italian fleet. There had already been some fighting between British and Italian ships, but the single most effective strike against the Italian fleet was made by naval airpower. On 11 November twenty-one obsolescent Swordfish torpedo bombers sank three Italian battleships at their moorings in the Italian base at Taranto. This was followed in March 1941 by the Royal Navy's victory off Cape Matapan in Crete, when three Italian cruisers and two destroyers were sunk.

However, events off Greece and Crete in April and May 1941 showed just what could happen to ships without adequate air cover. Exasperated by Italian defeats in Greece, Hitler invaded the country in April 1941, and soon Greek and British forces were being driven back. By this stage, the German Afrika Korps had been sent to North Africa to stiffen the Italian war effort there: the balance of forces was

116 HMS *Exeter* firing at Japanese aircraft in the Java Sea, 15 February 1942. Two weeks later the *Exeter*, damaged in the Battle of the Java Sea, was caught and sunk by the Japanese, along with the British destroyer *Encounter* and the American destroyer USS *Pope*. The *Exeter* was a famous ship, having taken part in the destruction of the *Graf Spee* in 1939. The Allied sailors in the Far East had fought bravely, but were overwhelmed by superior Japanese forces. Although the Japanese were eventually defeated, the Second World War marked the beginning of the end for the European maritime empires in the Far East.

moving against Britain. The navy was soon hard-pressed by the need to attack Axis convoys to Africa, with submarines and aircraft based on Malta taking the brunt of the action and the island suffering constant punishing air raids in return (the raids made Malta untenable as a base for surface ships for a long time). The German onslaught led to the evacuation of British forces from Greece to Crete; Crete itself fell to a German airborne invasion in May 1941 and another evacuation was organized. The Germans had command of the air, and the Royal Navy lost three cruisers and six destroyers off Greece and Crete, with sixteen other ships suffering major damage. Just under two-thirds of the 30,000 men on Crete were rescued by the navy, but the campaign had left the British Mediterranean fleet seriously weakened.

At the time same as the Cretan campaign, the navy succeeded in sinking the German battleship *Bismarck* in the Atlantic. The *Bismarck* was a powerful commerce raider and its destruction was of the first priority. In an epic sea chase the *Bismarck* sank the battleship HMS *Hood*, which blew up with the loss of almost all her crew. However, a combination of Swordfish and warship attacks eventually sank the *Bismarck* three days later. The great German capital ships, such as the *Bismarck*, *Scharnhorst* and *Tirpitz*, caused enormous concern to the Royal Navy, for these powerful vessels could outgun all but the largest Allied ships and were a menace to all naval and merchant ships operating in their vicinity. The very existence of these ships tied down major Allied forces for long periods.

After the outbreak of war, the United States had moved from a position of neutrality to one of support for Britain, supplying weapons, military stores, aircraft and (in September 1940) fifty old destroyers and ten other warships, the latter helping to reinforce the navy's depleted convoy escort forces. However, these were not free gifts and the destroyers came in exchange for rights to establish US bases in British overseas possessions and other concessions. The United States was brought into the war by the Japanese attack on Pearl Harbor on 7 December 1941. The attack was one element of a massive Japanese offensive that saw invasions of Burma, Malaya, the Philippines and islands in the Pacific. By April 1942 the Europeans and Americans had been routed in the Far East.

Neither the British, the Americans nor the Dutch (who had survived as an independent enclave in the Far East, despite the occupation of their homeland) had sufficient military, naval or air forces in the region to successfully oppose the Japanese. Britain's two most powerful warships in the area, the battleship *Prince of Wales* and the battlecruiser *Repulse*, were sunk by air attack in December 1941 with the loss of 800 men. A unified American, British, Dutch and Australian Command (ABDACOM) was set up in January 1942 to co-ordinate Allied operations, but it had few forces with which to operate. On 27 February a force of fourteen Dutch, British, American and Australian warships moved to attack a Japanese invasion convoy heading for the Dutch-held island of Java. The unit, which had not trained together and was not well co-ordinated, ran into four Japanese cruisers and thirteen destroyers. By early March ten Allied ships had been sunk in the battle of the Java Sea and the actions that followed. Along with them went the fortunes of ABDACOM.

A Japanese foray into the Indian Ocean in April 1942 drove the surviving British Eastern Fleet from its temporary base in the Maldive Islands near Sri Lanka to the coast of East Africa. It would be more than two years before the Royal Navy could return to the region in force, and the brunt of the naval war against Japan was borne by the Americans. The Japanese victories of 1941 and 1942 were the worst naval and military defeats ever suffered by Britain. It had become clear to the Admiralty in the 1930s that, for all its reputation as a great seapower, Britain did not have the naval forces to fight major sea wars in both Europe and the Far East. Australia and New Zealand were now left exposed and had to rely on America and their own efforts for their defence. The Second World War in the Far East revealed, in a very direct and brutal way, the limits of British seapower. The rapid collapse of the European colonies under the Japanese onslaught also fatally undermined the aura of invincibility that surrounded the European maritime empires in Asia. This encouraged the growth of post-war nationalism that led to wholesale decolonization in the Far East in the two decades after 1945.

As in the First World War, the most effective and dangerous part of the German navy was its U-boat arm. Despite the fact that Germany had been barred from possessing submarines by the Versailles Treaty, the German navy had kept abreast of technical developments by running a clandestine design bureau in Holland. The

Anglo-German naval treaty of 1935 allowed Germany to have a submarine fleet equivalent to 45 per cent of the Royal Navy's. The Kriegsmarine had only forty-six operational boats at the start of the war in 1939, operating from Baltic and North Sea bases. Unrestricted submarine warfare was waged from the outset, and by mid-1940 just over a million tons of shipping (300 vessels) had been sunk. The fall of France in 1940 provided the U-boats with forward operating bases on the French coast. Again, as in 1914–18, the Atlantic was a vital supply route for Britain, the more so because most of Europe was under Axis control. Iceland was occupied by Britain in May 1940 and used as an air and naval base, and both Iceland and St John's in Newfoundland became convoy escort bases. Both the Royal Navy and the Royal Canadian Navy undertook convoy escort using a variety of escort types, including the famous *Flower*-Class corvettes, tiny warships based on the design of a whaler. The escort crews, and the merchant seamen they defended, had to face some of the worst weather conditions in the world, as well as the constant possibility of attack. Part of the problem for the Atlantic convoys was the vast 'air gap' in mid-Atlantic, which made it possible for U-boats to surface at night and conduct attacks without fear of aircraft (all submarines of the time had to surface at night to recharge their batteries; they were also faster on the surface). Ultra long-range patrol aircraft were in very short supply until midway through the war, as were escort carriers.

German U-boats sank nearly 14.7 million tons of Allied shipping (2,828 ships) during the war, about two-thirds of the total Allied tonnage lost. Air attacks and mines were the next most common causes of ships lost, followed by the German commerce-raiding surface ships, which were mainly sunk or neutralized by the Royal Navy. The British tonnage destroyed in the war (11.4 million tons, 2,714 ships) was equivalent to 54 per cent of the total of the Merchant Navy on the outbreak of war. Just over 30,000 merchant seamen were killed in action in British ships during the war, about 17,000 of them in the North Atlantic, the main convoy battleground, where more than half of all Allied merchant ship losses took place.[7]

The British-controlled merchant marine actually grew by about 3 million tons between 1939 and late 1941 because of the addition of shipping belonging to countries occupied by the Germans and new constructions built in the UK or bought from the United States. The U-boat campaign was eventually out-fought by Allied naval and air forces, and out-built by Allied (particularly American) shipyards. However, the campaign brought periods of enormous crisis for the Allies, as well as a great deal of human suffering. German tactics changed in 1941 with the introduction of the 'wolf pack', which concentrated groups of U-boats in the suspected paths of convoys. As well as using sonar detection equipment (Asdic), radio location and other technical aids, the Admiralty introduced other less complex measures which helped to protect ships, such as evasive routeing.

Another critical factor in the sea war was that from June 1941 the British code-breakers at Bletchley Park were able to decipher every message being sent in the German naval Enigma code by U-boats on patrol. Code-named 'Ultra', the intelligence gained from the Enigma codes was of vital importance to the Allied war effort in most fields. This made it possible to reroute convoys out of harm's way or at least to reinforce those in danger. The sinking of merchant ships by U-boats declined markedly in the second half of 1941. However, in February 1942 the U-boat Enigma code was upgraded and it remained unreadable by the Allies until December 1942. Disastrously, this coincided with a period (February 1942 to June 1943, with a few short breaks) during which the German code-breaking service was able to read the main Royal Navy code.

The entry of America into the war in December 1941 was followed by a major U-boat campaign off the east coasts of Canada and America, which took the submarines away from the main transatlantic convoy routes. The situation changed in August 1942 when the U-boats returned to ocean convoy attacks. A great deal of information about the U-boats was still coming from versions of the Enigma codes and other sources, but the critical information about the routeing and location of enemy submarines in the Atlantic was still lacking. By October 1942 just over a hundred U-boats were operating in the Atlantic; in November they sank over 721,000 tons of shipping, the worst month for shipping losses of the whole war. Shipping losses were running ahead of the ability of either Britain or the USA to replace them, and the British government became very fearful that the Atlantic lifeline could be broken if they continued at this level. In December the British Government Code and Cypher School again cracked the naval Enigma. The crucial period of the Battle of the Atlantic was from December 1942 to May 1943:

117 The end of *U454*, 1 August 1943. This submarine was depth-charged and sunk in the Bay of Biscay by a Sunderland flying boat operated by 10 Squadron, Royal Australian Air Force, based at Mount Batten near Plymouth.

as F.H. Hinsley remarked, 'the severe mauling of a convoy was the equivalent of a lost battle on land'.

Enigma was not some dramatic cure-all. Delays in decipherment, the need to keep Ultra secret and other factors meant that information did not always reach operational commanders in time, or even had to be withheld to prevent the Germans from learning that Enigma had been compromised. At this period of the naval war, 'the value of Enigma must be judged not by its failure to eliminate disasters to convoys, but by the extent to which it reduced the frequency and scale of the disasters' (Hinsley). Many U-boats were withdrawn to the Mediterranean in an unsuccessful attempt to attack the Anglo-American landings in North Africa, and the sinking of merchant ships declined in December. U-boats began to return to northern seas in some numbers in January and February 1943 (rising to about 116 by February, with some 60 in the North Atlantic), but evasive rerouteing based on Enigma decrypts meant that the sinking of ships remained at a relatively contained level. However, with increasing numbers of submarines and convoys, plus German signals intelligence regarding convoy routes, matters were reaching a crucial point. Forty-two ships were sunk in March, twenty-two of them (about 146,000 tons) in the convoys HX229 and SC122, which were attacked by some forty U-boats.[8]

Events started to move against the U-boats. The Admiralty, by now aware that the Germans were reading its main cipher, changed the code in April. More escorts were becoming available as ships were released from the Mediterranean. There was also more widespread use of radar and radio-location devices, as well as new anti-submarine weapons. Air cover was crucial. Escort carriers were used on Atlantic convoys from late March, and by this stage more very long-range aircraft (American-built Liberators) were available to conduct oceanic reconnaissance from shore bases. The deadly 'air gap' was closed. When air and surface forces were able to operate together against a submarine, the chances of destroying it were greatly increased. Through the war aircraft sank something in the region of 290 U-boats, surface vessels sank 245 and a further 50 'kills' were shared between aircraft and ships. An unknown number of submarine attacks were averted by the mere presence of aircraft over a convoy.

Sinkings in all areas (but mainly the Atlantic) by German and Italian submarines reached another peak in March 1943: 110 vessels totalling nearly 634,000 tons. Thereafter the numbers began to decline to 287,000 tons in April and 237,000 in May. Apart from a brief rise in July (nearly 238,000), the monthly sinking of merchant ships never rose above 100,000 tons for the rest of the war and mostly declined far below this. Fifty-six U-boats were sunk between late February and late May 1943, and losses were on such a scale that the U-boats were temporarily withdrawn for refitting. They would return, but never again in such numbers. The total Allied and neutral merchant tonnage sunk in the whole of 1944 was little more than the total for the terrible March of 1943. The U-boat war would continue until the very end of the Third Reich in May 1945, but it was effectively won in the Atlantic in the spring of 1943.

The Atlantic was not the only major convoy route for British and other

Allied shipping. Between August 1941 and May 1945, ninety-eight Allied convoys sailed to Arctic Russia with military supplies for the Soviet war effort on the Eastern Front, through some of the worst seas in the world. Over the course of the war, 104 merchant ships and 23 Allied naval vessels were sunk on the Russian convoys. Aside from the enemy, the weather could be deadly. Edward Young, an RNVR officer of HM Submarine *Sealion*, *en route* to Murmansk in October 1941, wrote later of 'a desolation of tossing water' visible through the periscope, and storms so powerful that wave motion could be felt even 80 feet (23 m) below the surface.[9]

The RN Submarine Service in the Second World War suffered the loss of just over 12 per cent of the 25,000 men who served in British submarines during the conflict. The loss rate of the submarines was much higher: out of a total of 215 boats in service, 75 were sunk (35 per cent). The scale of casualties did not approach that of the German U-boat service, but it was bad enough. Due to the largely successful blockade of Germany, Axis merchant vessels were not at sea as often as their Allied counterparts, but British submarines were able to sink about 1.5 million tons of enemy merchant shipping and to damage another half a million tons. The Submarine Service also directly or indirectly (through mining) sank 174 enemy warships and damaged 55 others. British submarines probably made their most effective contribution in the Mediterranean, where they operated against the shipping that took reinforcements and supplies to the Afrika Korps in North Africa.[10]

Allied sea- and airpower eventually came to dominate the Mediterranean. Ships, submarines and aircraft hit the supply lines of the German and Italian forces in North Africa, and the Axis navies were unable to prevent the landing of Allied forces in North Africa. British aircraft and submarines on the island of Malta played a vital role in attacking enemy supply shipping. The North African campaign ended in May 1943 with the surrender of the German and Italian armies there, and major Allied seaborne landings in Italy followed, on Sicily (July) and the mainland (September).

The biggest single naval operation of the war was Operation 'Overlord', the Allied invasion of Normandy on D-Day, 6 June 1944. The need for a 'Second Front' against Germany (as well as the Eastern Front in Russia) had been recognized for years past, and had been contemplated in 1943, but sufficient resources were not available until 1944. The aim of Overlord was to land British, American and other Allied forces on five beaches in Normandy, from which they would fight inland, liberate France and then move on to Germany. The naval part of Overlord was codenamed 'Neptune', and in all it involved the use of 1,213 warships and just over 4,100 landing craft. Some 958 of the ships came from the Royal Navy or the Royal Canadian Navy, with 200 from the US Navy and 55 from other Allied navies. About three-quarters of the landing craft belonged to the Royal Navy. In addition, there were hundreds of supply ships drafted in, to supply the assault forces and the fleet. The purposes of the warships were to protect the invasion forces and supply vessels, and to provide gunnery support to the troops in the early stages of the invasion.

Ships for the invasion were based in many parts of the UK, but the most significant invasion ports were on the south coast – a dozen places, from Falmouth to Newhaven, including Plymouth, Poole, Portsmouth and Shoreham. To make up for the lack of a suitable harbour on the beaches, two 'Mulberry harbours'– huge artificial harbours made up of concrete sections and old ships – were constructed. These were towed across the Channel and put in place to provide docking facilities for supply ships. The landings achieved complete strategic surprise: by the end of 6 June more than 130,000 soldiers had gone ashore. Such was the strength of the Allied naval and air forces that the Kriegsmarine was never able to inflict serious damage on the invasion force or the supply ships. Cherbourg was captured in late June and was available from mid-July as a deep-water port.

A large Allied seaborne landing took place in the south of France in August 1944, and by September the Allied armies were in Brussels. However, the German army demonstrated remarkable powers of survival, and the Allies were not able to cross the Rhine until March 1945. The war at sea continued, with the U-boats and (in the Channel and North Sea) the E-boats (torpedo boats) still constituting a threat, but what was left of the German navy could not influence the outcome of the war.

The Royal and Merchant Navies played an enormous part in the Allied victory. The Atlantic lifeline and the Allied position in the Mediterranean could not have been maintained without Allied seapower, most of it British. The transatlantic convoy routes were fundamental: without the men, weapons and supplies that they brought, Britain could not have continued to fight. If Britain had surrendered, the Second World War could have had a very different outcome.

The Royal Navy lost over 350 major warships and more than 1,000 smaller vessels during the war. Most of the losses were in escort vessels (such as destroyers, frigates and corvettes – 132 destroyers, for example) and in submarines (74). The merchant fleet lost 2,714 ships. The human cost was terrible. Fifty-one thousand Royal Navy sailors and 30,000 British merchant seamen perished, along with 102 Wrens. In addition, 14,663 naval seamen were wounded. In land battles the injured usually far outnumber those killed; modern sea warfare kills more and leaves fewer wounded.

For Britain, the last major naval campaign of the war was against Japan. Since 1942 the sea war in the Far East had been largely an American undertaking, supported by Australia and New Zealand. Both of these countries became major bases for the Allied offensive in the Pacific. A series of bloody 'island-hopping' campaigns and major naval and air battles gradually pushed the Japanese back, and by 1944 the United States Navy had amassed vast amphibious fleets in the Pacific, equipped with modern warships and thousands of aircraft. In October 1944 American forces began landing in the Philippines.

The British Eastern Fleet was gradually reinforced in 1944 with more modern warships and aircraft. The aim of reviving British naval forces in the region was partly military – to assist in the defeat of Japan in the Pacific and Indian Ocean – and partly political, to stake a better claim for Britain in post-war peace negotiations. In November 1944 the Americans agreed to British participation in the

Pacific, and the Eastern Fleet was reformed to create the British Pacific Fleet (BPF) and the East Indies Fleet. The East Indies Fleet was used primarily against the Japanese in the Indian Ocean and in operations supporting the Allied advance into Burma.

The BPF grew in size from 52 warships, 43 support vessels and 258 aircraft in January 1945 to a force of 84 warships, 106 support ships and close on 600 aircraft by the time Japan surrendered on 15 August 1945. Although the fleet included some battleships, a major part of its striking power was carried in four (later five) large fleet carriers. The BPF was equipped with significant numbers of purpose-designed, American-built carrier aircraft such as Hellcat fighters and Avenger bombers, which were rather more effective than their British counterparts. The pre-war neglect of naval aviation had saddled the wartime navy with many obsolescent and inadequate British types, which were nowhere as successful as those designed and built for the RAF. By 1945 nearly two-thirds of the aircraft on British carriers were American-built. The BPF was one of the single most powerful fleets ever put together by the Royal Navy during the war, and it was soon in action. In January the largest air strikes ever undertaken by the Fleet Air Arm were

118 Fleet Air Arm Seafire fighters running up their engines prior to take off from the carrier HMS *Implacable*, Pacific Ocean, 1945. *Implacable* was part of the powerful British Pacific Fleet, created in 1944. However, the BPF formed just one task force of the vast American armada in the Pacific: the Royal Navy, at the height of its powers, was being eclipsed by the United States. Nearly half of the aircraft in this photograph were US-built Avengers (at the back, with wings folded). Pre-war neglect of naval aviation in Britain left the wartime Fleet Air Arm heavily dependent on US designs.

mounted against Japanese oil refineries in Sumatra, destroying about two-thirds of the total Japanese capacity to make aviation fuel.

The BPF sailed on to Australia in February, where it was now based. In March 1945 it was attached to the US Fifth Fleet as Task Force 57, and in March and April provided air cover for the American landings on Okinawa and carried out air strikes on Japanese airfields. All of the British carriers involved in these operations were hit by Japanese kamikaze (suicide) aircraft, but survived because of their armoured flight decks (British carriers were designed to operate close to shore-based airpower). During the Okinawa campaign FAA aircraft from the five carriers involved flew over 5,300 sorties. In July and August Task Force 57 was assigned to the US Third Fleet, to conduct air attacks and later bombardment of the Japanese mainland. These operations were still in progress when the dropping of the atomic bombs brought about Japan's surrender.

Powerful as the BPF and the East Indies Fleet were, the fact that the BPF constituted but one task force out of the US Navy in the Pacific (which had numerous task forces) underlines the shift in power that had taken place during the war. Britain played a pivotal role in the defeat of Germany and Italy, but was only able to survive and partake in the victory thanks to American support. By 1944 the United States was very much the senior partner in the alliance against the Axis. Britain was bankrupted by the war, its stresses uncovering unpleasant facts about the limitations of the economy on which Britain's power had rested. Post-war Britain had neither the means nor the will to hold on to much of its overseas territories; within twenty years of 1945 most of the empire created by seapower had ceased to exist. The Second World War left two superpowers – the USA and the USSR – with Britain in decline as a force in the international community.[11]

The Royal Navy, the Cold War, and the Korean War, 1945–60

The Second World War saw the Allies emerge as victors, but perhaps with the United States as the only clear and unequivocal winner. Without the USA, Britain and the other Allies would probably have lost. Such was the extent of American power that even at the height of the conflict, fighting major campaigns on several fronts, the USA never had to devote more than 43 per cent of its economy to war production. The Soviet Union was militarily strong in 1945, but had lost 20 million of its people and its economy had been devastated. Britain was the leading military and political power in Western Europe, but was economically exhausted and in the twenty years after the war would see its former position as an imperial power virtually disappear.

The seeds of the East-West confrontation went back to the period before the war. The parliamentary democracies and capitalist economies of the West were not compatible with the centralized political and economic systems of the Soviet Union, and in any event, traditional communist doctrine held that the two would always be at war in some form or another before the eventual triumph of socialism. Added to that, the Soviet Union was ruled by Josef Stalin, a paranoid autocrat who feared plots among his own people, let alone foreigners. Even so, confrontation of the dangerous and potentially apocalyptic kind that did develop was not necessarily a foregone conclusion. Each side's view of the other was marked by suspicion and miscalculation, which served to make a bad situation worse.

Despite hopes of a post-war rapprochement, relations between the West and the Soviet Union deteriorated rapidly, particularly as countries occupied by the Red Army fell under communist governments. In 1948–9 the Soviets instituted a land blockade of the western enclave in Berlin, but West Berlin was successfully sustained by the Berlin Airlift and eventually the blockade was called off. The fear of a third world war was high, and in April 1949 the United States, Britain, Canada and eight other nations formed the North Atlantic Treaty Organization (NATO), for mutual assistance against Soviet expansion in the North Atlantic region, including continental Europe. The Soviet Union formed its own alliance, the Warsaw Pact, with the new communist regimes of Eastern Europe, which was basically a means for implementing the strategy of the Soviet general staff. NATO, although dominated by the USA from the outset, is an alliance of democratic states and has so far outlasted the Warsaw Pact by more than a decade.

In June 1950 the army of communist North Korea invaded South Korea and came very close to driving South Korean and US forces into the sea. Thanks to a temporary Russian boycott of the United Nations, the Americans succeeded in getting the UN to approve the war to retake Korea as a United Nations operation. A seaborne landing at Inchon on the west coast of Korea in September 1950 drove the communists back, but the UN forces then proceeded to overreach themselves in the pursuit north, and came close a second disaster later in the year when communist China intervened on behalf of the North Koreans. The war cost the lives of about 20 per cent of the Korean population, as well as the lives of hundreds of thousands of servicemen. It ended eventually in a stalemate, followed by an uneasy truce.

The US and South Korean armed forces supplied most of the UN manpower, but the UK contributed a sizeable contingent, along with other Commonwealth nations such as Australia, Canada and New Zealand. Units of the Royal Navy were already on station in the region when the war broke out, and the first British casualties of the war were suffered by the cruiser HMS *Jamaica* on 8 July 1950 when the ship was hit by fire from shore batteries. Shore bombardment of troops, installations and transport links was one of the main tasks of the UN naval forces off Korea. Other functions included air attacks by carrier aircraft, minesweeping and the landing of secret agents or commandos. Inshore action was particularly difficult and dangerous, and was made worse by out-of-date charts and, in winter, sub-zero temperatures and ice floes.

Aside from a small number of RAF personnel operating with the Australians, the only British air forces used in Korea were those of the Fleet Air Arm. Fireflies from the FAA were active throughout the conflict, taking part in dangerous ground attacks on the Korean mainland, often escorted by Sea Fury fighters. Both types were piston-engined, but in 1952 naval Sea Furies from 802 Squadron, based on HMS *Ocean*, were successful in shooting down some of the feared Chinese MiG jet fighters.

The UN naval forces rapidly eliminated North Korea's small fleet, and instituted a sea blockade that remained effective throughout the war. The blockade meant that all troop reinforcements and supplies from China had to come overland, which forced the Chinese into reliance on land attacks. This cost them huge numbers of casualties that in the long run even the massive Chinese army could not sustain. The Chinese themselves secretly admitted that the strategy forced on them by the naval blockade was ultimately unsupportable, and that this led them to call for an armistice in 1953.[12]

The post-war Royal Navy was rapidly reduced in size, like the military forces of other nations. The fleet shrank from over 600 major warships and 865,000 men in 1945 to 122 ships and 142,000 men by 1950. As in previous periods of peace, the navy was involved in one form or another of imperial policing. Its grimmest task in the immediate post-war period was the interception of ships carrying Jewish immigrants to Palestine, as the British authorities had declared such immigration illegal. However, the British Mandate in Palestine came to an end in 1948 following a bloody guerrilla war, and the state of Israel was created soon after. The Labour government elected in 1945 wanted to concentrate on rebuilding the British economy, and part of this process relied on reducing Britain's military commitments and spending. India and Pakistan gained their independence in 1947. Given that one of the planks of British naval policy since the nineteenth century had been the defence of India, this was the beginning of a profound shift in British defence strategy that culminated in the withdrawal of most British forces from bases east of the Suez Canal.

Wartime experience confirmed that the main capital ship in world navies was no longer the battleship but the aircraft carrier. For Britain the problem was that it could not afford to build or maintain many of the largest version of this vessel, the fleet carrier. The Royal Navy had one fleet carrier by 1950 and four smaller light carriers; the US Navy had eleven fleet carriers, despite having been drastically reduced in size since 1945. Most British battleships were rapidly decommissioned after the war, having lost their value as fighting units. The Royal Navy's submarine force was gradually modernized in the late 1940s and early 1950s, much having been learned from captured German technology. The navy also started to receive its first jet fighters, and in 1947 formed its first helicopter squadron (used for air-sea rescue). The Fleet Air Arm's name was abolished in 1946 and replaced by that of 'Naval Aviation', to signify that aviation was now an integral part of naval power; the FAA name was restored in 1953 to encourage recruitment.

Although Britain had participated in the development of the wartime atomic bomb, the United States ended co-operation in nuclear matters after the war. In 1947 the Attlee government took the decision that Britain would have to develop its own nuclear weapon in order to stand any hope of hanging on to its fading 'great power' status. The first bomb was tested in 1952, but the early atomic (and the first hydrogen) bombs were designed to be dropped by aircraft. The idea of nuclear deterrence was current in military thinking from the 1940s, but until the late 1960s

Britain's nuclear deterrent was principally based on RAF bombers, although in 1959 a nuclear bomb type called Red Beard went into production for the Royal Navy's Scimitar jet aircraft.[13]

The nuclear navy, 1960–2001

The navy's first nuclear-powered submarine, HMS *Dreadnought*, was completed in 1963. From the 1960s to the early 1990s nuclear-powered attack (SSN) submarines gradually replaced diesel-powered submarines in the Royal Navy. The adoption of the wartime German Schnorkel design from the 1940s made it possible for diesel boats to run their diesel engines when submerged, rather than relying on their quieter but slower electric motors, but nuclear boats were significantly faster. For example, even the *Swiftsure* Class of nuclear boats, completed between 1974 and 1980, could achieve more than 30 knots when dived, while the last class of diesel boats built for the navy – the ill-fated *Upholder* Class of the 1980s and 1990s – could only reach an underwater speed of 20 knots. A nuclear submarine can outpace many potential surface targets (even a modern destroyer can only reach about 30 knots), whereas a diesel boat, as in the two world wars, is much better adapted for lying quietly in wait for a target that comes towards it.

The last active-duty diesel submarine in the Royal Navy was paid off in 1993, and the four *Upholder*-Class submarines departed for lay-up at Barrow-in-Furness, despite the fact that they were all new craft, completed between 1989 and 1993. These boats may have been disposed of because the Cold War came to an end in the late 1980s and early 1990s: they were designed specifically to fight Soviet submarines in the so-called 'GIUK Gap' (the sea areas between Greenland, Iceland and Britain), and once this threat evaporated, they were among the first in line for the defence cuts of the 'peace dividend', possibly a sacrifice by the navy to prevent cuts to the nuclear submarine fleet.

Since the late 1960s the Royal Navy has been the mainstay of Britain's nuclear forces. With the failure of various airborne nuclear weapons projects, the navy was able to present a case to the government that it could provide Britain with a nuclear deterrent. In 1962 President Kennedy agreed to make American submarine-launched Polaris missiles available to Britain, with the British providing the nuclear warheads and the boats to launch the missiles. The first British Polaris boat, HMS *Resolution*, went on its first patrol in 1968; the last of the four boats, HMS *Repulse*, was paid off in 1996, after a total of 229 Polaris patrols over twenty-eight years. Polaris underwent a modernization programme called Chevaline in the early 1980s, but the government decided that eventually the system would be replaced by the even more destructive American Trident missile. The first of the *Vanguard*-Class Trident boats was ordered in 1986 and commissioned in 1993.

The actual effectiveness of the 'independent nuclear deterrent' is open to question. At the height of the Cold War, it only equated to a small fraction of the nuclear forces at the command of the USA and USSR, although the fact that Britain is a nuclear power has conferred benefits in diplomatic terms. A dark suspicion has been raised many times that the British nuclear force is maintained

119 Rear view of HMS *Vanguard*, the first of the four Trident submarines commissioned for the Royal Navy between 1993 and 1999. Replacing the earlier Polaris submarines, each Trident boat is armed with sixteen Trident II DS ballistic missiles. The missiles have a range of over 4,000 miles and can carry up to twelve nuclar warheads apiece, although at present each boat has no more than 48. This apocalyptic firepower – equivalent to 384 Hiroshima bombs – is carried behind the submarine's sail or conning tower.

more because it gives added prestige to British politicians, rather than because it in any material way protects the British people. Since the formation of the Campaign for Nuclear Disarmament in the 1950s, nuclear weaponry has been the focus of pacifist protest, most notably in the 1960s and 1980s, and there is still a peace camp outside the submarine base at Faslane on the Clyde, which in 2001 was the scene of active protest.

Most of the British attack submarine fleet was laid up in 2000 with nuclear reactor problems, depriving the Royal Navy of a vital part of its striking force. It was perhaps the most serious technical fault in British naval history. Outside of a few politicians, defence journalists and anti-nuclear activists, this attracted relatively little attention, perhaps a sign of general public apathy towards matters of maritime defence and wider concerns about the world's marine environment.

Aside from the reactor problems of the attack submarines, one of the more pressing problems created by the nuclear submarine force is that of what to do with the decommissioned boats – sealed radioactive relics that can never find their way safely into any museum.[14]

The Falklands War to the 'War on Terrorism', 1982–2001

'Gunboat diplomacy', a term first coined in the nineteenth century as the diplomat and historian Sir James Cable pointed out, it is still very much alive today. As a naked exercise of force, or the threat of force, it is not a pleasant activity, although it has sometimes been used to save lives rather than take them.

The nuclear deadlock of the Cold War meant that military conflicts between the 1950s and 1980s were so-called 'limited wars', fought in closely defined geographical areas such as Korea and Vietnam. However, 'gunboat diplomacy' still flourished then, as it does today. The Royal Navy took part in numerous operations that could be defined in this way, from the futile Anglo-French Suez War against Egypt in 1956, to the 'cod wars' of the 1950s and 1970s, in which the navy attempted to stop Icelandic gunboats from harassing British trawlers.[15]

Between 1945 and 1982 none of the Royal Navy's deployments involved operations against a serious naval opponent and no British warship was sunk in action. The year 1982 was advertised by the English Tourist Board as 'Maritime England Year'. By a horrible irony, it was also the year of Britain's first maritime war since 1945. Argentina has long held a territorial claim to the Falklands Islands, which had led to moments of tension with Britain, but in 1982 the military *junta* that ruled Argentina decided to take the initiative and seize the Falklands. On 2 April an Argentine force invaded the islands and quickly overwhelmed the small Royal Marine garrison stationed there, although fortunately without loss of life to the Falkland Islanders or the Marines. The Falklanders suddenly found themselves ruled by a foreign military dictatorship and the government in London had suffered a major humiliation. On 3 April the prime minister, Mrs Thatcher, announced that a Task Force would sail south to retake the islands, under the code-name Operation 'Corporate'. The force was readied with impressive speed, and by 6 April the aircraft carriers *Invincible* and *Hermes*, accompanied by fifteen other warships and fleet auxiliaries, were on their way to the British-owned Ascension Island, which was to serve as a staging post during the campaign. Many other warships, Royal Fleet Auxiliary support vessels and merchant ships were to follow.

Feverish international diplomacy failed to achieve a political compromise, and on 24–5 April a small British force retook the remote and desolate island of South Georgia from the Argentinians. In the course of this Royal Navy helicopters disabled the Argentine submarine *Santa Fe*, forcing her crew to beach and abandon the boat. This was the first submarine to be destroyed by the navy since 1945. The first British submarine attack since 1945 followed a week later. On 2 May the Argentine cruiser *General Belgrano* was torpedoed and sunk by the nuclear attack submarine HMS *Conqueror*, killing 321 Argentine sailors. The attack on the *Belgrano* became the single most controversial action of the war. As well as the heavy loss of life, the cruiser was sunk outside the total exclusion zone declared by the British around the islands, and was headed towards the mainland. It has been claimed that the sinking of the *Belgrano* was authorized by the British government with the aim of making a peaceful solution impossible. Certainly, after the sinking, it looked as if the war would have to be fought to a conclusion. However, it should

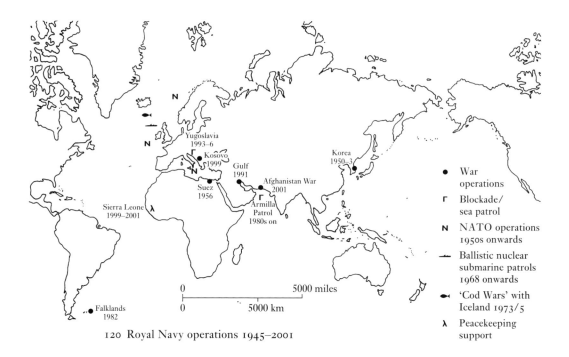

- • War operations
- Γ Blockade/ sea patrol
- N NATO operations 1950s onwards
- ◂ Ballistic nuclear submarine patrols 1968 onwards
- ◂● 'Cod Wars' with Iceland 1973/5
- λ Peacekeeping support

120 Royal Navy operations 1945–2001

also be pointed out that the *Belgrano* and her escorts were on an east-west patrol line at the time, and would have turned away from the mainland in due course. Also, to the north of the islands on that same day, the Argentine carrier *25 de Mayo* was preparing to launch an airstrike on the British Task Force. This failed to happen because there was insufficient wind for aircraft launches, but had it taken place, it would have pushed peace as far away as the sinking of the *Belgrano* was to do. Militarily the sinking had a crucial result: the Argentine surface fleet withdrew to the South American coastline and remained there until the end of the war.

Argentine airpower remained very effective, as the Falklands were within range of land-based aircraft. On 4 May the British destroyer *Sheffield* was hit and effectively destroyed by an air-launched Exocet missile. The Task Force temporarily withdrew eastwards, but on 21 May major elements of the fleet entered Falkland Sound, between the two islands, and began landing troops at San Carlos Water on East Falkland. The confined channel of San Carlos Water came under intense Argentine air attack. On that day the frigate HMS *Ardent* suffered such heavy damage that it had to be abandoned, and it later sank, with four other war-ships also taking some damage. Two days later HMS *Antelope*, a sister-ship of the *Ardent*, was also sunk. On 25 May the Type 42 HMS *Coventry* was sunk by the three bombs north of the Falklands, and the container ship *Atlantic Conveyor*, a requisitioned merchantman, was destroyed by an Exocet. Later, on 8 June, the RFA's *Sir Galahad* and *Sir Tristram* were bombed and set ablaze while they were at anchor, crowded with soldiers, causing deaths and dreadful injuries. The rescue of the survivors was marked by episodes of considerable bravery, particularly

121 HMS *Yarmouth* rescuing men from HMS *Ardent*, 21 May 1982. The main British landings during the Falklands War took place in San Carlos Water, off Falkland Sound. The landings came under heavy attack by Argentinian aircraft, and HMS *Ardent* was one of the warships stationed out in the Sound, providing gunfire support for the troops ashore and anti-aircraft cover. The ship was hit by two air attacks, which killed 22 men and wounded 37. The second attack started fires which could not be controlled, and it was decided to abandon ship. The *Yarmouth* came alongside the blazing vessel and evacuated 179 men.

on the part of helicopter crews who flew their machines into blinding smoke over blazing ships filled with ammunition. The last Royal Navy vessel to be attacked was the destroyer HMS *Glamorgan*, which was hit by a land-based Exocet on 12 June. The British land and air campaign, backed up by naval shore bombardments, eventually led to the surrender of the Argentine forces on 14 June.

Much still remains unclear about the Falklands War, especially at the level of political decision-making. At the time and since, parallels were drawn with the futile Suez campaign of 1956, questioning the expenditure of so many lives and so much money for remote islands populated by a couple of thousand people. For the Falkland Islanders, the war led to their liberation. In Argentina the military *junta*, undermined by its failure to be successful even in war, eventually crumbled. The Conservative government, buoyed up by the success of the war, was re-elected in 1983.

The Falklands War may have been the last conflict in which Britain was able to mount a maritime campaign on her own. Although there was undoubtedly much *matériel* and intelligence help from the United States, the combatant ships were all

British, as were the merchant ships, 'Ships Taken Up From Trade' (STUFT). By 14 June over 40 British merchant ships of varying sizes had sailed to the South Atlantic, including the liners *Queen Elizabeth II*, *Canberra* and *Uganda*, 14 oil tankers, 4 container ships and 6 roll-on/roll-off ferries.

Militarily the campaign was a major success for the armed forces who, operating 8,000 miles (12,880 km) from home, demonstrated considerable professionalism and courage, but the war could easily have had a disastrous outcome for Britain. Since the scrapping of the carrier *Ark Royal* in the 1970s, the Royal Navy had not had any carrier-based airborne early warning (AEW) aircraft, increasing the vulnerability of the Task Force to air attack, as events proved. The loss of one of the carriers would probably have compelled the Task Force to withdraw, as the Fleet Air Arm and Royal Air Force Harriers that they carried were vital for the protection of the fleet and for the prosecution of the land campaign.

The war also underscored the terrible effectiveness of both submarines and sea-skimming missiles. All told the Royal Navy lost two destroyers, two frigates and a landing ship, together with a merchant vessel. Four other ships were seriously damaged, and the majority of the thirty-four British aircraft lost were from the Fleet Air Arm. Over 10,000 Argentinian servicemen were taken prisoner on the Falklands, and the Argentinian forces lost an estimated 102 aircraft. The total number killed, on both sides, ran to more than a thousand.

In 1990 and 1991 substantial British land and other forces were sent to the Gulf to fight Iraq, after the latter had invaded Kuwait. The Royal Navy had been active in the region since 1980, maintaining the Armilla Patrol in the Gulf to protect British merchant ships during the Iran-Iraq war of 1980–8 and after. The Royal

122 HMS *Monmouth*, a *Duke*-Class frigate in Portsmouth Harbour, August 2001. The 3,500 (displacement)-ton *Monmouth* is an anti-submarine frigate, and was completed in 1993.

123 Aircraft carrier HMS *Illustrious* in Portsmouth Harbour, August 2001. *Illustrious* is one of the Royal Navy's three *Invincible*-Class carriers, which, at about 20,000 tons displacement, are among the largest vessels in the fleet, entering service between 1980 and 1985. The carriers operate Harrier jets and helicopters. A few weeks after this photograph was taken, *Illustrious* was serving as the flagship of a 24-ship fleet in a major exercise off Oman, the largest deployment by the Royal Navy since the Falklands War. The terrorist attacks in the United States on 11 September of that year meant that the fleet was soon put on a war footing, supporting United States attacks on the Taliban and Al-Qaeda in the Aghanistan War.

Navy deployed nineteen warships and fourteen support vessels to the Gulf at different times before and during the 1991 war. The navy played an important role in minesweeping operations, and RN helicopters sank a number of Iraqi surface vessels. The decline of the British merchant fleet in the 1980s meant that a large-scale merchant auxiliary did not exist by the early 1990s. The sea transport of the British forces (which included over 200 armoured vehicles) was undertaken by 110 chartered merchant ships, of which only five were British-registered. The contrast to the Falklands War of only eight years before could not have been greater. [16]

The years 1999–2001 saw British forces in action in several parts of the world. In 1999 the Royal Navy began taking delivery of American-built Tomahawk cruise missiles, armed with high-explosive warheads, for use by nuclear-attack submarines. The missile was first used against Serbian targets in the Kosovo war of 1999, and in October 2001 three Royal Navy submarines launched Tomahawks at targets in Afghanistan at the outset of Operation 'Veritas', the codename for British participation in the US-led war against international terrorism. The Tomahawks give the Royal Navy's submarine force the capability to mount conventional attacks on land targets hundreds of miles away, but this British contribution was dwarfed by the might of US sea- and airpower.

The horrific terrorist attacks on the USA in September 2001, and the 'war against terrorism' that has followed, have left the world in a very perilous state. Seapower has proved critical in enabling the Western nations to make a military response. Western seapower is also a physical embodiment of Western political and economic power, and is undoubtedly one of the things that has caused great resentment among non-Western nations. If the war continues, seapower may well become even more important. Whatever happens, it is clear that the story of sea warfare is not over.[17]

Men and women of the Royal Navy, 1914–2001

The twentieth century saw the manpower of the Royal Navy rise to its greatest level ever at the end of the Second World War. By the 1990s British naval manpower had fallen to levels not seen since the 1850s (see Table 18). However, sheer numbers of men (and latterly, women) are no longer as significant as they once were. Technological change has made the warship of the 1990s a far more destructive weapon than its mid-nineteenth century predecessor, and it is the Royal Navy that maintains the country's nuclear forces. In terms of training and organization, the modern navy is a world away from its Victorian forebear, and modern sailors are considerably better educated and cared for than Queen Victoria's Jack Tar.

The twentieth-century Royal Navy reached its manpower peaks during the two world wars, due in considerable measure to conscription. Apart from a few years in the 1920s and 1930s, naval manpower did not fall below 100,000 from 1900 to 1960, and was kept at or above this level by war or the fear of war. The fear of war did not of course magically disappear in 1960 – by then the fear was of nuclear annihilation – but the gradual shrinking of the navy was occasioned by the naval withdrawal from east of Suez, among other factors.

The navy that went to war in 1914 did so with many reservists. As long ago as 1859 the Royal Naval Reserve had been established, to provide the navy with a pool of trained manpower from the merchant and fishing fleets; by 1890 it had 20,000 men on its books. The Royal Fleet Reserve was later established for men who had completed their full-time naval service, and in 1903 the Royal Naval Volunteer Reserve (RNVR) was set up. Later known as the 'wavy navy' (RNVR officers' stripes were wavy, while RN officers' stripes were straight), large numbers of RNVR sailors served in both world wars. Conscription was introduced in 1916, but such was the horrendous death toll on the Western Front that all armed services faced a manpower crisis. The Women's Royal Naval Service (WRNS) was established in 1917 to recruit young women to undertake auxiliary work in the navy, eventually working in many areas, including administration, transport, stores and communications. By late 1918 the Wrens numbered some 7,000 and had freed up male sailors for combat duties.

The navy's soldiers, the Royal Marines, saw a great deal of fighting in the First World War. The Corps rose from 17,000 men in 1914 to 55,000 in 1918, and Marines were used both as infantry and to help operate the main and secondary guns of warships. Marines served in major sea battles such as Jutland, the land

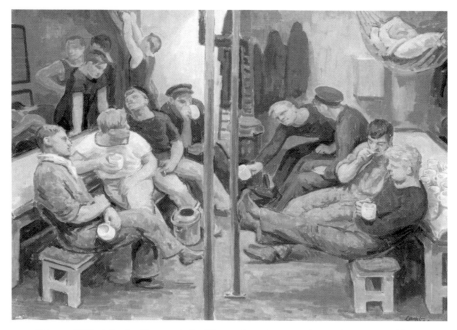

124 *Eleven O'Clock in the Forecastle*, by Henry Lamb, 1940. A wartime crew taking their tea break.

battles in France and Flanders, and in amphibious operations such as Gallipoli and the 1918 raid on the German-occupied port of Zeebrugge.

There were signs of growing discontent in the navy in 1917 among some ratings and non-commissioned officers regarding pay and conditions, which led to pay increases at the end of the year; the signs of unease on the lower deck were mainly confined to the presentation of demands for improvements. It was the German fleet that suffered mass mutinies in 1918 – the situation in the Royal Navy never even came close to this (although there were some small-scale mutinies and desertions among men sent to serve in the Baltic against the Bolsheviks in 1919).

Despite significant pay rises in 1919, pay cuts followed in the 1920s as governments reduced expenditure, and simmering discontent culminated in the Invergordon Mutiny of 1931. The crews of various Atlantic Fleet warships, anchored at Invergordon in Scotland, refused to sail on exercises and all of the ships were ordered to return to their home ports. Peaceful as it was, the mutiny caused considerable shock, and although further pay cuts were introduced, they were less severe than those originally proposed. The mutiny led to upheavals in the senior ranks of the navy and a good deal of soul-searching as to the breakdown in shipboard communications that had helped to lead to the situation. Some officers were seriously out of touch with their men: one captain at Invergordon was said to have told his men that everyone had to tighten their belts, and that his contribution was to tell his wife to sack one of the maids! The navy remained very class-ridden in the 1930s, although the pay cuts were reversed in 1934 and efforts were made to improve some other aspects of sailors' lives. However, life at sea remained hard and in some ways rather primitive. Shipboard conditions for eating, sleeping and washing only really began to improve after the Second World War, and the gradual replacement of the time-honoured hammock by bunks only started in the 1950s.

Royal Navy manpower increased nearly six and a half times during the war, the vast majority 'hostilities-only' (HO) ratings and officers who soon outnumbered the regulars. However, the navy generally maintained its professional standards despite the enormous influx of men and women with no nautical background whatsoever. By 1945 88 per cent of the navy's officers were from the RNVR rather than the RN. Demobilizing the 'hostilties-only' sailors took two years. Prize money was paid for the last time in 1946, ordinary seamen getting the princely sum of £6 each; modern war had seen many more ships sunk than captured. The WRNS had been demobilized after the First World War, but it was reactivated in 1938; by 1944 there were over 74,000 Wrens, performing a vast range of support duties for the navy. The service was made permanent in 1949.

The Royal Navy won the sea war against Germany through hard, sustained pressure, and long, wearying blockade patrols or convoy escort duties, with few spectacular or decisive battles. It is not easy for most people born after the war to appreciate the sheer physical hardships and dangers of war at sea in the Second World War, or the great spirit of comradeship that seems to have pervaded many warships. Boredom, exhaustion, terror and pain were the lot of many men, and

125 Wrens using a signal projector at Wee Fea Communications Centre, Lyness Naval Base, *c*.1943–5. As in other areas of military and industrial life in the World Wars, the Royal Navy employed women in areas that freed men up for combat. The Women's Royal Naval Service reached a peak strength of over 74,000 in 1944. Wrens worked in a very wide range of naval trades and professions, and enjoyed a high reputation for efficiency and dedication. Wee Fea was the main communications centre for the fleet base at Scapa Flow, and most of the communications staff were Wrens.

over 50,000 died. The sea itself, aptly described by the former RNVR officer Nicholas Monsarrat as 'the cruel sea', could at times be a worse opponent than the human enemy.

As in the First World War, Royal Marines served as both infantry and naval gunners. However, the development of landing craft and other vessels for amphibious warfare, and the increasing use of commando tactics, meant that Royal Marines saw a great deal of action in their amphibious role. Marines were involved in every major landing operation of the war, and 17,500 Royal Marines took part in the D-Day landings, the largest-ever Royal Marine group in a single battle. The Corps reached a peak strength of 78,000 men in 1945.

Naval pay was increased significantly in 1946 and 1950. National servicemen continued to serve in the navy until 1961, although the navy took fewer conscripts than the army or RAF. Social change also affected the navy. Officer-cadet intake from fee-paying public and independent schools declined, and by 1970 about 70 per cent of the new cadets were coming from state schools.

The 1957 Defence Review aimed at cutting defence expenditure, amongst other things, and total naval manpower had been reduced by nearly 10 per cent by the early 1960s. The popularity of service in the armed forces was declining by the 1960s, particularly in a period of low unemployment, and by the mid-1960s there was a serious problem with levels of recruitment, which were addressed to some extent by improvements to pay and conditions. The navy had done very little to accommodate the families of officers or men before the war. Post-war, in common with the rest of society, ratings and officers began marrying earlier. It was only in the 1950s and 1960s that serious efforts were made to remedy the situation with the construction of many large naval housing estates close to bases.

The traditional daily tot of rum was abolished in 1970, partly because of the effect it was having on sailors operating complex equipment, and partly because of fears of indiscipline and alcoholism. The £300,000 annual saving was put into providing shipboard bars for petty officers and an amenities fund for ratings.

The Board of Admiralty was amalgamated in 1964 with the other services' staff departments to form the Ministry of Defence. The navy withdrew from east of Suez in 1971, to concentrate in particular in patrolling the North Atlantic with NATO against the perceived threat of the Soviet navy. Naval manpower shrank by more than a quarter between 1960 and 1982, but managed to maintain high professional standards, as the Falklands War showed. Another manpower crisis loomed in the 1970s, partly due to low pay, but armed forces pay was increased by nearly one-third in 1979 and recruitment began to pick up. The Thatcher government of the time aimed to balance the books by reducing the size of the fleet under a Defence Review produced in 1981 by the then Minister of Defence, John Nott. The Falklands War put a stop to this, but the end of the Cold War a few years later led to inevitable cut-backs in the navy as the old Soviet threat disappeared. By 2002 the navy had about 40 per cent fewer personnel than in 1980, with just under 43,000 people in total (including the Royal Marines). The WRNS was merged with the rest of the navy and in 1991 (with trepidation in some circles) the first female sailors went to sea. By 1996 650 women were serving in RN ships; by 2002

20 per cent of the navy's officer intake was female. Women are currently excluded from frontline combat, although in a naval war airpower and long-range missiles can make the difference between combat and non–combat zones rather irrelevant. Although much has been made of a commitment to equal opportunities in recent years, the navy still has a long way to go in terms of having a representative ethnic mix: currently less than 1 per cent of the navy's service people are from non-white ethnic groups, a far lower proportion than the population as a whole.

The Royal Marines served in most of the post-1945 conflicts in which British forces were active, playing a major role in the Falklands War. Marines still serve aboard warships as boarding parties, but for many decades their primary tasks have been amphibious landings and special forces operations.

In common with the other armed services, the Royal Navy has been considerably stretched to cover the commitments of the past few years, which have included the war in Kosovo, the Afghan War and deployments to other places. In a few years time it appears that it will enter a period of some years without its own air cover, between the retirement of its Harrier jets and the arrival of American-built replacements. There are clearly dangers inherent in stretching the remit of a service that, despite the continuing professionalism of its service people, now has levels of manpower not seen for about 150 years.[18]

Table 18 Manpower in the Royal Navy, 1914–2001[19]

Date	No. of men*	
1914	250,000 }	First World War
1918	450,000 }	
1920	136,000	
1930	97,000	
1939	134,000 }	Second World War
1945	865,000 }	
1950	142,000 }	Korean War
1953	149,000 }	
1960	100,500	
1970	87,500	
1980	72,000	
1982	73,000	Falklands War
1991	63,000	Gulf War
1996	48,000	
2001	42,000	Afghan War

* Figures rounded up or down to nearest 1,000.

The royal dockyards

The royal dockyards experienced considerable fluctuations in their fortunes during this period. The 1914–18 war saw dockyard activity reach new peaks; new temporary base facilities were also developed at places like Harwich, which was used to repair and maintain smaller vessels operating in the North Sea. Post-war expenditure cuts led to the run-down of Pembroke and Rosyth (though Rosyth was later revived), and the sack for many dockyard workers. The only new naval dockyard developed in the inter-war period was at Singapore, which cost £20 million to build and had only been in service for some four years when the port fell to the Japanese in 1942. It was a terrible irony that so much had been invested in the creation of a huge Far Eastern dockyard when Britain already did not have sufficient naval power to defend its possessions in the region.

The Second World War witnessed an even greater rise in dockyard activity than the First, and temporary fleet bases appeared all over the world, in places such as Kenya and Ceylon. As in the First World War, many women came to work in the dockyards, but most left after 1945. The size of the female dockyard workforce did not begin to grow again until the 1970s.

The shrinking post-war navy inevitably led to dockyard closures. Pembroke closed in 1947 (although a small naval facility was maintained there for some decades afterwards), Bermuda in 1953, Malta in 1958 and Sheerness in 1960. Sheerness was later redeveloped as a commercial port, although all such closures had adverse effects on what had become traditional dockyard communities.

Devonport was extended in the 1950s and substantially rebuilt. In the 1960s the main yards were Portsmouth, Devonport and Rosyth, the latter becoming the navy's main refit base for nuclear submarines in 1963. Chatham, in decline after the war, acquired a centre for refitting and refuelling nuclear attack submarines in 1968, but was closed by defence cuts in 1984. Both Portsmouth and Devonport underwent further modernization in the 1970s.

The largest new naval shoreside development of the 1960s was Faslane on the Clyde, which opened in 1968 as a base for Polaris nuclear submarines, with a missile-storage facility at nearby Coulport. Both places are still used by the nuclear submarine fleet. Privatization and cost-cutting since the 1980s have considerably reduced the state's direct role in the maintenance of the Royal Navy's ships (although all dockyards and naval bases remain under RN command). The management of Devonport and Rosyth was taken over by private companies in the 1980s, and in 2002 a similar deal transferred 1,750 workers at HM Naval Base Clyde, plus others at Devonport and Portsmouth, to a private company. Rosyth lost the Trident nuclear submarine refit contract to Devonport in the late 1990s, and in 2002 the new facility opened in the south-west, some two and a half years behind schedule. Privatization has been accompanied by job losses in the past, and has met with a good deal of opposition from many dockyard workers and their trade unions. It remains to be seen how well the modern dockyard system would cope with the stress of a major war.[20]

Ports, sea trade and offshore industries

The patterns of sea trade and port development established in the nineteenth century persisted well into the twentieth. The great dock complexes, with their massive warehouses and forests of cranes, were symbols of trade, wealth and maritime might for 150 years and more.

British ports did not suffer any significant damage during the 1914–18 war, but for international trade and for millions of people around the world, the peace years of 1919–39 were mostly terrible. National and international economies went in to recession and slump at various times in the period (not just in the Depression years of the early 1930s), and although trade did increase in some areas, one of Britain's major exports was hit by technological change. Oil was increasingly replacing coal as a fuel across the world, and the tonnage of British coal exports in the late 1930s were almost half of what they had been just before the First World War. The coal ports such as Cardiff suffered badly as a result.

By 1920 there were 122 shipping companies in Cardiff, which was briefly 'the greatest steamship-owning centre in the world'. The booming Cardiff coal market collapsed in the early 1920s as oil began to take over as a shipping fuel and competition from foreign collieries grew. The shipping trade went down with the coal trade. By 1937 only fifty-seven shipping concerns survived; coal exports from Cardiff ended in 1964 and by 1986 only two shipping companies were left in the

126 Scottish emigrants dancing on board the liner SS *Montcalm* on their way to Canada, 1926. Large-scale seaborne emigration from the British Isles continued in the 20th century.

port. Subsequently many of the wharves and quays of Cardiff have been turned over to residential and commercial development, the fate of many nineteenth-century dock complexes.

However, ports such as London, Southampton, Manchester, Liverpool and Glasgow saw increases in their trade in the interwar period because they had the facilities to cope with the growing sizes of cargo ships and liners (average tonnage of British foreign trade ships rose by nearly a quarter between 1913 and 1923). Many of the larger ferry ports, such as Dover and Harwich, also grew because they could handle large throughputs of passengers and cargo at appreciable speed.

Britain, like other countries, needed increasing quantities of oil. For reasons of safety and ease of unloading and storage, specialized oil terminals were developed in the interwar years away from existing ports. The first British oil terminal was Skewen, near Swansea (opened 1922), but others followed in the 1920s and 1930s, such as Avonmouth, near Bristol.

Although the bigger ports were mostly able to cope with larger shipping, other new facilities were created in the 1920s and 1930s, such as the massive King George V Dock in London (opened 1921, with about three *miles* of quays), and the major developments at Southampton, including a dry dock big enough to take ocean liners.

127 The Royal Albert Dock, London, 1958. The forests of cranes and fleets of lighters were to be found in many world ports of this period. Towed by tugs, the lighters were used to move cargo around the port.

128 The passenger/cargo liner *St Essylt* being towed into Cardiff, 1948. The *St Essylt* was a modern design built in 1947 by Thompsons of Sunderland for the Cardiff-based South American Saint Line, and intended for between Cardiff and the River Plate in South America. In the event, most of the company's small fleet in the 1950s and 1960s was employed in the tramp trade in northern Europe.

The movement of cargo had been improved in the nineteenth century by the application of steam power and hydraulics, but in the decades after the Second World War 'palletization' (carrying goods on pallets that could be moved and stacked easily by fork-lift trucks) began to come in from about 1950, and the movement of goods, vehicles and people through ferry ports was revolutionized by the growing use of roll-on/roll-off ('ro-ro') ferries and the relatively simple port equipment that went with them. Ro-ro ships did exist before the 1939–45 war, but wartime experience of tank and other vehicle landing-craft made them much more feasible. The third major shipping and port revolution of the period was containerization, which became a reality in the second half of the 1960s. The first British container ports opened at Tilbury and Felixstowe in 1968. Although merchant ships became bigger and more complex during the twentieth century, most of the big ports remained places where hordes of dockers worked with relatively little mechanical assistance, apart from cranes, to unload ships that were packed with bulk cargoes like coal or else crates, barrels, lumps of machinery and other traditional forms of cargo. The advent of containerization in the 1960s led to radical changes in the design of ships, the layout and location of ports, and the numbers of people required to work in harbours. Containerization dealt a body-blow to the traditional dock trades. Most of the trade of the port of London was shifted eastwards to Tilbury with the space of a few years. The number of registered dockworkers in London peaked at 32,000 in 1955; by 1985 that figure had shrunk to about 3,000.

129 The Victoria Deep Water Terminal, Greenwich, River Thames, 1980.
Containerization radically changed the operation and appearance of ports, and in some
cases their locations.

The older ports were also affected by the growing size of oil tankers and other
bulk carriers. It became easier and more efficient for these ships to unload or load
at deep water terminals outside established dock or port areas. The traditional liner
berths at places such as Southampton also declined as intercontinental passenger
transport by sea fell victim to the development of mass air travel in the 1960s and
1970s (although in more recent years the growth of the holiday cruise market has
seen a renewed lease of life for the passenger liner).

Radical developments in port location were not just caused by containerization.
The Manchester Ship Canal, for example, opened in 1894 and gave the great
manufacturing city of Manchester access to the sea, making it cheaper and far
easier to import materials and export manufactured goods. However, by the 1960s
the increasing size of merchant ships, competition from road transport, and the
shift in the pattern of trade more towards Europe, began to adversely affect trade
on the canal. Despite this, the western stretch prospered after the construction of
container ports at Salford (1968) and Ellesmere Port (1972).

The upshot of these changes was to leave many of the traditional dock areas short
of trade and increasingly obsolete. The traditional dockland communities suffered
as business and jobs went elsewhere or just evaporated. Across Britain, from
Glasgow to the Thames, many of the derelict docks were turned into residential
and commercial areas. London's docklands, in common with many other derelict
dock areas in Britain, underwent major residential and commercial redevelopment
in the 1980s and 1990s, and the Royal Group became home to a new airport. The
'yuppification' of such areas was often met by resentment from local communities,

as homes went up that were far too expensive for locals to afford. However, redevelopment in some form was inevitable: either that or continued dereliction. In 1986 a major London redevelopment organization declared 'the major advantage of Docklands is its closeness to London': the area had ceased to have much significance for sea trade.

Some ports have undergone major changes in staffing, structure and infrastructure. London's dock workforce was far from being the only one to be radically affected by the transformation of port activities, and some dockers reacted by taking industrial action. At Liverpool, for example, there was a long-running and bitter dock dispute in the 1990s.

British merchant shipping may have declined in recent decades, but the business of the larger UK ports has grown over this period. Since the early 1990s, the tonnage of cargo passing through British ports (both imports and exports) has topped 500 million tonnes per year, and in 1997 stood at 522 million tonnes. Nearly three-quarters of the cargo comes in bulk form (mostly in the form of oil or its products), with just under a quarter in containers loaded as cargo or on lorries carried by ro-ro ships.

London remains the leading port in the United Kingdom, but unlike the sixteenth century, when it had no rivals, there are other major harbours now. London, handling 56 million tonnes of cargo in 1997, was closely followed by Tees and Hartlepool (51 million tonnes), Grimsby and Immingham (48 million), Forth in Scotland (43 million) and Milford Haven in Wales (38 million). In all, about three-quarters of all UK trade passed through these big ports and ten others, including Southampton, Sullom Voe oil terminal in Shetland and Liverpool.

The UK has had a major offshore oil and gas production industry since the 1960s. Natural gas has replaced the older, coal-produced 'town gas', and North Sea oil has been coming ashore in Scotland, which is the centre of Britain's oil industry, since 1975. These industries created a good deal of work, both on the drilling and production platforms, and in rig fabrication yards, but oil industry employment peaked at 90,000 in the mid-1980s and subsequently declined. The offshore industries have suffered a number of major disasters, the worst of which was the explosion of the oil platform *Piper Alpha* in July 1988, which killed 170 people.[21]

The shipbuilding industry, 1914–2001

In 1913 Britain had 61 per cent of the world's merchant shipbuilding market (see p. 231). One-sixth (16.6 per cent) of the world's merchant tonnage at this time thundered down the slipways of the Clyde shipyards. In 1997 Japan and South Korea took 80 per cent of new building orders, and the UK as a whole built about 0.7 per cent, with the entire Scottish shipbuilding industry contributing 0.14 per cent. In relative terms the output of new ships in Britain had shrunk some 87 times in a little over eighty years.

The First World War saw the shipbuilding industry geared to building and repairing warships and merchantmen. With so many men away in the armed forces, many women were temporarily employed. Ninety per cent of naval armament production was being carried out by female labour by 1918.

Britain's share of the world shipping market was down to 40 per cent in 1920, with the growth of new competitors. The short post-war boom evaporated and, as trade declined, so did demands for shipping services and new ships. The ship-building slump was long-lived and deep. John Brown's yard on the Clyde employed just over 9,000 men in 1920; by 1922 this was down to 3,600, and in the dark Depression year of 1932 the figure stood at 422. Harland & Wolff, the Belfast giant, managed to expand and prosper somewhat in the 1920s, and by 1927 was employing 35,000 men across the UK. The Royal Mail Group, the world's largest shipping concern, had had a controlling interest in the yard since 1919, but Harland & Wolff had deep-seated financial troubles and was a cash drain on its parent company. The bankruptcy of the Royal Mail Group in 1930 badly affected the Belfast yard, and came just after the Wall Street Crash of 1929 had inaugurated the Depression. As with many other yards, orders virtually dried up. In 1932–3 only the company's Clyde yards launched any ships – a mere ten and most of them small. Suffering was widespread in working-class areas during the

130 The nearly-completed oil rig *Drill Master* at Stornoway, 1980.

131 Shipbuilding on the Clyde, Glasgow, 1943. The Clyde rose to be the greatest shipbuilding area in the world in the 19th century. Despite a huge upsurge in activity during the Second World War, the Clyde shared in the long postwar collapse of the British shipbuilding industry.

Depression – in Belfast alone 28 per cent of the working population were unemployed and many lived on the edge of starvation. In the 1930s the Northern Ireland government helped to keep Harland & Wolff going as a means of creating employment; such help was not forthcoming from the national government.

The larger shipbuilders got together to buy up and close down rival shipyards that were in financial trouble. This in turn created more unemployment, and, for example, deprived the north-east town of Jarrow of its only industry. World trade began to increase towards the end of 1933, providing some work for shipbuilding, but British shipbuilding was suffering from the after-effects of having been the world's shipbuilder. There was a reluctance to invest in new technology or adopt new working practices, and conservatism among the management and the workforce, the former being inflexible and frequently dictatorial in outlook. The industry could still build ships such as the *Queen Mary* (launched 1934) and *Queen Elizabeth* (1938), the greatest liners of their time, but the industry itself was living on borrowed time.

The onset of rearmament before the Second World War helped to revive the industry: Brown's, for example, finally got back to 1920 employment levels in 1939. The war brought full order books but it did not bring in rapid change within the yards themselves. The introduction of new methods such as welding hulls (instead of riveting them) was slow, and the industry was plagued by demarcation disputes. The union rule books in the yards even specified which workers could use which tools, and major disputes could arise over seemingly minor issues. The postwar shipbuilding industries of former enemies like Germany and Japan rose to become serious competitors, while the British industry began to lose ground. This was not just a matter of cheaper wages abroad: the Japanese industry had to be rebuilt after the war and was re-created on better-organized lines, with innovation positively welcomed. There were moves towards large-scale modernization in some British yards in the late 1950s and early 1960s, but overall the industry was in dire straits.

The story of the shipbuilding industry at this time was repeated in other industries: insecurity of employment, low morale, entrenched and outdated attitudes

132 The launch of the supertanker *Myrina* at Harland & Wolff's yard, Belfast, 1967. The 95,450 grt (gross registered tons, or grt, denotes the volume of space available within a ship for cargo, storage, crew, passengers and fuel) supertanker was the first VLCC ('very large crude carrier') to be launched in Britain and, at the time, the largest vessel to be built in Europe.

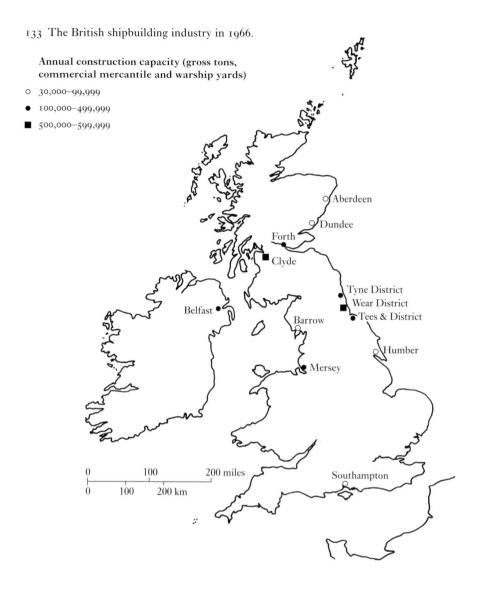

133 The British shipbuilding industry in 1966.

Annual construction capacity (gross tons,
commercial mercantile and warship yards)

○ 30,000–99,999

● 100,000–499,999

■ 500,000–599,999

Aberdeen

Dundee

Forth

Clyde

Tyne District

Wear District

Belfast

Barrow

Tees & District

Humber

Mersey

0   100   200 miles

0   100   200 km

Southampton

among management and workforce, coupled with a lack of investment or willing-
ness to devote enough time and money to research and planning. Attempts were
made to save part of the Clyde shipbuilding industry in 1966 by merging three
firms to become Upper Clyde Shipbuilders (UCS), but attempts to improve
management–union co-operation were not very successful. In 1971 the new
Conservative government withdrew support for UCS. In an attempt to keep the
yard afloat the workforce began their famous 'work-in' in July of that year, which
lasted until October 1972. It failed, and the yard was sold to oil-rig builders.

The 1973 'oil shock', when OPEC (Organization of Petroleum Exporting
Countries) cut production, and the economic downturn that resulted, saw British
yards lose yet more customers. The Labour government (elected in 1974) decided

to nationalize most of the industry in 1977 as British Shipbuilders, a large concern with 87,000 employees. However, the decline continued, with world orders for shipping sluggish, and the 1979 Thatcher government set about privatizing huge swathes of nationalized industry, including British Shipbuilders, in the 1980s. The reprivatized yards mostly suffered badly and many disappeared. Total employment in the British shipbuilding and ship-repair industries is now said to be about 26,000, but this figure apparently includes many working in small firms building yachts and motorboats. With a few exceptions, the old giant yards are gone.[22]

Ireland: trade and naval defence, 1921–2001

Irish trade after independence was dominated by certain factors. One of these was the economic relationship with Britain, which remained the main destination for Irish exports until both countries entered the European Economic Community (EEC) in 1973. Agricultural produce, particularly livestock, remained Ireland's main exports, but the volume of Irish trade was limited by policies of protectionism pursued by successive Irish governments from the early 1930s to the 1960s. Exports of industrial products did not overtake those of agricultural produce in value until the 1970s.

Ireland was forced to take measures to develop a small merchant fleet during the Second World War, when British ships (which had carried most of the Irish trade) were banned from carrying goods to Eire. Irish Shipping Ltd was set up in 1941 as a partly state-owned business, with a fleet of fifteen ships. The company existed for over forty years, until it over-extended itself and had to be wound up in 1984.

The Anglo-Irish Treaty of 1921 reserved the so-called 'Treaty Ports' of Berehaven, Queenstown (Cobh), Lough Swilly, Haulbowline and Rathmullen for Britain, and maintained British control over Irish waters. However, these bases proved costly to maintain and were potentially vulnerable to attack from inland. They were handed over to the Irish Free State in 1938, which became responsible for the first time for its own territorial waters.

The Irish state established a Marine and Coastwatching Service in 1939, together with a volunteer naval reserve. Irish opinion about the war was very divided, with much sympathy for the Allied cause, but there was still great resentment of Britain and, for a time, the fear of British invasion from the North. Ireland's official policy during the war was neutrality, although many Irish people served in the British armed forces and the Merchant Navy.

The Marine Service had ten vessels by 1941, including six torpedo boats, but was ineffective. It was replaced in 1946 by the Naval Service, which purchased three *Flower*-Class corvettes from Britain. The Naval Service suffered from a lack of funds and for a time in 1970 had no operational vessels. A revival began in the 1970s and new vessels were acquired, including the first naval vessels to be built in independent Ireland. Between 1972 and 1984 the Verlome Cork Dockyard built five craft for the Irish Navy. The modern Naval Service has a naval base at

Haulbowline, and operates seven ships, a helicopter, four offshore patrol vessels and two coastal patrol craft. The fleet's main purpose is national defence, although its activities are chiefly centred on fishery protection, search and rescue, aid to the gardai (police) and customs, and other forms of aid to the civil power.[23]

Merchant sailors, shipowners and the shipping industry 1900–2001

The late nineteenth and early twentieth centuries saw a marked growth in the unionization of British seafarers. The title National Union of Seamen (NUS) was adopted in 1926, but the union traced its origins to the National Amalgamated Sailors' and Firemen's Union of 1887, which was re-formed as the National Sailors' and Firemen's Union (NSFU) in 1893. Local unions also existed, and in 1922 the NUS absorbed the oldest and most powerful of these, the Hull Seamen's Union. The NUS was incorporated into the Rail, Maritime and Transport Union in 1990. The fragmented nature of seafaring employment, and the prevalence of much casual work, made union organization difficult in the shipping industry. However, by 1911 the NSFU represented the great majority of British seafarers; led by Havelock Wilson, the union staged the first national seamen's strike in 1911.

The First World War led to the creation of the National Maritime Board, which, under stringent wartime controls, imposed standard pay rates and conditions across the industry. The board became a permanent organization, a venue for consultations between the union and management. Unlike other industries, shipowners only had to deal with one trades union, in the form of the NUS, which from 1922 also represented ships' cooks and stewards. A short-lived post-war shipping boom lasted from 1918 to 1921, but collapsed because of economic downturn and the fact that too many ships were chasing too few cargoes. The economic crises of the 1920s and early 1930s had dire effects on the British shipping industry. Employment declined and total British shipping tonnage remained fairly static from 1919 to 1931; the relative world position of the Merchant Navy shrank in world terms as other nations, such as Germany, the USA and Japan, strove to build new merchant fleets, particularly in the passenger and cargo liner trades, supported by government subsidies. For lack of cargoes on the liner routes, the liners took part cargoes of bulk goods like rice and sugar, which were the staple of tramp shipping. Unsubsidized British tramp shipping suffered in particular, with many ships laid up for want of business. In 1935 the British Shipping (Assistance) Act was passed, to provide temporary government financial aid for tramp ships. The Act lapsed in 1938 as trading conditions began to improve.

The British merchant fleet had technological problems as well. The Royal Navy had mostly converted to oil power by the end of the First World War but, as Britain was a great coal producer, the Merchant Navy continued to rely on steamships. A diesel-engined motor ship could easily outsail a steamer, as the average steamer speed was 8–10 knots and the motor ship could make 12–17 knots. Oil was also increasingly competitive as a fuel. This technological stagnation and lack of investment led to lost trade for British ships and the steady relative decline of the

British merchant fleet, still the largest in the world in 1939, but only as a result of British maritime hegemony before 1914.

The inter-war period was a grim one for British merchant seamen, with pay cuts in the early 1920s and 1932 and a lack of employment. Pay and conditions did improve later in the 1930s, but life at sea in British merchant ships remained fairly basic for many seafarers.

The British and other Allied merchant fleets were critical elements in the eventual Allied victory in the Second World War. The British merchant service drew most of its pre-war manpower from traditional seafaring regions, not all of them in Britain. In 1938 just over two-thirds (68.6 per cent) of 192,000 people employed in the Merchant Navy came from the UK, but about 50,000 (26 per cent) came from India and China. This ethnic mix increased as a result of the wartime drive for manpower, and the Merchant Navy also received many recruits who signed up for the duration of hostilities from non-seafaring backgrounds in the UK.

Wartime building and other acquisitions made up for ships lost in the war, and in fact replaced many older ships. The ten years or so after 1945 was a good period for the British shipping industry, because of a lack of competition from foreign fleets and generally high freight rates. Crew accommodation and conditions aboard British merchant ships began to improve, but labour relations in the post-war shipping industry were not smooth. In 1966 the National Union of Seamen voted for a national strike for better pay and a forty-hour working week. The strike lasted six weeks, and although there have been subsequent strikes in the shipping industry, none has been on the scale of the 1966 conflict, partly because of the shrinking size of the sea-going workforce.

Excluding tanker tonnage and the US war reserve merchant fleet, Britain still had the world's largest merchant fleet in 1957. The fleet was divided up as follows:

Table 24 The British merchant fleet, 1957[24]

Type	No. of ships	Gross tonnage '000 tons	% of tonnage
Passenger-cargo liners	322	2,879	17.2
Cargo liners	1,145	6,344	37.3
Tramps	1,070	3,191	18.9
Tankers	575	4,528	26.6
Total	3,112	16,942	100

The composition of the fleet changed between the 1930s and the 1950s, with declines in passenger-cargo liner and tramp tonnage, and a rise in the size of the cargo-liner fleet. The tramp-shipping sector included many small companies (in 1957 nearly a third of Britain's tramp shipping was in companies with four ships or

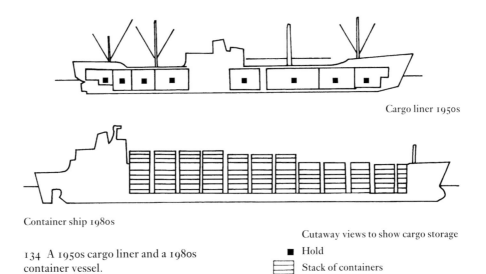

Cargo liner 1950s

Container ship 1980s

134 A 1950s cargo liner and a 1980s
container vessel.

Cutaway views to show cargo storage

■ Hold

▤ Stack of containers

less), which found it much less easy to survive than the larger firms, who had made economies of scale. In 1936 there were about 257 tramp-owning companies; by 1957 there were only 143. In the booming maritime economy of the early 1900s, with Britain as number one maritime nation, such firms would have prospered. In the late 1950s, with cheaper foreign competition growing, their days were numbered.

World merchant shipping underwent a tremendous revolution, driven in part by technology, from the 1960s onwards. One of the key changes was the development of containerization, in which cargoes such as manufactured goods, food and other products are packed into standard 20 ft or 40 ft (6 m or 12 m) steel containers, rather than broken down into individual small units such as sacks, boxes or barrels. Containers had profound effects on ports and shipping. Although developments in crane technology in the twentieth century made the movement of heavy cargoes easier, the loading and unloading of traditional cargoes, with thousands of small units, took a long time, involved a lot of labour and there were risks of damage and theft. Unloading a 10,000–15,000-ton cargo liner might take several days, and once the goods were ashore, they generally had to be warehoused. Containerization cut out whole areas of cargo-handling and reduced the need for conventional warehouses, as containers can be stacked in the open and then loaded directly on to road or rail transport. Containerization, amongst other things, led to the demise of the London docks closest to the City (see p. 269).

Containers also made it possible to build bigger ships, as the ships could be designed around standardized boxes. One container ship replaced between eight and ten conventional cargo liners, with consequent savings in crew costs. It was also faster and, in the opinion of many, far uglier. The search for ever greater economies of scale in world trade helped to drive the development of bigger tankers, great bulk carriers and other types.

The period between the end of the Second World War and the end of the twentieth century saw British shipping enter a period of relative decline, followed by a time of absolute decline. The relative decline took place as the fleet grew in size between the 1940s and the mid-1970s, while the rest of the world's merchant fleets also grew. In 1950 the UK merchant fleet had 3,092 ships of 17.2 million grt (gross registered tons). By 1975 the actual number of ships had declined, but the tonnage of the fleet was over 80 per cent greater, at 31.5 million grt. By 1986 flagging-out and other factors had reduced the fleet tonnage by three-quarters, to 7.7 million tons, slightly less than half of the 1950 tonnage. The fleet was even smaller by 2001, with 368 trading vessels registered in the UK, totalling 3,600,000 grt. The flagging-out of ships to the Crown Dependencies and other British Dependent Territories has grown apace, with the result that now the Channel Islands, Isle of Man and some other places have nominal merchant fleets totalling 90 ships of 3,200,000 grt. A further 165 British-owned ships sail under foreign flags, totalling nearly 2.5 million grt. In other words, less than 40 percent of British-owned shipping is British-registered. One wonders whether, in a world of economic 'globalization', the ships that do not fly the Merchant Navy's red ensign can be seen in any real sense as part of a 'British' fleet, although the earnings from these vessels do contribute to the British balance of trade (over £2,200 million in 1998). It is possible that in the new century, national merchant fleets will have less and less reality, as management becomes increasingly globalized. However, Britain still wields some influence in the world shipping business, for the City of London remains the world centre for shipbroking.

One of the reasons for the shrinkage of the UK fleet in recent decades is competition from ships run under flags of convenience, with poorly-trained, low-paid crews, which can undercut the rates of UK-owned and registered fleets with their higher service and training standards and better pay. Many shipowners have flagged their vessels out of the UK registry to cut costs and to make use of the plentiful market of cheap seafaring labour from the Third World. Tax and 'inflexible' (the government's own word) registration standards have also played their part in the decline, along with changing trade patterns and new electronic technology (modern ships require fewer seamen to run them), but the net result has been a major crisis in British merchant shipping. The situation is made all the more bizarre by the fact that in terms of its Gross Domestic Product, the UK is the fifth largest trading nation in the world, exporting 26 per cent of its GDP, and 95 per cent of its trade by volume travels by sea.

In 1999 the New Labour government introduced a 'tonnage tax', which offered tax incentives to shipowners to register their ships in the UK, as long as they also committed themselves to training new British seafarers. P & O, the largest UK shipping line, undertook to register fifty ships in mainland Britain and to make a substantial increase in their trainee intake. By 2001 twenty P & O ships had been re-registered. The government's initiative is the most significant of its kind in recent years, but it remains to be seen if it can reverse the long-term decline of the British shipping industry.

The number of British seafarers suffered a rapid fall between 1980 and the mid-

Table 25 Numbers and origins of UK seafarers, 1986 and 1995[25]

Year	Total UK seafarers	% of UK origin
1986	28,086	84%
1995	30,597	54%

1990s, from close on 30,000 officers and over 20,000 ratings in 1980 to fewer than 10,000 of either by 1997, with a substantial rise in the proportion of foreign seamen employed. The sudden drop in the numbers of British seamen may in part have been caused by cost-cutting, by flagging-out, by retirement and by the declining attractions of the sea as a career. Projections from a London Guildhall University study suggest that, if nothing is done to arrest the decline, by 2012 the process of retirement will leave the country with fewer than 6,000 merchant officers. This absolute shrinkage in the size of the seafaring workforce is perhaps more dangerous for the future of the British merchant fleet than flagging-out.[26]

Technology and ships

The technology of navigation was revolutionized in the twentieth century. The gyroscopic compass, invented in 1908, is an electrically-powered compass that always points to the true North Pole (unlike a magnetic compass, which always points to magnetic north). It makes navigation easier, eliminating the need to estimate compass error in a magnetic compass, caused by the earth's changing magnetic field, before one can estimate a true course.

Radar was invented in the 1930s and was soon being used on warships. Intensive wartime development produced radars that were useful for collision avoidance, the detection of ships and aircraft, and for the direction of guns. After the Second World War radar became common on merchant ships, making the seas somewhat safer (although far from eliminating the need for human lookouts, as many collisions have shown). Radio waves were also used for direction-finding at sea. The idea was first used before the First World War, but it was the Second World War that saw the construction of large systems of radio navigation transmitters, which enabled ships to fix their positions by triangulating different radio beams. After the war one such system became famous as the British-developed Decca Navigator. However, even this system was overtaken by changing technology. The development of satellites from the 1960s eventually made pinpoint navigational accuracy possible by direct radio feeds from space, and in 2000 the Decca system was finally switched off.

The twentieth century also witnessed revolutions in ship propulsion. Oil rapidly replaced coal as the primary marine fuel in the years after the 1918, both replacing coal as the fuel used to produce steam for turbines and powering the new marine diesel engine in 'motorships'. Oil was lighter than coal and took up less storage space, factors that were critical in merchant ship design, but the expense of oil and the cost of diesel engines did deter some owners from investing in motorships. High-power steam engines (and even triple expansion engines) were still being built for some merchant ships in the 1950s and 1960s, but diesels were developed in the 1950s that could burn cheaper types of oil. After 1970 steam power was virtually extinct in merchant ships.

Steam turbines continued in naval use after the Second World War, because of their reliability and the power they could develop. The Royal Navy began to introduce gas turbine propulsion in the late 1950s, at first in conjunction with steam turbines. The gas turbine is a jet engine, powered by kerosene, in which the jet blast, rather than steam, is used to turn the turbine blades. Gas turbines proved to be highly efficient, and from the early 1970s they were installed in all major British surface warships. Steam power still survives in the Royal Navy in the form of the power plants of its nuclear submarines, where the heat from nuclear reactions is used to raise steam to run a turbine.[27]

Fishing

The British herring industry prospered until the First World War, but the economic disruption that followed the conflict led to a steady decline thereafter. English and Welsh herring fishing had more or less stopped by the early 1960s. New technology gave it a second lease of life in Scotland in the mid-1960s, but the near-extinction of the herring stock led to the closure of the North Sea herring fishery in 1977 and that off the west Scotland in 1978, although some limited fishing later resumed.

Other parts of the British fishing industry prospered, but it was affected by a slowness to invest in new technology. In 1952 just over three-quarters of British fishing vessels of 70 feet (21 m) or more in length were more than thirty years old. Owners were slow to buy the more efficient and reliable diesel and diesel-electric boats; catches by boats using these newer forms of propulsion did not exceed those of steam vessels until 1963. Britain was also slow to adopt factory-freezer ships, which only began to be more common in the 1960s. Other forms of new technology, such as radio navigation aids, radar and echo-sounders (used to locate fish shoals) were introduced, however, and made fishing somewhat safer and more efficient.

By the 1960s the British fishing industry was being affected by foreign competition. In the 1970s politics affected it even more. After three 'cod wars' with Iceland from the 1950s to the 1970s, British trawlers were finally excluded from a 200-mile (324-km) territorial waters zone round Iceland in 1976. It dealt a body blow to the UK's long-distance fishing fleet. In 1977 the European Economic Community introduced a common 200-mile (324-km) limit for EEC-nation fishing grounds. Traditional British fishing grounds were opened up to various forms of competition from other countries. Over-fishing became a major problem, with some fish stocks near extinction. Catch quotas were imposed for different species. It is a tangled and unhappy story that one way or another has impacted, or will impact,

135 Steam trawlers at the North Wall, Grimsby Fish Dock, 1948. Britain had the most advanced trawling fleet in the world in 1914, but by 1948 under-investment had left the country with a large number of ageing trawlers, the vast majority still powered by steam. Programmes of modernization were introduced, but landings by diesel-powered trawlers did not exceed those of steam trawlers until 1963.

adversely on the fishing fleets of every nation in the present European Union. The British industry has shrunk significantly. Between 1967 and 1997 British fish landings fell by 28 per cent, numbers of fishermen by 22 per cent (to about 18,600) and the tonnage of the larger parts of the fleet by 44 per cent. There were also major job losses in the processing industries that supported the old industry; for each job afloat, there are several more ashore. All is not doom and gloom, however, for the present fleet includes many more modern boats than its predecessors.

Head for head of population, Scotland is a much greater fishing nation than either England or Wales. In 1997 about 50 per cent of UK fishermen were living in England and Wales (and most of those in England), but about 44 per cent (8,200) were in Scotland, which has a much smaller population (the remaining 6 per cent of fishermen were in Northern Ireland). The three top fishing ports in Britain are all Scottish – Peterhead, Aberdeen and Fraserburgh – while Newlyn is the leading English port.

Irish fishing remained rather underdeveloped into the twentieth century, but Ireland has benefited from membership of the EEC and later the European Union in terms of an expanded fishing zone and other economic benefits. The fishing fleet of Eire numbered 1,240 vessels in 1998, but many of the boats were old, with only about 4 per cent built in the previous decade. The main fishing ports of Eire are Castletownbere in County Cork and Killibegs in County Donegal. In 1997

136 Traditional inshore fishing: Scottish cobles on Skye, 1981. Inshore fishing in Britain and Ireland is still carried out by some traditional types of craft, vessels adapted to meet local traditions. However, most are powered by inboard or outboard motors, rather than traditional sail or oar.

Donegal was also home to the most modern fishing vessels in the Irish fleet, seiners and pelagic trawlers.

The problems being encountered by the European Union seem to be part of a global problem affecting all fisheries. At its heart is over-fishing that aims to satisfy the demands of industrialized or industrializing societies. For the average consumer the result may be a rise in the cost of part of their diet; for the fishermen and ports that rely on fishing for their livelihoods the price is a good deal higher.[28]

Conclusion

Trying to form some hard-and-fast conclusion about 1,600 years of maritime history is not only difficult, but also may suggest that I somehow feel that the maritime history of Britain and Ireland is over. Certainly the trends of recent decades have indicated that it might be coming to an end: after all, with air travel and the Channel Tunnel (opened 1994), are maritime matters relevant any more? Geography, economic fact, strategic necessity and common sense, however, suggest that the answer is 'yes'. It is axiomatic that Britain, Ireland and the other parts of this archipelago are surrounded by water; whether they know it or not, the sea has a greater impact on the lives of the average British or Irish person than it does, say, on the average inhabitant of Switzerland or the American Midwest. The vast majority of Britain's trade, for example, still travels by sea, and the country is heavily dependent on foreign earnings. As two world wars demonstrated, if the country's sea-lanes are threatened, its future can be put at risk. One might argue that in the context of the European Union and Britain's defence alliances, there is less need to worry about that aspect of things. At the moment there seems little cause for concern, but recent history has shown that the future is terrifyingly unpredictable, all the more so in a complex multipolar world where undeclared wars can be waged in the heart of cities.

I am not arguing for 'making Britain great again' (a phrase that used to win applause in radio discussion programmes in the 1960s) in the sense of the country having a huge navy or once again being the world leader in merchant shipping and shipbuilding. These historical phenomena relied on sets of circumstances that no longer exist, and there is no point in getting too nostalgic about them; they were also, in many ways, related to Britain ruling and exploiting large numbers of previously independent peoples.

However, if this book has a message, it is that the peoples of Britain and Ireland should take much more notice of the seas around them, of the people who work on them and of what happens there. The sea has been, and remains, a highway, a source of food, a battleground, a dumping-ground and a playground. It is also on our front doorstep.

Notes and references

Abbreviations

BCS British Chamber of Shipping

DETR Department of the Environment, Transport and Regions

NMM National Maritime Museum, Greenwich

RMM Royal Marines Museum, Eastney, Portsmouth

PRO Public Record Office

CPR Calendar of Patent Rolls (PRO)

CCR Calendar of Close Rolls (PRO)

E101 Exchequer, King's Remembrancer, Accounts Various (PRO)

E351 Exchequer, Pipe Office, Declared Accounts (PRO)

E364 Exchequer, Lord Treasurer's Remembrancer, Foreign Accounts (PRO)

Most other publications are cited by author/editor or date only; full publication details are supplied in the bibliography.

Page 7

1 Quoted in Davis 1972, p. 107.

2 Eames 1980, p. 140.

3 Peter Scott, *The Battle of the Narrow Seas*, 1945, p. xi.

Introduction

1 Murray 1972, pp. 96–7.

2 Crystal 1995, pp. 6–7, 106–9.

1 A boat to the island of ghosts

1 Ure 1951, p. 246.

2 Frere 1974, pp. 253–2, 379–80; Snyder 1998, pp. 19, 173–4.

3 Swanton 1996, pp. xviii, 12–15.

4 Swanton 1996, pp. 14–20; Snyder 1998, pp. 50, 249; Filmer-Sankey 1999, p. 47.

5 Crystal 1995, p. 7.

6 Thomas 1971, p. 68; Snyder 1998, pp. 67–8; Thomas 1990, p. 5; Loyn 1994, pp. 90–1, 97; Richards 1992, p. 89.

7 Alcock 1973, pp. 201–21; Laing 1975, p. 133; Haslam 1984, pp. 276–7; Snyder 1998, pp. 152 and 243–4; Medieval Archaeology Newsletter, 25 October 2001 (online) p. 5; atlas of Roman pottery: www.potsherd.uklinux.net/atlas.

8 Haywood 1991, pp. 61–2.

9 Alcock 1973, pp. 209–13; Snyder 1998, p. 174.

10 Rodger 1997, p. 6; Falkus and Gillingham 1981, p. 37; Fulford 1990; Thomas 1990 (quotation p. 10); Alcock 1999, p. 208.

11 Thomas 1971, pp. 62–7; Snyder 1998, pp. 40–3.

12 Farmer 1979, 54, pp. 87–8.

13 Rodger 1997, p. 5; Fulford *et al.* 2000; Edwards 2001.

14 Davies 1991, pp. 3–4.

15 McGrail 1981, pp. 26–9; Swanton 1996, p. 82.

16 McGrail 1981, pp. 30–1, 81.

17 Haywood 1991, p. 73; Roberts 1999, pp. 195–6.

2 *Wics*, wars and heathen men

1 Drewett, Rudling and Gardiner 1988, pp. 258, 309–11; Hodges 1989, pp. 69–114; Wood 1999, pp. 235, 239.

2 Haslam 1984, *passim*; Scull 1999, p. 22; Stevenson 1999, p. 181; Hines 1999; Gardiner *et al.* 2001.

3 Tatton-Brown 1984, pp. 2–21.

4 Tatton-Brown 1984, pp. 16–21.

5 Holdsworth 1984, pp. 332–7.

6 Walker 2000, pp. 11–12, 16, 149–54, 171–4; Vince 1990; Sherley-Price 1968, p. 104; Haslam 1984, *passim*; Lapidge 1999, pp. 255, 296, 451–4; Loyn and Percival 1975, pp. 113–14; Loyn 1994, pp. 90–1, 97; Richards 1997, p. 89.

7 The narrative of this section is substantially based on Stenton 1971 and Swanton 1996, using Swanton's corrected dates.

8 Roesdahl 1998, pp. 4–11, 83–93, 187–94.

9 Loyn and Percival 1975, p. 108.

10 Hill 1981, pp. 92–3.

11 Stenton 1971, p. 413.

12 Higham 1997, p. 200.

13 Ritchie 1993, *passim*.

14 Redknap 2000, *passim*.

15 Richards 1992, pp. 74, 87–9; West 1983, p. 70; Gardiner 1997.

16 Richards 1992, pp. 11, 87.

17 See Sandahl 1951, 1958 and 1982, *passim*.

18 Friel 1995, p. 16.

19 Delgado 1997, pp. 175–6, 388–9; Loyn 1994, p. 97.

20 Haywood 1991, p. 93.

21 Hollister 1962, pp. 103–26 and 1965, pp. 14–15, 29–30, 120–1, 248–9, 257; Hill 1981, pp. 92–3; Rodger 1997, pp. 19–21.

3 Wars and trade

1 Swanton 1996, p. 249.

2 Rodger 1997, pp. 45–6.

3 Warren 1966, pp. 137–42; Laughton 1942.

4 Warren 1966, pp. 222–4; Rodger 1997, pp. 53–4.

5 Rodger 1997, p. 55.

6 Rodger 1997, p. 77.

7 Rodger 1997, pp. 83–90.

8 Rodger 1997, pp. 131–6; Richmond 1971.

9 Rodger 1997, pp. 446–9.

10 Runyan 1977, pp. 3–4; Rodger 1997, p. 118.

11 Platt 1973, pp. 107–12.

12 Dobson 1970, pp. 126–7.

13 Runyan 1977, p. 16.

14 Friel 1995, pp. 150–6.

15 Rodger 1997, p. 147; Rose 1982, pp. 237–8, 241.

16 Rodger 1997, p. 113; Mackie 1978, pp. 62–158.

17 Rodger 1997, pp. 138–40; PRO E364/43, D, m.1v.

18 Rodger 1997, pp. 488–9.

19 Burwash 1969, pp. 67–9.

20 Robinson 1974, pp. 21 and 660–1; Runyan 1977;
Rodger 1997, pp. 141–2.

21 Bolton 1980, pp. 274–5, 287–319; Carus-Wilson
1937, p. 79; Hatcher 1973, pp. 21–6, 89–132; Rodger
1997, pp. 79–80; Dyer 1989, p. 62.

22 Duffus Hardy 1833, pp. 177b–178.

23 Dyer 1989, pp. 62, 104–5.

24 Veale 1971, pp. 119–24; Childs 1992, p. 80.

25 Bridbury 1955, pp. 56–133.

26 Friel 1995, pp. 96–8; Zins 1972, p. 9; Childs 1981.

27 Platt 1973, p. 198.

28 Marcus 1980, pp. 125–73; Jones 2000.

29 Platt 1973, p. 161.

30 Zins 1972, pp. 22–3; Bolton 1980, pp. 305–6, 310–11.

31 Kowaleski 1992, p. 67; Platt 1973, p. 159.

32 Blake 1967.

33 Reknap 1998; Davies 1991, pp. 164–71.

34 Hutchinson 1997, pp. 129–30; Childs 2000;
Kowaleski 2000; Woolgar 2000.

35 Clout 1991, pp. 52–3; Osler and Barrow 1993,
pp. 8–11; McDonnell 1978, 90–108; Platt 1973,
pp. 76, 83–4.

36 Burwash 1969, map facing p. 146; Rodger 1997,
pp. 490–7.

37 Gosford: CPR 1401–5, 281; CCR 1402–5, 102;
Hewitt 1929; Beresford 1988, pp. 415–16, 497–8.

38 Childs 1982; Hewitt 1929, pp. 78–83, 123–5;
Bernard 1980; Graham 1980; Carus-Wilson 1954.

39 Lavery 2001, pp. 18–20.

40 Friel 1995, pp. 39–67.

41 Grant and Cheape 1987, p. 163.

42 Scammell 1961, p. 332; Friel 1995, *passim*.

43 Bernard 1980; Davis 1972, pp. 300–2.

44 CPR 1338–40, 491–2; Rodger 1997, p. 147.

45 Gairdner 1983, vol. 2, p. 136.

46 Ford 1979; Appleby 1992; Rose 1982, pp. 245, 250;
Rodger 1997, pp. 199–200.

47 Friel 1995, p. 30.

48 Scammell 1962; Kowaleski 1992; Friel 1995,
pp. 27–32.

49 Based on an analysis of the records of English royal
ships in PRO classes E101 and E364, 1399–1422.

50 Hutchinson 1997, pp. 164–82; Burwash 1969, 33–4.

51 Naish 1985, pp. 43–4, 82–4; Hutchinson 1997.

52 Harris 1969, *passim*.

4 Into the Ocean

1 This section is substantially based on Loades 1992
and Rodger 1997, pp. 164–346; the Scots navy section
is largely based on Macdougall 1989, pp. 223–46, and
Lavery 2001, pp. 20–3.

2 Morley 1976, pp. 8–9.

3 A very great deal has been written about Drake; see
Cummins 1995 for a recent study.

4 *The Times*, 17 September 1987.

5 The literature of the Armada is considerable;
see Martin & Parker 1988 and NMM 1988, amongst
others.

6 Dietz 1991.

7 Scammell 1970, pp. 140–1, 147.

8 NMM 1988, p. 153.

9 Rodger 1997, p. 306; NMM 1988, p. 203.

10 PRO E351/2193, m. 2r.

11 Laughton 1981, vol. 2, pp. 96, 138–9, 183.

12 Harris 1969, p. 251.

13 Heidenreich 2001; Stirland 2000.

14 Dietz 1986, *passim;* Jackson 1983, pp. 19–22.

15 Dudley-Edwards 1991, pp. 209–23.

16 Cullen 1968, pp. 21–2, 137–8; Devine 1996c.

17 Loades 1992, p. 120; Cordingly 1995, p. 236.

18 Loades 1992, p. 156.

19 Tenenti 1967, pp. 56–86.

20 Starkey 2000.

21 NMM 1988, pp. 209–10.

22 Andrews 1985, p. 8.

23 Loades 1992, p. 254.

24 For the most recent studies of the Frobisher voyages,
see Symons 1999, vols 1 and 2.

25 Quinn 1985, *passim.*

26 Andrews 1985, pp. 256–79.

27 Quinn 1985, pp. 163–4; Rich and Wilson 1980,
p. 278; MacGregor 1997.

28 Oppenheim 1988, pp. 171–7; Williams 1988, pp. 200–1.

29 Dietz 1991; ships 1509–1603 based on Rodger 1997, pp. 475–80.

30 Morris 1998; Banbury 1971, pp. 24–32; Burton 1994, pp. 34–8; Rodger 1997, pp. 230–2; *Fragments of Ancient English Shipwrightry*: NMM facsimile PST20 A and B.

31 Hakluyt 1932, pp. 248–60.

32 Rodger 1998.

33 Rodger 1997, pp. 218–19.

5 Fall and rise

1 This section is based on Harding 1995, pp. 31–72; Everitt 1973, pp. 66–7, 71; Powell 1962, *passim*; Rodger 1997, pp. 347–426; Capp 2001; Edwards 2001; Carlton 2001.

2 Davis 1972, pp. 305–12; Harding 1999, pp. 59–120; Sanderson 1975, pp. 77–8, 79–80, 136–8, 165–7.

3 Harding 1999, pp. 289–90.

4 Harding 1995, pp. 97–113; Harding 1999, pp. 149–82; Sanderson 1975, pp. 26, 28, 31–2, 47, 102, 188.

5 Harding 1995, pp. 114–36; Harding 1999, pp. 183–255; Sanderson 1975, pp. 43–4, 75, 88–9, 147–8, 150–2.

6 Harding 1995, pp. 135–43; Harding 1999, 257–79; Duffy 1992; Coad 1992; Lyon 1996, pp. 69–172; Sanderson 1975, 38–9, 45–6, 80–2, 130–2, 153–4, 179–82.

7 Harding 1995, pp. 70–1, 89–90, 126.

8 Lavery 1989, p. 118.

9 Harding 1995, pp. 70–1; Henderson and Carlisle 1999.

10 This and preceding sections based on Lavery 1989, pp. 88–144; Cannon 1997, pp. 768–9; Rodger 1986, pp. 164–5.

11 Lloyd 1968, pp. 286–9.

12 Rodger 1986, 344 and *passim*; RMM n.d., pp. 2–11.

13 Data based on an analysis of Lyon 1993.

14 Lyon 1993, pp. 129–31; Lyon 1996, pp. 23–6.

15 Lyon 1993, pp. 17, 63–4, 104.

16 Lavery 1992b.

17 Rodger 1997, pp. 498–501.

18 Lavery 1992b, 19.

19 Figures based on Lyon 1993; Gardiner 1992a.

20 This discussion of ship and weapon development is based substantially on Gardiner 1992a, b and c; Lavery 1992b and c; Tracy 1992; Marquardt 1992; Harland 1992a and b; Lees 1984; Howard 1979; signalling based on Wilson 1986, pp. 77–84.

21 This section is based on Davis 1972, pp. 300–10; Jackson 1983, pp. 22–33; Braddick 1998; Andrews 1984, pp. 256–79; Canny 1998; Dietz 1986; Cullen 1968, pp. 21–2 and 137–8; Devine 1996b and c, pp. 1–36; Devine 2000, pp. 5, 13, 54–61; Dudley Edwards 1991, pp. 209–23.

22 Jackson 1983, pp. 22–64; Brown 1981, pp. 34–7; Whincop and White 1986, pp. 29–32; Farrant 1976, pp. 3–15; Davies-Shiel and Marshall 1969, p. 115; Dudley Edwards 1991, pp. 209–23.

23 Tattersfield 1998; Elder 1996; Richardson 1998; Morgan 1998.

24 Mainwaring and Perrin 1922, p. 14.

25 Cordingly 1995, p. 5.

26 Cordingly 1995, *passim*; Rogozinski 1997; IMO 2001/2.

27 Berg 1994, p. 54; Osler and Barrow 1993, pp. 24–7.

28 Davis 1972, pp. 44–80; Osler and Barrow 1993, pp. 20–4.

29 Coad 1983, *passim*; Macdougall 1982; Banbury 1971; Gilbert 1965.

30 Data compiled from Lyon 1993.

31 Holland 1971, pp. 171, 174, 179–80.

32 Gardiner 1992b; Baynes and Pugh 1981, pp. 71–83.

33 Sadler 1968; Naish 1985, pp. 92–106.

34 Jackson 2000; Jones 2000; Starkey 2000; Haines 2000a and b; Robinson 2000a and b; Gray 2000a and b; Pawlyn 2000a.

35 Appleby 1998; Anderson 1998; Beckles 1998; Braddick 1998; James 1998; Mancall 1998; Marshall 1998 a and b; Sinclair 1980.

36 Davis 1972, 90; this section is based on Davis 1972, pp. 81–109.

37 Davis 1972, p. 38.

38 Blake 1960, facing p. 1.

39 Blake 1960, p. 54.

40 Earle 1998, pp. 110–11.

41 Rediker 1987, pp. 169–79; Harris 1969, p. 47.

42 Rediker 1987, p. 174; Mathias 1969, p. 216.

43 Rediker 1987, pp. 118–21.

44 Smith, Watts and Watts 1998, pp. 104–5.

45 Rediker 1987, pp. 299–300.

46 Davis 1972, pp. 135–7.

47 Earle 1998, pp. 22–4, 200–1; Rediker 1987, p. 307.

48 Davis 1972, pp. 122–6.

49 Lavery 1989, pp. 88–90.

50 Lloyd 1968, pp. 184–7.

51 Kelly 1899, Littlehampton entry.

52 Littlehampton Museum, Maritime History File.

53 Cordingly 2001, pp. 11–14; Wells 1994, p. 30.

54 Cordingly 2001, pp. 78–82; Stark 1996, pp. 82–3.

6 Pax Britannica

1 Sanderson 1975, pp. 73–4, 126–8; Mitchell 1974, pp. 154–72; Lyon 1996, pp. 173–85.

2 Tucker 2000, pp. 186–93; Kennedy 1982, 205–37.

3 Macdougall 1982, pp. 155–7.

4 Coad 1983; Macdougall 1982.

5 Lyon 1993, p. 169.

6 Tall and Kemp 1996; Griffiths 1997, pp. 71–84, 98, 140–53; Lyon 1980, *passim*; Preston 1980, pp. 5–13.

7 Wells 1994, pp. 269–73.

8 This section largely based on Wells 1994, pp. 1–91; Lloyd 1968, pp. 267–84.

9 Smith, Watts and Watts 1998, p. 34.

10 Eames 1980, pp. 34–40, 44–8.

11 Peters 1975, pp. 40–2 and *passim*; Thornton 1959, pp. 69–72; Smith, Watts and Watts 1998, pp. 19–38, 43–4, 47–62.

12 Middleton 1977, pp. 84–5, 94–117.

13 Jenkins 1986, pp. 3–7; Crouzet 1982, pp. 10, 342–70; Starkey 1999; Jackson 1983, pp. 54–139.

14 Dudley Edwards 1991, pp. 209–23; Foster 1989, pp. 345–72.

15 Pudney 1975, pp. 14–151; Brown 1981, pp. 34–7; Barker 1986; Hadfield 1994; Crowe 1994; Jackson 1983, pp. 73–139.

16 Mumby-Croft and Barnard 2000; Jarvis 2000; Reid 2000a; Robinson 2000b and c.

17 O Grada 1995, pp. 146–52, 234, 484–5.

18 Crouzet 1982, p. 306.

19 Crouzet 1982, p. 306.

20 Crouzet 1982, pp. 306–16; Greenhill 1980, pp. 5–19; Starkey 1999, pp. 354–5; Griffiths 1997, p. 98.

21 Currie 1988, pp. 31–5; Jenkins 1986, p. 64.

22 Jenkins 1986, pp. 3–6; Eames 1980, pp. 18–19; Crouzet 1982, p. 86.

7 Flagging-out

1 This account of the 1914–18 naval war is substantially based on Halpern 1995, *passim*; Chandler 1987, pp. 170–1; Sanderson 1975, pp. 60–2, 94–7.

2 Pope 1989, p. 13.

3 Cable 1981, pp. 68–71.

4 Preston 1980, pp. 24–32, 37.

5 Cable 1981, pp. 196, 202, 205, 213–18.

6 Wells 1994, p. 178.

7 Roskill 1998, p. 447.

8 Hinsley 1994, pp. 128, 307, 310–11.

9 Ruegg and Haig 1993, *passim*; Young 1983, p. 75.

10 Tall and Kemp 1996.

11 This narrative of the 1939–45 naval war is substantially based on Roskill 1998; Ireland 1998; Heneghan 1993; Kaplan and Currie 1998; Blair 2000; Spector 1985, pp. 123–44; Brown 1995, pp. 537–8.

12 Hickey 1999, pp. 300–7.

13 Watson 1991, pp. 48–52, 76–9, 104–9; Grove 1987, pp. 14, 32, 81, 44–5, 155–8, 212.

14 Watson 1991, pp. 151–3, 182–6; Grove 1987, pp. 218–44, 347–50, 355–6; Beaver 1996, pp. 14–16, 42–53; *BBC News Online* 1999–2001.

15 Cable 1981, pp. 23–4, 72–4, 253–4.

16 Brown 1987; Ethell and Price 1985; Beaver 1996, p. 30; Watson *et al.* 1991, pp. 121–34; Hansard 1992.

17 *BBC News Online* 1999–2001.

18 This account is substantially based on Wells 1994; RMM n.d., pp. 14–17, 20–3, 26–9, 34–5; Beaver 1996, pp. 175–6; *BBC News Online* 1999–2001; www.royal-navy.mod.uk.

19 Wells 1994, pp. 273–80.

20 Macdougall 1982; *BBC News Online* 1998–2001.

21 Adams 1986, p. 98; Jenkins 1986, pp. 6–7; Jackson 1983, pp. 140–67; Hadfield 1994; Crowe 1994; London Docklands 1986; DETR 1998a; Lee 1995.

22 Based on Burton 1994, pp. 177–245; Moss and Hume 1986, pp. 208–322; Dodds and Maguire 1998; www.tradepartners.gov.uk: Marine Sector Overview 2002.

23 Connolly 1998; Irish Naval Service and Irish Naval Association websites.

24 Thornton 1959, p. 121.

25 BCS 1996.

26 Thornton 1959, pp. 82–122; Madge 1993, pp. 147–69; DETR 1998b; *BBC News Online* 1998–2002; British Chamber of Shipping website: www.british-shipping.org.uk, 2002.

27 Griffiths 1997, pp. 198–229; Craig 1980, pp. 54–6.

28 Reid 2000b; Pawlyn 2000b; Haines 2000c; Robinson 2000c; Ashcroft 2000; Whitmarsh 2000; Holm 2000; O Grada 1995, pp. 151–2; White 1973; European Commission Directorate General XIV Fisheries, MARSOURCE website. MAFF UK (now DEFRA), Fisheries website; *BBC News Online* 1998–2002.

Bibliography

Abbreviation

MM Mariner's Mirror, Journal of the Society for Nautical Research

The place of publication is London unless otherwise stated.

Reference works

In terms of setting this book in its wider general and maritime setting, the following works of reference have been of immense value. Such is their ubiquity that they have generally not been referenced separately.

Cannon 1997. J. Cannon (ed.), *The Oxford Companion to British History*, Oxford.

Connolly 1998. S.J. Connolly (ed.), *The Oxford Companion to Irish History*, Oxford.

Falkus and Gillingham 1981. M. Falkus and J. Gillingham (eds), *Historical Atlas of Britain*.

Kemp 1979. P. Kemp (ed.), *The Oxford Companion to Ships and the Sea*, Oxford.

McEvedy and Jones 1978. C. McEvedy and R. Jones, *Atlas of World Population History*.

Palmer 1992. A. and V. Palmer (eds), *The Chronology of British History from 250,000 BC to the Present Day*.

— 1996. Alan Palmer, *Dictionary of the British Empire and Commonwealth*.

Storey 1994. R.L. Storey, *Chronology of the Medieval World, 800–1491*.

Williams 1966. N. Williams, *Chronology of the Modern World 1763 to the present time*.

— 1969. N. Williams, *Chronology of the Expanding World 1492–1762*.

Other works consulted

Adams 1986. G Adams, 'Cargo handling', in NELP 1986, pp. 97–109.

Alcock 1972. L. Alcock, *'By South Cadbury is that Camelot....': Excavations at Cadbury Castle 1966–70*.

— 1973. L. Alcock, *Arthur's Britain*.

— 1999. L. Alcock, 'Message from the Dark Side of the Moon: western and northern Britain in the age of Sutton Hoo', in Carver 1999, pp. 205–16.

Anderson 1998. V. DeJohn Anderson, 'New England in the seventeenth century', in Canny 1998, pp. 193–217.

Andrews 1984. K.R. Andrews, *Trade, Plunder and Settlement: Maritime Enterprise and the Genesis of the British Empire 1480–1630*, Cambridge.

— 1985. K.R. Andrews, 'Elizabethan privateering', in Youings 1985, pp. 1–20.

Appleby 1992. J.C. Appleby, 'Devon privateering from early times to 1688', in Duffy *et al.* 1992, pp. 90–7.

— 1998. J.C. Appleby, 'War, politics and colonization, 1558–1625', in Canny 1998, pp. 55–78.

Ashcroft 2000. N. Ashcroft, 'The diminishing commons: politics, war and territorial waters in the twentieth century', in Starkey, Reid and Ashcroft 2000, pp. 217–26.

Banbury 1971. P. Banbury, *Shipbuilders of the Thames and Medway*, Newton Abbot.

Barker 1986. T. Barker, 'Dockland: origins and earlier history', in NELP 1986, pp. 13–19.

Baynes and Pugh 1981. K. Baynes and F. Pugh, *The Art of the Engineer*, Guildford.

Beaver 1996. P. Beaver, *Britain's Modern Royal Navy*, Sparkford.

Beckles 1998. H.McD. Beckles, 'The "Hub of Empire": the Caribbean and Britain in the seventeenth century', in Canny 1998, pp. 218–40.

Beier and Finlay 1986. A.L. Beier and R. Finlay (eds), *London 1500–1700: The Making of the Metropolis*.

Beresford 1988. M. Beresford, *New Towns of the Middle Ages*, Gloucester.

Berg 1994. M. Berg, *The Age of Manufactures 1700–1820: Industry, Innovation and Work in Britain*.

Bernard 1980. J. Bernard, 'The maritime intercourse between Bordeaux and Ireland *c.*1450–*c.*1520', *Irish Economic and Social History*, 7, pp. 7–21.

Blair 2000. C. Blair, *Hitler's U-Boat War: The Hunted 1942–1945*.

Blake 1960. G. Blake, *Lloyd's Register of Shipping 1760–1960*.

Blake 1967. J.B. Blake, 'The medieval coal trade of north-east England: some 14th-century evidence', *Northern History*, 2, pp. 1–26.

Bolton 1980. J.L. Bolton, *The Medieval English Economy 1150–1500*.

Braddick 1998. M.J. Braddick, 'The English Government, war, trade and settlement, 1625–1688', in Canny 1998, pp. 286–308.

Bridbury 1955. A.R. Bridbury, *England and the Salt Trade in the Later Middle Ages*, Oxford.

BCS 1996. British Chamber of Shipping, *Fleet and Manpower Enquiry*.

Brown 1981. D. Brown, *Bristol and How it Grew*, Bristol.

— 1995. D. Brown (ed.), *The British Pacific and East Indies Fleet: The Forgotten Fleets' 50th Anniversary*, Liverpool.

— 1987. D. Brown, *The Royal Navy and the Falklands War*.

Burton 1994. A. Burton, *The Rise and Fall of British Shipbuilding*.

Burwash 1969. D. Burwash, *English Merchant Shipping 1460–1540*, Newton Abbot.

Cable 1981. J. Cable, *Gunboat Diplomacy 1919–1979*.

Canny 1998. N. Canny (ed.), *The Origins of Empire. The Oxford History of the British Empire*, Oxford.

Capp 2001. B. Capp, 'Naval operations', in Kenyon and Ohlmeyer 2001, pp. 156–91.

Carlton 2001. C. Carlton, 'Civilians', in Kenyon and Ohlmeyer 2001, pp. 272–305.

Carus-Wilson 1954. E.M. Carus-Wilson, *Medieval Merchant Venturers*.

Carver 1999. M.O.H. Carver (ed.), *The Age of Sutton Hoo. The Seventh Century in North-Western Europe*, Woodbridge.

Chandler 1987. D.G. Chandler, *The Dictionary of Battles*.

Chartres 1986. J. Chartres, 'Food consumption and internal trade', in Beier and Finlay 1986, pp. 168–96.

Childs 1981. W.R. Childs, 'England's iron trade in the fifteenth century', *Economic History Review*, 2nd
— series, 34, pp. 25–47.

— 1982. W.R. Childs, 'Ireland's trade with England in the later Middle Ages', *Irish Economic and Social History*, 9, pp. 5–33.

— 1992. W.R. Childs, 'Devon's overseas trade in the late Middle Ages', in Duffy *et al.* 1992, pp. 79–89.

— 2000. W.R. Childs, 'The eastern fisheries' and 'Conflict, control and international trade', in Starkey, Reid and Ashcroft 2000, pp. 19–23 and 32–35.

Clout 1991. H. Clout (ed.), *The Times London History Atlas*.

Coad 1983. J.G. Coad, *Historic Architecture of the Royal Navy: An Introduction*.

– 1992. J.G. Coad, 'The development and organisation of Plymouth Dockyard, 1689–1815', in Duffy *et al.* 1992, pp. 192–200.

Corbett 1905. J.S. Corbett (ed.), *Fighting Instructions 1530–1816*, Navy Records Society, 29.

Cordingly 1995. D. Cordingly, *Life Among the Pirates: The Romance and the Reality*.

— 2001. D. Cordingly, *Heroines & Harlots: Women at
— Sea in the Great Age of Sail*.

Corlett 1978. E. Corlett, *The Iron Ship*, Bradford-on-Avon.

Craig 1980. R. Craig, *Steam Tramps and Cargo-Liners 1850–1950*.

Crouzet 1982. F. Crouzet, *The Victorian Economy*.

Crowe 1994. N. Crowe, *Canals*.

Crystal 1995. D. Crystal, *The Cambridge Encyclopaedia
— of the English Language*, Cambridge.

Cullen 1968. L.M. Cullen, *Anglo-Irish Trade 1660–1800*, New York.

Cummins 1995. J. Cummins, *Francis Drake: The Lives
— of a Hero*.

Currie 1988. A. Currie, *Henleys of Wapping: A London Shipowning Family 1770–1830*, National Maritime Museum Monographs and Reports, no. 62.

Davies 1991. R.R. Davies, *The Age of Conquest: Wales 1063–1415*, Oxford.

Davies-Shiel and Marshall 1969. M. Davies-Shiel and J.D. Marshall, *The Industrial Archaeology of the Lake Counties*, Newton Abbot.

Davis 1972. R. Davis, *The Rise of the English Shipping Industry in the 17th and 18th Centuries*, Newton Abbot.

— 1975. R. Davis, *English Merchant Shipping and Anglo-Dutch Rivalry in the Seventeenth Century*.

Delgado 1997. J.P. Delgado (ed.), *Encyclopaedia of Underwater and Maritime Archaeology*.

DETR 1998a. Department of Environment, Transport and the Regions, *Maritime Statistics 1997*.

— 1998b. Department of Environment, Transport and the Regions, *British Shipping – Charting a New Course*.

Devine 1996a. T.M. Devine, *Exploring the Scottish Past: Themes in the History of Scottish Society*, East Linton.

— 1996b. T.M. Devine, 'The Cromwellian Union and the Scottish burghs', in Devine 1996a, pp. 1–16.

— 1996c. T.M. Devine, 'The merchant class of the larger Scottish towns in the later seventeenth and early eighteenth centuries', in Devine 1996a, pp. 17–36.

— 2000. T.M. Devine, *The Scottish Nation 1700–2000*.

Dietz 1986. B. Dietz, 'Overseas trade and metropolitan growth', in Beier and Finlay 1986, pp. 115–40.

— 1991. B. Dietz, 'The royal bounty and English shipping in the sixteenth and seventeenth centuries', *MM*, 77, pp. 5–22.

Dobson 1970. R.B. Dobson (ed.), *The Peasants' Revolt of 1381*.

Dodds and Maguire 1998. C. Dodds and B. Maguire, 'The Scottish shipbuilding industry', *Scottish Economic Bulletin*, no. 57, The Scottish Office, www.scotland.gov.uk.

Drewett, Rudling and Gardiner 1988. P. Drewett, D. Rudling and M. Gardiner, *The South East to AD 1000*.

Dudley Edwards 1991. R. Dudley Edwards, *An Atlas of Irish History*, 2nd edn.

Duffus Hardy 1833. T. Duffus Hardy (ed.), *Rotuli Litterarum Clausarum* I, 1204–1224.

Duffy 1992. M. Duffy, 'Devon and the naval strategy of the French wars 1689–1815', in Duffy *et al.* 1992, pp. 182–91.

Duffy *et al.* 1992. M. Duffy, S. Fisher, B. Greenhill, D.J. Starkey and J. Youings, (eds), *The New Maritime History of Devon*, vol. I: *From Early Times to the Late Eighteenth Century*.

Dyer 1989. C. Dyer, *Standards of Living in the Later Middle Ages: Social Change in England c.1200–1520*.

Eames 1980. A. Eames, *Ship Master: The Life and Letters of Capt. Robert Thomas of Llandwrog and Liverpool 1843–1903*, Denbigh.

Earle 1998. P. Earle, *Sailors: English Merchant Seamen 1650–1775*.

Edwards 2001. N. Edwards, 'Early medieval inscribed stones and stone sculpture in Wales', *Medieval Archaeology* XLV, pp. 15–39.

Edwards 2001. P. Edwards, 'Logistics and supply', in Kenyon and Ohlmeyer 2001, pp. 2 ??–7 ?.

Elder 1996. M. Elder, *Lancaster and ??e African Slave Trade*, Lancaster City Museum?, ???? ?????s No. 14, Lancaster.

Ethell and Price 1985. P. Ethell ??? ?. ?????, ?ar South Atlantic.

Everitt 1973. A Everitt, *The C?????? ???? ?? ??? the Great Rebellion 1640–60*, L??????.

Farmer 1979. D.H. Farmer (e?. ??? ?????? ?????nary of Saints*, Oxford.

Farrant 1976. J.H. Farrant, *Th? ??????? ?? ??????? 1700–1914*, Brighton.

Filmer-Sankey 1999. W. Filmer-?????? '?????? Anglo-Saxon cemetery: the current stat? ?? ?????????', in Carver 1999, pp. 39–52.

Firth 1908. C.H. Firth (ed.), *Naval Songs and Ballads*, Navy Records Society, 33.

Ford 1979. C.J. Ford, 'Piracy or policy: the crisis in the Channel 1400–1403', *Transactions of the Royal Historical Society*, 5th series, vol. 29, 6?–78.

Formoy 1926. B.E.R. Formoy, 'A maritime indenture of 1212', *English Historical Review*, 41, pp. 556–9.

Foster 1989. R.F. Foster, *Modern Ireland 1600–1972*.

Fowler 1971. K. Fowler (ed.), *The Hundred Years War*.

Frere 1974. S.S. Frere, *Britannia*.

Friel 1995. I. Friel, *The Good Ship: Ships, Shipbuilding and Technology in England 1200–1520*.

Fulford 1989. M.G. Fulford, 'Byzantium and Britain: a Mediterranean perspective on post-Roman Mediterranean imports in western Britain and Ireland', *Medieval Archaeology* XXXIII, pp. 1–6.

Fulford et al. 2000. M. Fulford, M. Handley and A. Clark, 'An early date for Ogham: the Silchester Ogham stone rehabilitated', *Medieval Archaeology* XLIV, pp. 1–24.

Gairdner 1983. J. Gairdner (ed.), *The Paston Letters* (consolidated edn), Gloucester.

Gardiner 1997. M. Gardiner, 'The exploitation of sea-mammals in medieval England: bones and social context', *Archaeological Journal* 154, pp. 173–95.

Gardiner et al. 2001. M. Gardiner et al., 'Continental trade and non-urban ports in Mid-Saxon England. Excavations at Sandtun, West Hythe, Kent', *Archaeological Journal* 158, pp. 161–290.

Gardiner 1992a. R .Gardiner, 'The frigate', in Lavery 1992a, pp. 27–45

— 1992b. R. Gardiner, 'Design and construction', in Lavery 1992a, pp. 116–24.

— 1992c. R. Gardiner, 'Guns and gunnery', in Lavery 1992a, pp. 146–63.

Gilbert 1965. K.R. Gilbert, *The Portsmouth Blockmaking Machinery*.

Graham 1980. B.J. Graham, *Medieval Irish Settlement*, Historical Geography Research Series, 3, Norwich.

Grant and Cheape 1987. I.F. Grant and H. Cheape, *Periods in Highland History*.

Gray 2000a. T. Gray, 'Inshore fisheries of the south west, c.1530–1630', in Starkey, Reid and Ashcroft 2000, pp. 82–5.

— 2000b. T. Gray, 'Fisheries to the east and west', in Starkey, Reid and Ashcroft 2000, pp. 96–100.

Greenhill 1980. B. Greenhill, *The Life and Death of the Merchant Sailing Ship 1815–1965*.

Griffiths 1997. D. Griffiths, *Steam at Sea*.

Grove 1987. E.J. Grove, *Vanguard to Trident: British Naval Policy since World War II*.

Hadfield 1994. C. Hadfield (rev. by J. Boughey), *Hadfield's British Canals: The Inland Waterways of Britain and Ireland*, Stroud.

Haines 2000a. M. Haines, 'The herring fisheries 1750–1900', in Starkey, Reid and Ashcroft 2000, pp. 64–71.

— 2000b. M. Haines, 'Local diversity in Wales c.1530–1880', in Starkey, Reid and Ashcroft 2000, pp. 87–91.

— 2000c. M. Haines, 'The Welsh fisheries', in Starkey, Reid and Ashcroft 2000, pp. 201–5.

Hakluyt 1932. R. Hakluyt, *The Principall Navigations, Voiages, Traffiques and Discoveries of the English Nation*, vol. 1.

Halpern 1995. P.G. Halpern, *A Naval History of World War I*.

Hansard 1992. *House of Commons Hansard Debates*, 9 July 1992, coll. 554.

Harding 1995. R. Harding, *The Evolution of the Sailing Navy 1509–1815*, Basingstoke and London.

— 1999. R. Harding, *Seapower and Naval Warfare 1650–1830*.

Harland 1992a. J.H. Harland, *Seamanship in the Age of Sail*.

— 1992b. J.H. Harland, 'Seamanship', in Lavery 1992a, pp. 172–80.

Harris 1969. G.G. Harris, *The Trinity House of Deptford 1514–1660*.

Haslam 1984. J. Haslam (ed.), *Anglo-Saxon Towns in Southern England*, Chichester.

Hatcher 1973. J. Hatcher, *English Tin Production and Trade before 1550*, Oxford.

Haywood 1991. J. Haywood, *Dark Age Naval Power: A Reassessment of Frankish and Anglo-Saxon Seafaring Activity*.

— 2001. J. Haywood, *The Historical Atlas of the Celtic World*.

Heidenreich 2001. C.E. and N.L. Heidenreich, 'A nutritional analysis of food rations of Martin Frobisher's second expedition, 1577', *Polar Record*, 38, no. 204, pp. 23–8.

Henderson and Carlisle 1999. J. Welles Henderson and R.P. Carlisle, *Jack Tar: A Sailor's Life 1750–1910. Marine Art and Antiques*, Woodbridge.

Heneghan 1993. C. Heneghan (ed.), *Battle of the Atlantic: 50th Anniversary*, Liverpool (articles by D. Brown, W.J.R. Gardner and A. Lane).

Hewitt 1929. H.J. Hewitt, *Medieval Cheshire: An Economic and Social History of Cheshire in the Reigns of the Three Edwards*. Chetham Society, new series, vol. 88, Manchester.

Hickey 1999. M. Hickey, *The Korean War: The West Confronts Communism 1950–1953*.

Higham 1997. N.J. Higham, *The Death of Anglo-Saxon England*, Stroud.

Hill 1981. D. Hill, *An Atlas of Anglo-Saxon England*, Oxford.

Hines 1999. J. Hines, 'The Scandinavian character of Anglian England: an update', in Carver 1999, pp. 315–30.

Hinsley 1994. F.H. Hinsley, *British Intelligence in the Second World War* (abr. edn).

Hodges 1989. R. Hodges, *The Anglo-Saxon Achievement*.

Holdsworth 1984. P. Holdsworth, 'Saxon Southampton' in Haslam 1984, pp. 331–43.

Holland 1971. A.J. Holland, *Ships of British Oak: The Rise and Decline of Wooden Shipbuilding in Hampshire*, Newton Abbot.

Hollister 1962. C.W. Hollister, *Anglo-Saxon Military Institutions on the Eve of the Norman Conquest*, Oxford.

— 1965. C.W. Hollister, *The Military Organisation of Norman England*, Oxford.

Holm 2000. 'An international perspective on Britain's fisheries in the new millennium', in Starkey, Reid and Ashcroft 2000, pp. 235–41.

Howard 1979. F. Howard, *Sailing Ships of War 1400–1860.*

Huggett 1988. J.W. Huggett, 'Imported grave goods and the early Anglo-Saxon economy', *Medieval Archaeology* XXXII, pp. 63–96.

Hutchinson 1997. G. Hutchinson, *Medieval Ships and Shipping.*

IMO 2001/2. International Maritime Organization, United Nations, IMO MSC.4/Circ.16, 31 March 2002, and press release on the 74th session of the Maritime Safety Committee, 2001.

Ireland 1998. B. Ireland, *Jane's Naval History of World War II.*

Jackson 1973. K. H. Jackson, *A Celtic Miscellany.*

Jackson 1983. G. Jackson, *The History and Archaeology of Ports*, Tadworth.

— 2000. G. Jackson, 'State concern for the fisheries 1485–1815', in Starkey, Jackson Reid and Ashcroft 2000, pp. 46–53.

James 1998. L. James, *The Rise and Fall of the British Empire.*

Jarvis 2000. A. Jarvis, 'Dock and harbour provision for the fishing industry since the eighteenth century', in Starkey, Reid and Ashcroft 2000, pp. 146–56.

Jenkins 1986. J. Geraint Jenkins and D. Jenkins, *Cardiff Shipowners*, Cardiff.

Jones 1966. A.H.M. Jones, *The Decline of the Ancient World.*

Jones 2000. E. Jones, 'England's Icelandic fishery in the early modern period', in Starkey, Reid and Ashcroft 2000, pp. 105–10.

Kaplan and Currie 1998. P. Kaplan and J. Currie, *Convoy: Merchant Sailors at War 1939–1945.*

Kelly 1899. *Kelly's Directory for Sussex.*

Kennedy 1982. P.M. Kennedy, *The Rise and Fall of British Naval Mastery.*

Kenyon and Ohlmeyer 2001. J.P. Kenyon and J. Ohlmeyer (eds), *The Civil Wars: A Military History of England, Scotland, and Ireland, 1638–1660*, Oxford.

Kowaleski 1992. M. Kowaleski, 'The port towns of fourteenth-century Devon' in Duffy *et al.* 1992, pp. 62–72.

— 2000. M. Kowaleski, 'The western fisheries' and 'The internal fish trade', in Starkey, Reid and Ashcroft 2000, pp. 23–32.

Laing 1975. L. Laing, *Late Celtic Britain and Ireland, c.400–1200 AD.*

Lapidge 1999. M. Lapidge *et al.* (eds), *The Blackwell Encyclopaedia of Anglo-Saxon England*, Oxford 1999 (articles by K. Wade on Ipswich, A. Vince on London, J. Blair on Towns and G. Astill on Trade).

Laughton 1942. L. G. Carr Laughton, 'Naval accounts for 1209–1211', *MM*, 28, pp. 74–7.

Laughton 1981. J.K. Laughton (ed.), *State Papers Relating to the Defeat of the Spanish Armada Anno 1588*, Navy Records Society, vols 1 and 2, 2nd edn, Havant.

Laurence 1994. A. Laurence, *Women in England: A Social History 1500–1700.*

Lavery 1989. B. Lavery, *Nelson's Navy: The Ships, Men and Organisation, 1793–1815.*

— 1992a. B. Lavery (ed.), *The Line of Battle: The Sailing Warship 1650–1840.*

— 1992b. B. Lavery, 'The ship of the line', in Lavery 1992a, pp. 11–26.

— 1992c. B. Lavery, 'Ships' fittings', in Lavery 1992a, 137–45.

— 2001. B. Lavery, *Maritime Scotland.*

Lee 1995. C. H. Lee, *Scotland and the United Kingdom*, Manchester.

Lees 1984. J. Lees, *The Masting and Rigging of English Ships of War 1625–1860.*

Lloyd 1968. C. Lloyd, *The British Seaman 1200–1860: A Social Survey.*

Loades 1992. D. Loades, *The Tudor Navy: An Administrative, Political and Military History*, Aldershot.

London Docklands 1986. *London Docklands. Exceptionally Placed.*

Loyn 1994. H.R. Loyn, *Anglo-Saxon England and the Norman Conquest.*

Loyn and Percival 1975. H.R. Loyn and J. Percival (eds), *The Reign of Charlemagne: Documents on Carolingian Government and Administration.*

Lyon 1980. D.J. Lyon, *Steam, Steel and Torpedoes: The Warship in the 19th Century.*

— 1993. D.J. Lyon, *The Sailing Navy List: All the Ships of the Royal Navy – Built, Purchased and Captured – 1688–1860.*

— 1996. D.J. Lyon, *Sea Battles in Close-Up: The Age of Nelson.*

McDonnell 1978. K.G.T. McDonnell, *Medieval London Suburbs*, London and Chichester.

Macdougall 1982. P. Macdougall, *Royal Dockyards.*

Macdougall 1989. N. Macdougall, *James IV*, Edinburgh.

McGrail 1981. S. McGrail, *Rafts, Boats and Ships from Prehistoric Times to the Medieval Era.*

MacGregor 1997. A. MacGregor, *Ark to Ashmolean: The Story of the Tradescants, Ashmole and the Ashmolean Museum*, Oxford.

Mackie 1978. J.D. Mackie *et al.*, *A History of Scotland.*

Madge 1993. T. Madge, *Long Voyage Home: True Stories from Britain's Twilight Maritime Years.*

Mainwaring and Perrin 1922. G.E. Manwaring and W.G. Perrin (eds), *The Life and Works of Sir Henry Mainwaring*, vol 2, Navy Records Society, 56.

Mancall 1998. P.C. Mancall, 'Native Americans and Europeans in English America, 1500–1700', in Canny 1998, pp. 328–50.

Marcus 1980. G.J. Marcus, *Conquest of the North Atlantic*, Woodbridge.

Marquardt 1992. K.H. Marquardt, 'Rigs and Rigging', in Lavery 1992a, pp. 125–36.

Marshall 1998a. P.J. Marshall (ed.), *The Oxford History of the British Empire, vol. II: The Eighteenth Century*, Oxford.

— 1998b. P.J. Marshall, 'The British in Asia: trade to dominion, 1700–1765', in Marshall 1998a, pp. 487–507.

Martin and Parker 1998. C. Martin and G. Parker, *The Spanish Armada.*

Mathias 1969. P. Mathias, *The First Industrial Nation: An Economic History of Britain 1700–1914.*

Middleton 1977. E.W. Middleton, *Lifeboats of the World*, Poole.

Mitchell 1974. D.W. Mitchell, *A History of Russian and Soviet Seapower*.

Morgan 1998. P.D. Morgan, 'The Black Experience in the British Empire, 1680–1810', in Marshall 1998a, pp. 465–86.

Morley 1976. B.M. Morley, *Henry VIII and the Development of Coastal Defence*.

Morris 1998. M. Morris, 'The rise of the English sailcloth industry 1565–1643: coastal trade records as an indicator of import substitution', *MM*, 84, pp. 139–51.

Moss and Hume 1986. M. Moss and J.R. Hume, *Shipbuilders to the World: 125 Years of Harland and Wolff, Belfast 1861–1986*, Belfast.

Mumby-Croft and Barnard 2000. R. Mumby-Croft and M. Barnard, 'An antiquated relationship? Trawler owners and trawlermen, c.1880–1980', in Starkey, Reid and Ashcroft 2000, pp. 119–26.

Murray 1972. J.J. Murray, *Antwerp in the Age of Plantin and Breughel*, Newton Abbot.

Naish 1985. J. Naish, *Seamarks: Their History and Development*.

NELP 1986. North East London Polytechnic, *Dockland: An Illustrated Historical Survey of Life and Work in East London* (papers by various authors, especially those by T. Barker and Lord Howie, and the Gazetteer of sites).

NMM 1988. National Maritime Museum, *Armada 1588–1988: The Official Catalogue*.

O Grada 1995. C. O Grada, *Ireland: A New Economic History 1780–1939*, Oxford.

Oppenheim 1988. M. Oppenheim, *A History of the Administration of the Royal Navy 1509–1660*.

Osler and Barrow 1993. A. Osler and A. Barrow, *Tall Ships Two Rivers: Six Centuries of Sail on the Rivers Tyne and Wear*, Newcastle-upon-Tyne, pp. 8–11.

Pawlyn 2000a. A. Pawlyn, 'The south west pilchard, trawl and mackerel fisheries, 1770–1850', in Starkey, Reid and Ashcroft 2000, pp. 85–7.

— 2000b. A. Pawlyn, 'The westcountry', in Starkey, Reid and Ashcroft 2000, pp. 197–200.

Peters 1975. G. Peters, *The Plimsoll Line: The Story of Samuel Plimsoll, Member of Parliament for Derby from 1868 to 1880*, Chichester and London.

Platt 1973. C. Platt, *Medieval Southampton: The Port and Trading Community, AD 1000–1600*.

Pope 1989. R. Pope (ed.), *Atlas of British Social and Economic History since c.1700*.

Powell 1962. J.R. Powell, *The Navy in the English Civil War*.

Preston 1980. A. Preston, *Dreadnought to Nuclear Submarine*.

Pudney 1975. J. Pudney, *London's Docks*.

Quinn 1985. D.B. Quinn, *Set Fair for Roanoke: Voyages and Colonies, 1584–1606*, Chapel Hill and London.

Rediker 1987. M. Rediker, *Between the Devil and the Deep Blue Sea: Merchant Seamen, Pirates and the Anglo-American World 1700–1750*, Cambridge.

Redknap 1998. M. Redknap, 'An archaeological and historical context for the medieval Magor Pill boat', *Maritime Wales – Cymru A'r Mor*, 19, pp. 9–29.

— 2000. M. Redknap, *The Vikings in Wales: An Archaeological Quest*, Cardiff.

Reid 2000a. C. Reid, 'From trawler to table: the fish trades since the late nineteenth century', in Starkey, Reid and Ashcroft 2000, pp. 157–65.

— 2000b. C. Reid, 'From boom to bust: the herring industry in the twentieth century', in Starkey, Reid and Ashcroft 2000, pp. 188–96.

Rich and Wilson 1980. E.E. Rich and C.H. Wilson (eds), *The Cambridge Economic History of Europe, vol. IV: The Economy of Expanding Europe in the Sixteenth and Seventeenth Centuries*, Cambridge.

Richards 1992. J.D. Richards, *Viking Age England*.

Richardson 1998. D. Richardson, 'The British Empire and the Atlantic slave trade, 1660–1807', in Marshall 1998, pp. 440–64.

Richmond 1971. C.F. Richmond, 'The war at sea', in Fowler 1971, pp. 96–121.

Ritchie 1993. A. Ritchie, *Viking Scotland*.

Roberts 1999. J. Roberts, 'Anglo-Saxon vocabulary as a reflection of material culture', in Carver 1999, pp. 185–202.

Robinson 1974. F.N. Robinson (ed.), *The Complete Works of Geoffrey Chaucer*, 2nd edn.

Robinson 2000a. R. Robinson, 'The line and trawl fisheries in the age of sail', in Starkey, Reid and Ashcroft 2000, pp. 72–80.

— 2000b. R. Robinson, 'The Yorkshire coast 1780–1880', in Starkey, Reid and Ashcroft 2000, pp. 91–5.

— 2000c. R. Robinson, 'Steam power and distant-water trawling', in Starkey, Reid and Ashcroft 2000, pp. 206–16.

Rodger 1986. N. Rodger, *The Wooden World: An Anatomy of the Georgian Navy*.

— 1997. N. Rodger, *The Safeguard of the Sea: A Naval History of Britain. Vol. 1, 660–1649*.

— 1998. N. Rodger, 'Guns and sails in the first phase of English colonization, 1500–1650', in Canny 1998, pp. 79–98.

Roesdahl 1998. E. Roesdahl, *The Vikings*.

Rogozinski 1997. J. Rogozinski, *The Wordsworth Dictionary of Pirates*, Ware.

Rose 1982. S.P. Rose (ed.), *The Navy of the Lancastrian Kings: Accounts and Inventories of William Soper, Keeper of the King's Ships 1422–1427*, Navy Records Society, 123.

Roskill 1998. S. Roskill, *The Navy at War 1939–1945*.

Rowse 1947. A.L. Rowse, *Tudor Cornwall*.

Ruegg and Hague 1993. B. Ruegg and A. Hague, *Convoys to Russia: Allied Convoys and Naval Surface Operations in Arctic Waters 1941–1945*, rev. edn, World Ship Society, Kendal.

Runyan 1977. T.J. Runyan, 'Ships and mariners in later medieval England', *Journal of British Studies*, 16, pp. 1–17.

Sadler 1968. D.H. Sadler, *Man is not Lost*.

Sandahl 1951, 1958 and 1982. B. Sandhal, *Middle English Sea Terms*, 3 vols, Uppsala.

Sanderson 1975. M. Sanderson, *Sea Battles: A Reference Guide*, Newton Abbot.

Scammell 1961. G.V. Scammell, 'English merchant shipping at the end of the Middle Ages: some east coast evidence', *Economic History Review*, 2nd series, 13, pp. 327–41.

— 1962. G.V. Scammell, 'Shipowning in England *c*.1450–1550', *Transactions of the Royal Historical Society*, 5th series, vol. XII, pp. 105–22.

— 1970. G.V. Scammell, 'Manning the English Merchant Service in the sixteenth century', *MM*, 56, 131–54.

Scull 1999. C.J. Scull, 'Before Sutton Hoo: structures of power and society in early East Anglia', in Carver 1999, pp. 3–24.

Sherley-Price 1968. L. Sherley-Price (ed. and trans.), Bede, *A History of the English Church and People*.

Shipbuilding 1966. The Shipbuilding Conference *et al.*, *British Shipbuilding Facilities and Services 1966*.

Sinclair 1980. K. Sinclair, *A History of New Zealand*.

Smith, Watts and Watts 1998. K. Smith, C.T. Watts and M.J. Watts, *Records of Merchant Shipping and Seamen*, Public Record Office Readers' Guide, no. 20.

Snyder 1998. C. Snyder, *An Age of Tyrants: Britain and the Britons AD 400–600*, Stroud.

Spector 1985. R.H. Spector, *Eagle Against the Sun: The American War with Japan*, New York.

Stark 1996. S.J. Stark, *Female Tars: Women Aboard Ship in the Age of Sail*.

Starkey 1999. D.J. Starkey (ed.), *Shipping Movements in the Ports of the United Kingdom 1871–1913: A Statistical Profile*, Exeter.

— 2000. D.J. Starkey, 'The Newfoundland trade', in Starkey, Reid and Ashcroft 2000, pp. 100–4.

Starkey, Reid and Ashcroft 2000. D. J. Starkey, C. Reid and N. Ashcroft (eds), *England's Sea Fisheries: The Commercial Sea Fisheries of England and Wales since 1300*.

Stenton 1971. F.M. Stenton, *Anglo-Saxon England*, Oxford.

Stirland 2000. A.J. Stirland, *Raising the Dead: The Skeleton Crew of Henry VIII's Great Ship, the* Mary Rose, Chichester.

Swanton 1996. M. Swanton (trans. and ed.), *The Anglo-Saxon Chronicle*.

Symons 1999. T.H.B. Symons (ed.), *Meta Incognita: A Discourse of Discovery. Martin Frobisher's Arctic Expeditions, 1576–1578*, 2 vols, Canadian Museum of Civilization Mercury Series Directorate Paper 10, Hull.

Tall and Kemp 1996. J.J. Tall and P. Kemp, *HM Submarines in Camera: An Illustrated History of British Submarines 1901–1996*, Thrupp.

Tattersfield 1998. N. Tattersfield, *The Forgotten Trade*.

Tatton-Brown 1984. T. Tatton-Brown, 'The towns of Kent' in Haslam 1984, pp. 1–36.

Tenenti 1967. A. Tenenti, *Piracy and the Decline of Venice 1580–1615*.

Thomas 1971. C. Thomas, *Britain and Ireland in Early Christian Times*.

Thomas 1990. C. Thomas, '"*Gallici Nautae de Galliarum Provinciis*" – a sixth/seventh century trade with Gaul reconsidered', *Medieval Archaeology* XXXIV, pp. 1–26.

Thornton 1959. R.H. Thornton, *British Shipping*.

Tracy 1992. N. Tracy, 'Naval Tactics', in Lavery 1992a, pp. 181–9.

Tucker 2000. S.C. Tucker, *Handbook of 19th Century Naval Warfare*, Thrupp.

Ure 1951. P.N. Ure, *Justinian and his Age*.

Veale 1971. E. M. Veale, *Studies in the Medieval Wine Trade*, Oxford.

Vince 1990. A .Vince, *Saxon London*.

Walker 2000. I.W. Walker, *Mercia and the Making of England*, Stroud.

Warren 1966. W.L. Warren, *King John*.

Watson 1991. B.W. Watson, *The Changing Face of the World's Navies, 1945 to the Present*.

Watson *et al.* 1991. B.W. Watson, B. George, P. Tsouras and B. L. Cyr, *Military Lessons of the Gulf War*.

Wells 1994. J. Wells, *The Royal Navy: An Illustrated Social History 1870–1982*, Stroud.

West 1983. J. West, *Town Records*, Chichester.

Whincop and White 1986. A. Whincop and A. White, *Lancaster's Maritime Heritage*, Lancaster.

White 1973. E .W. White, *British Fishing-Boats and Coastal Craft*.

Whitmarsh 2000. D. Whitmarsh, 'Adaptation and change in the fishing industry since the 1970s', in Starkey, Reid and Ashcroft 2000, pp. 227–34.

Williams 1988. N. Williams, *The Maritime Trade of the East Anglian Ports 1550–1590*, Oxford.

Wilson 1986. T. Wilson, *Flags at Sea*.

Wood 1999. I.N. Wood, 'Frankish hegemony in England', in Carver 1999, pp. 235–42.

Woolgar 2000. C.M. Woolgar, '"Take this penance now, and afterwards the fare will improve": seafood and medieval diet', in Starkey, Reid and Ashcroft 2000, pp. 36–44.

Youings 1985. J. Youings (ed.), *Raleigh in Exeter 1985: Privateering and Colonisation in the Reign of Elizabeth I*, Exeter Studies in History, 10, Exeter.

Young 1983. E. Young, *One of Our Submarines*.

Zins 1972. H. Zins, *England and the Baltic in the Elizabethan Era*, Manchester.

Websites

A number of websites have been consulted in the course of research for this book. They are:

Atlas of Roman pottery: www.potsherd.uklinux.net/atlas.

BBC News Online: www.bbc.co.uk/news

British Chamber of Shipping website: www.british-shipping.org.uk

Irish Navy: www.military.ie/naval

Royal Navy: www.royal-navy or www.royal-navy.mod.uk

Scottish Cultural Resources Access Network: www.scran.ac.uk

Scottish Economic Bulletin: www.scotland.gov.uk

DETR: www.detr.gov.uk

Index